T0331065

"*The New MBA Playbook* provides a good overview of the strategy, organizational, and branding elements of business integrated into a comprehensive business model that leads to a thriving business while still addressing societal challenges. With illustrative case studies, it's easy to read."

— **Professor David Aaker**, hailed as the "father of modern branding",
E.T. Grether Professor Emeritus of Marketing Strategy and Public Policy
at the University of California, Berkeley-Haas School of Business,
Vice Chairman at Prophet, a global consultancy, and author of 18 books,
including *The Future of Purpose-Driven Branding*

"This book will help MBAs in translating what they are getting in the classroom with the real world of work. It highlights many of the important aspects of management and organizational behavior today and in the future."

— **Professor Sir Cary Cooper**, Alliance Manchester Business School,
University of Manchester

"*The New MBA Playbook* offers a refreshing take on executive development and education, addressing the evolving standards of leadership and business strategies in our hyper-connected world. Dr. Tkaczyk's comprehensive approach integrates diverse disciplines, from behavioral economics to brand storytelling, and guides readers through essential MBA concepts with a fresh perspective. This book fosters self-insight and personal adaptation, allowing readers to tailor their learning experience to their unique needs. With its engaging style and practical insights, *The New MBA Playbook* is an invaluable resource for those seeking to excel in today's dynamic business landscape."

— **Dr. Marshall Goldsmith**, *Thinkers50* #1 Executive Coach
and *New York Times* bestselling author of *The Earned Life*,
Triggers, and *What Got You Here Won't Get You There*

"In *The New MBA Playbook*, Bart Tkaczyk brings a new energy and excitement to the fundamentals of management by approaching the core issues and challenges of business as seen through a lens of positivity, creativity and motivating ideals. Filled with real world examples; opportunities for individual engagement and reflection; and accessible introductions to some of the latest research insights and practical tools, the Playbook's operating and motivating premise is that business can be a positive force in the world and that these tools can help readers make that happen."

— **Mary C. Gentile**, PhD, Inductee into the *Thinkers50* Hall of Fame and
author of *Giving Voice To Values: How To Speak Your Mind When You Know
What's Right*. Formerly, the Richard M. Waitzer Bicentennial Professor of
Ethics at the University of Virginia Darden School of Business

"Why spend two years and a ton of money for an MBA when you can get the most important concepts from this book? *The New MBA Playbook* cuts through the unnecessary parts and gets right to the core concepts that can make for a successful business leader."

– **Professor Patrick M. Wright**, Thomas C. Vandiver Bicentennial Chair in Business, Chair, Department of Management, Darla Moore School of Business, University of South Carolina

"A brand-new take on a well-established topic of global relevance! Bart Tkaczyk applies some fabulous creativity and some pretty bold and imaginative thinking to refresh the concept of the MBA and corporate strategy. This is perfect reading for any executive or aspiring executive building on their professional and academic education. I particularly really loved the 'Your Take' on integrative thinking, absolutely spot on in how to turn 'strategy setting' from theoretical into practical. Very highly recommended!"

– **Professor Moorad Choudhry**, University of Kent Business School; formerly, CEO of Habib Bank AG Zurich, Treasurer at The Royal Bank of Scotland, Head of Treasury at Europe Arab Bank, Head of Treasury at KBC, Vice President at JPMorgan Chase, and author of *The Principles of Banking*

"In *The New MBA Playbook*, Dr. Bart Tkaczyk redefines leadership engagement leveraging both deep research expertise and significant practical global leadership experience to accelerate managerial careers. He distills the essence of practical leadership success to create an approachable, useful, and highly credible guide for managers at any point in their pursuit of professional excellence."

– **Professor Jeff Flesher**, iMBA faculty at the University of Illinois Urbana-Champaign (Gies School of Business). Formerly, VP of Learning & OD at Underwriters Laboratories

"*The New MBA Playbook* is a leadership primer that meets this complicated moment. In it, Bart Tkaczyk blends theory and practice, idea and application, to help individuals bring empathy, creativity and thoughtfulness to their management approach. The world will be better off if we can bring ever more humanity to business leadership, and this book provides very helpful guidance in that direction."

– **Jennifer Riel**, COO of IDEO, the global design and innovation firm, and author of *Creating Great Choices: A Leader's Guide to Integrative Thinking.* Adjunct Professor at the Rotman School of Management, University of Toronto

"If you are interested in concise descriptions of the differences between traditional economics and behavioral economics, between leadership and followership and the importance of kindness to organizational sustainability, I highly recommend *The New MBA Playbook* by Dr. Bart Tkaczyk."

– **W. Glenn Rowe**, PhD, Professor Emeritus, Professor of Strategy, Ivey Business School at Western University, and coauthor of *Cases in Leadership* and *Strategic Analysis and Action*. Formerly, the director of Ivey's Executive MBA Program

"The MBA degree is a key that will open many career doors and opportunities. However, that key stays in the door and the individual needs to be able to present and apply their experience and MBA learning to the role and task at hand. *The New MBA Playbook* is a superb aide memoire for someone starting their MBA journey or having achieved it, are well into their career. The topic areas covered go beyond the technical business topics and delve into the behavioral science of how people communicate, connect, build trust and develop healthy and harmonious relationships. The old saying is that 'People join brands and organizations but they leave because of managers'. *The New MBA Playbook* is an essential companion guide that can bring out the best in all of your people and provides an updated perspective about business knowledge and practical application."

– **Dil Sidhu**, Professor of Management Practice, Head of the Birkbeck Business School, University of London

The New MBA Playbook

The job market is heating up, standards are higher – and competition is becoming fiercer. Want to accelerate your *professional* development but can't because life is moving fast and time is short? As long as you have *The New MBA Playbook*, an innovative "MBA in a book", now is the ideal moment to, at your own pace, anywhere and anytime, boost your managerial proficiency so as to move forward positively, strategically, sustainably and ethically.

By an award-winning industry expert and executive educator who's had success in both corporate boardrooms and executive classrooms worldwide, *The New MBA Playbook* is a different kind of MBA sourcebook. It is humanity-centered (and beyond the AI hype!) and is organized into seven relevant, rigorous and readable two-unit modules ("mini-lectures"). This educational package condenses key MBA disciplines and topics into a playbook format that fits the work schedules of busy executives and professionals on the go, and delivers top MBA-quality intelligence in a matter of days, not years. Through *The New MBA Playbook*, you can deep dive into the essentials of business, creative strategies and fresh new thinking, and gain effective working knowledge of behavioral economics and policy, positive leadership and followership, strategic transformation, dialogic organization development, design thinking and innovation execution, brand coolness and storytelling, modern management consulting and executive coaching, global management strategies, cultural intelligence, and behavioral ethics, among other issues. The playbook, although designed to be worked through systematically, provides room for critical interpretation, enabling learning by "self-insight" and personal adaptation (the easy-to-use material is an "on-demand" resource from which you can "mix and match" modules freely and in any order, as all modules can stand alone, and you can customize the course to your needs).

Re-imagining MBA education and challenging existing business practice, *The New MBA Playbook*, designed to bridge the gap between the MBA classroom and real life, will be invaluable to potential and current MBA students, seasoned business executives seeking to refresh and update their skills, management consultants, successful entrepreneurs – and to anyone who simply refuses to stop learning.

Bart Tkaczyk, Fulbright Scholar at the University of California, Berkeley (the No. 1 public university in the world), and Managing Member with Energizers, LLC (the premier North American provider of positive organization development, executive leadership and strategic human resource development consulting services), has extensive experience in executive education/MBA teaching gained in Europe, the Middle East and North America, moving new concepts from the academic to daily application in highly interactive environments. He is also an executive coach, trusted leadership, organization development and strategy advisor to major corporations and governments worldwide, and the bestselling author of *Leading Positive Organizational Change* (Routledge). **Email:** bart_tkaczyk@ berkeley.edu **Visit:** www.drtkaczyk.com **Follow:** @DrBTkaczykMBA

The New MBA Playbook

An Updated Skills Mix for
the Future Business World

Bart Tkaczyk

Routledge
Taylor & Francis Group

LONDON AND NEW YORK

Designed cover image: Bart Tkaczyk

First published 2025
by Routledge
4 Park Square, Milton Park, Abingdon, Oxon OX14 4RN

and by Routledge
605 Third Avenue, New York, NY 10158

Routledge is an imprint of the Taylor & Francis Group, an informa business

© 2025 Bart Tkaczyk

British Library Cataloguing-in-Publication Data
A catalogue record for this book is available from the British Library

Library of Congress Cataloging-in-Publication Data
Names: Tkaczyk, Bart, author.
Title: The new MBA playbook: an updated skills mix for
the future business world / Bart Tkaczyk.
Description: Abingdon, Oxon; New York, NY: Routledge, 2025. |
Includes bibliographical references and index.
Identifiers: LCCN 2024029259 (print) | LCCN 2024029260 (ebook) |
ISBN 9781032805559 (paperback) | ISBN 9781032832081 (hardback) |
ISBN 9781003508274 (ebook)
Subjects: LCSH: Management—Study and teaching. |
Executive ability. | Career development.
Classification: LCC HD30.4 .T583 2025 (print) |
LCC HD30.4 (ebook) | DDC 658.4/07124—dc23/eng/20240711
LC record available at https://lccn.loc.gov/2024029259
LC ebook record available at https://lccn.loc.gov/2024029260

ISBN: 9781032832081 (hbk)
ISBN: 9781032805559 (pbk)
ISBN: 9781003508274 (ebk)

DOI: 10.4324/9781003508274

Typeset in Times New Roman
by codeMantra

Access the Support Material: www.routledge.com/9781032805559

To my beloved wife and life partner, Oleńka, and our precious little girl, Zosia, whose boundless love, warmheartedness, radiant smiles, and unwavering support and belief in me and in this project have illuminated every step of this journey. Your positive energy and sparkles have been my source of motivation and inspiration. *I love you, sweethearts.*

To my dearest mom and dad, whose constant encouragement and empowerment to pursue my dreams have been the foundation of everything I am today. *With the deepest gratitude.*

To the esteemed scholars, my publisher, editors, reviewers, teachers, mentors, and predecessors whose work fills the pages of this book. Your contributions have paved the way for this endeavor, and I stand humbly on your shoulders – you are true giants. You will undoubtedly smile when you recognize your imprint in the pages ahead. *With my sincere appreciation.*

To the very many talented MBA students, executives, business associates and clients I've been fortunate to work with – worldwide. Your insights and perspectives have enriched my thinking and fueled my personal growth. *With my heartfelt thanks.*

To my true friends, your companionship has made this process all the more meaningful. *I am much obliged to you.*

And to my readers, I hope it sparks a bit of magic in your lives. *Enjoy!*
– BT

P.S. Zosia, my dearest, may you one day discover this book and find value in it. Though it may not rival the beauty of the timeless Bible stories for little ones or the bedtime stories by Hans Christian Andersen, the Brothers Grimm or Charles Perrault that once lulled you to sleep as a child, it might inspire you to pursue your own MBA journey someday—if that's your dream. Know that I will *always* be your loving and affectionate dad. *Big hugs.*

Contents

Abbreviations

AI	artificial intelligence
AOM	Academy of Management
A.S.S.E.T.	attract attention, streamline, socialize, energize, timing counts
BAU	business as usual
BC	Before Christ
BGs	born globals
BPR	business process reengineering
B2B	business-to-business
B2C	business-to-consumer
CAGE(er)	cultural, administrative, geographic, economic (environmental, risk) distance framework
CAR	case analysis record
CE	circular economy
CEO	chief executive officer
CFO	chief financial officer
CFO	chief future officer
COO	chief operating officer
COVID-19	coronavirus disease 2019
CPD	continuing professional development
CQ	cultural intelligence
CSO	chief strategy officer
CSO	chief sustainability officer
CSR	corporate social responsibility
DJSI	Dow Jones Sustainability World Index
ELT	executive leadership team
EOC	Economy of Communion
ERG	energize, redesign, and gel
ERM	enterprise risk management
ESG(T)	environmental, social, corporate governance (and technology)
FCV	fragility, conflict, and violence
FTSE	Financial Times Stock Exchange-Russell Group
HBS	Harvard Business School
HMW	how might we...?
HQCs	high-quality connections

HR	human resources
HRD	human resource development
HRM	human resource management
H2H	human-to-human
ICF	International Coaching Federation
IMC	Institute of Management Consultants
INVs	international new ventures
IP	intellectual property
JV	joint venture
L&D	learning and development
M&A	mergers and acquisitions
MBA	master of business administration
MCII	mental contrasting with implementation intentions
NACD	North American Commercial Division
NFT	non-fungible token
NGO	nongovernmental organization
NYSE	New York Stock Exchange
OD	organization development
PDA	public displays of affection
PDSA	plan–do–study–act cycle
PfP	pay for performance
PMP	performance management process
POB	positive organizational behavior
POS	positive organizational scholarship
PPPPP	people, planet, prosperity, peace, and partnership
PSFs	professional service firms
PsyCap	psychological capital
PwP	performance with purpose
R&D	research and development
RBV	resource-based view of strategy
RCTs	randomized controlled trials
RICE	Respect, Integrity, Communication, Excellence
ROE	return on expectations
ROI	return on investment
S-A-P	strategy as practice
SIT	systematic inventive thinking
SME	small to medium-sized enterprise
SOAR	strengths, opportunities, aspirations, results
SWOT	strengths, weaknesses, opportunities, threats
TLA	test, learn, adapt
TLAs	three-letter acronyms
TMW	take–make–waste
UX	user experience
VRIN	valuable, rare, costly to imitate, non-substitutable
VUCA	volatility, uncertainty, complexity/chaos, and ambiguity
WHOOP	wish, happy outcome, obstacle, plan

Introduction

Welcome to *The New MBA Playbook* – the ideal antidote to the bland discussion materials in most coursebooks – fresh new thinking

The power of the individual, the hyper-connected workplace, the impact of globalization, and the omnipresence of the digital and the virtual are expeditiously effecting changes in executive human resource development and education – not to mention, organizational methodologies, corporate parlance, and leadership strategies. In the present climate, leaders are thus confronted with the imperative task of harmonizing and balancing the daily demands of a thriving career with the necessary investment in continuing professional development to meet these new expectations and evolving standards.

Seeking to lead in your field and positively impact your organization – and humanity?

To succeed in today's fast-paced, challenging workplace, you need to develop solid business skills and strategies – beyond standard economics or business administration. *The New MBA Playbook*, your new, informative and easily digestible guide to getting ahead – human-centered, strategically-integrated and results-driven – will give you a broad business perspective and help you to become fluent in the language of business. You'll quickly become more successful as you progress through critical MBA areas, adding greater value every day.

The New MBA Playbook, a complete integrated course (or a supplement) for learners at the MBA level or above, presents a novel set of skills and effective strategies that respond to the specific requirements of the advanced professional. It explores the essential components of a full MBA degree through condensed two-unit modules ("mini-lectures") – from a new angle. The cross-section of high-quality research-based and practice-informed material builds your complete skill set in a diverse spectrum of integrated disciplines. Moreover, *The New MBA Playbook* addresses a variety of crucial and timely business topics. While executive learners often complain that learning materials are bland, these topics are "different" – and are not often found in standard business coursebooks. For example, *behavioral* economics and policy, *positive* leadership and *followership*, *strategic* transformation, *dialogic* organization development, *creative* and *design* thinking and *innovation execution*, brand *coolness* and brand *storytelling*, *modern* management consulting and *executive* coaching, *global* management strategies,

DOI: 10.4324/9781003508274-1

born-global firms and organizational *cultural intelligence*, and *behavioral* ethics, among others. Accordingly, the stimulating, topic-based units will enable you to build on your previous knowledge while simultaneously developing your executive potential and skills.

Across all modules and units in *The New MBA Playbook*, bitesize research and theories related to business and management are harmoniously integrated with creative, game-changing strategies and benchmarks into a real-world, solution-focused approach to learning and development, delivering current theory through professional best- as well as "next-" practice. The selected best need-to-know frameworks provide you with the opportunity to critically reflect on and talk about your own work/business situation in a structured way. What is more, the book will help you to make better strategic business decisions, by expanding your knowledge of what really works in digestible form within a clearly defined and focused context.

What will you gain? Top ten reasons to choose and learning outcomes

Discover the key benefits and special learning features of *The New MBA Playbook*:

I **Understand the modern-day** principles behind an MBA and how they rise to contemporary business challenges and to "what's next". Broaden your horizons and gain today's expert knowledge, with a high-level executive focus on meeting tomorrow's challenges.

II **Get the full picture of business** and develop integrated management competencies. The text puts all the pieces of the management puzzle together by embracing a comprehensive business model designed for the "greater good" – and for future growth.

III **Structure-powered learning.** Each person has their hobby-horse, and a how-to guide rarely suits everyone (except its author). Playbooks should serve as useful tools to assist individuals in their learning journey, rather than being tyrants over them, cracking a whip and forcing conformity and group-think. The playbook, although designed to be worked through systematically, provides room for critical interpretation, enabling learning by "self-insight" and personal adaptation (the easy-to-use, authentic, flexible material is a resource from which you can also just select topics of interest freely – so you can "mix and match" modules in any order, as all modules can stand alone, and you can customize the course to your needs). Methodologically speaking, each unit is accompanied by explanatory text that is organized into clear and concise sections. All follow this pattern:

- **An opening quote** – which inspires and relates to the unit and helps to contextualize your learning.
- **Sneak peek** – enables you to focus on key unit concepts and terms that you will have learned by the end of each unit.
- **Pause 'n' reflect: Integrative thinking** – represents "your take" on the current issues and emerging trends by means of thought provoking

points – turned over in your mind at least twice ("before" and "after" completing each unit).

- **Lead-in** – general discussion points that serve as a springboard to a unit and a way of bringing resources, in terms of experience, to bear on a topic – to be worked on individually or in buzz groups.
- **Idea watch** – a concept, model, framework, or method that provides the basis or purpose of the unit.
- **Assumptions** – underpinning ideas that are essential for the concept, model, framework, or method to remain valid.
- **Key elements** – a description or definition of the distinct components comprising the concept, model, framework, or method.
- **Thinking critically: Issues** – the analysis of existing evidence and arguments in order to help form informed judgments by the application of unbiased evaluation.
- **Applications** – the ways in which the concept, model, framework, or method can be put into actual practice. In certain cases, these applications may extend beyond the original intent of development, offering a more innovative analytical approach within a specific domain.
- **Case Alert! Case classics** – providing a range of quick case studies and intriguing topical illustrations of unit content in practice and giving you the opportunity to apply your understanding of the concepts to actual business scenarios and real-life examples.
- **Greater good corner: Get ready to exercise your ethics** – here, the learner is presented with a dilemma and is prompted to respond to questions and to think ethically about how to address and resolve these complex situations.
- **Time out: Journal entry** – reflection pauses are incorporated within each unit to prompt learners to pause, re-think and reflect in writing on the material covered in the light of their own experience and learning needs.
- **Making connections: Related units and models** – identifying other concepts, models, frameworks, or methods within the playbook that have some form of correlation and can potentially enhance a more comprehensive analytical approach – via associations. Accordingly, strategic organizational and management analysis and development can be enhanced by developing new linkages between elements, or between frameworks, without losing their integrity.
- **Industry snapshot links** – web links at various points in the text containing useful information relating to the pertinent topics covered. You can easily supplement your lessons with the online material.
- **Deep dive: Main references and recommended resources** – the original references or those that most effectively go into greater detail and describe background to the concept, model, framework, or method – included at the end of each unit so as to help you take your learning further. This "Resource bank", also expanding on material in the book, forms a major product in its own right.

Plus, the **Module Monitor: Consolidation**, after every module, a section placed so as to encourage you to take greater responsibility for your own learning, that comes with review and self-check assessment exercises, including:

- **Self-check questions** (both true or false and multiple choice) – to help you review your understanding of the presented core concepts before moving on to study further materials. Note: all of the self-check assessment exercises are supported by an answer key at the back of the book.
- **Individualized learning record** – with thought questions and micro-assignments, to help you to re-contextualize, apply the module concepts, and substantially boost consultancy and research-based skills.
- **Can-do checklist** – to look back on the key terms you have learned in every two-unit module. Essentially, systematic "recycling" reinforces your knowledge and creates confidence.

IV **Gain real-world skills you can use on "Monday morning".** You leave every unit with new frameworks, processes and tools you can use at work right away, that enable you to think critically and act ethically, and to develop and execute successful strategies.

V **Become a "thinking performer".** The intent of this book is to help you modernize your approach and elevate your role to a thinking performer who can become more effective in optimizing day-to-day operations; approach challenges with an entrepreneurial mindset; design impactful solutions for the greater good; take the fear out of decision-making and make better informed decisions; take intelligent risks; strategize with all aspects of the business in mind; and understand managerial responsibilities as they relate to the entire business enterprise – and beyond.

VI **Enjoy increased confidence** in your ability to speak up in meetings, engage in effective executive dialogue, connect with colleagues and senior management, ask more thoughtful and insightful questions, champion your cause, recognize problems, and convey potential advantages within cross-functional departments and teams and to articulate to stakeholders using contemporary business language that aligns with the present standards and interpretations of success. This book allows you to do so.

VII **Maximize your return on investment (ROI).** By means of *The New MBA Playbook*, you've got the opportunity to better manage your day-to-day professional commitments and add value to your organization while acquiring practical know-how in a format that maximizes a limited schedule and minimizes your time away from the office. Through this text, you gain relevant industry know-how at a fraction of the time and cost, and can apply the greatest ideas and insights, breakthrough strategies and techniques taught in the best business schools – in the world.

VIII **Get a theoretically solid and applications-based perspective.** This playbook is written by a Fulbright scholar with real-world consulting and executive experience, which balances rigorous classroom theory with actual applications, to give you the most holistic education. It's the best of both worlds – a mix of cutting-edge, rigorous academic research with real-world business best practices – and through it, you've got a potent fusion!

IX **No entrance exams**, no grades – just fast, effective executive learning from an award-winning scholar-facilitator who can translate academic expertise into transformative knowledge and extend textbook topics into real-world strategies.

X **Support material accompanying the course.** Learn from an array of additional innovative resources, extra activities, assignments and exercises to continue your learnings independently and to keep you at the cutting edge of business research and practice.

Reader/learner profile

The New MBA Playbook, the ideal way to supplement and extend standard MBA course material, will be useful to several types of readers and learners:

- **MBA students** seeking stimulating, theoretically solid, focused, and applications-based material and "real-world" skill-building tools so as to figure on and be at the fore-front of upcoming industry trends and gain a competitive edge. The text can help with written assignments, projects, case studies, open-book examinations, and dissertations.
- **Potential students** thinking about doing an MBA or EMBA who want to find a quick (and budget-friendly!) way to obtain an overview of MBA essentials and get a world-class learning "trial" – without even paying for a plane ticket (or breaking the bank account in the process!).
- **Seasoned business executives**, including those who have already graduated from an MBA degree program and are now ready to "dust off" their degree and who want to "refresh" and "update" their skills, and to gain a new perspective on how business knowledge is evolving – without even setting foot inside a classroom.
- **Practicing managers and directors** who wish to apply a more rigorous and critical approach in their work.
- **Professionals from early to mid-career** looking to take on new responsibilities, to learn how to think cross-functionally, to increase their upward mobility, and to accelerate their careers.
- **Technically trained leaders** who seek to enhance their business knowledge and refine their business acumen.
- **Non-business professionals** seeking to understand business fundamentals in order to work more effectively with senior management or transition into management or leadership roles.
- **Individuals in government and nonprofit roles** looking to master the language of business and to gain a greater perspective on how organizations succeed – including learners on other higher-level courses that include business, organization and management units.

- **Management consultants and executive coaches** concerned with management or business.
- **Extremely busy entrepreneurs** who want to follow a course at MBA level so as to fine-tune their entrepreneurial thinking and learn to be catalysts for organic radical innovation, who wish to gain a better understanding of each area in the business ecosystem and who are looking for immediate results, but who don't wish to invest time (and money!) on a full MBA.
- **Change-makers and constant learners – anyone** who simply refuses to stop learning!

So, are YOU ready to re-invent yourself, your team, and your organization, to spruce up and leverage your newfound business management skills in current or future business endeavors, step up, and thrive? If so, take a bit of a deeper dive and enjoy your learning journey – and breathe easy with better knowledge and strategies for the new business world, gaining an in-depth understanding of the pillars of business, with *The New MBA Playbook* – the ideal stepping stone for the next phase of your continuing *professional* development.

Bart Tkaczyk, MSc (HRD & Consultancy),
PMSc (HRD), MBA (HR), PhD (HMN)
Berkeley, California, Brooklyn, NY & London, UK
drtkaczyk.com
@DrBTkaczykMBA
bart_tkaczyk@berkeley.edu

Module I

Breathing humanity and new life into organizations

Humanizing the enterprise

1 Behavioral economics and policy 101

For humans

"It's nonsense to say money doesn't buy happiness, but people exaggerate the extent to which more money can buy more happiness" – Daniel Kahneman

Sneak peek

Focus on: Key concepts and terms

Unit 1

- Attract attention, Streamline, Socialize, Energize, Timing counts (A.S.S.E.T.)
- Choice architect/architecture
- Cognitive (bias, ease, errors, heuristics, overload, shortcuts)
- Default
- Economics (behavioral, conventional, econ-, good, human-, humanistic, narrative, positive, standard, traditional)
- "Econs" vs. "humans"
- Friction (costs)
- Habits
- Hyperbolic discounting
- Initial information effect ("anchoring" effect)
- "Last mile"
- Libertarian paternalism
- Loss aversion
- Mental accounting
- "Motivational fee"
- Networks
- Norms
- Nudge (for good; helpful; nudging strategy) vs. "noodge"
- Over-choice

DOI: 10.4324/9781003508274-3

- Randomized controlled trials (RCTs)
- Reminders
- Salience
- Social proof
- Status quo
- Test, learn, adapt (TLA)

Pause 'N' reflect: On the current issues and trends

Before you complete this unit, think about each of the following statements. Mark each statement:

V – if you *agree.*
X – if you *disagree.*
? – if you are *undecided.*

Your take: Integrative thinking	*Before doing Unit 1*	*After doing Unit 1*
1 Customers, employees, and managers all engage in rational decision-making.		
2 Every business is in the business of changing someone's behavior.		
3 Offering too many choices to individuals raises the chances of them switching to a product category or brand with fewer alternatives.		
4 Saving money is painful and unnecessary.		
5 The medium-sized coffee cup enjoys the highest level of popularity. Well, the small size *always* has too little coffee and the large one *always* has too much coffee.		
6 The way prices are displayed holds equal or possibly greater significance compared to the actual setting of prices.		
7 Policymaking can be enhanced by adopting a more accurate model of human behavior. For instance, the inclusion of a statement like "the majority of people pay their tax on time" can increase repayment rates.		

Your take: Integrative thinking	*Before doing Unit 1*	*After doing Unit 1*
8 A "nudge" fundamentally involves encouraging or guiding behavior, but without mandating or instructing, and preferably without relying on substantial financial incentives or sanctions.		
9 Practical "choice architecture", which refers to designing user-friendly environments, can effectively nudge individuals toward the best decision without limiting their freedom to choose.		
10 The majority of businesses invest a significant portion of their resources at the beginning of the value creation process, such as crafting a strategy, developing new products or services, and conducting market analysis. However, they tend to allocate far fewer resources to the final stage: the pivotal "last mile", where consumers interact with their website, store, or sales representatives and make actual decisions.		

After you have done the unit, repeat "Your Take". How has reading the unit clarified the ideas herein? How have your views, feelings and thoughts changed over time?

Lead-in

General discussion points

Individually or in buzz groups, work on the following:

1 "If economics is not behavioral, then what is it? We're all behavioral economists now" – Economist. Why or why not?
2 Why do individuals often fail to act in a manner that is in their best interest even when they know what to do?
3 How might a lawyer, an economist, a marketer, and an applied behavioral scientist (often referred to as a "choice architect") address the same challenge of promoting behavior change, such as:

- encouraging healthy eating habits to prevent illness in people's old age,
- boosting voter turnout,
- motivating individuals to initiate retirement planning,
- advocating for organ donation,
- promoting flu shots, or
- fostering a consistent exercise routine?

4   How can governments incorporate behavioral insights into their operations so as to create more social and economic value? What resources and capabilities must they develop to fully adopt and utilize behavioral insights?

5   "Behavioral economics is just another fad" – Psychologist. Do you agree?

 Idea watch

The discipline of economics can be traced back to Adam Smith's influential publication from 1776, "An Inquiry into the Nature and Causes of the Wealth of Nations". In contrast, behavioral economics has a relatively shorter history of around 50 years. Israeli-born psychologists Daniel Kahneman and Amos Tversky are credited with originating behavioral economics within human behavior studies in the 1960s.[1] Over the subsequent three decades, their research played a pivotal role in the development of a field that has directly or indirectly contributed to Nobel Prizes in economic science. Notably, Daniel Kahneman, author of the popular book *Thinking, Fast and Slow*, received the Nobel Prize in 2002, and Richard Thaler, author of the widely read book *Nudge*, was awarded the Nobel prize in 2017. Recently, behavioral economics, a more *humanistic* economics, has revolutionized the field. This positive transformation stems from its emphasis on putting the "human" back into economics and on acknowledging that individuals can occasionally err, take care of others, and are generally not as cold, detached, and willfully calculating as economists have traditionally attributed to them. In his Nobel Laureate address, Thaler emphasized, "in order to do good economics, you have to keep in mind that people are *human*". Unlike "econs" (always perfectly rational decision-makers and self-interested utility maximizers) who are analytical, reflective, effortful, deliberate, patient (and well-versed in probability theory and rational optimization), "humans" are emotional, reflexive, effortless, impulsive, and rather short-sighted.

Briefly, *behavioral* economics ("human-economics") is built upon the notion that real human beings deviate from the idealized models presented in traditional "econ-economics" textbooks. Instead, we often exhibit inherent irrationality, relying on a range of cognitive, say, shortcuts to "navigate" daily life. Additionally, our decisions are influenced by unconscious cognitive biases, which are systematic thinking errors that impact our decision-making in almost every scenario.

Consider, for example, the "initial information effect", a cognitive thinking bias in which people fixate on an initial piece of information ("anchoring"), failing to appropriately adjust their judgments when presented with new and different data. There's also the "status quo" tendency, where individuals prefer maintaining their current situation even if changing circumstances could actually offer better options. "Loss aversion" is another concept, highlighting that people dislike losses more than they enjoy gains. "Mental accounting" involves mentally labeling money and allocating it to various "accounts", like *clothing, college savings*, or *entertainment*, instead of viewing it as fungible (the moment people label money differently, it gets spent differently). Lastly, there's "social proof", where individuals look to their peers' behavior to inform their decision-making and often conform to the actions of their peers. This emerging field of study presents a markedly different perspective on how both individuals and organizations operate – and *truly* behave.

Imagine you have a stakeholder who has initially opted for Option A, but you wish to encourage them to choose Option B. These choices could pertain to various things, including products, services, or behaviors. In this scenario, a lawyer would consider making Option A illegal, either by *banning* it outright or imposing *restrictions* that compel *compliance*. An economist, on the other hand, would advise using *incentives*, employing a mix of rewards and penalties (the "carrot-and-the-stick" strategy), such as introducing an economic *tax* on Option A to make it a costly choice, or offering economic *benefits* for choosing Option B to make it more financially attractive. A marketer would focus on *persuasion* tactics, like *advertising*, to sway individuals toward choosing Option B. Lastly, a behavioral scientist would recommend *simplifying* the decision-making process for the individual, making it easier to opt for Option B over Option A, following the principles of the "nudge", or "choice architecture", approach.

Technically, a *nudge* refers to any element of the choice architecture that alters people's behavior in a predictable way without forbidding any choices or substantially altering their economic consequences. To be considered a helpful nudge, the intervention should be simple and cheap to avoid. It's important to note that nudges are *not* mandates.

Let's now zoom in on a concrete situation, appraised by Richard Thaler and Cass Sunstein, behavioral scientists, involving two cafeterias aiming to reduce students' consumption of *un*healthy food. *Cafeteria I* addresses the issue through financial means, either by increasing the cost of junk food through a tax – or by deciding on a complete ban on its sale, which doesn't qualify as a nudge since it eliminates freedom of choice. In contrast, *Cafeteria II* takes a different approach by deciding to re-arrange and change the way in which food is displayed ("choice architecture") so that junk foods will be less likely to be reached for and picked. More specifically, they intentionally get to position fruits and vegetable snacks at eye level and near the front of the shelves, making them easily accessible to customers. On the other hand, junk foods are deliberately placed on higher shelves that are more challenging to reach. This approach qualifies as a "nudging strategy". The key takeaway from this is that school kids, much like adults, can be significantly influenced by small changes in the context.

Assumptions

In the *traditional* economic framework known as "rational choice theory", fundamental assumptions about human behavior are employed to simplify the model of how an economy works. Conversely, *behavioral* economics relies on assumptions that better reflect how people actually behave.

Predictably, the recent worldwide economic crises have undermined two core principles of conventional economic theory: the belief that humans typically make perfectly rational choices and that the invisible hand of the market reliably corrects imbalances. It is imperative that we discard these and other similar assumptions and embrace a more fresh approach. By merging elements from both psychology and economics, often applying experiments, behavioral economics, a more humanistic economics, operates on the premise that cognitive biases frequently hinder individuals from consistently making entirely rational choices, even when they exert their utmost effort. It posits that *ir*rationality is the real invisible hand driving human decision-making.

In contemporary societies, the idea of choice, along with the ability to exercise it, is widely regarded as a fundamental aspect of people's autonomy, well-being, and overall happiness.

The fields of economics and public policy have been significantly influenced by these concepts of freedom of choice. Within economics, the standard belief is that offering a greater array of choices enables individuals to discover options that better match their genuine preferences. In the realm of public policy and governance, the rights and capabilities of individuals to select what suits them best form the cornerstone of libertarianism.

On that account, nowadays, an effective leader is someone who serves as an innovative decision framework designer – a creative choice architect. They are tasked with structuring the environment in which individuals make choices. These "designers" nudge (they nudge *for good*!) – they energize people (let's call them "choosers") to lead healthier and wealthier lives, or to transform casual browsers into buyers. Apparently, humans are truly influenced by these gentle nudges.

Ultimately, by tapping into behavioral insights and adopting an experimental approach (for example, through randomized controlled trials (RCTs)), firms can uncover the reality behind their beliefs about customers, employees, operations and policies – they can do a better job of making their products and services more effective, their customers happier, and their employees more engaged and productive, and they can steer clear of disastrous errors.

 Key elements

If you want to activate (*or* inhibit) a behavior, make your interventions an A.S.S.E.T.

A.S.S.E.T. represents a mental shortcut among various cognitive shortcuts. While the A.S.S.E.T. framework doesn't encompass every subtlety found in behavioral literature, it does serve as a valuable initial reference point. Here's how it works:

Attract attention – individuals are naturally inclined toward things that capture their attention. For instance, you can *personalize* a message (by including the recipient's name) and/or emphasize essential points to make them more noticeable and *stand out* (salience).

Streamline – when aiming to encourage a specific action (such as tax compliance or hiring more staff), *simplify* the process and minimize inconvenience (e.g., simplify tax regulations for easier, low-hassle filing). Additionally, "defaults" often represent the easiest, healthiest, and the most secure choices. Defaults can be very effective indeed – for example, default consent rules can increase organ donations (in some countries, people are automatically registered as organ donors and have to "opt out" if they do not want to donate, but in other countries, people have to "opt in" by registering as an organ donor. Note: "opt-out" countries have substantially higher donor and transplant rates). Keep in mind, however, that if you intend to *inhibit* a behavior, add "friction costs" (e.g., positioning unhealthy snacks in harder-to-reach places, using speed bumps to discourage speeding, or segregating funds into separate accounts to reduce spending tendencies).

Socialize – humans are inherently social beings. People are strongly *influenced* by what their *peers* are actually doing or have done (think: norms). For example, advertising that highlights the majority of people participating in recycling to boost recycling efforts, or employing descriptive social norms to boost voter turnout (e.g., high-turnout script). Other strategies include: reciprocity and making active commitments (promises), receiving recommendations from friends or colleagues (networks), or utilizing reminders and cues related to others (like displaying eyes and faces) – see in "Case Alert! Box" below.

Energize – *invigorating* and initiating a targeted behavior, often accomplished by enhancing one's self-discipline and boosting one's self-control so as to rectify the misalignment between people's desired actions and their actual behavior. Besides, try making things "use*fun*" – useful *and* fun to do such as a "lottery" (e.g., while ongoing disputes revolve around the expansion of new airports, you can encourage potentially affected residents to see the advantages of a new airport by providing them with annual travel vouchers for flights departing from the airport, and/or example, by way of a "lottery" with prizes such as vacation giveaways). Lotteries can further infuse incentives with energy, too. Note that *emotions* hold as much significance as logical reasoning.

Timing counts – interventions tend to yield better results when applied *before* habits are established or when behavior has been disrupted due to external factors (e.g., altering human behavior before or during the arrival of a new baby). Additionally, it is beneficial to assist individuals in overcoming their own issues with "time inconsistency" (take, for example, "hyperbolic discounting", a mental model, that posits that humans are hardwired to value *immediate* rewards over *long-term* rewards. This could help explain why we opt for fruit over chocolate when the reward is set to be delivered next week, but we choose chocolate when given the choice at the moment of delivery. Moreover, expenses incurred in the future are not as strongly experienced as immediate costs).

Now, to assess the effectiveness of a policy or intervention, choice architects/ designers might want to begin using experiments more often through, for example, RCTs, which have become commonplace in fields like medicine and international development to identify which policies, medications or sales strategies are working. While it's important to note that no single study is likely to definitively establish causation, the process of randomization serves to minimize bias and offers a robust method for investigating the cause-and-effect relationships between an intervention and its outcomes. This occurs because the act of randomization balances participant characteristics (both observed and unobserved) between the groups, thus allowing attribution of any disparities in outcomes to the study intervention. The "Test, Learn, Adapt" (TLA) methodology outlines distinct phases and components essential for setting up any RCT.

Test

1 Selection: Choose at least two policy interventions for comparison (e.g., comparing an old policy with a new one or different policy variations).
2 Intended outcome definition: Define the intended outcome the policy aims to affect and specify how it will be measured during the trial.
3 Randomization unit: Decide on the level at which randomization will occur, whether it's at the individual level, within institutions (e.g., schools), or across geographical areas (e.g., local authorities).
4 Sample size determination: Determine the number of units (which could be individuals, institutions, or areas) needed to ensure robust and statistically significant results.
5 Random assignment: Use a rigorous randomization method to assign each unit to one of the policy interventions.
6 Implementation: Introduce the selected policy interventions to their respective assigned groups.

Learn

7 Learning impact: Measure the results and determine the impact of the policy interventions.

Adapt

8 Adaptation: Adapt your policy intervention to reflect your findings.
9 Circling back: Return to Step 1 to continuously enhance your comprehension of effective strategies and identify what works.

To conclude, this will be grounds for super-flexibility – a structural framework incorporating operational procedures that facilitate the seamless integration of rapid feedback loops and enable the organization to change when necessary, facilitating the execution of a TLA strategy.

◀))) Thinking critically: Issues

Behavioral economists reveal that individuals, enterprises, specific markets, and economies all frequently behave in ways that deviate from what traditional thinking would predict. To put it bluntly, they study why people act in ways that contradict the expectations of "Homo *economicus*" and instead behave more like "Homo *moralis*", "Homo *animalus*", "Homo *positivus*", "Homo *empathicus*", or more commonly "Homo *socialus*", representing different manifestations such as moral orientation, cheerful and exuberant boisterousness and the irrationality of animal spirits, positivity, empathy, and social manifestation – beyond just an economic one.

Although, earlier on, classical economic views on rational behavior were questioned by, for example, Herbert Simon (who won the Nobel Prize in Economic Sciences in 1978), who argued that individuals do not make fully rational decisions due to cognitive limitations (the difficulty of gathering and processing all necessary information) and social constraints (personal and social connections between people), in recent decades, behavioral economics, a more humanistic economics, has often been regarded as a peripheral field, somewhat distant from the mainstream of traditional economics. While practitioners of standard economics have reluctantly acknowledged that humans can occasionally act irrationally, they have largely adhered to their established theoretical frameworks. They argue that the experiments conducted by behavioral economists (and psychologists), while thought-provoking, do not undermine rational models because when they are conducted in controlled settings, they lack the crucial influence of the competitive market environment, which they consider the primary driver and regulator of rational behavior.

Primarily, the nudging approach adopted in this unit counts as "libertarian paternalism", the term coined by Richard Thaler and Cass Sunstein. The *libertarian* aspect of these strategies emphasizes the fundamental principle that, in most cases, people should be "free to choose". Ergo, designed policies ought to maintain or increase freedom of choice. On the other hand, the *paternalistic* aspect asserts that it is acceptable for those designing policies, known as choice architects, to attempt to influence people's behavior with the goal of improving their overall well-being, such as increasing their longevity and health. Essentially, a policy is considered *paternalistic* when it seeks to influence choices in a way that will make choosers better off, as judged by themselves. Drawing on established insights from social science, it is evident that individuals often make *sub*optimal decisions – choices they wouldn't have made if they had: (a) paid full attention and possessed complete information, (b) unlimited cognitive abilities, and (c) perfect self-control.

When *libertarian* is applied to qualify the word *paternalism*, it signifies a commitment to preserving individual liberty. In this light, libertarian paternalism is a relatively weak, soft, and nonintrusive type of paternalism because it doesn't block choice-making. If individuals wish to engage in behaviors like heavy smoking, consuming excessive candy, choosing an inappropriate healthcare plan, or neglecting to save for retirement, libertarian paternalists will not force them to do otherwise. Instead, they may gently nudge them to influence their behavior.

Explicitly, while the majority of organizations allocate a significant portion of their resources to addressing "first mile" problems (think: strategy development, new product creation, policy formulation, or welfare program design), it is equally crucial for them to pay attention to the "last-mile" aspects (think: tactics, the adoption and utilization of new products, policy execution and delivery, as well as the acceptance and uptake of welfare programs). In actuality, as informed by Dilip Soman, the "last mile" is super tricky since it relies on understanding human behavior, which exhibits considerable variability. Although we possess well-established theories in the realm of strategy, we lack a comparable wealth of sound theories when it comes to tactics…

In the realm of decision-making, the principle that choice is good holds true, but *over*-choice is not beneficial. Presenting individuals with (*too*) many options can induce confusion and cognitive overload. This phenomenon can be seen, for instance, when observing children making selections at an ice cream parlor. As they progress through a lengthy display of flavors, they tend to forget the initial few flavors they encountered. This can result in a state of preference uncertainty, where they second-guess their choices, such as debating between "White Chocolate" and "Peanut Butter 'n' Chocolate", and experience subsequent regret, contemplating whether they should have opted for "Mint Chocolate" instead of "Chocolate Almond". This phenomenon, often referred to as "analysis paralysis", frequently leads individuals, including children and adults alike, to revert to familiar and tried-and-tested flavors (just "Chocolate"). Comparably, similar dynamics are evident in various decision contexts, such as the selection of pain and fever medications, the choice of retirement investment funds, the configuration of software settings, or the purchase of automobiles with multiple available versions, including basic, basic plus, and an array of increasingly enhanced options. In situations characterized by complex decision-making, individuals often find solace in the presence of a sensible "default" option. Defaults carry substantial influence due to the human predisposition toward cognitive ease and the inclination to minimize effort, which is further compounded by a social normative element. It is noteworthy that prevailing indicators suggest that decision complexity will only escalate over time. Consequently, individuals are more inclined to gravitate toward brands that offer a limited set of well-defined branded variants, as this simplifies the decision-making process and aligns with their inherent preference for ease in choice selection.

Concerning nudging and choice architecture, there's no such thing as a "neutral" design. This observation raises concerns about the utilization of behavioral economics to subtly influence seemingly inconsequential decisions, as it may encroach upon the sphere of private decision-making, especially when employed by governmental entities. A fundamental attribute of a bona fide "nudge" lies in its preservation of open avenues for individuals to exercise their free will. For example, individuals who genuinely do not wish to opt into a retirement plan still have that choice under automatic opt-in. However, when an ostensibly innocuous choice becomes mandatory, the nudge turns into a more forceful push – a shove, or a "noodge" (the "Yiddishism *noodge*" is a noun meaning "a bore, nuisance or pest", which in turn comes from similar terms in Slavic languages, for example, *nuda; nudzić/nużyć* in Polish, meaning "a tedious situation or a thing"; "to bore/

to make (someone) feel weary/to turn someone off"). Therefore, it is incumbent upon nudges to possess qualities that are not only choice-enhancing but, at a minimum, abstain from restricting individuals' choices while simultaneously maintaining a high degree of transparency (nudging-style approaches should never be manipulation or propaganda!). When contemplating the ramifications of behavioral science, particularly in the context of widely adopted policies, it becomes evident that the potency of behavioral insights carries with it the potential for misuse. The primary apprehension lies in the absence of adequate accountability measures, emphasizing the necessity for those behavioral scientists and decision-makers who employ these strategies to be more responsive to the interests and concerns of the individuals impacted by their actions (the concern shared by *both* liberals and democrats).

In essence, efficacious nudges are those that steer individuals toward decisions that are inherently beneficial and conducive to their well-being, vitality and flourishing, viz. helpful nudges nudge *for good.*

Applications

A nudge can be considered one of the most powerful instruments for helping enterprises and their stakeholders navigate the "last mile". Nudges come in a diverse range, encompassing subtle text tweaks to fresh product innovations, and exhibiting various execution methods and features of application.

Let's now take a look at a lot more examples of applications.

Attract attention

- *Tax*: Encourage greater income declaration through attention-grabbing, *salient* letters.
- *Legal system*: Enhance fine payment compliance by sending *personalized* text messages.
- *Giving*: Increase contributions to emergency appeals by sharing the *story* of an individual child in need rather than presenting statistics of thousands affected.

Streamline

- *Retirement savings*: Significantly increase the number of individuals saving through *auto*-enrollment in employer-sponsored pension plans.
- *University admissions and higher education access*: Boost college attendance among low-income students by *pre*-filling college application forms based on their tax and income data.
- *Suicide risk management*: Decrease suicide rates by implementing preventive measures, such as *blocking* "easy" routes, e.g., packaging paracetamol in blister packs instead of loose bottles.

Socialize

- *Tax compliance*: People are more inclined to fulfill their tax obligations when they are informed that the *majority* of patriotic individuals "pay on time".
- *Charitable contributions*: People are more likely to donate when they discover that a *coworker* has already made a contribution.
- *Littering*: Volunteer to clean up. Individuals are more inclined to drop litter on the ground if they observe *others* doing it or if they see litter *already* on the ground.

Energize

- *Promoting children's healthy lifestyles*: Increase kids' consumption of wholegrain brown bread by cutting it into *fun* shapes. To further boost the well-being of children, produce an entertaining show tailored to youngsters that makes healthy-living *fun*.
- *Preventing drunk driving*: Steer clear of driving under the influence by *pre*-arranging a rest and recreation limousine service.
- *Workout routine*: Sustaining a regular exercise regimen by *committing to a minor penalty* ("motivational fee") for missing a gym session.

Timing counts

- *Taxation*: Encourage newly established small businesses to file their initial tax returns *accurately and promptly during their first year* of operation since individuals are less likely to respond to nudges if they were late in paying taxes the previous year – establishing *good* record-keeping *habits from the outset* makes it considerably easier to file tax returns on time in the future).
- *Agricultural development*: To boost production, increase the adoption of fertilizer offers (with *free* delivery) among farmers *after the harvest* season, *when cash-rich.*
- *Child development*: Nurse family partnership – a nursing practitioner forming a supportive relationship with a young, *first-time, at-risk* mother starting from the *pre*-natal stage and continuing until the child's second birthday (with the goal of reducing domestic violence, and child abuse, and enhancing educational achievement); language acquisition – language development in children who are exposed to more than one language *at a young age* may initially result in a delay in language acquisition, but it ultimately results in lifelong fluency in both languages and ease in acquiring further languages.

A.S.S.E.T. serves as a mental heuristic within the realm of humanistic economics. Similar to other cognitive heuristics, it may fail to encompass certain facets, but it is expected to provide substantial utility in advancing one's understanding and problem-solving endeavors.

Case alert! Case classic

Local government

LOOK IT UP: Dorling, T., & Tatam, S. (2017, November 29). *Babies of the borough – Using behavioural insights to reduce anti-social behaviour.* London: Local Government Association. Retrieved from: www.local.gov.uk/case-studies/babies-borough-using-behavioural-insights-reduce-anti-social-behaviour

Read the case study on "Babies of the Borough – Using Behavioural Insights to Reduce Anti-social Behaviour".

During the 2011 riots in Greenwich, London, rioters were causing significant harm to their own community. They were violently tearing apart shop shutters, setting fire to pubs, and causing chaos in the streets, making it an undesirable place to be at that time.

The solution to this problem may have initially seemed straightforward – increasing the presence of police officers on the streets. However, this approach could have been quite expensive. Instead, an innovative (*and* cost-effective) solution emerged. Behavioral scientists stumbled upon a fascinating study that highlighted a natural human instinct: the round face and big eyes of babies elicit a natural caring response from people. This response is hardwired into our psychology.

Taking inspiration from this insight, a creative approach was taken to address the situation. Instead of deploying a large number of police officers, which could potentially escalate violence and damage, a "nudge" strategy was implemented. In areas with high foot traffic and the potential for social unrest, shop front shutters were painted with images of baby faces.

This simple yet ingenious intervention resulted in a remarkable 24% reduction in crime, all without the need for a significant police presence or the associated costs.

Thought questions:

1 Are we all emotional? Do those feelings actually make us act?
2 Was the nudging-style intervention a success?
3 As regards changing behavior that is based on certain emotions, like anger, could neutralizing those emotions first be the best way to do it?
4 Behavioral insights can be used for a *good* cause (as used in the intense context of London riots). Can they be *mis*used?
5 What else can the local government do to sustain the new approach? How can governments strategically build a Behavioral Economics Capability?

To record your critical insights, use the Case Analysis Record provided in Appendix 2.

Greater good corner: Get ready to exercise your ethics

Take a stance: What would *you* do?

Dilemma and Decision: Navigating the dilemma of speeding beyond fines and threats – You've been nudged!

Design an intervention aimed at curbing speeding among drivers that transcends the conventional approach of utilizing speed cameras for detecting and penalizing speed violators. Instead, propose a strategy that *rewards* individuals who adhere to speed limits (potentially incorporating a *lottery* system as part of the intervention).

Please keep in mind the following evaluation criteria: the feasibility and cost-effectiveness of the intervention, and whether the potential outcomes of the intervention extend beyond its immediate objectives.

Note 1: It is essential to emphasize the importance of piloting the proposed intervention, conducting trials, and closely monitoring its success. Through this iterative process, you can identify the key factors contributing to long-term success. Specifically, aim to refrain from relying on fines and sanctions, such as hidden police vehicles and concealed speed cameras, as these may excel at revenue collection but are less effective at genuinely reducing speeding or promoting safer driving behavior. For example, drivers often revert to speeding once they have passed speed feedback signs or cameras.

Note 2: Regarding the question of whether the use of a lottery in a public service context is controversial, some individuals may perceive lotteries as an unconventional method for promoting responsible behavior in the realm of public services, while others might view it as an innovative and potentially effective approach. Public perception, moral considerations, and the specific context in which the lottery is implemented will play pivotal roles in determining its level of ethicality.

Do *you* find the use of a lottery in public service scenarios controversial? Should public safety be gamified? Why or why not?

Time out: Journal entry

Thought Sparks: A few reflections, insightful ideas, actionable suggestions, strategic thinking, and key takeaways from this unit.

Learning never stops… So, pause for a few minutes and reflect in writing on your personal learning experience and beliefs. Through writing in your journal, you develop your awareness of your own beliefs and attitudes. Now, consolidate what you have learned in this unit.

1 How have your beliefs and ideas about applied behavioral science, behavioral economics, and behavioral insights changed since you began the unit?

....

....

2 Thinking about the problems presented in the unit, write about whether you have found solutions to these problems.

....

....

3 How confident do you now feel about capitalizing on behavioral insights?

....

....

4 What would you still like to have clarified? What remaining concerns do you have?

....

....

5 What more would you like to learn about the topic, now that you have completed this unit?

....

....

6 If you want, doodle/draw something you like about behavioral science, economics or insights. This can be as abstract as you wish.

....

....

Remember: It's particularly useful to re-visit journal entries several times and see how themes have recurred or your thoughts have changed over time. Now, repeat "Your Take".

Making connections: Related units and models

- U 2. **The kindness advantage**: Cultivating positively energizing leaders and followers (see pp. 27–53)
- U 3. **Strategic transformation**: Strategy choice-making (see pp. 61–81)
- U 5. **Dialogic organization development (OD)**: Leading positive organizational change (see pp. 103–121)
- U 6. **Design-driven organization**: Human-centered design thinking and innovation execution (see pp. 122–139)
- U 7. **WOW! It's cool!** Crafting a coolness strategy for your brand (see pp. 147–159)
- U 9. **Professional management consulting for real people**: The advice business demystified (see pp. 181–203)
- U 10. **Executive coaching**: Whoop it up! (see pp. 204–219)
- U 13. **Progress with purpose**: The "good" enterprise (see pp. 257–272)
- U 14. **Oops! I messed up.** Why good people do bad things every so often (see pp. 273–287)
- Add in more related models you may want to remember: _____.

Industry snapshot

Dorling, T., & Tatam, S. (2017, November 29). *Babies of the borough – Using behavioural insights to reduce anti-social behaviour*. London: Local Government Association.Retrievedfrom:www.local.gov.uk/case-studies/babies-borough-using-behavioural-insights-reduce-anti-social-behaviour

Note

1 Personal note: The author was deeply saddened by the news of Professor Daniel Kahneman's passing in 2024. Danny, a giant, a genuine human being – and a beacon of inspiration, was a dear friend whom the author first met at the University of California at Berkeley back in 2007. The author will greatly miss their chats about intuition (its marvels and the flaws) and happiness, Danny's optimism and his boundless kind-heartedness.

Deep dive: Main references and resources

Akerlof, G.A., & Shiller, R.J. (2009). *Animal spirits: How human psychology drives the economy, and why it matters for global capitalism*. Princeton, NJ: Princeton University Press.

Altman, M. (Ed.). (2006). *Handbook of contemporary behavioral economics: Foundations and developments*. Armonk, NY: M.E. Sharpe.

Ariely, D. (2010). *Predictably irrational: The hidden forces that shape our decisions* (Revised and expanded edition). New York, NY: Harper Perennial.

Bagozzi, R.P. (2020). Some thoughts on happiness, well-being, and a meaningful life for academics. In D. Iacobucci (Ed.), *Continuing to broaden the marketing concept* (*Review of marketing research, Vol. 17*) (pp. 137–169). Bingley: Emerald Publishing.

Barends, E., & Rousseau, D.M. (2018). *Evidence-based management: How to use evidence to make better organizational decisions*. London & New York, NY: Kogan Page Ltd.

Becker, G. (1976). *The economic approach in human behavior*. Chicago, IL: University of Chicago Press.

Bernheim, D.B., DellaVigna, S., & Laibson, D. (Eds.). (2018). *Handbook of behavioral economics – Foundations and applications 1*. Amsterdam & Oxford: North-Holland.

Bernheim, D.B., DellaVigna, S., & Laibson, D. (Eds.). (2019). *Handbook of behavioral economics – Foundations and applications 2*. Amsterdam & Oxford: North-Holland.

Brunnermeier, M.K., & Reis, R. (2023). *A crash course on crises: Macroeconomic concepts for run-ups, collapses, and recoveries*. Princeton, NJ: Princeton University Press.

Buttliere, B., Arvanitis, A., Białek, M., Choshen-Hillel, S., Davidai, S., Gilovich, T., … Weick, M. (2024). Kahneman in quotes and reflections. *Psychological Inquiry*, 35(1): 3–10.

Chabris, C., & Simons, D. (2011). *The invisible gorilla: How our intuitions deceive us*. New York, NY: Broadway Paperbacks.

Chataway, R. (2020). *The behaviour business: How to apply behavioural science for business success*. Hampshire: Harriman House.

Cialdini, R.B. (2021). *Influence: The psychology of persuasion* (New and expanded edition). New York, NY: Harper Business.

Duffy, B. (2019). *Why we're wrong about nearly everything: A theory of human misunderstanding*. New York, NY: Basic Books.

Eyal, N. (2020). *Indistractable: How to control your attention and choose your life*. London: Bloomsbury Publishing.

Flesher, J. (2023). *Through a paradox lens: An introduction to paradoxical thinking and problem solving*. Ninatic, CT: Wisdom Mates Press.

Friedman, M. (1953). *Essays in positive economics*. Chicago, IL: University of Chicago Press.

Gigerenzer, G. (2007). *Gut feelings: The intelligence of the unconscious*. London: Penguin Books.

Gladwell, M. (2005). *Blink: The power of thinking without thinking*. New York, NY: Little, Brown and Company.

Gneezy, U. (2023). *Mixed signals: How incentives really work*. New Haven, CT & London: Yale University Press.

Halpern, D. (2016). *Inside the nudge unit: How small changes can make a big difference*. London: WH Allen.

Haynes, L., Service O., Goldacre, B., & Torgerson, D. (2012). *Test, learn, adapt: Developing public policy with randomized control trials*. London: Cabinet Office Behavioural Insights Team.

Hershfield, H. (2023). *Your future self: How to make tomorrow better today*. London: Little, Brown Spark.

Iyengar, S. (2010). *The art of choosing*. New York, NY: Twelve.

Johnson, E.J. (2021). *The elements of choice: Why the way we decide matters*. New York, NY: Riverhead Books.

Kahneman, D. (2011). *Thinking, fast and slow*. New York, NY: Farrar, Straus and Giroux.

Kahneman, D., & Tversky, A. (1984). Choices, values, and frames. *American Psychologist*, 39(4): 341–350.

Keynes, J.M. (2018). *The general theory of employment, interest, and money*. Cham: Palgrave Macmillan. (Original work published 1936).

Levitt, S.D., & Dubner, S.J. (2006). *Freakonomics: A rogue economist explores the hidden side of everything*. London: Penguin Books.

Lewis, M. (2017). *The undoing project: A friendship that changed the world.* New York, NY: W.W. Norton & Company.

Luca, M., & Bazerman, M.H. (2020). *The power of experiments: Decision making in a data-driven world.* Cambridge, MA & London: The MIT Press.

Marshall, A. (2013). *Principles of economics.* London: Palgrave Macmillan. (Original work published 1890).

Mažar, N., & Soman, D. (Eds.). (2022). *Behavioral science in the wild.* Toronto: Rotman-UTP Publishing.

Mill, J.S. (1987). *Utilitarianism.* Buffalo, NY: Prometheus Books. (Original work published 1863).

Morson, G.S., & Schapiro, M. (2017). *Cents and sensibility: What economics can learn from the humanities.* Princeton, NJ: Princeton University Press.

Roberto, C.A., & Kawachi, I. (Eds.). (2015). *Behavioral economics and public health.* Oxford: Oxford University Press.

Schrager, A. (2019). *An economist walks into a brothel: And other unexpected places to understand risk.* New York, NY: Portfolio/Penguin.

Schwartz, B. (2016). *The paradox of choice: Why more is less* (Revised edition). New York, NY: Ecco.

Sharot, T., & Sunstein, C.R. (2024). *Look again: The power of noticing what was always there.* New York, NY: Atria/One Signal Publishers.

Shiller, R.J. (2019). *Narrative economics: How stories go viral and drive major economic events.* Princeton, NJ: Princeton University Press.

Simon, H.A. (1957). *Models of man: Social and rational.* New York, NY: Wiley.

Smith, A. (1759). *The theory of moral sentiments.* London: Pantianos Classics.

Smith, A. (1904). *An inquiry into the nature and causes of the wealth of nations,* 2 Vols., Everyman's library. London: Dent & Sons. (Original work published 1776).

Soman, D. (2017). *The last mile: Creating social and economic value from behavioral insights.* Toronto: Rotman-UTP Publishing.

Soman, D., & Yeung, C. (Eds.). (2021). *The behaviorally informed organization.* Toronto: Rotman-UTP Publishing.

Sunstein, C.R., & Reisch, L.A. (Eds.). (2023). *Research handbook on nudges and society.* Cheltenham: Edward Elgar Publishing Ltd.

Sutter, M. (2023). *Behavioral economics for leaders: Research-based insights on the weird, irrational, and wonderful ways humans navigate the workplace.* Hoboken, NJ: Wiley.

Thaler, R.H. (2015). *Misbehaving: The making of behavioral economics.* New York, NY & London: W.W. Norton & Company.

Thaler, R.H., & Sunstein, C.R. (2003). Libertarian paternalism. *The American Economic Review,* 93(2): 175–179.

Thaler, R.H., & Sunstein, C.R. (2009). *Nudge: Improving decisions about health, wealth, and happiness* (Revised and expanded edition). London: Penguin Books.

Thomke, S.H. (2020). *Experimentation works: The surprising power of business experiments.* Boston, MA: Harvard Business Review Press.

Tkaczyk, B. (2021). *Leading positive organizational change: Energize – redesign – gel.* London & New York, NY: Routledge.

Tversky, A., & Kahneman, D. (1974). Judgment under uncertainty: Heuristics and biases. *Science,* 185(4157): 1124–1131.

Williamson, O.E. (1985). *The economic institutions of capitalism: Firms, markets, relational contracting.* New York, NY: Free Press.

Zamir, E., & Teichman, D. (Eds.). (2014). *The Oxford handbook of behavioral economics and the law.* Oxford: Oxford University Press.

2 The kindness advantage

Cultivating positively energizing leaders and followers

Several years ago, management scholars asked the faculty of West Point (The United States Military Academy) the following question: "*Since developing leadership is what this place is all about, how do you go about doing that task?*"

The reply was as follows: "*We begin by teaching them to be followers*".

Sneak peek

Focus on: Key concepts and terms

Unit 2

- Behavior (loving, organizational, positive, prosocial, toxic)
- Capital (economic, financial, human, psychological, social, spiritual)
- Check-ins (daily)
- Energy (boost, drain, emotional, life-giving, level, management, mental, negative, network, organizational, personal, physical, positive, productive, relational, spiritual)
- Flow
- Followership (co-active, positive, positively energizing, strengths-based)
- Generosity spectrum ("givers", "matchers", "takers")
- Givers (selfless, self-protective)
- Gratitude (expression, journaling, writing)
- Heliotropic effect
- High-quality connections (HQCs)
- Kindness (as a small act, as an event, as an intervention; behaviors; celebrate; zone)
- Leadership (heart-based, humble, idealism, kind-hearted, positive, positively energizing, presence, realism, servant, strengths-based, toxic, tyrannical)

DOI: 10.4324/9781003508274-4

- Loving-kindness meditation
- Positive organizational behavior (POB)
- Positive psychological capital (PsyCap) (optimism, hope, confidence, and resiliency)
- Power (fear-based vs. respect-based)
- Strength
- Talent
- Thriving
- Zone (aggression, comfort, passion, resignation)

Pause 'N' reflect: On the current issues and trends

Before you complete this unit, think about each of the following statements. Mark each statement:

V – if you *agree.*
X – if you *disagree.*
? – if you are *undecided.*

	Your Take: Integrative Thinking	*Before doing Unit 2*	*After doing Unit 2*
1	"Leadership is love" – Mark Rittenberg		
2	Toxic co-workers aren't just irritating – they affect your work quality too.		
3	Kids know what makes a great leader more than some adults… A great leader puts others' interests first. By way of illustration, 5- to 6-year-old kids view leaders as more responsible (not more entitled!), relative to non-leaders. Even infants distinguish between "leaders" and "bullies", and they expect leaders to actually right wrongs.		
4	Everyone deserves to flourish at work.		
5	"Good fences make good neighbors" – Robert Frost		

Your Take: Integrative Thinking	*Before doing Unit 2*	*After doing Unit 2*	
6 Performing random acts of kindness (such as giving away a cup of hot chocolate in a park) increases happiness in both givers and receivers, but people who perform a random act of kindness tend to undervalue their positive impact on recipients.			
7 Individuals do not uncritically continue the cycle of low-quality, toxic leadership. They imitate it when they lack concern for others. Following an experience with an abusive supervisor, those who prize kindness can break the cycle. Conversely, individuals who idealize self-centeredness do not. The role models we choose to follow mirror our personal values.			
8 Positive energy is strongly related to performance – success through individual and collective goal achievement, engagement, job satisfaction, and firm performance.			
9 Extremely good organizational leaders are primarily behavioral and organizational psychologists – they have an exceptional understanding of real human nature and behavior. Leadership is chiefly a communication quality, disposition or habit possessed by leaders.			
10 "Kindness?! Kind-hearted leadership feels good, but it won't win the day. Don't you know we are trying to sort out unprecedented cuts now and you're talking about this? I'm the boss! Why should I care if they like me? Intelligence helps more" – Chief executive officer			

After you have done the unit, repeat "Your Take". How has reading the unit clarified the ideas herein? How have your views, feelings and thoughts changed over time?

Lead-in

General discussion points

Individually or in buzz groups, work on the following:

1 Are leaders *born* or *made*?
2 *Investment* or *cost*? How important is this litmus test for leadership and talent development, and why? How does *your* organization develop C-suite executives, leadership cadre, high-potentials, and all employees?
3 There is no greater thing that you can tell someone than, "*I believe in you, you're good, I'm there for you*" – Coach K, quoted in *Time* magazine's selection of America's Best 2001. Discuss the point the sentence is making.
4 Kindness is contagious! Just observing acts of kindness makes people feel good and inspires them to want to behave more kindly. Do you agree? Are people kinder in the city or the countryside? What are the benefits of talking to strangers? Why is being kind to yourself so important, too?
5 Can bosses be kind? What are the benefits of being a kind boss, with a heart that listens? How to re-imagine the concept of kindness in a business context?
6 Describe a time when you felt most alive and vibrant at work. How do you create energizing, generative relationships in the workplace? Can building and sustaining high-quality connections (HQCs) created in everyday positive interactions with others at work be taught at business schools? If yes, what activities could you suggest?
7 Recall an instance when you brought out the best in someone and thus inspired the "peak performance" in them. Describe the actions you took and the methods you used to achieve this outcome.
8 Suffering in the workplace can rob you of humanity, dignity, and motivation, and it remains an unrecognized and costly drain on organizational energy and organization's full potential. How to deal with arrogance, low-quality and corrosive relationships at work? Provide an instance in which you have observed the successful management of toxic behavior within a professional setting. Why did it work?
9 What might be the reasons employees often don't ask for help from each other? What might prevent them from asking for help at work? What kind of help might you call on a co-worker for? Is asking for help a sign of weakness in your country/culture?
10 Do we need leaders at all? Discuss what alternatives there might be.

Idea watch

Until now, a significant portion of the academic focus within organizational studies and management research has been dedicated to the examination of leaders. Most assume that organizations succeed or fail, compete or crumble, on the basis of how effectively they are led. However, it's important to remember that leadership is only one part of the equation. Positive followers play an equally vital role too – without co-active followership, leadership is nothing. Yet, the concept of followership has remained largely overlooked.

The etymological roots of the words *leadership* and *followership* are of interest. The word *leader* first appeared in the English language in the 1300s, deriving from the root word *leden*, which conveys a sense of "to show the way". Subsequently, approximately five centuries later, the term *leadership* came into existence. The action verb *to follow* is rooted in the Old English *folgian, fylgian, fylgan*, which means "to accompany (especially as a disciple), move in the same direction as; follow after, pursue, move behind in the same direction"; rooted in the Old German word *follaziohan*, which means "to help", "serve" and "assist".

In reality, no matter what job title and company appear on your business card, on occasion, each one of us leads, and each one of us follows. In effective partnerships, there are instances where we lead and then seamlessly transition to following. To be a good leader, one might want to start by being a good follower. In essence, the connection between leading and following is dynamic, fluid, context-specific, and continually changing. This empowering interpretation makes leadership accessible to all, removes the stigma from followership, and facilitates more productive and creative collaborations.

As it happens, leaders are only ever as effective as their ability to harmoniously engage and connect with followers. Positive leadership – heart-based leadership – within *positive* organizational behavior (POB) that studies and applies positively oriented human resource strengths, talents and psychological capacities, is the process of energizing others to work together collaboratively to accomplish great things and of leading people toward a better future. In fact, the desire to have a positive impact on others for the good of the organization is a key predictor of "executive potential", understood as leading with strengths, continuously learning, maximizing their energy, connectedness, care and compassion, building trust, strategizing to win ethically, embracing new experiences and creating hope for the future, investing in and developing others, and bringing out strengths in others, among others.

A leader's level of positivity impacts how followers think, feel, and behave. Leading any organization involves the dissemination of positivity throughout the entire enterprise. When followers are in the presence of a positive leader, they can "catch" the leader's emotions. Effective people are high on, what Fred Luthans and POB colleagues call, positive "psychological capital" (PsyCap), namely *optimism, hope, confidence*, and *resiliency* – combined. PsyCap can serve as an intrinsically valuable human asset. Indeed, it's difficult to picture a successful person capable of energizing, mobilizing, inspiring and motivating others without having a positive and hopeful outlook, confidence in their team, and the resilience to withstand and bounce back.

Similar to the now well-acknowledged concepts of human and social capital, PsyCap is a takeoff from economic capital, where resources are invested and harnessed for future gains. Nevertheless, positive PsyCap extends beyond financial capital ("how much money one has"), human capital ("what you know") and social capital ("who you know"), focusing more directly on "who you are" and, crucially, "who you are becoming/evolving into" (in other words, the process of developing one's actual self to become one's best possible self).

In contrast to personality traits, which tend to be relatively fixed and resistant to change, hope, optimism, confidence and resiliency (PsyCap) – the positively oriented psychological capacities that can be measured, developed, and managed for performance enhancement – are seen as more malleable and amenable to learning and development (L&D). Additionally, they demonstrate performance impact. Brief training initiatives have proven effective in increasing participants' PsyCap levels and, as a result, their subsequent performance. In fact, recent utility analyses suggest that a 2.5-hour PsyCap training program for engineering managers with an average salary of $100,900 can generate a remarkable 270% return on investment (ROI).

Furthermore, when you factor in the concept of "spiritual capital" – which encompasses individuals' connection with God and their attempts to live it out and interact with others – it can serve as a reliable predictor for significant business outcomes. For instance, new research from Baylor University's Hankamer School of Business reveals that heightened levels of "spiritual capital" – the motivation, energy, and strong work ethic derived from one's relationship with God – can have a positive effect on business success, employment, and innovation, even after controlling for other forms of capital. Consequently, businesses are experiencing growth, attracting more workforce interest, increasing their sales, and having the confidence to try new things and venture out.

On an individual level, the "strengths" approach, when executed effectively, involves recognizing our naturally recurring patterns of thinking, feeling or behavior – otherwise known as "talents". These talents are then integrated into one's view of self, and lead to behavioral changes. Both individuals and organizations can nurture their strengths by enhancing their talents through knowledge and skill development. A strength, in this context, denotes the capability to consistently deliver high-quality (near-perfect) performance in a specific activity. It's important to note that a strengths-based organization doesn't ignore weaknesses, but, instead, aims for optimization and/or performance above the norm. This entails concentrating on and developing talents while understanding and effectively managing weaknesses. Fundamentally, individuals, teams and enterprises gain more by leveraging and building upon their talents and strengths, as opposed to expending comparable efforts to improve areas of weakness.

Customarily, "heroic" leadership paid little attention to kindness and care and a recognition of aspiring leaders who derive their strength from integrating kindness in their positive leadership approach. Though the world may not feel like an extremely kind place in the present climate (headlines speak of wars, hate crimes, social inequality and imbalance, and "us-versus-them" divisiveness), it could be precisely the moment when acts of kindness matter the most.

Kindness encompasses enduring aspects of character and behavior that promote social harmony and acknowledges that kindness is both innate and shaped through socialization. Kindness has "contagious" qualities – it helps to cultivate a compassionate and connected workforce, in other words, it helps to create and sustain, what Jane Dutton calls, "high-quality connections" (HQCs) at work – small bits of positively deviant everyday interactions with other people that are life-giving and that enhance organizational cooperation and L&D.

Additionally, kindness is strongly linked with well-being and gratitude. For example, "prosocial behavior" – voluntarily helping others – can help lower daily stress levels. Furthermore, research finds that feelings of caring predict health status in midlife. By way of illustration, in one study, 91% of participants who did not perceive themselves to have had a warm relationship with their mothers – assessed during college – had diagnosed diseases in midlife, including coronary artery disease, hypertension, duodenal ulcer, and alcoholism, as compared to 45% of participants who perceived themselves to have had a warm relationship with their mothers. A similar association between perceived warmth and closeness and future illness was obtained for fathers.

Now, take gratitude – the practice of appreciating positive life features. For instance, gratitude writing can improve the mental health, positively affect neural activity (subjects who participate in gratitude letter writing show both behavioral increases in gratitude and significantly greater neural modulation by gratitude in the medial prefrontal cortex three months later) as well as contribute to hearts having healthier resting rates (gratitude journaling may improve biomarkers related to heart failure morbidity, such as reduced inflammation). Moreover, gratitude can help increase longevity, too (e.g., positive emotional content in early-life autobiographies is strongly associated with longevity six decades later).

Ultimately, happy people become happier – through kindness. This fuels "upward spirals" toward optimal individual and organizational functioning.

Assumptions

Admittedly, leadership continues to be a very hot topic, and everyone wants to be a more effective leader, even if we now live in (supposedly) more "democratic" times with empowered staff and flatter and leaner enterprises. But without followers, there are no leaders or leadership. Given their need for joint participation and mutual responsiveness, leaders and followers require greater synchronization. Of note, the follower is not a passive part of the leadership formula. In truth, leadership/followership may be seen not as a role, but as a function or an activity that can be shared among members of a group or organization. Positive leaders and followers who are naturally co-creative, resourceful, and whole are active collaborators in an empowered and nurturing developmental partnership. Such a "shared partnership" approach can be technically neither leader-centered nor follower-centered.

Take the dancing team of Fred Astaire and Ginger Rogers – Fred and Ginger are among the most iconic dance couples in history. Was Ginger Rogers less of a dancer for being the follower? In an episode of BBC favorite *Talking Pictures*, Fred shared:

> Ginger was certainly the most effective partner I had – everybody knows that … It was a whole other thing, what we did. I just want to pay tribute to Ginger, because we did so many pictures together … And believe me, it was a value to have that girl. Oh, she had it! She was just great.

At bottom, it always "takes two to tango".

To tell the truth, you gain more by developing your gifts and leveraging your strengths than by repairing your weaknesses. When you give your employees the chance to learn and grow, they *thrive* ("vitality" – the sense that you're energized and alive + "L&D" – the gaining of knowledge and skills) – and so will your enterprise.

More than anything else, humans seek happiness. For example, the U.S. Declaration of independence, in 1776, declared that all have a right to the "pursuit of happiness"; the song "Happy Birthday" was composed in 1926; the yellow and black "smiley" face was invented in 1963; and McDonald's introduced the "Happy Meal" in 1977. As St Dwynwen, the Welsh patron saint of lovers, would famously say: "Nothing wins hearts like cheerfulness".

"All human beings flourish in the presence of light or of positive energy", emphasizes Kim Cameron. Optimistic, hopeful, confident, and resilient CEOs have higher performing organizations, too. Indeed, positive personal, relational, and organizational energy is the fuel that great enterprises run upon – positive, life-giving energy in organizations matters for performance, innovation, learning, and morale. What truly brings about a fulfilling experience is a state referred to as "flow". In this state, as informed by Mihaly Csikszentmihalyi, individuals usually encounter profound pleasure, unleash their creativity, treat others with kindness, and become fully engrossed in the present moment of life.

Even random acts of kindness and small gestures matter more than we may think. Income makes little difference to how kind people are. Living *kindly* is the key to your current and future well-being, happiness, better relationships, and future success. As Nelson Mandela so succinctly put it:

"What counts in life is not the mere fact that we have lived; it is what difference we have made to the lives of others that will determine the significance of the life we lead".

Key elements

You only have so many hours in the day. Positive *personal, relational* (see "Applications" below), and *organizational* energy is the fuel that keeps enterprises fired up – it can help boost kindness, empathy, care, helping, thoughtfulness, and compassion. Plus, energy can be systematically expanded and renewed.

Personal energy

Jim Loehr and Tony Schwarz speak of four dimensions of personal energy: physical, emotional, mental, and spiritual. Specifically:

- *Physical energy* (Stamina) – fuels and develops endurance and fitness. Physical energy boosts that will re-energize you include: regular sleep, exercise, and proper nutrition.
- *Emotional energy* (Relational harmony) – energizes and builds HQCs that enliven people. Emotional energy boosts that will re-energize you include being positive and caring, helping others or just undertaking random acts of kindness.
- *Mental energy* (Learning power and agility) – creates appropriate focus and generates attentiveness. Mental energy boosts that will re-energize you include taking breaks or ending multitasking and replacing this with sequential tasking.
- *Spiritual energy* (Purpose) – provides a powerful source of motivation, hope, true grit, centeredness, and positive executive presence. Spiritual energy boosts that will re-energize you include keeping a gratitude journal, imaginative contemplation exercises or praying.

Worth mentioning is the fact that effective energy management encompasses two primary elements: the utilization of energy ("stress") and its renewal ("recovery"). By way of illustration, let's look at the actual training and expected performance of a world-class athlete and of a typical executive. The challenges confronted by executives in sustaining peak performance on a daily, quarterly or yearly basis far exceed the demands on athletes … Consider this: a typical professional athlete predominantly dedicates their time to practice, with only a small portion – typically a few minutes/hours a day at most – actually spent in competitive situations. Conversely, a typical executive allocates minimal time to training and is required to perform promptly for extended periods, ranging from 10 to even 16 hours each day. Further, athletes benefit from several months of off-season break, whereas most executives are lucky to secure merely two to four weeks of annual vacation, if any. While the career span of an average professional athlete is approximately 4–7 years, a typical executive is expected to work for four through five decades…

Organizational energy

In similar fashion, as echoed in a number of studies, thinking about *organizational* energy is all-important. For example, as reported by Heike Bruch and Bernd Vogel, it's essential to keep track of the organizational energy that your enterprise is characterized by. So:

- If you're low on positive organizational energy ("comfortable inertia"), you are staying within your "comfort zone".
- Watch it, if you're consistently low but on negative organizational energy ("resignation inertia"), it's substantially a continuing "resignation zone". People may feel hopeless and defeated.

- Worse, if you're high on negative energy ("corrosive energy"), your enterprise is being dragged down into the "aggression zone". People may feel fearful, defensive, and resentful.
- Now, think of the opposite. If you're high on energy which is positive ("productive energy"), you're operating in a "kindness/passion/compassion zone", which is where you want to be – this is where people easily connect and flourish – and so do organizations (there's a positive relationship between the productive energy of firms and their overall performance).

Kindness meta-patterns

Last but not least, various patterns emerge that signify diverse ways of depicting kindness, as identified by Kristin Williams and Heidi Weigand. These kindness, or loving, behaviors include, for instance:

- *Kindness "as a small act"* – kindness as a small act, viewed as a minor gesture, isn't seen as a substantial obligation, yet it remains memorable and appreciated.
- *Kindness "as an event"* – kindness presented as an event necessitates co-ordination, guided by structure (and regulations), accompanied by a feeling of responsibility. It could be motivated by unfortunate events or significant moments, embodying the collaboration of one or numerous individuals who gather to meaningfully back up, recognize, or appreciate someone.
- *Kindness "as intervention"* – kindness as an intervention refers to purposeful acts of assistance where one or multiple parties intervene to provide (professional) aid. This may require life experience and preparedness (and, frequently, specialist expertise) when executing the behavior – people discern various complex social scenarios and take intentional measures to provide workable solutions. These actions often result in significant transformative effects.

 Thinking critically: Issues

Thus far, many organizational scholars and management researchers have concentrated primarily on the study of leaders, but leadership is only half the story. Indeed, there are no leaders without followers, yet the idea of followership has received very little attention.

While social researchers have suggested that expectations about imbalances in power attributed to leadership have slowly developed throughout the span of human history, we now know that leadership is more than a title or a position of privilege. Some of these expectations pertain to leaders' responsibilities to their followers.

More seriously, leadership tyranny represents an extreme manifestation of *leadership idealism*. Idealists, inspired by an elitist perspective akin to Plato's, assert that leadership is an inherent, inborn quality, signifying an elite status, and making them the "chosen" few. In instances of tyrannical leadership, a common thread is the leaders' perception of their superiority over followers, who are viewed as inferior subordinates. At its core, the essence of tyrannical leadership within an organization lies in the severe, sometimes oppressive, exercise of authority. Tyrants construct their own *utopian* organizational reality and invent their own ethics – this is not situation ethics but "ethics in the situation". Conversely, those who place confidence in *leadership realism*, influenced by Aristotle's rejection of Plato's elitist leadership, contend that leadership is something earned and developed. They believe that continuous learning, training, and education contribute to the formation of leaders. In both business and non-profit organizations, there is no room for narcissistic, pathological tyrants driving "productivity" at any organizational level.

Moreover, psychology research from the University of Illinois Urbana-Champaign and Bar-Ilan University finds that even children know that a genuine leader puts others' interests first. By way of illustration, 21-month-old infants(!) distinguish between "leaders" (*respect*-based power) and "bullies" (*fear*-based power). What's more, 17-month-old infants(!) expect leaders to intervene in within-group transgressions and confront the wrongdoers, yet they don't specifically expect non-leaders to step in during such situations. Further, five-year-olds(!) view leaders as more responsible (*not* more entitled), relative to non-leaders. Children of that age, too, recognize social hierarchies and are conscious when others fail to contribute equitably. At this developmental stage, to conclude, children only regard someone as a leader if that individual makes sacrifices to attain a shared objective – and "leaders" who take more than they give are considered unacceptable to young children – they are not actually leaders at all. The heart of the matter is: even very young infants prefer those who behave prosocially (a *helping* scenario) versus antisocially (a *hindering* scenario). Characteristically, human beings naturally gravitate toward positive energy and what is life-giving and away from negative energy and what is life-depleting. This is known as the "heliotropic effect" (compare with, in botany, the directional growth of a plant in response to sunlight, or, in zoology, the tendency of an animal to move toward light).

Unquestionably, leaders can gain valuable insights on how to lead not only from their followers but also from their own children. When very young children are exposed to *caring* parental leadership, they *trust* their parents completely – they believe in the good, reliability, truth, ability, and strength of their parents. Curiously, children are sometimes kinder and more understanding than adults and can teach adults how to foster harmonious relationships. An interesting comparison can also be drawn between the difficulties faced when learning to lead for the first time and the challenges of becoming a good parent. In both situations, and maybe somewhat unexpectedly, it's the junior who teach their superordinates the art of leadership.

Now, returning to the subject of leaders and their generosity, organizational "givers" (at the top) are often called humble "servant" leaders – they *altruistically* put the needs of others first, which contributes to the achievements of their enterprise. Similarly, research shows that before the age of two, toddlers experience more happiness when giving treats to others than when receiving them. Moreover, they feel even happier after engaging in *costly giving* – forfeiting their own resources – compared to giving the same treat without any cost. This suggests that the positive emotions associated with giving are a key factor in promoting human cooperation.

Be that as it may, as explained by Adam Grant, an organizational psychologist, generosity can have a dark side, too. People who are known for their *selfless* giving (e.g., willingly offering their time, energy, attention, and know-how – for instance, by arriving early and staying late, developing others' skills, facilitating connections, etc.) are specifically targeted for exploitation. By neglecting your own needs, exhibiting selflessness in the workplace might result in fatigue, lagging behind on your own professional goals, and experiencing stress and conflict at home. If you fail to establish boundaries around this, it will leave you exposed to "takers" (to identify takers, observe their behavior: *they behave as if they're entitled to your help and don't hesitate to intrude on your time*; and/or ask them: *can you give me the names of three people whose careers you've considerably improved?*), which will put you at the peril of burning yourself out – and, ironically, you may end up coming to others' help much less.

Alternatively, rather than choosing to be "givers" or "takers", on the "generosity spectrum", some opt to operate as "matchers", engaging in a balanced exchange of favors. They reciprocate in kind, anticipating some return of favors. However, matching *is* transactional – it adds comparatively less value for both you and others, yet it can be advantageous when dealing with someone who tends to take more than they give.

While it may be desirable to have a workforce primarily composed of givers, especially *self-protective* givers who are mindful of *self*-care (yes, be generous, but also recognize your boundaries – remember that saying "no" liberates you to actually say "yes" when it *truly* counts), it's critical to avoid selecting individuals who are solely focused on benefiting themselves, and who view every interaction as a chance to further their personal agenda.

The bottom line is, you may not want to choose to always be everything to everyone. *Reactive* helping (constant ad hoc requests for help can substantially drain people's energy) is fatiguing, yet *proactive* giving can be energizing.

 Applications

To cultivate positively energizing leadership and followership, you can, for example, use the following strengths-based practices and tools: (I) "Daily Check-ins", (II) "Loving-kindness Meditation", and (III) "Mapping a Positive Relational Energy Network".

I Daily Check-in

As part of your daily strengths-based leadership/followership development routine, here are some 12 self-coaching "check-in" questions.

In this context, you don't focus on primary competencies like understanding financial statements, and/or project valuations, planning and executing a merger deal, or using business analytics to predict unplanned downtime of capital-intensive assets and to identify inefficiencies in your operations. Instead, the interventions below are geared toward helping you build your capacity for more effective and positive "thinking performance", "talent development", "super-flexible strategizing", or "design thinking" (and "design doing"). By enhancing your dynamic capabilities across the board, you can develop your full potential and consistently sustain high performance.

Keep a logbook and "check in" with yourself daily by asking yourself the following 12 questions, registering, and reflecting on how you are developing:

Professionally as "Thinking Energizer". Did I bring my "A" game to:

* energize my workplace and home today?
* choose and show my positive leadership/followership presence today?
* develop some skill(s) or learn something new today?

Professionally as "People Operator". Did I bring my "A" game to:

* be a humble servant leader/follower today? Authentically listen, and demonstrate great empathy, care, and deep human understanding today?
* recognize or develop other people's talent today?
* build and sustain HQCs and model loving behavior today?

Professionally as "Strategic Navigator". Did I bring my "A" game to:

* have winning aspirations today?
* exercise super-flexibility today?
* lead change positively and sustainably today?

Professionally as "Innovator-Designer". Did I bring my "A" game to:

* use imagination today?
* design something new today?
* solve some complex problem creatively today?

Positive professional's notes

....

....

I solemnly promise to do my best to cultivate professionalism and positivity – every day.

Signed ....…… [Your name].

VARIATIONS/TIPS: For each question, you might want to score yourself on a 1–7 scale, comparing yesterday's effort with previous days. At the end of each week, you can create a Report Card – with your calculated results.

II A Loving-Kindness Meditation Practice

To appreciate and identify with co-workers, customers, and clients more empathically, you can check in with yourself daily with the help of "loving-kindness meditation", too.

Based in a meditative tradition, loving-kindness mediation is a contemplative practice that boosts relational energy and enhances social connectedness by directing good wishes toward yourself and other people. To find, build, deepen and maintain calm and compassion and connect better with others, devote some time each day (between meetings, design sprints, while commuting – whenever there is a free moment) and engage in this contemplative practice.

You can begin by directing the good wishes at yourself – *May I be happy and healthy. May I be filled with peace. May I pay attention to what has heart and meaning. May I always choose love, joy, gratitude.* After that, you can contemplate and direct your love toward someone you feel grateful for – your significant other, your daughter or son, perhaps – and say, *May she/he be happy and healthy. May she/he be filled with ease. May she/he always choose love, joy, gratitude.* Now, you can visualize your "difficult" direct report and extend the feeling of positive regard outward to her or him and repeat, *May she/he be happy and healthy. May she/he find calm. May she/he be full-, open-, clear-, and strong-hearted. May she/he always choose love, joy, gratitude.* Finally, to close the practice, you can reflect on all human beings and direct your unconditional well-wishes toward everyone universally: *May all human beings – everywhere – stay happy and healthy. May everyone pay attention to what has heart and meaning.*

III Mapping a Positive Relational Energy Network

To further help build and sustain HQCs that energize the workplace, you can adopt a technique known as "mapping a positive relational energy network". Relational energy is vital – it's positively associated with employee job performance through the mechanism of job engagement.

Every day, you can ask those who directly report to you to rate their level of physical, emotional, mental, and spiritual energy on a 10-point scale. To methodologically track trends, you can also ask your team to average out their results over the week. This will help you and all the team members better understand how people react to different critical incidents and what affects their productive energy levels.

To prevent burnout, monitor the acceleration trap – doing too much at the same time or constantly pushing to limits. Recognize that renewing energy is as important as expending it. On a weekly basis, you can ask your staff to actually jot down the names of three co-workers they would endorse for positive energy and identify as the most positively energizing in their work team. In the end, the scores are graded by determining the number of endorsements won by each employee.

This ritual can help you better capitalize on relational energy and workplace relationships, and more effectively deploy positive energizers so that they can energize others to support business objectives and organizational strategy, ultimately achieving spectacular results.

Case alert! Case classic

Starbucks corporation

LOOK IT UP: Rothaermel, F.T., & McBride, C. (2023). *Starbucks corporation*. New York, NY: McGraw-Hill Inc. Retrieved from: https://store.hbr.org/product/starbucks-corporation/MH0074

Read the case study on "Starbucks Corporation", Additionally, visit: https://stories.starbucks.com/stories/2023/a-little-kindness-is-never-really-little/.

Kindness uplifts us all. Starbucks' aspiration is to be "people positive" – **investing in humanity** and the well-being of everyone they connect with, from their "partners" (employees) to coffee farmers to the customers in their stores and beyond.

As Howard Schultz, former Starbucks CEO and now lifelong Chairman Emeritus, evangelizes: "Over a cup of coffee, we bring people together".

A little kindness is never really little – here are some inspiring stories of kindness heard from Starbucks partners and customers.

Kelsie, partner:

> When Robert walks into Kelsie's store, she greets him like she does every customer. Except Robert is Deafblind, and Kelsie communicates with him using a combination of American Sign Language and Tactile Sign Language that she learned from another barista who is Deaf. "It's very **life-giving** to be able to have that moment or be able to **connect** with someone.

she says. "That is something I don't want a customer to miss out on".
From a customer in Rye, NY:

> It had been another crazy morning getting the family up early. After I dropped the kids off at the bus stop, I went into my local Starbucks and ordered my usual. But when I reached into my jacket pocket, I noticed I had left my wallet and phone at home. Thankfully the **kindest** woman was standing behind me and **offered** to pay for my coffee. I don't know her name, but **thank you** so much to whoever you are.

Although when times are being tough and turbulent, moments of kindness can be harder to see, every day, in every community, they *are* happening.

1 Starbucks' leadership has long been believers in the "human connection". Now, how can they ensure the continued growth of *digital* connections?

2   How can kindness further fuel and inspire strategic leadership and strategy execution (positive organizational change, and organizational culture) at Starbucks?

3   Are there other companies where "heart-based leadership/followership" is practiced? Can you think of some examples?

4   How do *you* celebrate the kindness around you?

5   Pour yourself some kindness (and really good coffee!) – sit back, meditate, and relax. To help inspire moments of compassion, start with being kind to yourself…

To record your critical insights, use the Case Analysis Record provided in Appendix 2.

Greater good corner: Get ready to exercise your ethics

Take a stance: What would *you* do?

Dilemma and Decision: Give or take?
You and a stranger will both receive some cash. You have three choices about what you and the stranger will get, and you'll never see or meet the stranger. Which option would *you* choose?

a   I receive $50, and the stranger receives $50

b   I receive $80, and the stranger receives $40

c   I receive $50, and the stranger receives $70

Time out: Journal entry

Thought Sparks: A few reflections, insightful ideas, actionable suggestions, strategic thinking, and key takeaways from this unit.

Learning never stops… So, pause for a few minutes and reflect in writing on your personal learning experience and beliefs. Through writing in your journal, you develop your awareness of your own beliefs and attitudes. Now, consolidate what you have learned in this unit.

1 How have your beliefs and ideas about leadership and followership changed since you began the unit?

....

....

2 Thinking about the problems presented in the unit, write about whether you have found solutions to these problems.

....

....

3 How confident do you now feel about leading/following kindly and modeling loving behavior?

....

....

4 What would you still like to have clarified? What remaining concerns do you have?

....

....

5 What more would you like to learn about the topic, now that you have completed this unit?

....

....

6 If you want, doodle/draw something you like about human kindness and/or heart-based leadership/followership. This can be as abstract as you wish.

....

....

Remember: It's particularly useful to re-visit journal entries several times and see how themes have recurred or your thoughts have changed over time. Now, repeat "Your Take".

Making connections: Related units and models

- U 1. **Behavioral economics and policy 101**: For humans (see pp. 9–26)
- U 4. **SOAR:** Possibility thinking in positive strategic dialog (see pp. 82–95)
- U 5. **Dialogic organization development (OD)**: Leading positive organizational change (see pp. 103–121)
- U 6. **Design-driven organization**: Human-centered design thinking and innovation execution (see pp. 122–139)
- U 8. **Once upon a time…** Strategic brand storytelling (see pp. 160–174)
- U 9. **Professional management consulting for real people**: The advice business demystified (see pp. 181–203)
- U 10. **Executive coaching**: Whoop it up! (see pp. 204–219)
- U 12. **Small world**: Are you a culturally intelligent organization? (see pp. 238–250)
- U 13. **Progress with purpose**: The "good" enterprise (see pp. 257–272)
- U 14. **Oops! I messed up.** Why good people do bad things every so often (see pp. 273–287)
- Add in more related models you may want to remember: _____.

Industry snapshot

Snook, S.A., Perlow, L.A., & DeLacey, B. (2005). Coach Knight: The will to win. Harvard Business School Case 406–043. Retrieved from: https://store.hbr.org/product/coach-knight-the-will-to-win/406043?sku=406043-PDF-ENG

Snook, S.A., Perlow, L.A., & DeLacey, B. (2005). Coach K: A matter of the heart. Harvard Business School Case 406–044. Retrieved from: https://store.hbr.org/product/coach-k-a-matter-of-the-heart/406044?sku=406044-PDF-ENG

Reflective exercise

- Compare and contrast Coach K and Coach Knight. How are they different/similar? Discuss other leadership styles you know about.
- If you were a talented young basketball player, whom would you rather play for – Coach K or Coach Knight? Explain why.
- If you were an Athletic Director at a major university, whom would you hire as your college basketball coach – Coach K or Coach Knight? Explain why.

Deep dive: Main references and resources

Achor, S. (2012). Positive intelligence. *Harvard Business Review*, 90(1/2): 100–102.

Aknin, L.B., Hamlin, J.K., & Dunn, E. W. (2012). Giving leads to happiness in young children. *PLoS ONE*, 7(6): e39211.

Allen, T. (2010). You have to lead from everywhere. *Harvard Business Review*, 88(11): 76–79.

Altman, E.J., Kiron, D., Schwartz, J., & Jones, R. (2023). *Workforce ecosystems: Reaching strategic goals with people, partners, and technologies.* Cambridge, MA: The MIT Press.

Antonakis, J., Fenley, M., & Liechti, S. (2011). Can charisma be taught? Tests of two interventions. *Academy of Management Learning & Education*, 10(3): 374–396.

ATD. (2023). *Leadership development: Preparing leaders for success.* Alexandria, VA: Association for Talent Development.

Austin, R.D., & Pisano, G.P. (2017). Neurodiversity as a competitive advantage. *Harvard Business Review*, 95(3): 96–103.

Badaracco, J.L. (1998). The discipline of building character. *Harvard Business Review*, 76(2): 114–124.

Bagozzi, R.P. (2003). Positive and negative emotions in organizations. In K. Cameron, J. Dutton & R. Quinn (Eds.), *Positive organizational scholarship: Foundations of a new discipline* (pp. 176–193). San Francisco, CA: Berrett-Koehler.

Baker, S.D. (2007). Followership: The theoretical foundation of a contemporary construct. *Journal of Leadership & Organizational Studies*, 14(1): 50–60.

Baker, W. (2014, December 18). 5 ways to get better at asking for help. *Harvard Business Review*. Retrieved from: https://hbr.org/2014/12/5-ways-to-get-better-at-asking-for-help

Baker, W., Cross, R., & Wooten, L. (2003). Positive organizational network analysis and energizing relationships. In K. Cameron, J. Dutton & R. Quinn (Eds.), *Positive organizational scholarship: Foundations of a new discipline* (pp. 328–342). San Francisco, CA: Berrett-Koehler.

Barling, J. (2023). *Brave new workplace: Designing productive, healthy, and safe organizations.* Oxford: Oxford University Press.

Bernhardt, B.C., & Singer, T. (2012). The neural basis of empathy. *Annual Review of Neuroscience*, 35(1): 1–23.

Berry, L.L., & Seltman, K.D. (2017). *Management lessons from Mayo clinic: Inside one of the most admired service organization.* New York, NY: McGraw-Hill Education.

Blankenship, R.J. (2021). *Assessing CEOs and senior leaders: A primer for consultants (Fundamentals of consulting psychology series).* Washington, DC: American Psychological Association.

Blickle, G., Böhm, F., & Wihler, A. (2023). Is a little narcissism a good thing in leadership roles? Test of an inverted u-shaped relationship between leader grandiose narcissism and follower satisfaction with leader. *Personality and Individual Differences*, 210(2): 112230.

Blume, B.D., Ford, J.K., & Huang, J.L. (2024). Transfer of informal learning: The role of manager support in linking learning to performance. *Business Horizons*, 67(2): 125–136.

Boyatzis, R. (2011, January–February). Neuroscience and leadership: The promise of insights. *Ivey Business Journal.* Retrieved from: https://iveybusinessjournal.com/publication/neuroscience-and-leadership-the-promise-of-insights/

Brown, M.E., Treviño, L.K., & Harrison, D.A. (2005). Ethical leadership: A social learning perspective for construct development and testing. *Organizational Behavior and Human Decision Processes*, 97(2): 117–134.

Bruch, H., & Ghoshal, S. (2003). Unleashing organizational energy. *MIT Sloan Management Review*, 45(1): 45–51.

Bruch, H., & Vogel, B. (2011). *Fully-charged: How great leaders boost their organization's energy and ignite high performance.* Boston, MA: Harvard Business Review Press.

Bruning, P.F., Lin, H.C., & Hsu, C.Y. (2022). Crafting solutions to leadership demands for well-being and effectiveness. *Business Horizons*, 65(5): 603–615.

Cable, D. (2018, April 23). How humble leadership really works. *Harvard Business Review.* Retrieved from: https://hbr.org/2018/04/how-humble-leadership-really-works

Cable, D. (2019). *Alive at work: The neuroscience of helping your people love what they do.* Boston, MA: Harvard Business Review Press.

Cameron, K. (2021). *Positively energizing leadership: Virtuous actions and relationships that create high performance.* San Francisco, CA: Berrett-Koehler.

Cameron, K., & Caza, A. (2002). Organizational and leadership virtues and the role of forgiveness. *Journal of Leadership & Organizational Studies,* 9(1): 33–48.

Cheng, B.H. (2023). *The return on kindness: How kind leadership wins talent, earns loyalty, and builds successful companies.* Singapore: Penguin Random House.

CIPD. (2018, February 15). Neurodiversity at work. Retrieved from: www.cipd.org/en/knowledge/guides/neurodiversity-work/

Clayton, R., Artis, A., & Kong, D.T. (2023, June 7). Empower your team, empower yourself. *MIT Sloan Management Review.* Retrieved from: https://sloanreview.mit.edu/article/empower-your-team-empower-yourself/

Clements, C., & Washbush, J.B. (1999). The two faces of leadership: Considering the dark side of leader–follower dynamics. *Journal of Workplace Learning,* 11(5): 170–175.

Clifton, D. & Harter, J. (2003). Investing in strengths. In K. Cameron, J. Dutton & R. Quinn (Eds.), *Positive organizational scholarship: Foundations of a new discipline* (pp. 111–121). San Francisco, CA: Berrett-Koehler.

Cockayne, A., & Warburton, L. (2016, December 19). *An investigation of Asperger syndrome in the employment context.* London: CIPD Applied Research Conference. Retrieved from: www.cipd.org/globalassets/media/comms/get-involved/events/an-investigation-of-asperger-syndrome-in-the-employment-context_2016_tcm18-20003.pdf

Cole, M.S., Bruch, H., & Vogel, B. (2012), Energy at work: A measurement validation and linkage to unit effectiveness. *Journal of Organizational Behavior,* 33(4): 445–467.

Coller, K.E. (2022). Choosing kindness: Finding kindness in management and organization studies, In M. Thomason (Ed.), *Kindness in management and organizational studies (Kindness at work)* (pp. 13–27). Bingley: Emerald Publishing.

Conger, J.A. (1990). The dark side of leadership. *Organizational Dynamics,* 19(2): 44–55.

Cooper, C.L., & Dewe, P. (2021). *Work and stress: A research overview.* London & New York, NY: Routledge.

Cooper, C., Brough, P., & Anderson, V.L. (Eds.). (2024). *Elgar encyclopedia of occupational health psychology.* Cheltenham: Edward Elgar Publishing Ltd.

Cotney, J.L., & Banerjee, R. (2019). Adolescents' conceptualisations of kindness and its links with well-being: A focus group study. *Journal of Social and Personal Relationships,* 36(2): 599–617.

Crook, T., & McDowall, A. (2024). Paradoxical career strengths and successes of ADHD adults: An evolving narrative. *Journal of Work-Applied Management,* 16(1): 112–126.

Cross, R., Baker, W., & Parker, A. (2003). What creates energy in organizations? *MIT Sloan Management Review,* 44(4): 51–56.

Crossan, M., Seijts, G., & Furlong, B. (2024). *The character compass: Transforming leadership for the 21st century.* London & New York, NY: Routledge.

Csikszentmihalyi, M. (2008). *Flow: The psychology of optimal experience* (Harper Perennial Modern Classics). New York, NY: HarperCollins Publishers.

Cunha, Miguel Pina E., Rego, A., Simpson, A., & Clegg, S. (2020). *Positive organizational Behaviour: A reflective approach.* London & New York, NY: Routledge.

Danner, D.D., Snowdon, D.A., & Friesen, W.V. (2001). Positive emotions in early life and longevity: Findings from the nun study. *Journal of Personality and Social Psychology,* 80(5): 804–813.

Diener, E., Napa Scollon, C., & Lucas, R.E. (2009). The evolving concept of subjective well-being: The multifaceted nature of happiness. In E. Diener, E. (Ed.), *Assessing well-being (Social Indicators Research Series, Vol. 39)* (pp. 67–100). Dordrecht: Springer.

Diener, E., Sandvik, E., & Pavot, W. (2009). Happiness is the frequency, not the intensity, of positive versus negative affect. In E. Diener (Ed.), *Assessing well-being (Social Indicators Research Series, Vol. 39)* (pp. 213–23). Dordrecht: Springer.

DiGangi, J. (2023). *Energy rising: The neuroscience of leading with emotional power.* Boston, MA: Harvard Business Review Press.

Dutton, J. (2003). *Energize your workplace: How to create and sustain high-quality connections at work.* San Francisco, CA: Jossey-Bass.

Dutton, J. (2003, Winter). Fostering high quality connections through respectful engagement. *Stanford Social Innovation Review*, 1: 54–57.

Eckert, R.A. (2001). Where leadership starts. *Harvard Business Review*, 79(10): 53–61.

Emmons, R. (2008). *Thanks! How practicing gratitude can make you happier.* Boston, MA: Houghton Mifflin.

Fairholm, G.W. (1996). Spiritual leadership: Fulfilling whole-self needs at work. *Leadership & Organization Development Journal*, 17(5): 11–17.

Fernández-Aráoz, C., Groysberg, B., & Nohria, N. (2011). How to hang on to your high potentials. *Harvard Business Review* (The talent issue), 89(10): 76–83.

Finkelstein, S. (2004, January–February). The seven habits of spectacularly unsuccessful executives. *Ivey Business Journal.* Retrieved from: https://iveybusinessjournal.com/publication/the-seven-habits-of-spectacularly-unsuccessful-executives/

Fredrickson, B.L. (2003). Positive emotions and upward spirals. In K. Cameron, J. Dutton & R. Quinn (Eds.), *Positive organizational scholarship: Foundations of a new discipline* (pp. 163–175). San Francisco, CA: Berrett-Koehler.

Fredrickson, B.L., Cohn, M.A., Coffey, K.A., Pek, J., & Finkel, S. (2008). Open hearts build lives: Positive emotions, induced through loving-kindness meditation, build consequential personal resources. *Journal of Personality and Social Psychology*, 95(5): 1045–1062.

Gibb, S., & Rahman, S. (2019). Kindness among colleagues: Identifying and exploring the gaps in employment contexts. *International Journal of Organizational Analysis*, 27(3): 582–595.

Gilbert, D. (2012). The science behind the smile. *Harvard Business Review*, 90(1/2): 84–90.

Goffee, R., & Jones, G. (2000). Why should anyone be led by you? *Harvard Business Review*, 78(5): 62–70.

Gold, M., & Smith, C. (2022). *Where's the "human" in human resource management? Managing work in the 21st century.* Bristol: Bristol University Press.

Goldsmith, M. (2009). *Succession: Are you ready?* Boston, MA: Harvard Business Press.

Goleman, D. (1998). What makes a leader? *Harvard Business Review*, 76(6): 93–102.

Goleman, D. (2000). Leadership that gets results. *Harvard Business Review*, 78(2): 78–90.

Goleman D., & Boyatzis R. (2008). Social intelligence and the biology of leadership. *Harvard Business Review*, 86(9): 74–81.

Graham, C. (2023). *The power of hope: How the science of well-being can save us from despair.* Princeton, NJ: Princeton University Press.

Grant, A. (2014). *Give and take: Why helping others drives our success.* New York, NY: Penguin Books.

Grant, A., & Rebele, R. (January 23, 2017). Beat generosity burnout. *Harvard Business Review.* Retrieved from: https://hbr.org/2017/01/beat-generosity-burnout

Greene, C.N. (1975). The reciprocal nature of influence between leader and subordinate. *Journal of Applied Psychology*, 60(2): 187–193.

Groysberg, B., Hill, A., & Johnson, T. (2010). Which of these people is your future CEO? *Harvard Business Review*, 88(11): 80–85.

Gruman, J.A. & Budworth, M-H. (2022). Positive psychology and human resource management: Building an HR architecture to support human flourishing. *Human Resource Management Review,* 32(3): 100911.

Guarino, A. (2016). *Why CHROs really are CEOs.* Los Angeles, CA: The Korn Ferry Institute.

Hafenbrack, A.C., Cameron, L.D., Spreitzer, G.M., Zhang, C., Noval, L.J., & Shaffakat, S. (2020). Helping people by being in the present: Mindfulness increases prosocial behavior. *Organizational Behavior and Human Decision Processes*, 159: 21–38.

Hamlin, J.K. & Wynn, K. (2011). Young infants prefer prosocial to antisocial others. *Cognitive Development*, 26(1): 30–39.

Hammond, C. (2022). *The keys to kindness: How to be kinder to yourself, others and the world.* Edinburgh: Canongate Books.

Han, M., Hu, E., Zhao, J., & Shan, H. (2023). High performance work systems and employee performance: The roles of employee well-being and workplace friendship. *Human Resource Development International,* 1–20. https://www.tandfonline.com/doi/full/10.1080/13678868.2023.2268488

Harris, C.M., Wright, P.M., & McMahan, G.C. (2019). The emergence of human capital: Roles of social capital and coordination that drive unit performance. *Human Resource Management Journal*, 29(2): 162–180.

Harrison, R. (2009). *Learning and development* (5th edition). London: CIPD.

Harrison, R. & Kessels J. (2004). *Human resource development in a knowledge economy: An organizational view.* Hampshire & New York, NY: Palgrave Macmillan.

Haskins, G., Thomas, M., & Johri, L. (Eds.). (2018). *Kindness in leadership.* London & New York, NY: Routledge.

Hollander, E.P. (1992). Leadership, followership, self, and others. *The Leadership Quarterly*, 3(1): 43–54.

Hunter, E.M., Neubert, M.J., Perry, S.J., Witt, L.A., Penney, L.M., & Weinberger, E. (2013). Servant leaders inspire servant followers: Antecedents and outcomes for employees and the organization. *The Leadership Quarterly*, 24(2): 316–331.

Hunter, J.C. (1998). *Servant leadership: A simple story about the true essence of leadership.* New York, NY: Crown Business.

Hurwitz, M., & Hurwitz, S. (2017). *Leadership is half the story: A fresh look at followership, leadership, and collaboration.* Toronto: Rotman-UTP Publishing.

Hutcherson, C.A., Seppala, E.M., & Gross, J.J. (2008). Loving-kindness meditation increases social connectedness. *Emotion*, 8(5): 720–724.

Jackson, B., & Parry, K. (2018). *A very short, fairly interesting and reasonably cheap book about studying leadership* (3rd edition). London: Sage.

Kelemen, T., & Matthews, M. (2023, January 12). This new year, resolve against workaholism. *MIT Sloan Management Review.* Retrieved from: https://sloanreview.mit.edu/article/this-new-year-resolve-against-workaholism/

Kelley, R.E. (1988). In praise of followership. *Harvard Business Review*, 66(6): 142–148.

Kiecolt-Glaser, J.K., Bane, C., Glaser, R., & Malarkey, W.B. (2003). Love, marriage, and divorce: Newlyweds' stress hormones foreshadow relationship changes. *Journal of Consulting and Clinical Psychology*, 71(1): 176–188.

Kini, P., Wong, J., McInnis, S., Gabana, N., & Brown, J.W. (2016). The effects of gratitude expression on neural activity. *NeuroImage*, 128: 1–10.

Kumar, A., & Epley, N. (2023). A little good goes an unexpectedly long way: Underestimating the positive impact of kindness on recipients. *Journal of Experimental Psychology: General*, 152(1): 236–252.

Laker, B., Weisz, N., Pereira, V., & De Massis, A. (2023, December 7). The emotional landscape of leadership. *MIT Sloan Management Review*. Retrieved from: https://sloanreview .mit.edu/article/the-emotional-landscape-of-leadership/

Lafley, A.G., & Tichy, N.M. (2011). The art and science of finding the right CEO. *Harvard Business Review* (The talent issue), 89(10): 66–74.

Litzinger, W., & Schaefer, T. (1982). Leadership through followership. *Business Horizons*, 25(5): 78–81.

Loehr, J., & Schwartz, T. (2005). *The power of full engagement: Managing energy, not time, is the key to high performance and personal renewal*. New York, NY: The Free Press.

Logan, J.M., Holladay, C.L., Schumacher, A., & Simmons, D. (February 28, 2019). Assessment: How well does your team function? *Harvard Business Review*. Retrieved from: https://hbr.org/2019/02/assessment-how-well-does-your-team-function

Luthans, F. (2002). The need for and meaning of positive organizational behavior. *Journal of Organizational Behavior*, 23(6): 695–706.

Luthans, F. (2002). Positive organizational behavior: Developing and managing psychological strengths. *Academy of Management Perspectives*, 16(1): 57–72.

Luthans, F., Avey, J.B., Avolio, B.J., Norman, S.M., & Combs, G.M. (2006). Psychological capital development: Toward a micro-intervention. *Journal of Organizational Behavior*, 27(3): 387–393.

Luthans, F., Avolio, B.J., Avey, J.B., & Norman, S.M. (2007). Positive psychological capital: Measurement and relationship with performance and satisfaction. *Personnel Psychology*, 60(3): 541–572.

Margoni, F., Baillargeon, R., & Surian, L. (2018). Infants distinguish between leaders and bullies. *Proceedings of the National Academy of Sciences*, 115(38): E8835–E8843.

McDowall, A., Doyle, N., & Kiseleva, M. (2023). *Neurodiversity at work: Demand, supply and a gap analysis*. London: Birkbeck, University of London.

McVey, A.W. (2020). *Soulful organizational leadership*. St. Louis, MO: Enroute.

Medalie, J.H., & Goldbourt, U. (1976). Angina pectoris among 10,000 men. II. Psychosocial and other risk factors as evidenced by a multivariate analysis of a five year incidence study. *The American Journal of Medicine*, 60(6): 910–921.

Meuser, J.D. & Smallfield, J. (2023). Servant leadership: The missing community component. *Business Horizons*, 66(2): 251–264.

Mills, P.J., Redwine, L., Wilson, K., Pung, M.A., Chinh, K., Greenberg, B.H., Lunde, O., Maisel, A., Raisinghani, A., Wood, A., & Chopra, D. (2015). The role of gratitude in spiritual well-being in asymptomatic heart failure patients. *Spirituality in Clinical Practice*, 2(1): 5–17.

Mirivel, J.C., & Lyon, A. (2023). *Positive communication for leaders: Proven strategies for inspiring unity and effecting change*. Lanham, MD: Rowman & Littlefield.

Mitchell, T., Lemoine, G.J., & Lee, D. (2022). Inclined but less skilled? Disentangling extraversion, communication skill, and leadership emergence. *Journal of Applied Psychology*, 107(9): 1524–1542.

Moldoveanu, M.C., & Narayandas, D. (2022). *The future of executive development*. Stanford, CA: Stanford Business Books.

Nakamura, Y.T., Milner, J., & Milner, T. (2022). Leveraging neurobiology to develop empathetic leaders. *Organizational Dynamics*, 51(3): 100865.

Nakamura, Y.T., Gu, Y., Jin, H., Yu, D., Hinshaw, J., & Rehman, R. (2023) Introducing neuroscience methods: An exploratory study on the role of reflection in developing leadership from a HRD perspective. *Human Resource Development International*, 26(4): 458–470.

Neubert, M.J. (2019). With or without spirit: Implications for scholarship and leadership. *Academy of Management Perspectives*, 33(3): 253–263.

Neubert, M.J., Bradley, S.W., Ardianti, R., & Simiyu, E.M. (2017). The role of spiritual capital in innovation and performance: Evidence from developing economies. *Entrepreneurship Theory and Practice*, 41(4): 621–640.

Neubert, M.J., de Luque, M.S., Quade, M.J., & Hunter, E.M. (2022). Servant leadership across the globe: Assessing universal and culturally contingent relevance in organizational contexts. *Journal of World Business,* 57(2): 101268.

Oc, B., Chintakananda, K., Bashshur, M.R., & Day, D.V. (2023). The study of followers in leadership research: A systematic and critical review. *The Leadership Quarterly*, 34(1): 101674.

Otake, K., Shimai, S., Tanaka-Matsumi, J., Otsui K., & Fredrickson, B.L. (2006). Happy people become happier through kindness: A counting kindnesses intervention. *Journal of Happiness Studies*, 7(3): 361–375.

Owens, B.P., Baker, W.E., McDaniel Sumpter, D., & Cameron K. (2016). Relational energy at work: Implications for job engagement and job performance. *Journal of Applied Psychology*, 101(1): 35–49.

Pagonis, W.G. (2001). Leadership in a combat zone. *Harvard Business Review*, 79(11): 107–117.

Peters, K., & Haslam, S.A. (2018), I follow, therefore I lead: A longitudinal study of leader and follower identity and leadership in the marines. *British Journal of Psychology*, 109(4): 708–723.

Peterson, S.J., Balthazard, P.A., Waldman, D.A., & Thatcher, R.W. (2008). Neuroscientific implications of psychological capital: Are the brains of optimistic, hopeful, confident, and resilient leaders different? *Organizational Dynamics*, 37(4): 342–353.

Peterson, S.J., Galvin, B.M., & Lange, D. (2012). CEO Servant leadership: Exploring executive characteristics and firm performance. *Personnel Psychology*, 65(3): 565–596.

Piñon, N. (2022, December 23). Adam Grant says this skill can make you highly successful— but 'there's not a book' on how to do it properly. CNBC. Retrieved from: www.cnbc.com/2022/12/23/adam-grant-being-a-good-follower-can-make-you-highly-successful.html

Pitichat, T., Reichard, R.J., Kea-Edwards, A., Middleton, E., & Norman, S.M. (2018). Psychological capital for leader development. *Journal of Leadership & Organizational Studies*, 25(1): 47–62.

Porath, C. (2016). An antidote to incivility. *Harvard Business Review*, 94(4): 108–11.

Porath, C., & Boissy, A. (February 10, 2023). Practice empathy as a team. *Harvard Business Review*. Retrieved from: https://hbr.org/2023/02/practice-empathy-as-a-team

Psychological capital. (2023, August 21). Psychological capital: What it is and why employers need it now. American Psychological Association. Retrieved from: www.apa.org/topics/healthy-workplaces/psychological-capital

Pugh, A.J. (2024). *The last human job: The work of connecting in a disconnected world.* Princeton, NJ: Princeton University Press.

Raposa, E.B., Laws, H.B., & Ansell, E.B. (2016). Prosocial behavior mitigates the negative effects of stress in everyday life. *Clinical Psychological Science*, 4(4): 691–698.

Rath, T. (2015). *Are you fully charged? The 3 keys to energizing your work and life.* Arlington, VA: Missionday, LLC.

Raz, T. (2003, January 1). The 10 secrets of a master networker. *Inc. Magazine.* Retrieved from: www.inc.com/magazine/20030101/25049.html

Redwine, L.S., Henry, B.L., Pung, M.A., Wilson, K., Chinh, K., Knight, B., Jain, S., Rutledge, T., Greenberg, B., Maisel, A., & Mills, P.J. (2016). Pilot randomized study of a gratitude journaling intervention on heart rate variability and inflammatory biomarkers in patients with stage B heart failure. *Psychosomatic Medicine*, 78(6): 667–676.

Riggio, R.E., Chaleff, I., & Lipman-Blumen, J. (2008). *The art of followership: How great followers create great leaders and organizations.* San Francisco, CA: Jossey-Bass.

Rittenberg, M. (2017). Leadership is love: The power of human connections. TEDx Talks (TEDxCincinnati). Retrieved from: https://youtu.be/ZrdxOYEr9Bg

Roberts, L., Spreitzer, G., Dutton, J., Quinn, R., Heaphy, E., & Barker, B. (2005). How to play to your strengths. *Harvard Business Review*, (83)1: 74–80.

Rothaermel, F.T., & McBride, C. (2023). *Starbucks corporation.* New York, NY: McGraw-Hill Inc. Retrieved from: https://store.hbr.org/product/starbucks-corporation/MH0074

Rowe, G.W., & Nason, K.A. (2024, July–August). Failure is an option. *Ivey Business Journal.* Retrieved from: https://iveybusinessjournal.com/failure-is-an-option/

Russek, L.G., & Schwartz, G.E. (1997). Feelings of parental caring predict health status in midlife: A 35-year follow-up of the Harvard mastery of stress study. *Journal of Behavioral Medicine*, 20(1): 1–13.

Sadun, R., Bloom, N., & Van Reenen, J. (2017). Why do we undervalue competent management? *Harvard Business Review*, 95(5): 120–127.

Sanford F.H. (1958). The follower's role in leadership phenomena. In E.L. Hartley, T.M. Newcomb, & G.E. Swenson (Eds.), *Readings in social psychology* (pp. 257–259). New York, NY: Holt, Rinehart, & Winston.

Schein, E. (1990). *Career anchors: Discovering your real values.* San Francisco, CA: Jossey-Bass/Pfeiffer.

Schwartz, T., & McCarthy, C. (2007). Manage your energy, not your time. *Harvard Business Review*, 85(10): 63–73.

Schyns, B., Wisse, B., & Sanders, S. (2019). Shady strategic behavior: Recognizing strategic followership of dark triad followers. *Academy of Management Perspectives*, 33(2): 234–249.

Seppälä, E. (2015, May 7). Why compassion is a better managerial tactic than toughness. *Harvard Business Review.* Retrieved from: https://hbr.org/2015/05/why-compassion-is-a-better-managerial-tactic-than-toughness

Seppälä, E., & Cameron, K. (2015, December 01). Proof that positive work cultures are more productive. *Harvard Business Review.* Retrieved from: https://hbr.org/2015/12/proof-that-positive-work-cultures-are-more-productive

Shaw, D. (February 24, 2021). CEO secrets: "My billion pound company has no HR department". BBC. Retrieved from: www.bbc.com/news/business-56130187

Shults, S.G., Reichard, R.J., Diaz, J.B.B., Pitichat, T., & Kea-Edwards, A. (2022). Pursuing your leader development: Lessons from 101 executives. *Organizational Dynamics*, 51(3): 100894.

Smith, J.A., Newman, K.M., Marsh, J., & Keltner, D. (2020). *The gratitude project: How the science of thankfulness can rewire our brains for resilience, optimism, and the greater good.* Oakland, CA: New Harbinger Publications.

Snook, S.A., Perlow, L.A., & DeLacey, B. (2005). Coach Knight: The will to win. Harvard Business School Case 406–043. Retrieved from: https://store.hbr.org/product/coach-knight-the-will-to-win/406043?sku=406043-PDF-ENG

Snook, S.A., Perlow, L.A., & DeLacey, B. (2005). Coach K: A matter of the heart. Harvard Business School Case 406–044. Retrieved from: https://store.hbr.org/product/coach-k-a-matter-of-the-heart/406044?sku=406044-PDF-ENG

Spreitzer, G.M., & Grant, T. (2012). Helping students manage their energy: Taking their pulse ith the energy audit. *Journal of Management Education*, 36(2): 239–263.

Spreitzer, G., & Porath, C. (2012). Creating sustainable performance. *Harvard Business Review*, 90(1/2): 92–99.

Stanley, M.L., Neck, C.P., & Neck, C.B. (2023). The dark side of generosity: Employees with a reputation for generosity are selectively targeted for exploitation. *Journal of Experimental Social Psychology*, 108: 104503.

Stavans, M., & Baillargeon, R. (2019). Infants expect leaders to right wrongs. *Proceedings of the National Academy of Sciences*, 116(33): 16292–16301.

Stavans, M., & Diesendruck, G. (2021). Children hold leaders primarily responsible, not entitled. *Child Development*, 92(1): 308–323.

Stearns, P.N. (2012). The history of happiness. *Harvard Business Review*, 90(1/2): 104–109.

Stone, A.A., Mezzacappa, E.S., Donatone, B.A., & Gonder, M. (1999). Psychosocial stress and social support are associated with prostate-specific antigen levels in men: Results from a community screening program. *Health Psychology*, 18(5): 482–486.

Storey, J., & Wright, P.M. (2023). *Strategic human resource management: A research overview* (2nd edition). London & New York, NY: Routledge.

Sullivan, D.M., & Bendell, B.L. (2023). Help! Lonely at work: Managerial interventions to combat employee loneliness. *Business Horizons*, 66(5): 655–666.

Tkaczyk, B. (2014a). Crafting continuing learning and development: A positive design tool for leadership development. *Development and Learning in Organizations*, 28(4): 5–8.

Tkaczyk, B. (2014b). Daily check-ins stimulate self-improvement. *Talent Development (TD)*, 68(8): 72–73.

Tkaczyk, B. (2015). Leading as constant learning and development: The knowledge-creative enterprise. *Design Management Review*, 26(3): 38–43. Published in a special issue on Organization Development and Design Management.

Tkaczyk, B. (2018, July–August). Can HR level up, please? A case study. *The World Financial Review*: 66–68.

Tkaczyk, B. (2021). *Leading positive organizational change: Energize – redesign – gel.* London & New York, NY: Routledge.

Tu, M.-H., Bono, J.E., Shum, C., & LaMontagne, L. (2018). Breaking the cycle: The effects of role model performance and ideal leadership self-concepts on abusive supervision spillover. *Journal of Applied Psychology*, 103(7): 689–702.

Uhl-Bien, M., Riggio, R.E., Lowe, K.B., & Carsten, M.K. (2014). Followership theory: A review and research agenda. *The Leadership Quarterly*, 25(1): 83–104.

Unwin, J. (2018). *Kindness, emotions and human relationships*. Dunfermline: Carnegie UK Trust.

Useem, M. (2010). Four lessons in adaptive leadership. *Harvard Business Review*, 88(11): 86–90.

Wageman, R., Nunes, D., Burruss, J., & Hackman, R. (2008). *Senior leadership teams: What it takes to make them great*. Boston, MA: Harvard Business Press.

Warren, M.T., Braun, S.S., & Schonert-Reichl, K.A. (2023). A virtues approach to children's kindness schemas. *The Journal of Positive Psychology*, 19(2): 301–314.

Weiss, J., Donigian, A., & Hughes, J. (2010). Extreme negotiations. *Harvard Business Review*, 88(11): 66–75.

West, T. (2022). *Jerks at work: Toxic coworkers and what to do about them*. New York, NY: Portfolio/Penguin.

Williams, K.S., & Weigand, H. (2022). Patterns and possibilities: Exploring the meaning of kindness, In M. Thomason (Ed.), *Kindness in management and organizational studies (Kindness at work)* (pp. 1–12). Bingley: Emerald Publishing.

Wong, P., Donelly, M, Neck, P., & Boyd, W.E. (2018). Positive autism: Investigation of workplace characteristics leading to a strengths-based approach to employment of people with autism. *Review of International Comparative Management*, 19(1): 15–30.

Wong, Y.J., Owen, J., Gabana, N.T., Brown, J.W., McInnis, S., Toth, P., & Gilman, L. (2018). Does gratitude writing improve the mental health of psychotherapy clients? Evidence from a randomized controlled trial. *Psychotherapy Research: Journal of the Society for Psychotherapy Research*, 28(2): 192–202.

Wright, P.M., & McMahan, G.C. (2011). Exploring human capital: Putting 'human' back into strategic human resource management. *Human Resource Management Journal*, 21(2): 93–104.

Wright, P.M., Nyberg, A.J., Schepker, D.J., & Strizver, S. (2022). *Managing high potentials and executives (2022 CHRO survey report)*. Columbia, SC: The Center for Executive Succession, Darla Moore School of Business, University of South Carolina.

Wrzesniewski, A., Berg, J., & Dutton, J. (2010). Turn the job you have into the job you want. *Harvard Business Review*, 88(6): 114–117.

Zak, P.J. (2017). Neuroscience of trust. *Harvard Business Review*, 95(3): 44–103.

Zander, R.S., & Zander, B. (2002). *The art of possibility transforming professional and personal life*. London: Penguin Books.

Zenger, J.H., Folkman, J.R., & Edinger, S.K. (2011). Making yourself indispensable. *Harvard Business Review* (The talent issue), 89(10): 16–23.

Zenou, E., Allemand, I., & Brullebaut, B., & Galia, F. (2020). Board recruitment as a strategic answer: Do companies' strategies for innovation influence the selection of new board members? *Strategic Change*, 29(1): 127–139.

Zhang, R., Voronov, M., Toubiana, M., Vince, R., & Hudson, B.A. (2024). Beyond the feeling individual: Insights from sociology on emotions and embeddedness. *Journal of Management Studies*, 61(5): 2212–2250.

Module monitor and Consolidation I

Workshop I: Applications/review exercises

Self-check questions

You should now be able to answer Self-Check Questions 1–10

1 **True or false** *Humans* are not well described by the rational-agent model and therefore the *humanities* can provide *economists* with avenues to enhance the realism of their models, improve the precision of their forecasts, and create more effective and just policies.

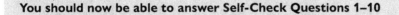

2 True or false Most individuals tend to think of themselves as primarily *rational* when it comes to their thoughts, choices, and behavior. However, even highly intelligent and well-educated individuals frequently fall prey to cognitive errors when navigating financial, medical, personal, and ethical decisions. These errors in reasoning, known as *cognitive biases*, impact virtually everyone across a wide range of situations. The bottom line is, inasmuch as people are *Humans*, not *Econs*, they make *predictable errors*.

3 True or false The designation of joining a pension plan as the *default* option is an example of a *nudge*.

4 True or false The *way the options are presented* describes *choice architecture*.

5 True or false The *A.S.S.E.T* framework can be utilized not only by policymakers but also anybody, really. If you wish to encourage a behavior – in yourself or in others – make it *attractive, streamlined, social, energizing,* and *timely*.

6 True or false It's the process of energizing others to work to meet specific objectives. This describes *positively energizing leadership*.

7 True or false Without followers who are ready to follow, leadership might prove rather hollow. It is the energetic and independent-thinking follower who says *yes* or *no* to leadership. This describes *followership*.

8 True or false You're en route to a rendezvous with a friend for a picnic, toting a basket brimming with delicious provisions. As you proceed, you encounter an individual seated alone on a bench, appearing skinny, dirty, and possibly hungry. You pause and offer them a share from your picnic hamper no problem. This describes *kindness as intervention*.

9 True or false We lost our baby in 2022. During that time, we experienced an overwhelming display of support and benevolence from our community. People went out of their way to help out – offering their companionship, providing co-ordinated assistance with various tasks, and even preparing meals for us. They would come visit us and simply spend time by our side. That was so, so, so uplifting! This describes *kindness as a small act*.

10 True or false In 2006, following the immense destruction caused by Hurricane Katrina, an executive felt compassion for the victims and was determined to help in any possible way. As a result, he took charge and organized a group of employees to travel to New Orleans with the purpose of aiding in the city's reconstruction efforts. This describes *kindness as an event*.

Individualized learning record

When you have finished Module I, try filling in this record of what you have learned.

1   What is a *nudge* and what is *choice architecture*? How do organizations that genuinely adopt *behavioral insights* distinguish themselves and excel in their operations?

  ....
  ....

2   Should organizational leaders prioritize the creation of *a comprehensive theory that unifies decision-making*, or should they instead concentrate on fostering an organizational culture that encourages *experimentation*?

  ....
  ....

3   Which is more effective in enhancing *welfare*, *nudging* or *promoting literacy*?

  ....
  ....

4   "*Please*", "*Thank you*", and "*Sorry*" should be simple things to say – polite and uncontroversial. However, for many people, that's far from the case. Why? What prevents people from being kinder?

  ....
  ....

5   Stop trying to raise successful kids and start raising *kind-hearted* ones. Write an argumentative essay arguing in favor of this proposition.

  ....
  ....

6   *Kindness* in the workplace is not solely a *virtue* ("it is good") but it is also a *value* ("it does good"). Do you agree?

  ....
  ....

7   For over 25 consecutive years, Benjamin Zander, renowned conductor of the Boston Philharmonic Orchestra and a professor at the New England Conservatory of Music, encountered a recurring challenge. He had to instruct students who were consistently burdened by anxiety over the

measurement of their performance, causing them to hesitate when it came to embracing creative experimentation.

One evening, he and his partner Roz Stone Zander, a therapist, came together to brainstorm a solution. They came to the conclusion that the most effective strategy would be to give everyone an "A", at the beginning of the course. This "A" wasn't meant to serve as a means of evaluating performance against established criteria, but as an instrument to open them up to new possibilities.

A Your task: "Give yourself an A" – to earn this grade, you're required to write a letter to yourself (*dated next year*) that begins with "Dear Professor, I got my A (for the course) because…", describing in as much detail as possible, how you came to achieve this extraordinary grade.

When composing your letter (phrases such as "I hope", "I intend" or "I will" must not appear; everything must be written in the past tense), imagine yourself in the future, looking back, and report on all the valuable insights you acquired and significant milestones you attained throughout the year, as though those accomplishments had already been realized.

B By automatically assuming the best and giving everyone an "A" from the start, you let the best come out in them. Now, how might the Zander's philosophy of "giving everyone an A" be applied to a workplace practice like Performance Management?

8 "Every block of stone has a statue inside it and it is the task of the sculptor to discover it" – Michelangelo. What significance does this quote hold in relation to strategic human resource and talent development, organization development, and to your personal leadership approach? Do you believe that leadership development contributes to superior organizational performance?

9 Why do certain groups or organizations radiate energy and productivity, while others appear to languish, lacking vigor, and gradually fade away? How can we develop *high-performing cultures of thriving* (high degrees of learning and positive energy)? How can we build *high-performing cultures of flourishing* (positive emotions, positive employee experience, HQCs, positive communication and meaning, and achievement)?

10 Read the article by Patrick Wright and Gary McMahan, "Exploring human capital: Putting 'human' back into strategic human resource management", and reflect on the authors' point that the "human" element should not be ignored in strategic HRM. Consider the importance of this perspective in

the context of modern leadership and followership. By the way, do you agree that the "human" aspect is crucial in strategic HRM? Why or why not?

Now, reflect on the statement by a CEO who claimed, "In my experience, HR departments don't make employees happier or more productive. So my billion-pound company has no HR department". Is it possible to effectively lead an organization without an HR department? Think about the implications of this approach. What challenges/risks and benefits/opportunities might arise? What alternatives to traditional HR could be implemented to support employee well-being and productivity in an organization? For example, decentralized people management, technology-driven HR solutions, or leadership-driven employee engagement initiatives.

Can-do checklist

Looking back, I have learned the following Key Terms:

Unit 1

- attract attention, streamline, socialize, energize, timing counts (A.S.S.E.T.)
- choice architect/architecture
- cognitive (bias, ease, errors, heuristics, overload, shortcuts)
- default
- economics (behavioral, conventional, econ-, good, human-, humanistic, narrative, positive, standard, traditional)
- "econs" vs "humans"
- friction (costs)
- habits
- hyperbolic discounting
- initial information effect ("anchoring" effect)
- "last mile"
- libertarian paternalism
- loss aversion
- mental accounting
- "motivational fee"
- nudge (for good; helpful; nudging strategy) vs. "noodge"

- over-choice
- randomized controlled trials (RCTs)
- reminders
- salience
- social proof
- status quo
- test, learn, adapt (TLA)

Unit 2

- behavior (loving, organizational, positive, prosocial, toxic)
- capital (economic, financial, human, psychological, social, spiritual)
- check-ins (daily)
- energy (boost, drain, emotional, life-giving, level, management, mental, negative, network, organizational, personal, physical, positive, productive, relational, spiritual)
- flow
- followership (co-active, positive, positively energizing, strengths-based)
- generosity spectrum (selfless, self-protective "givers", "matchers", "takers")
- gratitude (expression, journaling, writing)
- heliotropic effect
- high-quality connections (HQCs)
- kindness (as a small act, as an event, as an intervention; behaviors; zone)
- leadership (heart-based, humble, idealism, kind-hearted, positive, positively energizing, presence, realism, servant, strengths-based, toxic, tyrannical)
- loving-kindness meditation
- positive organizational behavior (POB)
- positive psychological capital (PsyCap) (optimism, hope, confidence, and resiliency)
- power (fear-based vs. respect-based)
- strength
- talent
- thriving
- zone (aggression, comfort, passion, resignation)

Module II

Strategizing for the future

Setting, communicating, and
executing a positive strategy

3 Strategic transformation

Strategy choice-making

"Strategy requires hard choices" – Michael Porter

Sneak peek

Focus on: Key concepts and terms

Unit 3

- Advantage (competitive, strategic, sustainable, true, winning)
- Aspiration (energizing, guiding, winning)
- Bounded rationality
- "Business as usual" (BAU) mindset
- Capabilities (distinctive, dynamic, hard-to-replicate, must-have)
- Chief strategy officer (CSO)
- Economic strategy approach
- Emergent strategies
- Entrepreneurial reconfiguration
- Factors (differentiation, firm, industry)
- Forces (economic, outside, the five)
- Home-base
- How-to-win choices
- Management systems
- Operational effectiveness
- Resource-based view (RBV) of strategy
- Scenario planning
- Strategic transformation
- Strategist

DOI: 10.4324/9781003508274-6

- Strategy (bold, bottom-up, business, coherent, competitive, economic, effective, executable, future perfect, open, successful, top-down, winning)
- Strategy as design
- Strategy as practice (S-A-P)
- Strategy choice-making
- Value proposition (winning)
- Valuable, rare, costly to imitate, non-substitutable (VRIN)
- Where-to-play choices

Pause 'N' reflect: On the current issues and trends

Before you complete this unit, think about each of the following statements. Mark each statement:

V – if you *agree.*
X – if you *disagree.*
? – if you are *undecided.*

Your Take: Integrative Thinking	*Before doing Unit 3*	*After doing Unit 3*
1 Strategy is becoming a lost art.		
2 There is a disconnect between managerial fantasy (rhetoric) and organizational capability (reality). Organizationally, front-line employees are unable to implement the fancy-schmancy (and often overly complex) strategies their executives have created.		
3 Strategy energizes an organization – it symbolizes an organization's dreams and, in scenario planning, a means of overcoming its worst nightmares.		
4 When it comes to involvement in business strategy (setting, communicating, and implementing), senior business leaders (senior decision-makers) and functional leaders (e.g., senior HR people) are not always connected. Similarly, the HR director is not seen as a "trusted advisor" to the CEO/board.		

Your Take: Integrative Thinking	Before doing Unit 3	After doing Unit 3
5 The future perfect strategy makes use of the imagination to picture future actions as though they had already occurred.		
6 Consider the Hard Rock Cafe restaurants in London, New Delhi, New York, NY, Toronto, Warsaw, and elsewhere, really. The value proposition remains the same – high-fat, high-cholesterol fast food. But, hold on! Mounted on cafe walls, however, there are autographed guitars previously played by legendary musicians, costumes from world tours, rare photographs, and other memorabilia. Now, it's fast food *plus* nostalgia and a cool sense of community.		
7 You can be both a cost leader *and* a differentiator with no problem.		
8 True competitive advantage develops when the enterprise does something unique that creates value. When copied, the uniqueness is lost and dynamic capability is gone. Capabilities are naturally dynamic as they frequently get imitated, substituted, and outmaneuvered by rivals. A company can gain a competitive edge from purposefully creating, extending, or modifying its resource base.		
9 There's been a subtle shift from planning to strategy. Ideologically, central planning was what socialists did, and they tried, and failed at it. So, central planning is certainly not something that should be practiced by strategists and senior management teams.		
10 Many pursue a Master of Business Administration (MBA) to become strategists. The "case-method" learning on MBA programs, combined with the topics covered in strategy courses, prepares MBAs for "doing strategy" in everyday life.		

After you have done the unit, repeat "Your Take". How has reading the unit clarified the ideas herein? How have your views, feelings and thoughts changed over time?

Lead-in

General discussion points

Individually or in buzz groups, work on the following:

1 You walk into a toy store with your child, and they quickly see that there are no LEGO products available. Your child cries out, "Daddy, can we go to a toy store, please!" Interpret what this reveals about how LEGO strategizes.
2 *Strategy is designed to guide an organization through changes and transitions in order to ensure its long-term growth and success. If it lacks a coherent strategy, an enterprise will go adrift – much like a tiny boat on a stormy sea with no sails or rudder.* What does this statement illustrate about (re)setting strategic direction?
3 Gary Hamel says that "strategy is revolution; everything else is tactics". Do you agree with this? Explain why.
4 Some say that strategists do not just advise on strategy; they "talk" strategy and its effects, into being. In anthropological terms, who is "homo strategicus"? What do strategists actually do when "doing strategy"? Who becomes strategists? Are you a "natural" strategist? Do you think *you* could become a strategist?
5 What would have happened had Henry Ford started out in *your* country? Would he have been successful – or failed there? What would have to be true for the strategic possibilities? Does the "home-base" matter?

Share your thoughts with your peers/team members. Discuss points of (dis)agreement.

Idea watch

Because of its distinctive nature, strategy has been dubbed "the queen of the management sciences", and the sovereign subject. Etymologically, the word "strategy" derives from ancient Greek and is composed of two parts: *stratos* meaning "army" and *agein* referring to "to lead".

Although strategy has claimed many parents, for example, Sun Tzu (a Chinese military strategist), Niccolò Machiavelli (a Florentine political philosopher and diplomat), Carl von Clausewitz (a Prussian general), Chester Barnard (an executive from AT&T), Alfred DuPont Chandler (a business historian, related to the DuPont Chemicals family), the field of strategic management has a relatively brief history.

The origins may be traced back to the launch of a Business Policy course at Harvard in the 1920s. Positioned near the end of the MBA program, the course was designed to put the learner in the shoes of a business's general manager and allow for the integration of all specialist business topic areas. At the outset, in the main, the business management curriculum was partially influenced by the teaching of individuals coming from strategy consulting firms, and, by the 1970s, Business

Policy courses were being delivered to undergraduate and MBA students across business schools, usually by senior faculty members who had spent some of their professional lives in different disciplines of business. Still, something was lacking. In March 1970, ten professors with interests in Business Policy met in Chicago, IL to discuss the formation of the Business Policy and Planning (BPP) Division of the Academy of Management (AOM) the next year (later on, known as Business Policy and Strategy [BPS], and, now, Strategic Management [STR]). In 1980, the Strategic Management Society and its *Strategic Management Journal* were launched; in that same year, the "embryonic" field was given a super boost when Michael Porter, one of the most influential voices in strategy, published his best-seller, *Competitive Strategy: Techniques for Analyzing Industries and Competitors*. As of 1981, there still wasn't an obligatory first year Strategy course at Harvard Business School (HBS), and there was only one Strategy elective in the second year, "Industry & Competitive Analysis", authored and delivered by Michael Porter. Today, however, strategy has become a popular topic of research and teaching at business schools worldwide; business schools also aim to train MBA students in strategy formally who are then eagerly recruited by management consulting firms worldwide.

With this history in mind, it's understandable that there are virtually as many approaches to strategy as there are strategists. Importantly, it is both what's *outside* the firm (the structure of the industry and the market you're operating in) and what's *inside* the firm (valuable resources, dynamic capabilities, management systems) that should and do drive the winning strategy of a firm. Therefore, in a fast-changing world, creating effective strategies necessitates an integrative perspective.

According to Michael Porter, strategy means positioning oneself in a competitive environment – there would be no need for strategy if there were no competition. Essentially, the potential of an organization is governed by the structure of the industry and the market in which it operates (an "outside-in" approach to strategy). The economic structure of an industry in not an accident, mind you (think: the bargaining power of suppliers, buyers; threat of new entrants, substitutes; and rivalry among competitors). Its complexities are the outcome of long-term social patterns and economic forces. Yet, its impact on your business is rather immediate, as it sets the competitive rules, strategies (and tactics) that you'll probably need to employ. Together, the strength of the forces determines the profit potential in an industry by influencing the prices, costs, and required business investments – the elements of return on investment (ROI). Put simply, the industry structure sets the limits for what your enterprise can (and cannot) do.

While Porter draws attention to the significance of the sector and external factors, he also makes a point of the region's and/or the nation's success within a specified industry. He urges that the "home-base" – where your enterprise starts out – matters (think, for instance: Apple in Cupertino, CA, music bands in Manchester or moviemaking in Hollywood).

On the other hand, leveraging what's inside the firm matters, too. The big idea is that enterprises can be regarded as a bundle of resources, which can help them to gain a competitive edge. This perspective is called the resource-based view (RBV) of the firm, regardless of the more macro-level characteristics. In a nutshell, resources ("firm factors" such as financial capital, human capital, knowledge, technology, culture, trust, brand reputation, efficient processes, speed, innovation capability, machinery, etc.) are the sum of all intangible and tangible assets that may enable the enterprise to develop a competitive advantage that arises when an organization does something distinctive that adds a unique mix of value. Moreover, to create and sustain a strategic advantage, the following VRIN traits are required:

- *V*aluable in energizing your enterprise to explore opportunities and to counter threats,
- *R*are among your competitor firms,
- *I*mperfectly imitable, and
- *N*ot easily substitutable.

At its most basic, the RBV is concerned with what an organization is capable of: it asks, "what are its capabilities"? The firm's ability to integrate, build, and reconfigure internal and external competences and to orchestrate the assets to address rapidly changing environments calls for "dynamic capabilities". As David Teece postulates, this can be thought of as falling into three clusters of dynamic capabilities:

- Sensing – identification of opportunities and threats at home and abroad,
- Seizing – mobilization of resources to deliver value and shape markets, and
- Transforming – continuous renewal and periodic major strategic shifts.

Noteworthy is the fact that strategic transformation, often in the form of super-flexible "entrepreneurial reconfiguration", is a proactive approach to reformulating strategy that cultivates growth. You can achieve a competitive re-positioning of your enterprise and growth (namely, "company growth"), through, for example, acquisition, and "collaborative growth" through strategic alliances, joint ventures (JVs), outsourcing, and radical innovation partnerships. This differs from two other orthodox turnaround options, viz., rebuilding your organization on its prior strategic footprint or simply maintaining efficiency.

Finally, when framing strategy, go beyond just being purely analytical, and also revolve around imagining possibilities, co-creating, designing experiments, testing, and continuous dialogic learning. Ultimately, strategizing to win should be "designerly" and fun too.

 Assumptions

Strategy is literally all over the place. Football teams have strategy playbooks. Political parties set strategies. Regions and nations develop strategies to attract visitors. Even individuals craft personal brand statements – to establish, position, and leverage their personal brand so that they play to win rather than play to play. Last but not least, enterprises (startups, SMEs, private, public, for-profits, and non-profits) strategize to win – or, at least, they're expected to.

Typically, although there's no such thing as an ideal strategy, it's all about boosting your chances of success. While size can be a luxury, strategy is the ultimate equalizer. After all, strategy is about making choices – in order to win, you must deliberately choose to do some things – and not others. Go-ahead enterprises, when crafting their strategies, mix discipline and rigor (industry analysis, customer value analysis, relative position analysis, competitor analysis) with imagination (fueling possibility thinking in positive strategic dialog, design thinking, immersive visualization sessions, social platforms, strategic simulations, storytelling, and other tools to energize conversation around strategy).

In today's context, radical times call for radical strategies. As proposed by Jeanne Liedtka, the field of business strategy also calls for new metaphors. For example. the metaphor of strategy as a process of design has thus been adopted. In this view, the main goal of strategy is to construct a meaningful space that enables certain actions, connections, and behaviors to thrive. Both "good strategy" and "good design" provide a polyphonic fusion of many components into a cohesive whole. "Strategy as design" addresses itself to developing such a harmonic system. Indeed, the actual generative design process is what makes this result possible. It's a powerfully co-creative, dialogic learning-oriented process – an important method for those successfully delivering value through organic radical innovation and for leveraging and liberating the entrepreneurial spirit inside all employees. It's more experimental and less "left brained", giving the go-ahead for the exploratory play of strategic choices, possibilities, ideas … and for failing fast, failing often…, which helps to truly future-proof your strategy.

Surprisingly, to create a successful strategy, some organizations open up their strategy and innovation processes and engage a lot more diverse sets of stakeholders – front-line employees, experts, suppliers, customers, entrepreneurs, extreme users, crowds, and even competitors. Technically, "open strategy" combines the principles of conventional business strategy with the potential of "open innovation", aiming to harness the advantages of openness to enhance value creation within organizations. Practically, a successful open strategy strikes a balance between capturing value and fostering value creation. For example, to master disruption from outside the C-suite, innovative companies, for instance, decide on open collaboration and build scalable crowdsourcing innovation platforms (so as to harness the wisdom of crowds), run strategy jams (virtually or in-person, lasting from a few hours to a few days), "nightmare competitor contests" (an imaginary competitor developed to confront the unthinkable), or develop "trend radars" (spotting core trends and evaluating preparedness).

In many cases, the strategic thinking ability of leaders, managers, and other employees can be developed by means of, for example, strategy coaching. Ultimately, strategy is everybody's job – if it exists only at the top, it's doomed to failure, as it happens…

Key elements

Everything in strategy is simple – but nothing in strategy is very easy. Strategy compels desired customer action. It's a problem-solving tool and it can help tackle your most thorny issues. Discomfort is part of the process though. Strategy doesn't mean performing similar activities better/cheaper/faster than rivals perform them (that's "operational effectiveness", which is necessary – but not sufficient). As Roger Martin evangelizes, a plan is not a strategy either; rather, strategy is about making choices – it's a pattern in a stream of decisions. It's not a wish list, though. So, when designing an effective strategy, you're strongly recommended to purposefully choose:

What is your guiding aspiration?

Think big and craft your organization's energizing aspiration – start with people (employees, clients, partners) rather than money (stock price). Why do you exist (= purpose)? Consider what kind of organization you want yours to be. By the way, if your organization disappeared today, how different would the world be tomorrow? Can you paint a picture of the future for your enterprise (= vision)? What does winning mean for you? What do you believe in (= values)? What are you proud to accomplish? What is an easy/hard-earned win for you? Against whom? What are your non-financial goals? What's your risk "appetite"? In thinking about aspiration, remember to pair the "soft" aspiration with some concrete metric.

Where to compete (and where not to play) so as to achieve your winning aspiration?

Define your playing field. Consider what fits your strategic aspiration – think: product/service portfolio, industry sectors or product categories, customer segments, distribution channels, geographies, key markets, and vertical stages of production.

How to win on the playing field you've chosen?

Why choose you over the competition? The value offered is deemed the "value proposition". What is the unique "value proposition" to your potential customer (vs. the competition)? What is your *sustainable* winning advantage (a particular way to win, i.e., the way in which true advantages are leveraged to produce superior value for a customer and superior returns for a business)? A competitive advantage is the way a value proposition is delivered – and when it's difficult to be replicated, the value proposition is a winning one. How is it linked to your chosen playing field? Do you compete on low cost (thoroughly study cost drivers and drive costs down, and offer standard products and/or sacrifice nonconforming customers) *or* differentiation (e.g., be distinctive, really understand customers' needs, and offer the products they adore, enabling your enterprise to charge a price premium)? A reality check: if you claim to be "the most innovative company in our industry", why don't customers see you that way? And if you claim to have "the lowest cost position", why do your competitors continue to reduce their prices?

What hard-to-replicate capabilities/reinforcing activities must be in place?

What are some specific four/five must-have capabilities (e.g., the quality system, tech transfer, continuous process improvement, design thinking, paradoxical inquiry, innovation execution, high-performance HR practices, talent development, organizational unlearning, brand building), and their configuration!, that you must be extremely good at as a means to win in this way?

What management systems, structures, and measures are required?

What management systems support your capabilities and strategic choices? How can you evaluate whether your strategy is working? Also think: delivery accountability, priority efforts, disciplined change readiness, and change leadership process.

Thinking critically: Issues

Strategizing can be both intellectually and emotionally demanding. Most people lack the proper educational foundation for it, and organizations don't typically provide the necessary training either. Even numerous "strategy consulting" firms have largely shifted away from *true* strategy work, prioritizing areas like digital transformation, post-merger integration, and other services. As a result, strategizing remains a difficult and often daunting process.

Although it has its own justification, winning does not guarantee *continued* success, though it may increase its likelihood.

Without a doubt, figuring out what is going on outside the firm is critical. Michael Porter's economic strategy approach is heavily focused on an enterprise's external environment and uses this to identify the strategy that a company should pursue. Indeed, the economic structure of an industry is not an accident. Nonetheless, major issues may arise when an organization's strategy is framed in accordance with the structure of its market, as it may be based on the presumption that the market is generally static or unchanging.

As advocated by Henry Mintzberg, because of the great complexity and rapid rate of change, "emergent strategies" are required. While for generally steady conditions with little complexity, a top-down strategy-making process works well, in chaotic, and "stormy", conditions with high uncertainty, the process of creating a strategy becomes experimental, and rather messy – bottom-up driven. As it happens, when senior management, encased in boardrooms – and disconnected from the corporate "every day", formulates an apparently "perfect" strategy, further complications can develop when people on the ground are tasked with executing that strategy on a daily level.

Don't forget that issues are often unclear and open to more than one interpretation. Outside of the essential textbooks of economic studies, "rational actors" are quite rare; it's a little trickier in *real* life. Herbert Simon, the Nobel Economics laureate, was right! Decisions are rarely, if ever, made in an environment of pure rationality. We always make them with varying degrees of uncertainty and understanding. Frequently, the criteria for choosing are vague, and information regarding the options are often limited. Besides, others could have very different – and even conflicting – perspectives on the problems, solutions, and choices. Simply speaking, there may not be enough time, effort, or buy-in to bring disparate points of view together. Accordingly, instead of being purely "rational optimizers", analyzing every piece of information, awaiting the availability of all the evidence, we behave in a "bounded rational" manner – we don't try hard to make optimal decisions, but rather choices that basically "work". Simon called this "satisficing". His term was a combination of the words "satisfy" and "suffice."

Who would have known in, say, 2019, that enterprises, communities, industries, and economies throughout the world would be on lockdown because of a novel coronavirus (COVID-19) – within a matter of weeks? Or that, as a result, the transition to digitally enabled online working, studying, and communicating would happen almost overnight? One effective method for developing strategies around the unknown unknowns (*the past does not process linearly into the future!*) and trying to envision a range of futures for the enterprise, is "scenario planning". This is a reflexive exercise of understanding what the future *might* look like by enquiring into social dynamics, economic, environmental, political, and tech issues and trends, among others. Yes, gather information, structure scenarios, write them and use them. Yet, scenario planning must go beyond the standard "base case/best case/worst case" planning. By way of illustration, Shell plc scenarios team helps explore possible versions of the future by identifying drivers, uncertainties, enablers, and constraints and unearthing potential issues and their implications. Importantly, when putting scenarios into practice to develop a much broader view of strategy, you need to zoom in on:

- What elements of your enterprise's environment are causing you to feel so deeply uncertain?
- To better make sense of the possible consequences of the uncertainty, whom could you tap for information and intel, and which of these can you use into your scenarios?
- How might you think about tweaking your company's strategy so as take advantage of fresh chances and to make sure it holds up in all possible scenarios?
- What key signals do the scenarios suggest you use to track changes in your organization's environment?
- What essential signals should you employ to monitor variation in your organization's playing field – according to the scenarios?

As an alternative to Porter's and other market-driven approaches, the RBV of strategy has evolved. This perspective, based on works by Edith Penrose, Birger Wernerfelt, and Jay Barney, among others, argues that internal resources, strengths and "firm factors" (rather than "industry factors") are make-or-break characteristics. Despite having idiosyncratic capabilities that result in distinctive goods and services, you might, nonetheless, struggle in the market due to "outside" forces that you are unable to manage and/or that are unfavorable to your positioning. Besides, if strategy revolves around resource development, it's akin to saying that if you build resources, they will come. However, the challenge lies in the fact that a resource that's valuable in one area may not hold the same value in another context. This raises the question: how do you determine which resources are worth the investment to build? And where should you prioritize building and allocating them?

Ultimately, strategizing may be regarded as an important "social practice" – essentially, it's what strategists do. In fact, there are no great "natural" strategists; great strategists have one thing in common - they just practice it. Richard Whittington recommends following a "strategy as practice" (S-A-P) agenda, by seeking answers to the following questions:

- Where and how is the work of strategizing and organizing actually done?
- Who does this strategizing and organizing work?
- What are the skills for this work and how are they acquired?
- What are the common tools and techniques of strategizing and organizing?
- How are the products of strategizing and organizing communicated and consumed?

Practically speaking, although Chief Executive Officers (CEOs) hold both formal and final responsibility for strategy, nowadays, their available time to work on it is dwindling. Hence, Chief Strategy Officers (CSOs) are being appointed to the C-suite. While the CSO is a relatively new role, it is starting to play a more and more significant function in many organizations. By nature, to be set up for success, the CSO can serve as:

- an "internal strategy consultant" – concentrated chiefly on strategy formulation alone and/or with the chosen strategy, on rethinking the strategic planning process that is often "dry" by boosting the quality of the strategy dialog or by installing modern strategy crafting processes and high-level thinking. Here, the strategy implementation resides mainly with the business units. Of note, a background in consulting *will* help enormously here;
- a "strategy specialist" – dealing with mergers and acquisitions (M&A) activity, government and specific regulations;
- a "strategy coach" – facilitating the dialogic strategizing process; and
- a "change leader" or even "Chief Future Officer" (CFO) – focused on leading positive organizational change and renewal and on shaping the future.

Applications

Revolution, disruption, risk, speediness, crazy busyness, lack of certainty, surprise, and shock ... all are constants in the present climate. Given this, much broader strategy perspectives are required of leaders. Some go for designing and operating whole value-creating social-capital-based (digital) eco-systems – not just sectors, as well as scenarios – not forecasts that are not good at foreseeing unexpected or surprising events. Instead of plans that often just die in the boardroom, many co-create strategy playbooks (consider: in certain scenarios, which "plays" make the most sense? What strategic choices and possibilities are out there for these plays? How will you monitor events and developments to choose which play to run?).

The art of strategy and its practice is a genuinely applied process. As Roger Martin further recommends:

- You can start your strategy choice-making with articulating (or by trying to articulate) your current strategy.
- Next, check in with stakeholders, and define the strategic problem – carry out an industry analysis, customer value analysis, relative position analysis, and competitor analysis.
- Following this, frame your strategic choice(s).
- After that, generate possibilities, and cluster them by themes – for each possibility, answer the strategy elements questions (see below in "Key elements"). Check in with your stakeholders again.
- Then, specify conditions that must be true for each possibility to be a great choice – look at conditions in the following categories: industry segments, structure, customer value, your capabilities and costs vs. your competitors' capabilities and costs, and the competitors' reaction(s) to your actions.
- Afterward, identify the greatest barriers to choosing each possibility.
- Subsequently, design tests of those barriers (for example, guerilla-style, small-scale, pilot, and large-scale ones), and check in with stakeholders.
- Thereafter, conduct tests, analyze, and discuss test results.
- In the end, choose. If needed, tweak your strategy – here, continuous improvement, learning (and *un*learning) within the execution are vital.
- In due course, communicate your new strategy organization-wide (business leaders and functional leaders need to be connected), and build must-have capabilities and management systems.
- Remember: keep on strategizing to win.

Besides, to dismantle the "business as usual" (BAU) mindset and achieve spectacular results, perhaps try implementing a "future perfect strategy", a concept closely identified with thinkers such as Alfred Schütz, Harold Garfinkel, and Karl Weick. The future perfect strategy leverages the imagination to picture future events as if they had already occurred. To achieve this, you can employ the following creative methods. For example:

- The resourceful use of "strange conversations" – a process of asking "dumb" questions that generates feedback, which increases your awareness of the

hidden assumptions and challenges related to your strategy. This nurtures dialogic learning, too. Remember: deep listening may yield important and otherwise unknown information.

- The rehearsal of "end games and the practice of workshopping" – this methodo-
logical practice involves imagining and projecting into the desired future (and
generating positive strategic future scenarios), and then "building the rocket"
to get there, i.e., working backward to the present in order to come up with
concrete (and realistic) actions maps in the available time, and
- "Projecting feelings, concerns, and issues" – where a lot of effort is spent figuring
out how people feel about various elements of your strategy – both among your
own leadership team, users, experts, extreme users, and more broadly – in the
community. Rather than bureaucratic formal strategy plans, "social empathy" is
prioritized.

Ultimately, to excel at both strategy and execution, you need to be an integrative
thinker (and doer) – be both a visionary and a resourceful operator. Specifically:

1 Raise aspirations. Make big moves early and often. Build a bold but executable
strategy.
2 Translate the coherent strategy into the everyday – invest behind leading positive
organizational change and link the budget closely to the strategy.
3 Energize the entire organization to execute it.

Case alert! Case classic

Tennis Canada

LOOK IT UP: Martin, R. (2015, January–February). Strategic transformation at
Tennis Canada. *European Business Review*: 44–49.

Your task: Read the article on Tennis Canada (the governing body of tennis in
Canada) in *European Business Review* and learn how a small organization can start
playing to win in an ultra-competitive global arena.
 What challenges did Tennis Canada face before crafting a new strategy? How
did the strategic transformation at Tennis Canada, and a novel approach to
reformulating strategy, help cultivate strategic organization development and to
build a sustainable platform for success? How did the five key strategy playbook
questions used support this strategic transformation? How is Tennis Canada
doing these days?
 To record your critical insights, use the Case Analysis Record provided in
Appendix 2.

Greater good corner: Get ready to exercise your ethics

Take a stance: What would *you* do?

Dilemma and Decision: Do we become an innovator or an imitator?
You'd like to break into a new marketplace. You may want to create an entirely new product/service, and innovation will be a vital ingredient for success. Yet, if your products/services closely resemble those of a rival, you will need to distinguish yourself with differentiation factors like quality and safety, pricing, customer care, and "adding value", which will be critical.

You're now having a meeting. Your Chief Marketing Officer (CMO) states, "Strategy is really all about being different. We must be distinct ... or we'll be extinct!". Now, your CSO suggests: "Well, we may actually gain a competitive edge by becoming a "fast copier" (follower), and scaling, imitating the market leader – at a much lower price".

You're thinking,

> There are so many successful businesses that didn't create anything radical or new. Airbus didn't design the first wide-bodied passenger jet. Campbell Soup Company didn't pioneer the concept of canned soup. Dell didn't invent the personal computer. McDonald's didn't invent the hamburger or the fast-food restaurant. Still, all four have been flourishing. Hmm, how have they been thriving imitators, rather than innovators...? Is copying others ethical?

Now, what do you do?

Note: Among other things, assess your marketplace. To analyze the structure of your industry, you may want to consider the following Five Forces that determine the profit potential and attractiveness of your industry and counter them with specific tactics:

1 How will the greater power of suppliers affect your business? (List the major inputs needed for your business. For each input, list possible suppliers. Think up how you can work best with each supplier to maximize your bargaining power?)
2 How will the greater power of buyers affect your business? (List the types of customers that you (expect to) have. What alternatives might these customers have for your product/service? How can you build loyalty for your product/service to reduce the customer bargaining power?)

3 How might the threat of new entrants affect your business? (How would a new entrant affect your business? What will your competitor(s) do if there's a new entrant into your marketplace? How will you respond to a new competitor?)

4 How will the threat of substitutes affect your business? (List possible substitutes that your customers could use in place of your product/service. How easy would it be for your customers to consider this alternative? How can you differentiate your products/services or build customer loyalty to manage the threat of substitutes?)

5 How does rivalry among competitors affect your business? (List your major competitors. What business and growth strategies does each competitor use? How will each competitor affect your business? What actions will you take in response to your competitors' actions?)

Thought questions:

1 How do ethical considerations shape the balance between innovation and imitation?

2 How might the pursuit of profit through imitation impact the ethical standards of the industry as a whole?

3 What ethical responsibilities does a company have in ensuring that its strategic choices, whether innovative or imitative, promote fair competition and do not lead to monopolistic practices or the exploitation of smaller businesses?

Time out: Journal entry

Thought Sparks: A few reflections, insightful ideas, actionable suggestions, strategic thinking, and key takeaways from this unit.

Learning never stops… So, pause for a few minutes and reflect in writing on your personal learning experience and beliefs. Through writing in your journal, you develop your awareness of your own beliefs and attitudes. Now, consolidate what you have learned in this unit.

1 How have your beliefs and ideas about strategy changed since you began the unit?

....

....

....

2 Thinking about the problems presented in the unit, write about whether you have found solutions to these problems.

....

....

....

3 How confident do you now feel about making choices when ethically strategizing to win?

....

....

....

4 What would you still like to have clarified? What remaining concerns do you have?

....

....

....

5 What more would you like to learn about the topic, now that you have completed this unit?

....

....

....

6 If you want, doodle/draw something you like about proactive strategic transformation. This can be as abstract as you wish.

....

....

....

Remember: It's particularly useful to re-visit journal entries several times and see how themes have recurred or your thoughts have changed over time. Now, repeat "Your Take".

Making connections: Related units and models

- U 1. **Behavioral economics and policy 101**: For humans (see pp. 9–26)
- U 4. **SOAR**: Possibility thinking in positive strategic dialog (see pp. 82–95)
- U 5. **Dialogic organization development (OD)**: Leading positive organizational change (see pp. 103–121)

- U 6. **Design-driven organization**: Human-centered design thinking and innovation execution (see pp. 122–139)
- U 7. **WOW! It's cool!** Crafting a coolness strategy for your brand (see pp. 147–159)
- U 9. **Professional management consulting for real people**: The advice business demystified (see pp. 181–203)
- U 10. **Executive coaching**: Whoop it up! (see pp. 204–219)
- U 11. **So, you want to go global?** Becoming an instant international (see pp. 227–237)
- U 13. **Progress with purpose**: The "good" enterprise (see pp. 257–272)
- Add in more related models you may want to remember: _____.

Industry snapshot

www.tenniscanada.com

Deep dive: Main references and resources

Adner, R. (2023). *Winning the right game: How to disrupt, defend, and deliver in a changing world*. Cambridge, MA: The MIT Press.

Aguesse, M., & Decreton, B. (2022, June 14). Using fiction to find your strategy. *Harvard Business Review*. Retrieved from: https://hbr.org/2022/06/using-fiction-to-find-your-strategy

Aversa, P., Bianchi, E., Gaio, L., & Nucciarelli, A. (2022): The grand tour: The role of catalyzing places for industry emergence. *Academy of Management Journal*, 65(6): 2058–2091.

Barnard, C. (1938). *The functions of the executive*. Cambridge, MA: Harvard University Press.

Barney, J.B. (1991). Firm resources and sustained competitive advantage. *Journal of Management*, 17(1): 99–120.

Berenschot. (2002). *Het strategieboek I*. Amsterdam: Nieuwezijds. [*The strategy book I.*]

Berenschot. (2006). *Het strategieboek II: Nieuwe speelvelden*. The Hague: SDU. [*The strategy book II: New playing fields.*]

Bogers, M., Chesbrough, H., Heaton, S., & Teece, D.J. (2019). Strategic management of open innovation: A dynamic capabilities perspective. *California Management Review*, 62(1): 77–94.

Breene, R.T., Nunes, P.F., & Shill, W.E. (2007). The chief strategy officer. *Harvard Business Review*, 85(10): 84–93.

Browne, S., Sharkey Scott, P., Mangematin, V., & Gibbons, P. (2018). Shaking up business models with creative strategies: When tried and true stops working. *Journal of Business Strategy*, (39)4: 19–27.

Bungay, S. (2011). How to make the most of your company's strategy. *Harvard Business Review*, 89(1–2): 132–140.

Bungay, S. (2019, April 19). 5 myths about strategy. *Harvard Business Review*. Retrieved from: https://hbr.org/2019/04/5-myths-about-strategy

Campbell, A., Lancelott, M., & Gutierrez, M. (2018). *Operating model canvas: Aligning operations and organization with strategy*. 's-Hertogenbosch: Van Haren Publishing.

Carter, C., Clegg, S., & Kornberger, M. (2008). *A very short, fairly interesting and reasonably cheap book about studying strategy*. London: SAGE.

Casadesus-Masanell, R., & Ricart, J.E. (2011). How to design a winning business model? *Harvard Business Review*, 89(1/2): 100–107.

Casey, A.J., & Goldman, E.F. (2010). Enhancing the ability to think strategically: A learning model. *Management Learning*, 41(2): 167–185.

Chandler, A.D. (1962). *Strategy and structure: Chapters in the history of the American industrial enterprise*. Cambridge: Massachusetts Institute of Technology.

Chermack, T. (2022). *Using scenarios: Scenario planning for improving organizations*. Oakland, CA: Berrett-Koehler Publishers.

Chesbrough, H.W., & Appleyard, M.M. (2007). Open innovation and strategy. *California Management Review*, 50(1): 57–76.

Clark, D. (2018, June 21). If strategy is so important, why don't we make time for it? *Harvard Business Review*. Retrieved from: https://hbr.org/2018/06/if-strategy-is-so-important-why-dont-we-make-time-for-it

Collis, D.J., & Rukstad, M.G. (2008). Can you say what your strategy is. *Harvard Business Review*, 86(4): 82–90.

Csaszar, F.A. (2018). What makes a decision strategic? Strategic representations. *Strategy Science*, 3(4): 606–619.

Day, G.S., & Schoemaker, P.J.H. (2018). How to sense and seize opportunities–and transform your organization. *Rotman Management,* 4: 68–74.

Deneffe, D., & Vantrappen, H. (2020). *Fad-free strategy: Rigorous methods to help executives make strategic choices confidently*. London & New York, NY: Routledge.

Duggan, W. (2007). *Strategic intuition: The creative spark in human achievement*. New York, NY: Columbia Business School Publishing.

Eyring, M.J., Johnson, M.W. & Nair, H. (2011). New business models in emerging markets. *Harvard Business Review*, 89(1–2): 88–95.

Felin, T., & Powell, T.C. (2016). Designing organizations for dynamic capabilities. *California Management Review*, 58(4): 78–96.

Felin, T., & Zenger, T. (2018). What sets breakthrough strategies apart. *MIT Sloan Management Review*, 59(2): 86–88.

Flyvbjerg, B., & Gardner, D. (2023). *How big things get done: The surprising factors that determine the fate of every project, from home renovations to space exploration and everything in between*. New York, NY: Currency.

Galpin, T. (2023). *The strategist's handbook: Tools, templates, and best practices across the strategy process*. Oxford: Oxford University Press.

Goldman, E.F. (2007). Strategic thinking at the top. *MIT Sloan Management Review*, 48(4): 75–81.

Goldman. E.F., Scott, A.R., & Follman, J.M. (2015). Organizational practices to develop strategic thinking. *Journal of Strategy and Management*, 8(2): 155–175.

Greene, R. (2007). *The 33 strategies of war.* London: Profile Books.

Hamel, G. (1996). Strategy as revolution. *Harvard Business Review*, 74(4): 69–82.

Hax, A.C. (2014). *The delta model: Reinventing your business strategy*. New York, NY: Springer.

Heikkinen, K., Kerr, W., Malin, M., Routila, P., & Rupponen, E. (2023, April 21). When scenario planning fails. *Harvard Business Review*. Retrieved from: https://hbr.org/2023/04/when-scenario-planning-fails

Heshmati, M., & Csaszar, F.A. (2024). Learning strategic representations: Exploring the effects of taking a strategy course. *Organization Science*, 35(2): 453–473.

Horn, J. (2023). *Inside the competitor's mindset: How to predict their next move and position yourself for success*. Cambridge, MA: The MIT Press.

Johnson, M.W., Christensen, C.M., & Kagermann, H. (2008). Reinventing your business model. *Harvard Business Review*, 86(12): 50–59.

Kilduff, G.J. (2019). Interfirm relational rivalry: Implications for competitive strategy. *Academy of Management Review*, 44(4): 775–799.

Knight, E., Daymond, J., & Paroutis, S. (2020). Design-led strategy: How to bring design thinking into the art of strategic management. *California Management Review*, 62(2): 30–52.

Lafley, A.G., & Martin, R. (2013). *Playing to win: How strategy really works*. Boston, MA: Harvard Business Review Press.

Lang, T., & Whittington, R. (2022, May 23). The best strategies don't just take a long view. They take a broad view. *Harvard Business Review*. Retrieved from: https://hbr .org/2022/05/the-best-strategies-dont-just-take-a-long-view-they-take-a-broad-view

Leinwand, P., & Rotering, J. (2017, November 17). How to excel at both strategy and execution. *Harvard Business Review*. Retrieved from: https://hbr.org/2017/11/ how-to-excel-at-both-strategy-and-execution

Leinwand, P., Naujok, N., & Rotering, J. (2019, January 15). Memo to the CEO: Is your chief strategy officer set up for success? *Strategy+Business*. Retrieved from: www .strategy-business.com/article/Memo-to-the-CEO-Is-Your-Chief-Strategy-Officer-Set-Up-for-Success

Lenox, M. (2023). *Strategy in the digital age: Mastering digital transformation*. Stanford, CA: Stanford University Press.

Liedtka, J. (2000). In defense of strategy as design. *California Management Review*, 42(3): 8–30.

Mankins, M.C., & Steele, R. (2005). Turning great strategy into great performance. *Harvard Business Review*, 83(7): 64–72.

Martin, R. (2015, January–February). Strategic transformation at tennis Canada. *European Business Review*: 44–49. https://rogerlmartin.com/docs/default-source/default-document-library/tebr-jan-feb-2015-strategic-transformation-at-tennis-canada.pdf? sfvrsn=be803e82_0

Martin, R. (2018, December 28). The board's role in strategy. *Harvard Business Review*. Retrieved from: https://hbr.org/2018/12/the-boards-role-in-strategy

Martin, R. (2022, June 29). A plan is not a strategy. *Harvard Business Review*. Retrieved from: https://youtu.be/iuYlGRnC7J8

Martin, R. (2023, January 16). Sticking with strategy: How to hold on to give it a chance. Retrieved from: https://rogermartin.medium.com/sticking-with-strategy-100bc94d26ed

Mintzberg, H. (1990). The design school: Reconsidering the basic premises of strategic management. *Strategic Management Journal*, 11(3): 171–195.

Montgomery, C.A. (2008). Putting leadership back into strategy. *Harvard Business Review*, 86(1): 54–60.

Muthusamy, S.K. (2015). Shoaling (school of fish) as competitive strategy. *Strategic Change*, 24(6): 499–507.

Nooteboom, B. (2022). *Dynamic capabilities: History and an extension*. Cambridge: Cambridge University Press.

Ohmae, K. (1982). *The mind of the strategist: The art of Japanese business*. New York, NY: McGraw-Hill.

Osterwalder, A., & Pigneur, Y. (2010). *Business model generation: A handbook for visionaries, game changers, and challengers*. Hoboken, NJ: Wiley.

Osterwalder, A., Pigneur, Y., Bernarda, G., & Smith, A. (2014). *Value proposition design: How to create products and services customers want.* Hoboken, NJ: Wiley.

Pearce, J.A., II, & Robbins, D.K. (2008). Strategic transformation as the essential last step in the process of business turnaround. Business Horizons, 51(2): 121–130.

Penrose, E. (2009). *The theory of the growth of the firm* (4th edition). Oxford: OUP.

Pitsis, T.S., Clegg, S.R., Marosszeky, M., & Rura-Polley, T. (2003). Constructing the Olympic dream: A future perfect strategy of project management. *Organization Science*, 14(5): 574–590.

Pope, S., & Wæraas, A. (2023, October 31). How to create company values that actually resonate. *Harvard Business Review.* Retrieved from: https://hbr.org/2023/10/how-to-create-company-values-that-actually-resonate

Porter, M. (1980). *Competitive strategy: Techniques for analyzing industries and competitors.* New York: Free Press.

Porter, M. (1996). What is strategy? *Harvard Business Review*, 74(6): 61–78.

Porter, M. (2008). The five competitive forces that shape strategy. *Harvard Business Review*, 86(1): 78–93.

Powell, T.H., & Angwin, D.N. (2012). The role of the chief strategy officer. *MIT Sloan Management Review*, (54)1: 15–16.

Ramirez, R., Churchhouse, S., Palermo, A., & Hoffmann, J. (2017). Using scenario planning to reshape strategy. *MIT Sloan Management Review*, 58(4): 31–37.

Ramirez, R., Lang, T., Finch, M., Carson, G., & Fisher, D. (2023). Strategizing across organizations. MIT Sloan Management Review, 64(3): 62–65.

Rogers, P., & Blenko, M. (2006). Who has the D? How clear decision roles enhance organizational performance. *Harvard Business Review*, 84(1), 52–61.

Schoemaker, P.J.H., Heaton, S., & Teece, D. (2018). Innovation, dynamic capabilities, and leadership. *California Management Review*, 61(1): 15–42.

Shaw, G., Brown, R., & Bromiley, P. (1998). Strategic stories: How 3M is rewriting business planning. *Harvard Business Review*, 76(3): 41–50.

Shih, W. (2016). The real lessons from Kodak's decline. *MIT Sloan Management Review*, 57(4): 11–13.

Simon, H.A. (1945). *Administrative behavior* (2nd edition). New York, NY: Free Press.

Stadler, C., & Reeves, M. (2023, May 30). Three lessons from chatting about strategy with ChatGPT. *MIT Sloan Management Review.* Retrieved from: https://sloanreview.mit.edu/article/three-lessons-from-chatting-about-strategy-with-chatgpt/

Stadler, C., Hautz, J., Matzler, K., & Friedrich von den Eichen, S. (2023). *Open strategy. Mastering disruption from outside the c-suite.* Cambridge, MA & London: The MIT Press.

Subramaniam, M. (2022). *The future of competitive strategy: Unleashing the power of data and digital ecosystems.* Cambridge, MA: The MIT Press.

Sull, D., & Turconi, S. (2017, September 28). How to recognize a strategic priority when you see one. *MIT Sloan Management Review.* Retrieved from: https://sloanreview.mit.edu/article/how-to-recognize-a-strategic-priority-when-you-see-one/

Sull, D., Turconi, S., Sull, C., & Yoder, J. (2017). Four logics of corporate strategy. *MIT Sloan Management Review*, 59(2): 38–44.

Sull, D., Sull, C., & Yoder, J. (2018). No one knows your strategy—Not even your top leaders. *MIT Sloan Management Review*, 59(3): 179–184.

Sull, D., Turconi, S., Sull, C., & Yoder, J. (2018). Turning strategy into results. *MIT Sloan Management Review*, 59(3): 1–12.

Teece, D.J., Pisano, G., & Shuen, A. (1997). Dynamic capabilities and strategic management. *Strategic Management Journal*, 18(7): 509–533.

Tkaczyk, B. (2021). *Leading positive organizational change: Energize – redesign – gel.* London & New York, NY: Routledge.

Wernerfelt, B. (1984). A resource-based view of the firm. *Strategic Management Journal,* 5(2): 171–180.

Whittington, R. (2003). The work of strategizing and organizing: For a practice perspective. *Strategic Organization,* 1(1): 117–125.

Whittington, R. Yakis-Douglas, B., & Ahn, K. (2015, December 28). Wall Street rewards CEOs who talk about their strategies. *Harvard Business Review.* Retrieved from: https://hbr.org/2015/12/wall-street-rewards-ceos-who-talk-about-their-strategies

Zenger, T. (2016). *Beyond competitive advantage: How to solve the puzzle of sustaining growth while creating value.* Boston, MA: Harvard Business Review Press.

4 SOAR

Fueling possibility thinking in
positive strategic dialog

"If you want something new, you have to stop doing something old" – Peter Drucker

Sneak peek

Focus on: Key concepts and terms

Unit 4

- Balanced scorecard
- "Blue/red ocean" strategy
- Open inquiry
- Positive strategy
- Positive dialogic strategizing
- Positive organizational scholarship (POS)
- Possibility thinking (positive, positively deviant, strategic)
- Strengths, opportunities, aspirations, results (SOAR)
- Strengths, weaknesses, opportunities, threats (SWOT)

Pause 'N' reflect: On the current issues and trends

Before you complete this unit, think about each of the following statements. Mark each statement:

V – if you *agree.*
X – if you *disagree.*
? – if you are *undecided.*

DOI: 10.4324/9781003508274-7

Your Take: Integrative Thinking	*Before doing Unit 4*	*After doing Unit 4*
1 The pressures to make strategy energizing and creative are grounds for novel approaches to framing it. *Positive* strategy contrasts with the traditional, formal, centralized, bureaucratic, mechanistic, reactive view of strategy by paying much more attention to positive processes that capacitate organic collective resourcefulness and generative dynamics, resulting in positive conditions as well as measurable and meaningful results.		
2 SWOT (*strengths*, *weaknesses*, *opportunities*, *threats*) focuses more on analysis and planning than on planning and execution.		
3 SOAR (*strengths*, *opportunities*, *aspirations*, *results*) is a positive, alternative approach to strategy development that goes beyond a problem-solving mindset by intentionally appreciating and getting immersed in strengths to build a shared image of potential.		
4 Maximum productivity can be gained by elevating strengths and managing weaknesses.		
5 In *standard* strategic planning, managers use problem-solving methods that they have previously used to address the same or related issues. In *positive* possibility strategizing, leaders often focus on exploring future possibilities, building value-creating strategies, and facilitating positively enhancing innovations.		
6 Strengths analysis can help develop a deeper understanding of what separates *good* from *great*.		
7 A strategic aspiration is an organization's bold and compelling dream that energizes stakeholders and supplies the physical, emotional, mental, and spiritual energy for the journey into the future.		

Your Take: Integrative Thinking	*Before doing Unit 4*	*After doing Unit 4*
8　All team/enterprise members need to engage in positively deviant possibility thinking. Strategy conversations and creative dialog nurture positive strategies, actions, and outcomes; they fuel and sustain positive strategizing.		
9　Visioning can inspire and guide positive action. Strategic vision stories provide a vividly detailed portrayal of an ideal future that everyone can easily picture and imagine.		
10　Cut-throat competition culminates in nothing but a "bloody red ocean" of rivals fighting over a shrinking profit pool. Yet, sustainable success lies not in beating off competitors but in creating "blue oceans" – untapped new market spaces ripe for growth.		

After you have done the unit, repeat "Your Take". How has reading the unit clarified the ideas herein? How have your views, feelings and thoughts changed over time?

Lead-in

General discussion points

Individually or in buzz groups, work on the following:

1　*The "strengths-based" enterprise does not ignore weaknesses, but rather it optimizes where strengths are focused and developed upon, while weaknesses are known and managed.* How do you interpret this opinion? Do you agree with it? Explain why.
2　Have you ever either conducted or reviewed a SWOT (*s*trengths, *w*eaknesses, *o*pportunities, *t*hreats) analysis? If yes, can you share any profound or penetrating insights that came out of any such SWOT analysis?
3　Have you ever tried performing a dynamic, strengths-based SOAR (*s*trengths, *o*pportunities, *a*spirations, *r*esults) analysis? If yes, is doing SOAR more energy-boosting or energy-depleting than doing SWOT?
4　Strategic vision is a snapshot of the ideal future state you want to co-create and work toward. What other attributes of an effective vision could you suggest? How would you best map out a strategy?
5　*Although the company's core purpose itself does not change (the purpose defines the reason for the enterprise's existence – it's something that ought to endure for at least 100 years and contrasts with goals and business strategies,*

which are continually changing over time), it does inspire positive change. Because purpose can never be completely realized, an enterprise can never stop stimulating change and development. What do you think?

Share your thoughts with your peers/team members. Discuss points of (dis) agreement.

Idea watch

According to strategy and organization development (OD) scholars and practitioners, we're in need of fresh methods for strategizing, so we might want to rethink our strategy and OD notions, models, and tools.

SOAR, created by Jacqueline Stavros, is a dynamic, strengths-based, and solution-oriented framework with a participatory, whole system (stakeholder), co-creative approach to framing strategic thinking. It focuses on the formulation and implementation of a *positive* strategy by finding **strengths**, boosting imagination and innovation in the form of **opportunities**, energizing individuals and teams to share **aspirations**, and delivering positively deviant performance that is far above the norm – leading to spectacular **results**.

Characteristically, backed by Positive Organizational Scholarship (POS) (POS, a sub-field in the area of Management and Organizations Studies founded by Kim Cameron, Jane Dutton and Robert Quinn, is the science and practice of that which is positive, flourishing and life-giving in organizations), the SOAR framework provides a flexible, positive OD and learning, and dialogue process to complete a strategic assessment and to create innovative strategies for action.

An essential component of this POS method to strategizing is the human capacity of the workforce to frame strategy by inquiring into and appreciating its positive core – the sum of an organization's distinctive capabilities, valuable assets, superior strengths, high potentials, high-quality networks, and vital resources – to work together to build a brighter future for the enterprise. This necessitates strategic conversations among employees, i.e., generative structures for articulating the organization's strategic intent (usually incorporating stretch targets, which force companies to lead in innovative ways) and for sustaining positive strategy.

Assumptions

While traditional SWOT analysis (e.g., *Where can we outperform others? Where can others outperform us? How might we exploit the market? What/who might take our market?*), based on research carried out at Harvard Business School and Stanford Research Institute in the period of 1955–1965 (which has, in effect, been the standard for performing a strategic assessment since then), frames strategy from the assumption that there is an actual environment in which the company competes (SWOT is mainly *rivalry*-centered – "just beat them!"), SOAR is instead *potential*-centered ("always aim higher"). Moreover, rather than a problem to be solved, an enterprise is a mystery to be embraced and appreciated.

Furthermore, the greatest gains in talent and OD are based on investment in what individuals and organizations do best naturally (organizations gain more when they build on their strengths) – far more than when enterprises make proportional efforts to improve their areas of weakness.

In addition, high performers have a *higher purpose*, an awareness of one's *strengths*, winning *aspirations*, and positively energizing leaders who are extremely good at firing the imagination (*opportunities*) with a *result*-driven process.

Consequently, positive strategizing, addressing itself to positive processes that enable collective resourcefulness as well as generative dynamics that bring about positive conditions and meaningful results, is a living, co-creative, value-adding activity. Thus, it becomes everyone's responsibility to choose which strategies will best enable the enterprise to achieve the intended outcomes.

Finally, through a continuous process of experimenting and dialogic learning, SOAR facilitates organizational super-flexibility as strategy emerges and develops through appreciation, discovery, strategic conversations, learning (and *un*learning), dreaming, design thinking (*and* doing), and reflection and reflexivity.

Key elements

The life-giving SOAR elements include:

Strengths (S) serve as the basis for strategic growth by finding and synchronizing an enterprise's best capabilities to center on performance drivers and on a more sustainable future. To identify how strengths can be capitalized on to attain the intended outcomes, a positive strengths-based strategic dialog is entered into.

Opportunities (O) expand into the world of identifying potential and positively complementing uncharted projects – and breakthrough innovations. Positive strategic dialog concentrates on opportunities to execute innovations in products, services, processes, and experiences.

Aspirations (A) further energize those who pay particular attention to the future of the enterprise. Positive strategic dialog revolves around strategic efforts that will serve different stakeholders' aspirations (for example, current and prospective clients).

Results (R) positively enhance and renew the drive and commitment to action of those involved in achieving the intended outcomes. To boost positive results, the enterprise must identify and tap into the necessary assets and incentives to engage its employees.

Thinking critically: Issues

Despite the fact that the term "positive strategy" might be unfamiliar to some organizational leaders, perhaps the phrase "strengths-based" is better recognized in this context (think, e.g., organizational high performance, high-quality connections and interpersonal communication, thriving, successful teams, positive organizational energy and change, resilience, organizational virtuousness, excellence, mindfulness, forgiveness, healing, compassion, gratitude, hope, self-efficacy, et cetera).

Admittedly, the typical method for strategic thinking entails conducting a SWOT analysis, which, in theory, starts with strengths, but often devolves into making a list of weaknesses and threats, often resulting in a downward spiral of negative energy. In contrast to a standard SWOT analysis, a positive alternative approach to strategic thinking utilizes the SOAR analysis where, in reality, using an appreciative intent (e.g., What is our desired future? What do we want to be known for?), a strategic inquiry (e.g., What are our greatest assets? How can we best partner with others?) serves as its first step. SOAR encourages and fuels strategic conversations to positively move from weaknesses to strengths and from threats to opportunities. Rather than instantly dealing with weaknesses and threats, SOAR, through positive dialogic strategizing, reframes these as circumstances that allow the enterprise to continuously grow.

Some may contend that the key drawbacks of a SOAR analysis are as follows: SOAR does not properly examine weaknesses or threats. While POS does not reject the examination of dysfunctions, SOAR does represent an affirmative bias and orientation. Additionally, some elements appear to cross over and recur in other strategy frameworks (e.g., aspirations are frequently articulated as an organization's vision). Moreover, as opposed to formal strategic plans, the SOAR approach strongly promotes creating strategies for action.

More practically, Jeff Flesher, a strategic human resource development (HRD) professor and global OD consultant, highlights more critical SWOT limitations. In particular, those conducting SWOT analyses often lack sufficient knowledge of the context to accurately represent the real situation. Frequently, these analyses are completed solely by senior leaders during planning sessions. The process becomes even less effective when the results are passed on to even more senior decision-makers, who weren't involved in the discussions but later base plans and next steps on them as gold standard data sources. Additionally, session timing tends to dictate the process ("we have an hour planned") rather than allowing the time needed for generating meaningful insights. Facilitators also influence the outcomes, and social dynamics play a role in the process depending on how well the session is facilitated and the level of risk (the elephants may still be in the room). What's more, the tool relies heavily on judgment, with observations being made in real-time. Data collection and analysis are condensed into a single, fast session, often driven by good/bad characterizations. While this may seem efficient, it lacks a structured approach to first understanding the situation, then comparing it to defined objectives, and finally contrasting the current state with the desired outcome. On top of that, since SWOT is based on paradoxical premises, most aspects can be (and are) both strengths and weaknesses, with their value often independent of the labels that infer good and bad.

Broadly, the majority of SWOT analyses fail to include how employees ought to renew their business because they are not meant to *energize* the organizational stakeholders to "*soar*" to a level of engaged high performance. Consequently, the product of a SWOT analysis may be insufficiently relevant, insightful, or committed, which is, in some measure, due to the fact that organizational members lack a meaningful means to frame the strategy and bring to light how they make for strategy formation, communication, and execution.

While it's not claimed here that either model is right or wrong, SOAR is a significant advance as a paradigm for strategic thinking because of its development from SWOT and its use of positive OD practice. Ultimately, SOAR can actually leverage SWOT (in reality, the appropriate framework will be determined by the circumstances, and in some circumstances, both SWOT and SOAR can be applied when strategizing) Plus, the very flexibility of SOAR allows for easy integration with other strategic management, *dialogic* OD and positive change methods.

 ## Applications

Plans *often* die in the boardroom. Instead of developing formal strategic plans, various SOAR practitioners have used the framework to craft innovative strategies for action around an issue or to challenge stakeholders who are looking for a strategic answer. Indeed, SOAR enables possibility thinking in positive strategic dialog.

To make the most of your SOAR analysis and to turn insights into concrete results, follow these 5 steps:

1 Review your current state and think about intended performance going forward;
2 Craft a strategic plan with a list of areas of concentration;
3 Execute your strategy;
4 Measure and evaluate your performance; and
5 Adapt and adjust to capture new possibilities.

Significantly, to enhance the greater fidelity of this process:

• Incorporate multiple groups, levels, and review stages;
• Utilize additional methods, such as environmental scans; and
• Engage in extensive discussions and debates, although this inevitably sacrifices the speed of results.

Now, to grease the wheels of SOAR strategizing, you can use the following **SOAR questions**. The four sets of questions can be covered in one- or two-day strategic dialog sessions. Remember to invite a broad representation of stakeholders – more than just top leadership – into the strategic thinking, positive dialog, and groundwork process.

Strengths questions

• What *energizes* our organization and gives it life?
• What are our current strengths, greatest assets, and "super powers"?
• What do we do very well? What's already working well – at first glance... at second glance?

- Without being humble, share a story about when our enterprise performed at its peak and completed a task that made us feel proud and had a particularly positive impact. What were the circumstances during that time? What made that possible?
- What is our enterprise's greatest achievement?
- How do our strengths match up with the demands of the environment and the business strategy?
- Why choose us over the competition?

An extra tip: The framework highlights the positives in an enterprise, yet it must still be executed rigorously and with sound business judgment. You must deal only with evidence-based elements, not just spurious impressions, or the outcomes will be too ambiguous to be of use. Remember to involve your clients in the process by asking them what they appreciate the most about your product or service. Doing this will enable your enterprise to double down on strengths, plus boost sales and profits. Be prepared for learning some information you might not have realized before.

Opportunities questions

- Considering our strengths, what are the best possible opportunities? Can we *co*-create them?
- What would have to be true about the industry dynamics, customer needs, company capabilities, cost position, and competitor moves for this possibility to be the optimal choice?
- How might we…?
- What are our stakeholders asking for?
- Where do we (not) play?
- Through what channels?
- What potential can we see or recognize?
- What current gigatrends are radically changing the world that our enterprise can capitalize on?
- Is there a market gap that we might be able to fill? Are there any new markets we should enter?
- Do our customers have unfulfilled needs?
- Could any of the threats to our business be turned into an opportunity?
- How might we best pool resources and partner with others?
- What if…?

An extra tip: Avoid the overwhelming temptation to jump at any opportunity that your rivals might also be rushing to seize ("Red Ocean"). Instead, try expanding into the "Blue Ocean" of exciting new possibilities that your company would excel at exploring. Blue Ocean strategy is the simultaneous pursuit of differentiation and low cost to open up a new market space and create new demand; it's about creating and capturing uncontested market space, thereby making the competition irrelevant. Consider what you can build upon in the long term.

Aspirations questions

- Reviewing our strengths and opportunities conversations, what do we exist to do (purpose)?
- What is the "Everest goal"/"moonshot" that we want to pursue and achieve in a short time... in the distant future?
- If there were no limits, what would we dare to do?
- What should our desired future look like? Let's describe the future we want for our organization... Let's use words, expressions, or images that capture our desired future, task outcomes, goals, and objectives.
- What is our winning aspiration? Who are we winning against? What is an obvious win for us?
- What do we want to be (vision)?
- What do we *genuinely* care about? What do we believe in (values)? Do we assume that all human systems are inclined toward the highest aspirations of humankind?
- What are we proud to accomplish? What do we hope to achieve?
- What are our financial and non-financial goals (e.g., environmental, social, and governance (ESG); brand, market position)?
- What are our stakeholders asking for?
- Is our "risk appetite" small, medium, large, or healthy?
- What vital projects, programs, or processes will likely support our aspirations?
- If we could not fail, what would be our strategic choices, and which of those choices would add the most value? What would have to be true?

An extra tip: Play to win rather than play to play.

Results questions

- Reflecting on our strengths, opportunities, and aspirations, how do we know we are succeeding? How can we define success?
- What action steps will we take right now (today, tomorrow, next week, next month) to accomplish our goal(s)? What milestones, measures, and metrics can we implement to accelerate progress toward our goal(s)?
- How do we convert our winning aspirations into measurable data and insights?
- How do we track our performance? Is it positively deviant, spectacular, surprising or extraordinary?
- Do we have clear objectives, targets, and measures? What are our measurable results?
- What are the tools, rewards, and resources required to achieve tangible results?
- What management systems build our dynamic capabilities and support our strategic choices?
- Of all the choices we have considered, which ones will we pursue?
- What will look different when we've gotten there? What elements of our enterprise and its processes will change – and how?

- What are three to five indicators that would create a scorecard that addresses people, planet, prosperity, peace, and partnerships?
- *Who* exactly is going to do *what* exactly and *by when* exactly?
- How will you keep on strategizing to win?

An extra tip: To monitor progress, ensure you have the appropriate tools in place. Manage accurate data, and make informed choices by means of some strategy performance management tool that is known to work – such as a Balanced Scorecard. Accordingly, consider: *How should we appear to our customers? What internal business processes must we excel in? How will we sustain our ability to learn, change, grow, innovate, and continuously improve? How should we appear to our shareholders/other stakeholders?*

To facilitate the whole process, **positive dialogic strategizing** can help your team willingly, genuinely, non-judgmentally, and, without interference, advance your learning and understanding through the free exchange of ideas and intellectual interventions. To enable this type of open dialog, five strategies of open inquiry can fundamentally shape and transform your team dynamics. These are:

- **Advocate for outcomes by means of suggestions and open inquiry**, e.g., "Here's a strategic possibility…", or "What might be (in)appropriate here?"
- **Obtain genuine buy-in by asking the team members**, "What could we do?" and "How can each of us explain this to colleagues?"
- **Clarify by paraphrasing**, e.g., "It seems to me that this is what you mean… To what extent does that capture your point?"
- **Resolve differences by asking for more information**, e.g., "It seems that you think this argument is not a super idea. I'm not exactly sure how you understand it. Could you help me understand how you see the situation?"
- **Deepen understanding by uncovering causes and justifications**, e.g., instead of asking "What do you want?" ask, "Why do you want that?" or "Why is that important to you?"

Ultimately, the beauty of SOAR is that it allows for integration with other strategic transformation techniques.

Case alert! Case classic

John Deere

LOOK IT UP: Hinrichs, G. (2010). SOARing for sustainability: Longitudinal organizational efforts applying appreciative inquiry. *International Journal of Appreciative Inquiry*, 12(3): 31–36.

Your task: Read "SOARing for sustainability" on how John Deere (in the case study described as EarthCo), an American corporation and a world leader in agricultural, construction, forestry, and turf care equipment, has been using SOAR for many years. Both leading and lagging indicators turned out to be decidedly impressive. In what way did SOAR generate positive energy? Do you think the same results could have been achieved at Deere by using SWOT alone? Now, search for their "Higher Purpose" and "Purpose Principles" on the Internet. Could SOAR help fulfill the aspirations of Deere? Why (not)? Can you perhaps use SOAR to help craft yours? Report back.

   To record your critical insights, use the Case Analysis Record provided in Appendix 2.

Greater good corner: Get ready to exercise your ethics

Take a stance: What would *you* do?

Dilemma and decision: "Sunnier side of life?"

As one of the merger's assets, your business has recently acquired a villa in Kolymvari, Greece, a wonderfully pretty coastal fishing village in Crete, with its breathtaking coastline and rocky hillsides, nestled between the sea and the cliffs. You are now in a critical phase, preparing to renew a significant contract with the local government. As part of your strategizing, you analyze all angles that could impact the negotiation, and during this process, you learn that their top negotiator's daughter is ill and would benefit greatly from spending some time in the warm climate and sunshine of the scenic Aegean Sea.

   Do you let him use your vacant villa in this unspoiled Cretan village – an absolutely ideal place for a delightful island getaway and for convalescing?

Time out: Journal entry

Thought Sparks: A few reflections, insightful ideas, actionable suggestions, strategic thinking, and key takeaways from this unit.

Learning never stops... So, pause for a few minutes and reflect in writing on your personal learning experience and beliefs. Through writing in your journal, you develop your awareness of your own beliefs and attitudes. Now, consolidate what you have learned in this unit.

1 How have your beliefs and ideas about positive, dialogic strategizing changed since you began the unit?

....
....
....
....

2 Thinking about the problems presented in the unit, write about whether you have found solutions to these problems.

....
....
....
....

3 How confident do you now feel about using SOAR?

....
....
....
....

4 What would you still like to have clarified? What remaining concerns do you have?

....
....
....
....

5 What more would you like to learn about the topic, now that you have completed this unit?

....
....
....
....

> **6** If you want, doodle/draw something you like about positive strategy. This can be as abstract as you wish.
>
> ....
> ....
> ....
> ....
>
> **Remember**: It's particularly useful to re-visit journal entries several times and see how themes have recurred or your thoughts have changed over time. Now, repeat "Your Take".

Making connections: Related units and models

- U 2. **The kindness advantage:** Cultivating positively energizing leaders and followers (see pp. 27–53)
- U 3. **Strategic transformation**: Strategy choice-making (see pp. 61–81)
- U 5. **Dialogic organization development (OD)**: Leading positive organizational change (see pp. 103–121)
- U 6. **Design-driven organization**: Human-centered design thinking and innovation execution (see pp. 122–139)
- U 7. **WOW! It's cool!** Crafting a coolness strategy for your brand (see pp. 147–159)
- U 8. **Once upon a time…** Strategic brand storytelling (see pp. 160–174)
- U 9. **Professional management consulting for real people**: The advice business demystified (see pp. 181–203)
- U 10. **Executive coaching**: Whoop it up! (see pp. 204–219)
- U 11. **So, you want to go global?** Becoming an instant international (see pp. 227–237)
- U 13. **Progress with purpose**: The "good" enterprise (see pp. 257–273)
- Add in more related models you may want to remember: _____.

Industry snapshot

www.deere.com/en/our-company/higher-purpose/

Deep dive: Main references and resources

Cameron, K., Dutton, J., & Quinn, R. (Eds.). (2003). *Positive organizational scholarship: Foundations of a new discipline*. San Francisco, CA: Berrett-Koehler Publishers.

Cameron, K., & Spreitzer, G. (Eds.). (2012). *The Oxford handbook of positive organizational scholarship*. New York, NY: Oxford University Press.

Cameron, K.S., & Caza, A. (2004). Introduction: Contributions to the discipline of positive organizational scholarship. *American Behavioral Scientist*, 47(6): 731–739.

Chermack, T.J., & Kasshanna, B.K. (2007). The use and misuse of SWOT analysis and implications for HRD professionals. *Human Resource Development International*, 10(4): 383–399.

Collins, J., & Porras, J. (1996). Building your company's vision. *Harvard Business Review*, 74(5): 65–77.

Furr, N.R., & Furr, S.H. (2022). *The upside of uncertainty: A guide to finding possibility in the unknown*. Boston, MA: Harvard Business Review Press.

Hinrichs, G. (2010). SOARing for sustainability: Longitudinal organizational efforts applying appreciative inquiry. *International Journal of Appreciative Inquiry*, 12(3): 31–36.

Kaplan, R.S., & Norton, D. (1992). The balanced scorecard: Measures that drive performance. *Harvard Business Review*, 70(7/8): 172–180.

Kaplan, R.S., & Norton. D. (1996). Using the balanced scorecard as a strategic management system. *Harvard Business Review*, 74(1): 75–85.

Kaplan, R.S., & Norton, D.P. (2000). Having trouble with your strategy? Then map it. *Harvard Business Review*, 78(5): 167–176.

Kim, C., & Mauborgne, R. (2015). *Blue ocean strategy: How to create uncontested market space and make the competition irrelevant* (expanded edition). Boston, MA: Harvard Business Review Press.

Malnight, T.W., Buche, I., & Dhanaraj, C. (2019). Put purpose at the core of your strategy. *Harvard Business Review*, 97(5): 70–78.

Puyt, R.W., Lie, F., & Wilderom, C.P.M. (2023). The origins of SWOT analysis. *Long Range Planning*, 56(3): 102304.

Simons, R. (2010). Stress-test your strategy: The 7 questions to ask. *Harvard Business Review*, 88(11): 92–100.

Stavros, J.M., & Cole, M.L. (2013). SOARing towards positive transformation and change. *Development Policy Review*, 1(1): 10–34.

Stavros, J.M., Cooperrider, D., & Kelley, L. (2007). SOAR: A new approach to strategic planning. In P. Homan, T. Devane, & S. Cady (Eds.), *The change handbook: The definitive resource on today's best methods for engaging whole systems* (2nd ed., pp. 375–380). San Francisco, CA: Berrett-Koehler Publishers, Inc.

Stavros, J.M., & Hinrichs, G. (2009). *Thin book of SOAR: Building strengths-based strategy*. Bend, OR: Thin Book Publishing.

Stavros, J.M., & Saint, D. (2010). SOAR: Linking strategy and OD to sustainable performance. In W. Rothwell, J. Stavros, R. Sullivan, & A. Sullivan (Eds.), *Practicing organization development: A guide for leading change* (3rd ed., pp. 377–394). San Francisco, CA: Jossey-Bass.

Stavros, J.M., & Wooten, L. (2012). Positive strategy: Creating and sustaining strengths-based strategy that SOARs and performs. In K.S. Cameron, & G.M. Spreitzer (Eds.), *Oxford handbook of positive organizational scholarship* (pp. 825–842). New York, NY: Oxford University Press.

Sull, D., & Sull, C. (2018). With goals, FAST beats SMART. *MIT Sloan Management Review*, 59(4): 1–11.

Tawse, A., & Tabesh, P. (2023). Thirty years with the balanced scorecard: What we have learned. *Business Horizons*, 66(1): 123–132.

Tkaczyk, B. (2021). *Leading positive organizational change: Energize – redesign – gel*. London & New York, NY: Routledge.

Zarestky, J., & Cole, C.S. (2017). Strengths, opportunities, aspirations, and results: An emerging approach to organization development. *New Horizons in Adult Education and Human Resource Development*, 29(1): 5–19.

Module monitor and Consolidation II

Workshop II: Applications/review exercises

Self-check questions

You should now be able to answer Self-Check Questions 1–10

1 **True or false** In essence, *strategy* and *planning* are the same.
2 **True or false** *Operational effectiveness* means performing *different* activities from rivals' or performing similar activities in *different* ways.
3 **True or false** To achieve a *sustainable competitive advantage*, you shouldn't be everything to everyone. To win, you must *choose* to do some things – and not others. At the end of the day, when everything is considered a priority, nothing truly holds priority.
4 **True or false** It's a dark little secret: most executives cannot *articulate* the objective, scope, and advantage of their business in plain English. If they can't, neither can anybody else.
5 **True or false** The art of *strategy* is gradually being forgotten. Long live *scenario planning*!
6 **True or false** *Positive organizational scholarship (POS)*, a new movement in organizational science, uses science-backed methods to promote a broad vision of "the sunnier side of life". *Positive* relates to the elevating processes and results in enterprises. *Organizational* relates to the interpersonal and structural dynamics activated in and through organizations, especially considering the conditions in which positive phenomena emerge. *Scholarship* relates to the scientific, theoretically derived, and rigorous investigation of that which is positive in organizational settings.
7 **True or false** *It addresses itself to peak organizational experiences and to what "wows" in organizations. It's energy boosting. It engages and makes out different stakeholders' aspirations and it's potential-centered. It focuses on planning and execution. Organic radical innovation is promoted.* This describes the SWOT framework.
8 **True or false** *It wrestles with the question of what's wrong in organizations and focuses on "gaps". It's energy depleting. It's top down and rivalry-centered. It focuses on analysis and planning. Incremental improvement is promoted.* This describes the SOAR framework.
9 **True or false** *Create uncontested market space. Create and capture new demand. Always aim higher.* These recommendations relate to *Red Ocean*

strategy. Still and all, *competing in existing market space, exploiting existing demand, and beating the competition* relate to *Blue Ocean* strategy.

10 True or false There's no such thing as an *absolutely perfect strategy*. Discomfort is a natural component of the process. It's always a work in process...

Individualized learning record

When you have finished Module II, try filling in this record of what you have learned.

1 *Strategy* is neither an art nor a science. Rather, it's a reflective practice. Do you agree? Explain why.

....

....

2 Can you say what your strategy is in 35 to 100 words or less? If so, would your colleagues put it the same way? Next, compare yours with that of two or three other similar organizations in your sector. What are the similarities/differences? Whose is the most/least successful strategy and why?

....

....

3 *Startups* just don't have time to "*do strategy*". What do you think?

....

....

4 Your *CEO* has recently asked you to develop a strategy for the company. You're not a *chief strategy officer (CSO)*. What do you do?

....

....

5 Regarding the role of a *board/CEO* with respect to strategy, if the board that gets together just a few days annually reckons it must do strategy for the enterprise or can do a better job of setting strategy than the CEO who

runs the business 24/7, then the board should fire the CEO, period. Do you agree? Explain why.

....

....

6 *SWOT* is an awful way to start a strategy process. What are the arguments for and against this point of view?

....

....

7 Strategizing is a *"team* sport" and so all organizational members need to work together to develop, communicate and execute a strategy. Explain why. By the way, to what extent are business leaders (senior decision-makers) and functional leaders (e.g., senior HR people) in your organization "connected"?

....

....

8 Creating a *positive strategy* requires building a positive, sustainable organizational culture first. This takes positively deviant possibility thinking, strategic conversations and dialogic learning skills. How would this work in practice?

....

....

9 *SOAR* is a strengths-based framework with a highly participatory approach to strategizing that enables stakeholders in an organization to *co*-create and execute its most preferred future via high-quality partnering, common knowledge, and a commitment to action. SOAR-enabled businesses can experience an abundance of advantages by adopting a strengths-based, solution-oriented approach to strategic thinking. Illustrate the potential benefits.

....

....

10 *OD scholars and practitioners argue that the science and practice of thriving organizations provide the field of strategic management with a positive, alternative perspective through which to analyze processes connected with formulating, communicating and executing strategy. Yet, it is sometimes said that the increased emphasis on the human side has neglected certain critical strategic management issues. In contrast, a significant portion of strategic management research has ignored the human processes that make clear the behavioral*

dynamics that guide an organization's strategic efforts. Thus, in order to offer an
effective, dynamic perspective on strategy development, we need to bring these
two viewpoints together. Do you agree with this? Explain why.

....

....

Can-do checklist

Looking back, I have learned the following Key Terms:

Unit 3

- advantage (competitive, strategic, sustainable, true, winning)
- aspiration (energizing, guiding, winning)
- bounded rationality
- "business as usual" (BAU) mindset
- capabilities (distinctive, dynamic, hard-to-replicate, must-have)
- chief strategy officer (CSO)
- economic strategy approach
- emergent strategies
- entrepreneurial reconfiguration
- factors (differentiation, firm, industry)
- forces (economic, outside, the five)
- home-base
- how-to-win choices
- management systems
- operational effectiveness
- resource-based view (RBV) of strategy
- scenario planning
- strategic transformation
- strategist
- strategy (bold, bottom-up, business, coherent, competitive, economic, effective, executable, future open, perfect, successful, top-down, winning)
- strategy as design
- strategy as practice (S-A-P)
- strategy choice-making

- value proposition (winning)
- valuable, rare, costly to imitate, non-substitutable (VRIN)
- where-to-play choices

Unit 4

- balanced scorecard
- "blue/red ocean" strategy
- open inquiry
- positive strategy
- positive dialogic strategizing
- positive organizational scholarship (POS)
- possibility thinking (positive, positively deviant, strategic)
- strengths, opportunities, aspirations, results (SOAR)
- strengths, weaknesses, opportunities, threats (SWOT)

Module III

Organization development and design innovation

Tools for dramatic change

5 Dialogic organization development (OD)

Leading positive organizational change

"The best of OD is like a jazz ensemble; it's a multiple set of skills – harmonizing. The best of OD, to me, has always been interdisciplinary" – David Jamieson

Sneak peek

Focus on: Key concepts and terms

Unit 5

- Change (generative, organizational, positive, sustainable; aversion, confidence, drivers, failure, leadership, management, readiness)
- Design thinking (collective)
- Energize, redesign, and gel (ERG)
- Learning (adaptive, continuous, culture, dialogic, emergent, generative, organizational, planned, vigilant)
- Organization development (OD) (diagnostic, dialogic, generative, humanistic, positive, strategic)
- Organizational energy (depleted, dysfunctional, negative, personal, positive, relational)
- Organizational (un)learning vs. organizational forgetting
- Organizational renewal (strategic)
- Psychological safety (team)
- Resistance to change (active, passive, constructive)
- Response to change (affective, behavioral, cognitive, emotional, physical)
- Super-flexibility (strategic)

DOI: 10.4324/9781003508274-9

Pause 'N' reflect: On the current issues and trends

Before you complete this unit, think about each of the following statements. Mark each statement:

V – if you *agree.*
X – if you *disagree.*
? – if you are *undecided.*

Your Take: Integrative Thinking	*Before doing Unit 5*	*After doing Unit 5*
1 Traditional organization development (OD) is primarily an effort that is *planned, organization-wide,* and *managed* from the *top,* to improve *organization effectiveness* and *health* through *planned interventions* in the organization's processes, utilizing *behavioral-science* knowledge.		
2 Well, there's too little O in OD.		
3 Positive OD moves away from the tendency to want to "fix" what is wrong with organizations and people. By identifying what "wows"/works best and transferring those ingredients into other situations, strengths-based development builds energy for positive change.		
4 Expect change to be a constant. You'll never run out of change to lead. Basically, you must lead it or die.		
5 Dialogic OD is seen as a humanistic response to the de-humanizing effects of scientific management practices, wherein workers are treated as small cogs in the well-oiled machinery of organizational bureaucracies.		
6 It's possible to design enterprises to be super-flexible and optimized for change and changing.		

Your Take: Integrative Thinking	Before doing Unit 5	After doing Unit 5
7 OD is in crisis. Very few change programs produce an improvement in bottom-line, surpass the company's cost of capital, or even bring about improvements in service delivery. The ramifications of such programs exert a heavy toll, both human and economic.		
8 "Effective change has to be planned and dictated from the top otherwise the organization would be out of control and become unmanageable" – CEO		
9 If the humanistic/democratic/ developmental values at the core of OD are compromised, its distinctive contribution to the organization will diminish, and preserving this unique contribution is of utmost importance.		
10 Change is energizing when done by us and disturbing when done to us.		

After you have done the unit, repeat "Your Take". How has reading the unit clarified the ideas herein? How have your views, feelings and thoughts changed over time?

Lead-in

General discussion points

Individually or in buzz groups, consider the following discussion prompts:

1 Can all organizations learn and develop? Is all learning "good"? Now, reflecting on your development over the past year: do you feel that your strengths are in planning your learning ("planned learning") or in learning opportunistically ("emergent learning")? Identify your weaker approach and devise individual and organizational strategies to enhance and strengthen it.
2 "Change starts with changing everyday conversations". Do you agree or disagree with this perspective as it points to *dialogic* organization development (OD)?
3 Dominant images and mental models: The metaphor of the "organization as a machine" emphasizes (technical) rationality and ignores emotion (*controlling* actions and activities). An alternative approach to change is based on reconceptualizing the "organization as a living, breathing organism" (*shaping* capabilities). What are the strengths and constraints of each image? What skills do you

believe are associated with each image in order to apply it effectively? To what degree do you find yourself more at ease with one of the two conceptualizations concerning your own approach to leading change? Is your organization dominated by a particular image or approach to change?

4   Recall a significant change that you have experienced at work (you might even regard your family as an organization). First, discuss different aspects of the change: structure, size and shape; (in)formal systems, processes and procedures; culture, values and beliefs; individual perceptions of and reactions to change; and behaviors at all levels. Next, recognize the emotions you encountered and describe how you managed them. Finally, identify both the (un)intended impacts/consequences of these on different parts of the organizational system and/or on the whole system. By the way, did you instigate it or was it forced upon you? Does it matter?

5   There's a need for stability – as well as for change…

Share your thoughts with your peers/team members; discuss points of agreement/ disagreement.

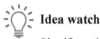

Idea watch

Significantly, there are numerous drivers that propel the need for a business to change and undergo transformation, including operational process changes, organizational restructuring, organizational design and flexibility, technological change, new competitor behavior, mergers and acquisitions (M&A), expansion (local, regional or global), evolving economy and customer needs and tastes, advancements in technology and social communication, cost savings, workforce downsizing, revenue, growth – and the imperative to maximize shareholder value.

At times, change is initiated proactively to seize opportunities and drive progress, while in other instances, it is a reactive effort to catch up with existing developments or trends. Other classifications of change are established, such as whether the impetus for change originates from external or internal sources (both internal planned and internal unplanned changes). The change can manifest as either revolutionary and all-embracing, or evolutionary and incremental. Both revolutionary and evolutionary change can be transformational. Organization-wide changes include structural, cultural, economic, political – and changes in top leadership. Nevertheless, at the core of all these considerations lies the fundamental purpose of change, which is to foster positive organizational development and boost competitiveness in the intricate and interconnected global landscape we have shaped.

Conveniently, strategic change leadership has the potential to enable positive transformation within an organization by employing positive, structured approaches to shift individuals, teams and organizations from a current state – to a desired future state. After its initiation, change may take on a nonlinear trajectory, responding to uncertainties, reactions and guidance from those engaged.

In line with this, OD, based on the concept of the organization as a living system, is an ongoing, holistic, systemic, and action-oriented process of planned and emerging interventions that are in line with behavioral and organizational science principles. The intent of its application is to change a system and improve its effectiveness and health. As suggested by David Jamieson, this is done in accordance with values of humanism, participation, choice, and development so that organizations and their members continuously learn and develop and renew.

Moreover, dialogic OD, as originated by Gervase Bushe and Robert Marshak, holds the perspective that sustainable change primarily happens when shifts in mindsets take place. This transformation is more apt to be achieved through "generative conversations" rather than attempting to persuade based solely on "facts". Edgar Schein characterizes dialogic OD as a return to the roots of OD's original "spirit of inquiry". The dialogic approach signifies a departure from perceiving change as a moderately manageable, linear progression, toward one that can be characterized by unpredictability and unexpected shifts.

Ultimately, OD work is expressed strategically as the process of developing an organization so that it's more effective in achieving its business goals. Change strategizing is a continuous forward-looking activity, rather than an annual or biannual one, encompassing a "test and learn (*and* test)" approach to drive growth. To do this, one needs to identify purpose, services, products, and other elements that will, under a range of conditions, create high reliability, high involvement, and positively deviant performance – in other words, performance far above the norm. These will become strategic imperatives where dynamic capabilities must be developed.

Assumptions

Organizations develop through continuous, adaptive, and generative learning. The OD and learning process is delivered as part of an overarching strategic development process.

The primary goal of OD work is to pragmatically enhance organizational capabilities, thereby improving efficiency and performance within the organization. This includes developing individual and organizational well-being and psychological safety. This last is a collective belief among team members that encourages and enables risk-taking, open expression of ideas and concerns, asking questions and speaking up, and admitting mistakes – all without the fear of facing negative consequences.

At its core, OD has two central focuses: a humanistic approach that empowers individuals to reach their full potential within the organization, and a business imperative to facilitate the organization's effectiveness and success in its environment – and beyond. Thus, this pursuit is often articulated as attaining the optimal alignment between organizational and individual objectives.

Moreover, change is inherent and can be self-organizing. It's continuous, cyclical, or both. With more than two-thirds of change efforts failing and even greater number of M&A deals not achieving their perceived synergies and promise, OD practitioners' expertise on organizational renewal and effective implementation is crucial.

Importantly, OD involves the "total system" – an organization-development effort that is related to a total organization change such as a change in the learning culture, the reward systems or the total managerial strategy.

OD also entails improving organization effectiveness and health – this means designing and developing a self-renewing system, continuous improvement mechanisms, and a healthy operating organization – it's like a hot spot buzzing with positive energy and innovation.

Methodologically speaking, design thinking fills the gap that exists in classic change management frameworks. Design thinking is a design-driven approach to change leadership that can be adopted to design, develop, and deliver a powerful learning-oriented organizational change program. It usually relies on some form of experienced-based learning activities (see below in Unit 6).

As might be expected, its intent is to change attitudes, mindsets, and/or behavior. Apparently, human beings are naturally change-averse. So the story goes, people tend to harbor a fear of the unknown – when confronted with change, individuals often imagine more negative than positive outcomes, and frequently assume the worst case scenarios. Evidently, the brain is hardwired for change aversion. Notably, part of the brain, the amygdala (a small part of your brain, but having a big job) perceives change as a threat and triggers the release of hormones linked to "fear", "fight" or "flight" responses – the body's defensive mechanisms. Your amygdala is a major processing center for your emotions. It also links your emotions to various brain functions, such as memories, learning, and your sensory experiences. When it malfunctions, it can lead to or exacerbate disruptive feelings and symptoms.

On occasion, resistance can "kill" change. People resist change in three distinct ways – actively, passively or constructively. *Active* resistors exhibit a "fight" response (active opposition), while *passive* resistors may display "flight" or "freeze" reactions (passive avoidance). In contrast, *constructive* resistors actively engage in the process, and their resistance is informed and grounded in knowledge and understanding of the impact of change on themselves and others (constructive engagement). Since people prefer the change they create, by involving constructive resistors in the process, challengers get "converted" into more enthusiastic champions of change.

To succeed in leading positive organizational change, organizations should fast-track:

Structure: people need substantial structure to feel reasonably comfortable with the messiness of the change context. A lot of what we deal with is habit. Coherent structure makes it much easier to keep people going when the going gets tough, which in turn creates psychological safety. So, worksheets, exercises, templates, tools, examples, and an in-place robust organizational capabilities framework (such as *Energize–Redesign–Gel*) might come in handy.

Training: promote training to employees at all levels, not just leaders. A popular training formula is: "A" (knowledge/skills/attitude required to do a job) minus "B" (employees' current knowledge/skills/attitude) is "C" (identified "needed training" skills gap). Training also helps scale the development of change leadership skills.

Yet, research finds that organizations aren't prepared to manage change – only 30% of organizations have professional change management teams.

In addition to these strategies, *building an organization-wide learning culture*: successful organizations champion an enterprise-wide learning and development culture. Strong cultures of learning are distinct hallmarks of organizations that consistently achieve exceptional business results. Specifically, top-performing enterprises are five times more likely to have extensive learning cultures. *Un*learning of orthodoxies and *re*learning of new approaches are critical, too.

It is also worth noting that *change doesn't* always *start at the top*: While the majority of change programs are designed and implemented top-down, certain change endeavors emerge from "below" and spiral upward throughout the organization. In other words, some initiatives start small and don't wait for permission from the higher-ups.

Key elements

While designing and executing organizational change is not easy, it *is* doable. OD is an effort that addresses itself to improving an organization's capability through the alignment of strategy, structure, people, rewards, metrics, and management processes. *Positive* OD – reforming and transitioning people, teams, and organizations to a desired future state – requires a shift toward *positive* personal, relational, and **organizational energy** (*energize*), *collective* **design thinking** (*redesign*), and an unprecedented level of flexibility – *strategic* **super-flexibility** (*gel*).

Significantly, *e*nergize, *re*design, and *g*el (ERG), a robust positive change methodology, is the express lane toward revitalizing collective leadership during these dynamic and unpredictable times. In these circumstances, this process serves as both a repeatable embedded dialogic approach and a design-inspired strategy, essential for re-imagining an organization, and for unlocking strategic innovation and unleashing the potential for dramatic change. By adopting ERG, you can pave the way toward a positive and creative future, achieving significant breakthroughs and tangible bottom-line results for your enterprise. More specifically:

Positive organizational energy nurtures and unleashes genuine positivity and engagement within the organization, leading to improved organizational health. Moreover, it helps to recognize strengths, opportunities, aspirations, and results (SOAR) while remaining curious and fully alert. This approach also encourages the challenging of old dominant logics or organizational mega-routines to drive positive change and progress.

Collective design thinking fosters a culture that embraces design principles and purpose-driven approaches within the organization. By harnessing collective intelligence and open innovation, this co-creative process becomes instrumental in achieving successful value delivery through organic radical innovation. Furthermore, it leverages and liberates the entrepreneurial spirit of all employees, unlocking their full potential for driving positive change and innovation.

Strategic super-flexibility enables organizations to effectively get on with their business while also inventing new business. It involves constant monitoring and improvement of processes, vigilant learning (including scanning for weak signals and properly interpreting the implications of these weak signals), and a willingness to unlearn outdated practices. Additionally, it encompasses the renewal of organizational and business models to be more responsive to change and changing patterns.

Of particular note is the fact that the super-flexible capabilities of energizing, redesigning, and gelling are integrated into the positive organizational culture and the strategy setting of the enterprise. They govern how the enterprise energizes, develops, mixes, reconfigures – and gels internal, external and collective assets to nimbly navigate today's environments that are volatile, uncertain, complex/chaotic, and ambiguous (VUCA) – and to attain real-time adaptation.

Thinking critically: Issues

The eclectic nature of OD, along with the existence of contradictory definitions and its perceived lack of a clear identity as a profession within corporate and academic realms, inevitably leads to a lack of understanding among those outside the field.

OD, instead of being a formal discipline, is more of a practical field, and when OD specialists are employed in-house, they don't often have an organizational home. Consequently, other concepts, such as human resource management (HRM), sometimes vie for the same territory (even though HRM has different theoretical foundations, like human capital theory). Indeed, OD has even been referred to as a "strategic HR tool". On-site, internal OD practitioners are often "buried" within the HR function and lack contact with senior executives. Practically speaking, to maintain sufficient distance from an organization, to retain an appropriate level of objectivity and the capacity to effectively challenge within an organization, it is recommended that an OD specialist should not serve in the same organization for more than five years. Concerning the future of OD, one potential direction for OD is the "strategy" model, where OD becomes an integral part of the strategy function, reporting directly to the CEO, rather than being a sub-function of HR.

Some say that, seemingly, OD is paradoxical: the term "Organization" suggests structure, predictability, and stability, while "Development" implies change, movement – and even turmoil.

Moreover, this is mirrored in the distinction between "change management" and "change readiness". Change management deals with change on a one-off basis, whereas change readiness involves addressing and leading change as an ongoing process. Initially, change management evolved to handle periodic change situations, such as restructuring due to market entry, diversification, or acquisition. Yet, in today's landscape, with triggers for change occurring daily, change is a continuous event – ranging from minor incremental adjustments to significant dramatic mega changes and transformations. Thus, change readiness fuels proactive engagement in driving positive change, acting as the drivers of change rather than passive participants, or merely "passengers", in the journey of change.

In contemporary OD approaches, creating new mindsets, possibly through negotiation, can lead to a state of continuous change. Although traditionally most change programs get designed and executed top-down (*diagnostic* OD), some purpose-driven change efforts can emerge from "below" and spiral upward throughout the enterprise (*dialogic* OD) –where bottom level changes build up and combine to create significant shifts at the organizational (as well societal) level over time.

Nevertheless, a noble purpose alone won't transform your organization. Hence, it's important for the organization to have organizational capabilities and a framework in place for the organization to work cohesively and prepare for transformative change and the unexpected. For instance, ERG, a positive OD strategy for leading change, can help organizations to become genuinely *change-able* organizations. A good example of a *change-able* organization is the so-called "knowledge-creative enterprise". This is a new kind of future-oriented organization, buzzing with positive energy and continuous learning-based process improvement, as well as organic radical innovation. In these organizations, everyone is considered talent, and change readiness, collective design thinking and dialogic learning are rooted in culture.

Deep down, however, most individuals tend to favor the status quo. Increased uncertainty regarding changes often leads employees to be concerned and fixate on potential negatives rather than potential positives. For this reason, it is crucial to highlight what will remain unchanged! Furthermore, addressing the employee experience of change is essential. Typically, employee experience to change is couched in terms of "resistance" to change, which can be unproductive because it may imply some inappropriate reaction. Instead, the term "response" (*behavioral, affective/emotional, cognitive*, and *physical*) can be applied, signifying a more neutral stance that suggests that this can be understood and developed. As humans, our responses to change are a mix of various elements that are bound up together, making it difficult to isolate them and/or view them in isolation.

By way of illustration, in change scenarios involving, say, M&A transactions, employees might find themselves assigned to a role they didn't originally apply for, in a company they never intended to work for. Therefore, it's not unexpected that employees would feel a sense of disappointment and experience a breach of the "psychological contract" they had with the organization, as the initial "deal" they signed up for seems to have been violated. These breaches can provoke *behavioral* symptoms, such as withholding information. Additionally, when an organization relocates geographically, employees may engage in a *cognitive* response to the change by re-evaluating the (dis)advantages of remaining with their current employer, and if they have great employability skills, the pros and cons of pursuing alternative employment opportunities.

To emphasize the significance of *cognitive* and *emotional* reactions, during a restructuring process involving the elimination or consolidation of work units, employees may experience a loss of their role identity. This uncertainty about their position in the new structure can lead to decreased confidence and may be perceived as a threat to their self-esteem and professional validation. It is posited that individuals progress through stages such as "denial", "resistance", "attitude trough", "exploration", "responsibility", and "commitment". Ethically, emotions play a crucial role in influencing our behavior, and they are deeply personal to each individual, making it important not to assume that emotions can be "managed" in line with organizational strategy.

Moreover, change can also trigger a diverse array of *physical* responses. For example, organizations implementing cost-cutting programs experience noticeably higher levels of absenteeism, and a larger percentage of managers report experiencing insomnia, headaches or chronic fatigue.

As an aside, cost-cutting through, for example, downsizing, in the longer term, might actually be a poor decision and a financially costly change effort. Wayne Cascio's research found that after looking at every publicly traded company on the New York Stock Exchange (NYSE) from 1980 to 2016, research found that companies who delayed layoffs – with salary cuts, furloughs or running in the red – saw higher stock returns two years later than companies who fired quickly.

Furthermore, when enacting organization-wide transformations, greater resistance may originate from sub-teams that lack alignment and exhibit incongruent team dynamics.

Interestingly, organizations with high ratings in change-related effectiveness are significantly more inclined to utilize simulations for both real-life and hypothetical change scenarios.

At bottom, acknowledging the diverse responses and perceptions employees may hold is the initial stride toward enhancing the success of change initiatives. Positive communication, especially in fostering supportive communication patterns, plays a vital role in addressing the uncertainties that accompany change.

Despite the challenges, although around 70% of change efforts fail to meet their goals, one might want to view hurdles as opportunities for adaptive and generative learning and growth and actually invest in building professional strategic OD and positive change leadership and change readiness capabilities.

Applications

Positive OD is an approach that cares about human beings – it advocates that people at *all* levels throughout an enterprise are, individually and collectively, both the drivers and engines of positive, generative change.

So how does a company jump-start strategic organizational renewal, link positive organizational dynamics to positive business outcomes, and fortify the organization's current process for design-driven innovation, adaptive learning, and dialogic OD?

Energize

First, **positive personal, relational, and organizational energy** is the fuel that keeps great enterprises fired up. Rather than fixating on deficits, problems and what's going wrong, redirect the focus toward strengths, what's working well – and what ignites renewed enthusiasm among individuals, teams, and the organization. This shift can bolster resilience, promote individual and organizational health, and unlock valuable strategic resources. By developing high-impact relationships, actively participating, and revitalizing depleted energy, new insights, co-operative behaviors, and fresh possibilities will emerge.

One way to begin this process is by getting involved in the co-creation of a purpose statement that exudes positive energy. Envision ambitious "Everest goals" and "moonshots" that your organization aspires to achieve. Engage in "backcasting" the future, which involves imagining the desired future state and crafting positive strategic scenarios to achieve it. This approach is akin to constructing the rocket that will propel the organization toward its envisioned destination.

Redesign

What's more, tap into the potential of **collective design thinking**, a potent co-creative process that serves as a vital tool for those who seek to deliver value through organic radical innovation and to unlock the entrepreneurial spirit residing within every employee.

In particular, engage in collaborative and generative conversations around sustainable change. Encourage the participation of your team, and even involve the entire organization in dialogic learning, experimentation, and visioning for the future. By embracing this approach, you, your team, and, indeed, the entire organization will rally behind the co-created purpose. To get this teamwork going, reach for and apply such truly effective tools as team coaching, hackathons, or team contracts. Be curious – empathize. Fearlessly ask questions (don't be afraid to ask "dumb" questions!) and radically synergize your efforts. Prioritize action, rapidly ideate, and prototype, but don't overlook the importance of testing and validation.

Gel

On top of that, strive for **strategic super-flexibility**. Get moving – shed old, dusty organizational logics and routines, and activate the engine of regenerative co-creativity. This will also help you run with the ball and nimbly strategize to win while avoiding chaos and disruption – or overwhelming competing priorities. Of note: organizational *unlearning* contrasts with its cousin *organizational forgetting*. Organizational forgetting is the unintentional degradation of established knowledge. Organizational unlearning, in contrast, is strategic – it is the "purposeful destruction" of embedded "ill" knowledge, which, paradoxically, is a positive action and so should be appreciated by the organization. As C.K. Prahalad would put it: "during a corporate transformation, the forgetting curve is sometimes more important than the learning curve".

Keep in mind that super-flexible organizations are "change confident" organizations. They adeptly lead and thrive through change and navigate through disruptions and uncertainties. This reflects their high level of change awareness and change readiness to embrace change and adapt to new circumstances with a positive and proactive mindset.

Although frequently depicted as a step process (*energize-redesign-gel*), this way of thinking of organizational change is, in reality, a dynamic and nonstop process – it follows a continuous flow. In the end, it is a day-to-day ritual that becomes ingrained in the business culture of the enterprise and is deeply integrated into its strategic thinking and activities.

Case alert! Case classic

General Motors (GM) Poland

LOOK IT UP: Dobosz-Bourne, D., & Jankowicz, A.D. (2006) Reframing resistance to change: experience from General Motors Poland. *The International Journal of Human Resource Management*, 17(12): 2021–2034.

Your task: Read an excerpt on change, language, and negotiating change in GM (Poland) – based on Dobosz-Bourne and Jankowicz (2006).

General Motors began developing its Opel Polska car plant on a greenfield site in Gliwice, Poland, in 1996. A critical responsibility for management was to establish work practices that aligned with a car plant capable of maintaining competitiveness in the 21st century. While some of the difficulties stemmed from the historical lack of exposure to competition during the country's time as part of the Soviet bloc, a deeper underlying issue appeared to be rooted in hundreds of years of Polish culture. Historically, Polish culture prized *fantazja* ("imaginativeness"), which was perceived as being fundamentally at odds with the notion of being disciplined, systematic or well-organized – the latter being equated with boring, monotonous, and unnecessary; the meaning also extended to a connotation of subjugation. The work practices designed for the new plant undeniably demanded a significant level of control and coordination. The managers feared that although *fantazja* could be advantageous in the continuous improvement processes integrated into the plant's operating model, the cultural tolerance for disorder could lead to disastrous outcomes.

GM held a strong position as there was an abundant pool of talented Polish employees eager to work in the new plant – 46,000 had applied for 1,800 positions – yet the company refrained from using the threat of being fired for noncompliance. Instead, a sequence of meetings took place between the European managers and the new workers, with the aid of interpreters. While cultural values and linguistic differences appeared to lie at the heart of employee resistance to working in the ways that managers felt were critically important, the resolution was also achieved within the same context. Similar to English, the word/concept "development" in the Polish language possesses a dual meaning, encompassing both "initiating something" and "making progress". In turn, "making progress" is the opposite of stagnation. For the Polish people, stagnation was something that lacked *fantazja*. Through "dialogic learning", the notion of a "disciplined organization" was reframed positively incorporating concepts and values already ingrained in Polish culture.

By the year 2000, the plant had achieved the highest quality and performance metrics among all General Motors facilities across the globe.

1 Is this a surprise to you? Why?
2 How can assuming the position of "functional persistence" (rather than "resistance to change") aid the development of new work attitudes, as opposed to constraining the old ones?
3 What else made the introduction of a change scheme in a General Motors factory plant in Gliwice, Poland successful?

To record your critical insights, use the Case Analysis Record provided in Appendix 2.

Greater good corner: Get ready to exercise your ethics

Take a stance: What would *you* do?

Dilemma and decision: Positive OD culture

Major organizational change typically necessitates a shift in workplace culture and the adoption of novel patterns of social organization. If possible, these should be carefully planned in advance, aligning closely with the organization's purpose and long-term development goals. In the present climate, however, the speed and unpredictability of internal/external events demand immediate responses at all levels of the organization, often without the luxury of detailed foresight, insight, and cross-sight. This unpredictability adds pressure on OD strategies to remain flexible and future-focused while still ensuring a positive, ethical work environment.

You recently joined a software company operating in such turbulent environments. The organizational culture is dysfunctional and high on negative organizational energy, which poses a serious threat to both employee well-being and overall productivity. Although its CEO announced a contentious new five-year strategy – one of "delivering a creative future", strong "positive OD culture" has been fairly rare therein. If, as the organization's new OD manager, you were to promote such a culture, what priorities would *you* set as a start, and why? For example, think: transparent communication, nurturing trust, cultivating an inclusive atmosphere where innovation can thrive free from the shadow of negativity, leadership gaps, misaligned incentives or toxic behaviors. Ensure your priorities are clear and targeted.

As you consider the steps to take in promoting a positive OD culture, it's important to reflect on the balance between different approaches in your OD work. Evidence-based practice or experimentation – how best to combine the two in OD work? What would *you* suggest, and why? In particular, could you use data to understand where the core issues lie, or introduce structured, ethics-driven team-building exercises or pilot new positively energizing leadership coaching/leading positive organizational change programs designed to enhance the positive energy within the company? Or perhaps explore other positive/dialogic OD interventions.

Time out: Journal entry

Thought Sparks: A few reflections, insightful ideas, actionable suggestions, strategic thinking, and key takeaways from this unit.

Learning never stops… So, pause for a few minutes and reflect in writing on your personal learning experience and beliefs. Through writing in your journal, you develop your awareness of your own beliefs and attitudes. Now, consolidate what you have learned in this unit.

1 How have your beliefs and ideas about OD/organizational change changed since you began the unit?

   ....

   ....

   ....

2 Thinking about the problems presented in the unit, write about whether you have found solutions to these problems.

   ....

   ....

   ....

3 How confident do you now feel about leading positive organizational change?

....

....

....

4 What would you still like to have clarified? What remaining concerns do you have?

....

....

....

5 What more would you like to learn about the topic, now that you have completed this unit?

....

....

....

6 If you want, doodle/draw something you like about dialogic OD/positive organizational change. This can be as abstract as you wish.

....

....

....

Remember: It's particularly useful to re-visit journal entries several times and see how themes have recurred or your thoughts have changed over time. Now, repeat "Your Take".

Making connections: Related units and models

- U 1. **Behavioral economics and policy 101**: For humans (see pp. 9–26)
- U 2. **The kindness advantage**: Cultivating positively energizing leaders and followers (see pp. 27–53)
- U 3. **Strategic transformation**: Strategy choice-making (see pp. 61–81)
- U 4. **SOAR**: Possibility thinking in positive strategic dialog (see pp. 82–95)
- U 6. **Design-driven organization**: Human-centered design thinking and innovation execution (see pp. 122–139)
- U 8. **Once upon a time**… Strategic brand storytelling (see pp. 160–174)
- U 9. **Professional management consulting for real people**: The advice business demystified (see pp. 181–203)
- U 10. **Executive coaching**: Whoop it up! (see pp. 204–219)
- U 11. **So, you want to go global?** Becoming an instant international (see pp. 227–237)

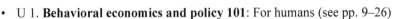

- U 13. **Progress with purpose**: The "good" enterprise (see pp. 257–272)
- Add in more related models you may want to remember: _____.

Industry snapshot

Dobosz-Bourne, D., & Jankowicz, A.D. (2006) Reframing resistance to change: Experience from General Motors Poland. *The International Journal of Human Resource Management*, 17(12): 2021–2034.

Tkaczyk, B. (2022). Positive organization development: Design-inspired strategizing for co-creating positive organizational change. *Design Management Review*, 33(4): 12–17. Published in a special issue on Supports and Barriers to the Business of Design.

Deep dive: Main references and resources

Anand, N., & Barsoux, J.-L. (2017). What everyone gets wrong about change management. *Harvard Business Review*, 95(6): 79–85.

Andersen, E. (2022, April 7). Change is hard. Here's how to make it less painful. *Harvard Business Review.* Retrieved from: https://hbr.org/2022/04/change-is-hard-heres-how-to-make-it-less-painful

ATD. (2014). *Change agents: The role of organizational learning in change management.* Alexandria, VA: The Association for Talent Development.

ATD. (2016). *Building a culture of learning: The foundation of a successful organization.* Alexandria, VA: The Association for Talent Development.

ATD. (2017). *Culture and change: Protecting and shaping culture during transitions.* Alexandria, VA: The Association for Talent Development.

ATD. (2018). *Change enablement: Skills for addressing change.* Alexandria, VA: The Association for Talent Development.

ATD. (2022). *Change management: Talent development's critical role.* Alexandria, VA: The Association for Talent Development.

Bahrami, H., & Evans, S. (2010). *Super-flexibility for knowledge enterprises: A toolkit for dynamic adaptation.* Heidelberg: Springer.

Bahrami, H., & Evans, S. (2011). Super-flexibility for real-time adaptation: Perspectives from Silicon Valley. *California Management Review*, 53(3): 21–39.

Bartunek, J.M., & Woodman, R.W. (2015). Beyond Lewin: Toward temporal approximation of organization development and change. *Annual Review of Organizational Psychology and Organizational Behavior*, 2(1): 157–182.

Beer, M., & Nohria, N. (2000). Cracking the code of change. *Harvard Business Review*, 78(3): 133–141.

Beretta, M., & Smith, P. (2023). Embarking on a business agility journey: Balancing autonomy versus control. *California Management Review*, 65(4): 93–115.

Binney, G., & Williams, C. (2005). The myth of managing change. In G. Salaman, J. Strorey & J. Billsberry (Eds.), *Strategic human resource management: Theory and practice. A reader* (pp. 295–317). London: Sage.

Björklund, T., Maula, H., Soule, S.A., & Maula, J. (2020). Integrating design into organizations: The coevolution of design capabilities. *California Management Review*, 62(2): 100–124.

Boland, R., & Collopy, F. (Eds.). (2004). *Managing as designing.* Stanford, CA: Stanford University Press.

Bright, D.S., Cameron, K.S., & Caza, A. (2006). The amplifying and buffering effects of virtuousness in downsized organizations. *Journal of Business Ethics,* 64: 249–269.

Bruch, H., & Ghoshal, S. (2003). Unleashing organizational energy. *MIT Sloan Management Review,* 45(1): 45–51.

Burke, W.W., & O'Malley, M. (2022). *Profitably healthy companies: Principles of organizational growth and development.* New York, NY: Columbia Business School Publishing.

Bushe, G.R. (2021). The generative change model: Creating the agile organization while dealing with a complex problem. *The Journal of Applied Behavioral Science,* 57(4): 530–533.

Bushe, G.R., & Marshak, R.J. (2009). Revisioning organizational development: Diagnostic and dialogic premises and patterns of practice. *Journal of Applied Behavioral Science,* 45(3): 348–368.

Bushe, G.R., & Marshak, R.J. (Eds.). (2015). *Dialogic organization development: The theory and practice of transformational change.* Oakland, CA: Berrett-Koehler.

Cameron, K.S., Bright, D., & Caza, A. (2004). Exploring the relationships between organizational virtuousness and performance. *American Behavioral Scientist,* 47(6): 766–790.

Cascio, W. (2002). Strategies for responsible restructuring. *Academy of Management Executive,* 16(3): 80–91.

Cascio, W., Chatrath, A., & Christie-David, R.A. (2021). Antecedents and consequences of employment and asset restructuring. *Academy of Management Journal,* 64(2): 587–613.

Cross, R., Edmondson, A.C., & Murphy, W. (2020). A noble purpose alone won't transform your company: Leadership behaviors that nurture interpersonal collaboration are the true drivers of change. *MIT Sloan Management Review,* 61(2): 37–43.

Cutcher, L. (2009). Resisting change from within and without the organization. *Journal of Organizational Change Management,* 22(3): 275–289.

Dobosz-Bourne, D., & Jankowicz, A.D. (2006). Reframing resistance to change: Experience from General Motors Poland. *The International Journal of Human Resource Management,* 17(12): 2021–2034.

e Cunha, M.P., Vera, D., Abrantes, A.C.M., & Miner, A. (2024). *The Routledge companion to improvisation in organizations.* London & New York, NY: Routledge.

Flores, B. (2023). *ATD's organization development handbook.* Alexandria, VA: The Association for Talent Development.

Ford, J.K., Lauricella, T.K., Van Fossen, J.A., & Riley, S.J. (2021). Creating energy for change: The role of changes in perceived leadership support on commitment to an organizational change initiative. *The Journal of Applied Behavioral Science,* 57(2):153–173.

Galbraith, J., Downey, D., & Kates, A. (2002). *Designing dynamic organizations: A hands-on guide for leaders at all levels.* New York, NY: Amacom.

Gallo, A. (2023). What is psychological safety? *Harvard Business Review.* Retrieved from: https://hbr.org/2023/02/what-is-psychological-safety

Gallos, J.V. (Ed.). (2006). *Organization development.* San Francisco, CA: Wiley & Sons.

Garrow, V. (2009). OD: Past, present and future. *Working Paper* 22. Brighton: Institute for Employment Studies.

Gittell, J.H., Cameron, K., Lim, S., & Rivas, V. (2006). Relationships, layoffs, and organizational resilience: Airline industry responses to September 11. *The Journal of Applied Behavioral Science,* 42(3): 300–329.

Hamlin, B. (2016). HRD and organizational change: Evidence-based practice. *International Journal of HRD Practice, Policy and Research,* 1(1): 7–20.

Hastings, B.J., & Schwarz, G.M. (2022). Leading change processes for success: A dynamic application of diagnostic and dialogic organization development. *The Journal of Applied Behavioral Science*, 58(1): 120–148.

Hillner, M. (2023). A prescriptive framework for the effective deployment of dynamic capabilities. *Design Management Review*, 34(2): 18–29.

Jamieson, D. (2015). Q&A: David Jamieson. *Design Management Review*, 26(3): 9–12. Published in a special issue on Organization Development and Design Management.

Kanter, R.M. (2003). Leadership and the psychology of turnarounds. *Harvard Business Review*, 81(6): 58–67.

Kim, W.C., & Mauborgne, R. (2003). Tipping point leadership. *Harvard Business Review*, 81(4): 60–9.

Liao, J., & Zhu, F. (2024). How to avoid the agility trap. *Harvard Business Review*, 102(6): 126–133.

MacLusky, G., & Hastrich, C. (2015). Co-creating organizational change with customers. *Design Management Review*, 26(3): 30–37. Published in a special issue on Organization Development and Design Management.

Manu, A. (2023). *The philosophy of disruption: From transition to transformational change*. Bingley: Emerald Publishing Limited.

Marks, M.L., & Mirvis, P.H. (2012). Applying OD to make mergers and acquisitions work. *OD Practitioner*, 44(3): 5–12.

Marshak, R.J. (2013). The controversy over diagnosis in contemporary organization development. *OD Practitioner*, 45(1): 54–59.

McCalman, J., & Potter, D. (2015). *Leading cultural change: The theory and practice of successful organizational transformation*. London: Kogan Page.

McGahan, A.M. (2018). Moonshots: Achieving breakthrough innovation in established organizations. *Rotman Management*, 4: 6–12.

Michels, D., & Murphy, K. (2021). How good is your company at change? *Harvard Business Review*, 99(4): 62–71.

Morton, J. (2023). Strategy making as polyphony: How managers leverage multiple voices in pursuing agility. *California Management Review*, 65(4): 22–42.

Paton, S., & Boddy, D. (2007). Stuck in the middle: A case study investigating the gap between top-down and bottom-up change. *Journal of General Management*, 32(4): 39–51.

Prahalad, C.K. (2010). Why is it so hard to tackle the obvious? *Harvard Business Review*, 88(6): 36.

Regan, A.-M.C., & Hobbs, L.M. 2012. Walter Reed Bethesda—much more than changing names. *OD Practitioner*, 44(3): 31–36.

Reeves, M., Faste, L., Whitaker, K., & Hassen, F. (2018). The truth about corporate transformation. *MIT Sloan Management Review*, 59(3): 1–7.

Rousseau, D.M., & ten Have, S. (2022). Evidence-based change management. *Organizational Dynamics*, 51(3): 1–13.

Sanchez, P. (2018, December 20). The secret to leading organizational change is empathy. *Harvard Business Review*. Retrieved from: https://hbr.org/2018/12/the-secret-to-leading-organizational-change-is-empathy

Sandberg, E., & Abrahamsson, M. (2022). Exploring organizational learning and experimental logistics development at the global fashion retailer H&M. *Global Business and Organizational Excellence*, 41(2): 6–20.

Self, D.R., & Schraeder, M. (2009). Enhancing the success of organizational change: Matching readiness strategies with sources of resistance. *Leadership & Organization Development Journal*, 30(2): 167–182.

Serdari, T. (2022). The role of cultural innovation in the success of luxury startups. *Strategic Change*, 31(3): 275–283.

Sirkin, H.L., Keenan, P., & Jackson, A. (2005). The hard side of change management. *Harvard Business Review*, 83(10): 108–118.

Tkaczyk, B. (2015). Leading as constant learning and development: The knowledge-creative enterprise. *Design Management Review*, 26(3): 38–43. Published in a special issue on Organization Development and Design Management.

Tkaczyk, B. (2021). *Leading positive organizational change: Energize – redesign – gel.* London & New York, NY: Routledge.

Tkaczyk, B. (2022). Positive organization development: Design-inspired strategizing for co-creating positive organizational change. *Design Management Review*, 33(4): 12–17. Published in a special issue on Supports and Barriers to the Business of Design.

Van de Ven, A.H. (2021). Projecting backward and forward on processes of organizational change and innovation. *The Journal of Applied Behavioral Science*, 57(4): 436–446.

Venus, M., Stam, D., & van Knippenberg, D. (2019). Visions of change as visions of continuity. *Academy of Management Journal*, 62(3): 667–690.

Vermeulen, F., Puranam, P., & Gulati, R. (2010). Change for change's sake. *Harvard Business Review*, 88(6): 70–76.

Warrick, D.D. (2023). Revisiting resistance to change and how to manage it: What has been learned and what organizations need to do. *Business Horizons*, 66(4): 433–441.

Warrick, D.D., & Cady, S.H. (2023). Is your organization prepared to manage tsunami change? *The Journal of Applied Behavioral Science*, 59(2): 337–340.

Weick, K., & Sutcliffe, K (2015). *Managing the unexpected: Sustained performance in a complex world* (3rd edition). Hoboken, NJ: Wiley.

Worley, C.G. (2014). OD values and pitches in the dirt. *OD Practitioner*, 46(4): 68–71.

Wrigley, C., Nusem, E., & Straker, K. (2020). Implementing design thinking: Understanding organizational conditions. *California Management Review*, 62(2): 125–143.

Wuertz, H., Eshbaugh, S., & Nelson, S.B. (2020). Design thinking for organizational change. *Design Management Review*, 31(4): 34–48.

6 Design-driven organization

Human-centered design thinking and innovation execution

"Design thinkers are human-centered. They don't care at all about mere customer satisfaction; they are in love with their customers. Try to translate this concept to your personal life. When you want to satisfy somebody, you do everything you can to fulfill all his or her needs. But when you love somebody—your spouse, your son, your mom—you do more, more than they may expect. You surprise him or her and enter the sacred field of the magic, of the extraordinary, of the memorable ... A designer without that flame inside is not a design thinker" – Mauro Porcini

Sneak peek

Focus on: Key concepts and terms

Unit 6

- Design (business/digital/service; human-/life-/user-centered; purpose-driven, responsible, strategic, sustainable)
- Design discipline
- Design ethnography
- Design function
- Design management
- Design maturity
- Design thinking (as mindset, as process)
- Innovation (empty, open, organic, radical, social),
- Organization (designful, design-driven, design-led, design-minded)
- Problem (ill-defined, well-defined, "wicked")
- Thinking (designerly, "inside the box", integrative, "outside the box", systems)

DOI: 10.4324/9781003508274-10

Pause 'N' reflect: On the current issues and trends

Before you complete this unit, think about each of the following statements. Mark each statement:

V – if you *agree.*
X – if you *disagree.*
? – if you are *undecided.*

Your Take: Integrative Thinking	*Before doing Unit 6*	*After doing Unit 6*
1 "Engineering, medicine, business, architecture and painting are concerned not with the necessary but with the contingent – not with how things are but with how they might be – in short, with design" – Herbert Simon		
2 "The future belongs to a different kind of person with a different kind of mind: artists, inventors, storytellers – creative and holistic "right-brain" thinkers whose abilities mark the fault line between who gets ahead and who doesn't … Design. Story. Symphony. Empathy. Play. Meaning – these are fundamentally human abilities that everyone can master" – Daniel H. Pink		
3 Design thinking points to thinking as a designer would.		
4 "The main tenet of design thinking is empathy for the people you're trying to design for" – David M. Kelley		
5 With the right type of thinking, *anyone* can be a "designer" or "creative" without a problem – and without permission from the supervisor. This equalizes creative chances. Everyone's experience matters. Everyone is in control and (as in a creative "sprint" process) no one is in control.		

Your Take: Integrative Thinking	*Before doing Unit 6*	*After doing Unit 6*
6 "The mission of design thinking is to translate observations into insights and insights into products and services that will improve lives" – Tim Brown		
7 "Where people aren't having any fun, they seldom produce good work" – David Ogilvy		
8 "Love your experiments (as you would an ugly child)" – Bruce Mau		
9 Thinking like a designer can create sustainable advantage – innovative design-led enterprises can maintain a significant stock market advantage (e.g., Apple, Coca Cola, Hyundai Motor Co., Nike, PepsiCo, Procter & Gamble, Samsung, Starbucks, Steelcase, or Walt Disney).		
10 Purpose-driven design will become the ultimate battleground for global competition in the 21st century. Human data and human behavior design will be prioritized.		

After you have done the unit, repeat "Your Take". How has reading the unit clarified the ideas herein? How have your views, feelings and thoughts changed over time?

 Lead-in

General discussion points

Individually or in buzz groups, work on the following:

1 *Design is much more than just making things look nice; it is also about making things work nicely.* Discuss the point the sentence is making.
2 *Businesspeople must begin to think like designers.* How far do you agree with this statement? Can design thinking skills be taught at business schools? If yes, what learning and development activities could you suggest?
3 *Design matters for management. If managers adopted a human-centered design attitude, the world of business would be different – and better.* Do you agree? Talk about how this statement makes you feel.
4 *The most successful companies in the world are design-driven organizations. They leverage design as an integrative resource to continuously*

innovate. However, most enterprises don't make it a priority to actually invest in design – frequently seeing that the value of design is difficult to quantify and define as a business strategy. Say why.

5 Explain in your own words what "design thinking" is.

Idea watch

Human-centered design starts with the human.

Intentionally or not, humans are constantly engaged in the act of designing something. Design is everywhere: think, for instance, of the products you use every day (e.g., your electric toothbrush – made easier to charge, especially when you're on the road), strategic human capital processes at work (e.g., employee engagement – employee engagement is an outcome; creating a positive employee experience is how you actually get there), or psychologically safe (and relaxing) air travel experiences (e.g., passenger experience is about more than just legroom; it's an emotional journey too). In each case, design shapes not only objects and processes but also experiences, underscoring its ubiquity and impact on modern life.

Amid this omnipresence, Design Thinking, a prominent innovation process, grounded in models of how people learn, seeks to understand core human experiences and to develop creative solutions in response to them. Design Thinking is an emerging field that applies the tools, mindsets and processes from the design disciplines (industrial design, design engineering, architecture, landscape architecture, interior design, graphic design, product design, apparel design, biophilic work design, cognitive science, artificial intelligence, and others) to complex, system-wide, human-, and life-centered challenges.

At its core, it uses the designer's sensibility and methods to match humans' needs with what is technologically feasible and what a viable business strategy can convert into customer value and market opportunity. This alignment involves critical steps and nuances vital to those design-driven organizations wishing to successfully deliver value through organic innovation, fortifying their organization's current processes for organization development (OD).

Evolutionarily, design as a field has undergone remarkable growth and development in recent decades, transcending its initial role as a mere styling tool to become a potent force for effecting social and cultural transformations. Similarly, within organizations, design has evolved from being an insignificant consideration to becoming an essential and core function. Companies are becoming more and more accustomed to the idea of including designers in the boardroom, achieving what is now referred to as "design maturity". This maturation reflects the growing recognition of design's strategic value. Increasingly, design is being promoted at the board level and embedded into organizational DNA. As a result, streamlined and strategically integrated design processes, policies, and practices lead to improved business performance and higher returns on investment (ROI).

To fully address the challenges and opportunities highlighted in this unit, design must function as a seamlessly integrated strategy across the entire organization. In its optimal state within design-driven enterprises, design positively impacts other functions, including corporate strategy, tech research, new business development, and the generation of new revenue streams. These impacts are clustered in the following roles: "strategic design as capability" (design skills, design thought leadership); "strategic design as approach" (design strategy, programming, delivery, supporting future value creation); and "strategic design as outcome" (design to innovate, champion new paradigms, and differentiate).

A C B   Assumptions

Design has emerged as a powerful catalyst for innovation – worldwide, shifting from a purely aesthetic function to a strategic focus. It has also broadened its horizons, encompassing not only products but also services, organizations, and society as a whole.

Get curious! Wonder – every day... Design Thinking emerges as a positive, proven, and repeatable creative problem-solving, innovation-boosting, sociocultural transformation-enabling, and value-creating protocol that *any* organization, *any* industry, or *any* profession can employ to achieve spectacular results – a new, rapid way to discover and validate innovations, including social innovations.

Fundamentally, Design Thinking can be characterized in two primary ways: as a rapid iterative process involving specific design activities, akin to a tool set (see "Applications" below), and as a broader pattern of thinking, reflecting a mindset (see "Elements" below). Both facets contribute to its growing contemporary relevance.

Design Thinking is of contemporary interest, because:

- The world is undergoing constant transformation, marked by heightened levels of chaos, unpredictability, and risk.
- The shifts in socioeconomic areas are affecting the role of design in business, e.g., "meaning is being sought in an "experience economy"", "business design/ digital design/service design are emerging as disciplines unto themselves", "innovation drives business, and design enables innovation", et cetera.
- There's a need for predictable processes to ethically design new systems.
- It's essential to elevate our collective creative capacities and systems thinking.
- It's said to have put the "human" back into the center of the design process.
- Radical innovation thinking mixes technology and a business model. Intrinsically, user-centered design balances business (*Should we do it?*), engineering/ technology (*How do we do it?*), and user (*What do they actually want?*).

Of note: this approach represents a new way to solve problems in life. While many ordinary problems are clearly defined, design problems that prioritize human-centeredness often lack clear boundaries and are ill-defined. This is because human needs and behaviors are complex and multifaceted, requiring solutions that go beyond simple functionality to create meaningful and lasting impact that resonates on both individual and societal levels.

Additionally, grand challenges like those outlined by the UN Sustainable Development Goals, such as "zero hunger", "affordable and clean energy", "decent work and economic growth", and "tackling rough sleeping and homelessness", are considered to be "wicked" problems – complex problems that are challenging or even impossible to resolve due to their incomplete, conflicting, and evolving nature, which can be difficult to discern ("wicked" denotes resistance to straightforward solutions rather than evil).

Both ill-defined and wicked problems can greatly benefit from the application of Design Thinking methodologies. These problems defy simple fixes as there is no one-size-fits-all solution. Therefore, they are best approached with a mindset of "systems thinking". Systems thinking is way of understanding the complexity of the world by viewing it as an interconnected whole and focusing on the relationships between its elements, rather than breaking it down into individual components.

For instance, to tackle rough sleeping and homelessness, it would actually take multiple stakeholders collaborating across public, private, and nonprofit sectors. Characteristically, the systems nature of the homelessness challenge needs to be addressed. Case in point: consider this reinforcing loop – when drug addiction increases (decreases), the duration of homelessness also increases (decreases). Likewise, as the duration of homelessness increases (decreases), drug addiction tends to increase (decrease) as well.

Ultimately, life-centered design and systems modeling can be a force for positive change and the common good.

Key elements

Design Thinking encompasses a distinct mindset, perspective, and cognitive approach that humanizes and inherently drives people's behavior and actions. These behaviors are directed toward developing and evaluating novel creations designed to address human-centric and real-world challenges.

The following are some of the fundamental components of the Design Thinking mindset: **optimism, experimentation, total empathy + compassion, radical collaboration, open innovation,** and **integrative thinking** – characteristics to look for in design thinkers, as shared by Tim Brown, Partner Emeritus of IDEO, a global innovation and design firm:

Optimism and positive energy are central to Design Thinking, making the act of designing a pleasurable, liberating experience. This empowering element is deeply rooted in the belief that individuals have the power to effect change, and it involves following a purposeful approach to generate fresh and meaningful solutions that bring about positive impact. It instills "creative confidence" in one's aptitude and provides a systematic (*and* scalable – optimism is contagious!) framework for converting complex problems into positively energizing design-driven opportunities.

Building on the foundation of optimism, **experimentation** takes this mindset further by actively encouraging risk-taking, exploration, and iterative learning. Design Thinking is inherently experimental and experiential, so dare to embrace ambiguity and paradox. This enables you to innovate, take risks, bounce back from failure (in fact, fail fast and cheaply!), as you generate new ideas, receive feedback on them, and then iterate repeatedly. Given the range of human needs, your work will never be finished or "solved"; it's always a "work in progress". You must learn – and *purposefully* unlearn.

Moreover, do rough prototypes. Be quick, dirty, and early. Rapid prototyping is not simply a way to just validate your idea; it is an integral part of your strategic innovation process. We build to think and learn – by doing. We prototype for empathy and prototype to test.

Just as optimism fuels creativity, **total empathy + compassion** focus on understanding the human element at the heart of every design challenge. Design Thinking is human-centered. Its fundamental tenet is that in order to tackle an issue, designers require more than just scientific or tech expertise; they must also be deeply attuned to the people affected by the problem and those who will benefit from the solution. Serving real people who face real challenges, rather than theoretical ones, requires developing empathy – the ability to understand and share the feelings of another.

When designers approach their work with deep empathy and genuine compassion, they recognize that they cannot simply generalize or assume that others share their personal experiences. Instead, they become keenly aware of their own biases and consciously work to minimize them by adopting a "newcomer" mindset, in which they train themselves to research each scenario as if they had never seen it before, without any preconceived beliefs.

Help is at hand from ethnography – a research method commonly used by anthropologists (people studying humanity via cultural anthropology, archaeology, linguistic anthropology, and biological anthropology) to understand behavior in context. In the realm of design, "design ethnography" becomes a powerful tool for understanding the nuances of daily life, which can maximize the success probability of a new product or service, while also reducing the risk of failure due to a lack of insight into consumers' basic habits. The key to developing true empathy lies in designers genuinely connecting with stakeholders – whether through in-depth interviews or observing participants in their everyday environments – and listening to their stories without any prior assumptions or expectations. So, Empathize… Observe and notice… Engage… Immerse… And always remember: while you can inspire the rich with passion, you can nourish the poor with compassion.

Furthermore, true **radical collaboration** ignites and facilitates breakthrough insights and solutions by seamlessly integrating diverse perspectives, experiences, and expertise. To fully harness the power of such radical collaboration, it is essential to cultivate a collective design culture and to assemble a team of innovators with mixed backgrounds. This multidisciplinary team must include "extreme" users as well, who in many cases, can tell you more than your "core" users, revealing unexpected opportunities for innovation.

The underlying principle of Design Thinking in relation to this element is that the complexity of design problems surpasses the capacity of a single designer to possess all the required knowledge and insight for their resolution. Therefore, the successful progress and execution of a project demands that every team encompasses a minimum of five essential archetypes. Although this does not imply that each team must consist of exactly five individuals, it does necessitate the inclusion of each archetype to be adequately represented, namely, "original thinkers", "positive energizers", "do-ers", "challengers", and "finishers". In sum, radical collaboration does more than just enhance creativity; it also ensures that solutions are well-rounded and inclusive, ultimately leading to more innovative and successful outcomes.

In today's rapidly evolving innovation landscape, **open innovation** has become absolutely vital. In the past, most companies followed a closed or "Do-It-All-Yourself" approach to innovation. However, to achieve truly spectacular and groundbreaking results, modern businesses have shifted toward "opening up" their innovation processes. In reality, innovation can arise from tapping into, leveraging, and absorbing diverse flows of knowledge across the boundary of the firm, whether incoming or outgoing.

Some of the transformative principles of "open innovation" found by Henry Chesbrough include:

- Recognizing that most of the smartest and most innovative people are employed someplace else.
- Leveraging external innovation can significantly contribute to value creation, but to secure and amplify that value, robust internal R&D efforts and a sound business model are essential.
- You can reap substantial benefits from research without necessarily being its originator.
- You can profit from others' use of your intellectual property (IP), and you can strategically acquire others' IP, if this advances your own business.
- Developing a superior and innovative business model is frequently more advantageous than simply being the first to enter the market.
- By seamlessly integrating internal and external ideas into cohesive platforms, architectures, and systems, you maximize your chances of sustained innovation success.

Finally, **integrative thinking** ties together the various elements. Integrative thinking is the meta-skill of being capable of simultaneously confronting conflicting ideas or models. Instead of simply choosing one over the other (it's OK to refuse to accept unpleasant trade-offs!), it involves generating a creative resolution that effectively addresses the tension. This resolution, in the form of a better model, incorporates elements from each model, but surpasses them individually or collectively. As elucidated by Roger Martin (the former Dean of the Rotman School of Management at the University of Toronto) and Jennifer Riel (Partner and COO at IDEO), integrative thinking can help create truly great choices.

Together, these components form the enabling and freeing mindset that not only drives extremely talented designers to take action but also positively energizes them to continuously push the boundaries of innovation and ingenuity.

Thinking critically: Issues

Capturing the essence of Design Thinking is no small feat, as design itself permeates all aspects of life and encompasses various dimensions. Indeed, there's no single definition for Design Thinking – it's an idea, a method, a strategy, and a way of seeing the world. As such, this can mean very different things to very different people.

Contrary to what the name might suggest, Design Thinking is more about doing than it is about thinking. Specifically, it has a bias toward action, doing, and making. In truth, Design Thinking and "design doing" are synonymous.

Naturally, design is commonly associated with creativity, and so many people just picture hipsters sitting on beanbag chairs and using Post-its to cover walls. While creativity *is* very much an element, it is erroneous to perceive Design Thinking solely as a manifestation of creativity. Rather, it is more accurate to regard it as a disciplined, iterative process that leverages extensive knowledge to foster creative insights.

In our current society, creativity (generation of new ideas) and innovation (developing and implementing those ideas to generate value for the organization, for example, new products and services, expanded markets, improved business models, and better processes) are often celebrated as positive forces that lead to progress and prosperity. Indeed, it's about solving unknown problems ("pain") with unknown solutions (innovation and experimentation). However, it is essential to recognize that innovation can also yield negative, unintended, and inefficient outcomes. This happens when policies are misguided and organizations prioritize superficial innovation simply to create an image, rather than genuinely seeking advancements in technologies, services, and products ("empty innovation"). As a result, corporate innovation projects are sometimes mere buzz phrases – meaningless acts of window-dressing – where a design-inspired approach to innovation results in beautifully elegant "designs" that … fail to pass the test of commercial viability, technological feasibility, or user desirability.

Moreover, according to conventional wisdom, it is believed that only thinking "outside the box" triggers original and creative innovation. Yet, some argue that working inside your familiar world – "inside the box" – and applying systematic inventive thinking (SIT) and a set of SIT techniques (for example, take your product and *subtract* a feature, or take a feature and *give it a different purpose*, etc.) can also foster creativity for breakthrough results.

At its core, Design Thinking is both a mindset and an exploratory process of stepping into the unknown. Those who experience it can change their views and come up with fairly unorthodox ideas. Consequently, it's not always a super comfortable process. While designers are accustomed to navigating ambiguity and embracing paradox and open-ended questions (note: there are no "dumb" questions!), industry leaders and managers tend to be more risk-averse, often harboring a fear of failure. Therefore, instituting a learnable, structured, and scalable methodology across the organization (see "Applications" below) should make even "non-designers" feel much more comfortable with executing innovation, engaging in designerly thinking, and making decisions.

From an organizational perspective, for the design function to be integrated into a business and secure a position at the strategic leadership table, or the board table, it is crucial to enhance communication of its value. This integration can be achieved by articulating the innovative design process and demonstrating how progress is measured through metrics and tangible business outcomes, rather than functioning in isolation as a sporadic service provider.

Furthermore, organizations that prioritize innovation tend to appoint directors with specialized skills, recognizing that various types of innovation call for distinct qualities in directors. Thus, board members can contribute human and social capital that bolster the innovative strategies of their firms.

In addition, design education requires an update, a refresh, and most critically, a redesign. While design is primarily taught in art schools, its future development heavily relies on integrating it more deeply with engineering, social sciences, and business disciplines. Occasionally, there's a tension between the fields of "design" (the humanist discipline born of the applied arts), "design management" (the business side of design – design with a focus on strategy), and "design thinking" – much like medical school (medicine) and public health (healthcare management).

Increasingly, innovation, particularly product innovation, brings in both human designers (engineers, developers, lead users, creative thinkers, and other innovators) and machine designers (software tools with algorithms that autonomously gather and interpret data to make innovative design choices). Top companies have, therefore, already harmonized the capabilities of human and machine designers to produce groundbreaking and ethically sound product innovations that were once unimaginable.

Ultimately, it's safe to say that design has never been presented as a way to save the world (e.g., environmental design, addressing shortages of food, helping people in psychological distress by designing a better, sustainable future) … until now. Only time will tell whether purpose-driven design will fulfill the expectations placed upon it.

Applications

The Design Thinking process guides the designer (as well as the non-designer!) what to do. As practiced at the Hasso Plattner Institute of Design (d.school) at Stanford University, it involves a series of actions and steps that are typically executed in the following order (dynamic iteration is implied throughout the creative "sprint" process, though):

1 **Empathize** with people experiencing the problem, to gain valuable insights.

Toolset:

- Observe directly,
- Conduct ethnographic interviews (not a questionnaire) – for empathy,
- Uncover emotions,
- Engage "extreme" users,

- Seek stories,
- Just love....

2 **Define** the problem in human-/life-centric ways.

Toolset:

- The "5 whys" activity,
- Journey mapping (e.g., in a flowchart) of the stakeholder's experience as they work to accomplish something of importance to them (the visual "experience flow"),
- Craft actionable "*How might we...?*" (HMW) statements,
- Immerse in the nature of the problem/zero in on the core problem,
- Identify meaningful surprises and tensions,
- Frame *and* reframe, and create human-centric problem definitions, such as (*X*/*user*) needs a way to (*user's need*) because/but/however (*insights from team experiences*),
- Infer insights.

3 **Ideate** human-/life-centered solutions.

Toolset:

- Brainstorm radical ideas to generate creative solutions – the more ideas, the better,
- Suspend judgment,
- Cultivate "Yes, let's..." and "Yes – and" thinking,
- Prioritize,
- Refine ideas.

4 **Prototype** potential solutions early and often to learn quickly and gain new understandings.

Toolset:

- Prototype for empathy/prototype to test,
- Think with your hands – it doesn't need to be fancy! Make things visible. Create low-res (*and* high-res) objects, mock-ups, and experiences,
- Role play to understand content and key features,
- Use storyboarding to capture the story in a series of sketches, photos, or key frames,
- Quickly build to think and learn.

5 **Test** solutions with actual customers/users to gain new insights about the solution and the problem.

Toolset:

- Test with real customers to refine solutions and gather ideas,
- Co-create with customers, and
- Launch learning.

The insights obtained from "Step 5" (*testing*) naturally trigger a re-start of the strategic process from "Step 1", forming a *continuous* "loop" in which fresh insights are pursued regarding the alignment of the proposed solution with the lives of its intended users. Over time, these insights drive revisions to the design.

At heart, play freely, for when humans are deprived of play, their well-being and creativity may suffer. Free play is not only a key to happiness and growth but also a vital force that helps people bond, build self-control, unlock their creative potential, and experience the joy that fuels both personal and collective innovation.

Case alert! Case classic

Hyundai motor company

LOOK IT UP: Chung, K.-W., Kim, Y.-J., & Bencuya, S. (2015). Hyundai motor company: Evolution of a design organization. *Design Management Review*, 26(3): 50–59.

Read the article about Hyundai as a design enterprise.

Report back on how a company with very little experience in designing automobiles, in a country still reeling from civil war, used design to bring itself to the forefront of the industry – and managed to do this over a scant four decades.

Can your enterprise become a designful organization, too?

To record your critical insights, use the Case Analysis Record provided in Appendix 2.

Greater good corner: Get ready to exercise your ethics

Take a stance: What would *you* do?

Dilemma and Decision: From waste to wear. Re-imagining sustainable design

The fashion and automotive industries face a common challenge: waste. Both industries produce significant amounts of discarded materials that often end up in landfills, contributing to environmental degradation. Astonishingly, a fusion of fashion and waste management could signal a shift toward a more circular economy (CE), where nothing goes to waste and everything has the potential for a second life.

Through creative collaboration, how can *conscious* designers and, say, automotive corporations re-imagine and re-purpose car waste into upcycled fashion? For example, think of collections featuring jewelry, jumpsuits, work vests, bags, and other clothing made from discarded materials such as seat belts, airbags, rubber tires, upholstery, and metal scraps produced during the automobile making and scrapping process.

Next, watch this "Idea Generation" video on Bloomberg (www.bloomberg .com/news/videos/2023-03-28/idea-generation-nicole-mclaughlin) to learn what Nicole McLaughlin, a designer who takes you on a journey from her start as a graphic design intern to becoming a viral sensation on social media by crafting creative upcycled shoes, does to promote "responsible design" and how she does it. Does her work prove that sustainability and creativity can co-exist in design? Are there any surprises in her approach? If yes, explain why.

Now, how would *you* address the problem of global waste if you were a purpose-driven designer? Consider, for example, sourcing materials from post-industrial and post-consumer waste; creating durable, stylish, and ethically produced fashion pieces that minimize environmental impact; educating consumers on the importance of sustainable fashion, promoting conscious consumption and advocating for a shift away from fast fashion toward more responsible practices, etc.

Time out: Journal entry

Thought Sparks: A few reflections, insightful ideas, actionable suggestions, strategic thinking, and key takeaways from this unit.

Learning never stops… So, pause for a few minutes and reflect in writing on your personal learning experience and beliefs. Through writing in your journal, you develop your awareness of your own beliefs and attitudes. Now, consolidate what you have learned in this unit.

1   How have your beliefs and ideas about human-centered design, design thinking, design-driven organization, and design management (the design with focus on strategy) changed since you began the unit?

....

....

2 Thinking about the problems presented in the unit, write about whether you have found solutions to these problems.

....

....

3 How confident do you now feel about design thinking and "design doing"?

....

....

4 What would you still like to have clarified? What remaining concerns do you have?

....

....

5 What more would you like to learn about the topic, now that you have completed this unit?

....

....

6 If you want, doodle/draw something you like about human-centered design, design thinking, or the design-minded enterprise. This can be as abstract as you wish.

....

....

Remember: It's particularly useful to re-visit journal entries several times and see how themes have recurred or your thoughts have changed over time. Now, repeat "Your Take".

Making connections: Related units and models

- U 1. **Behavioral economics and policy 101**: For humans (see pp. 9–26)
- U 3. **Strategic transformation:** Strategy choice-making (see pp. 27–53)
- U 4. **S.O.A.R:** Possibility thinking in positive strategic dialog (see pp. 82–95)
- U 5. **Dialogic organization development (OD):** Leading positive organizational change (see pp. 103–121)
- U 7. **WOW! It's cool!** Crafting a coolness strategy for your brand (see pp. 147–159)
- U 8. **Once upon a time…** Strategic brand storytelling (see pp. 160–174)
- U 9. **Professional management consulting for real people:** The advice business demystified (see pp. 181–203)

- U 10. **Executive coaching:** Whoop it up! (see pp. 204–219)
- U 11. **So, you want to go global?** Becoming an instant international (see pp. 227–237)
- U 13. **Progress with purpose**: The "good" enterprise (see pp. 257–272)
- Add in more related models you may want to remember: _____.

Industry snapshot

https://motorstudio.hyundai.com/itg/ln/main.do?lang=en
www.hyundai.com/worldwide/en/brand-journal/lifestyle
https://artlab.hyundai.com

Deep dive: Main references and resources

Aagaard, A. (Ed.) (2024). *Business model innovation: Game changers and contemporary issues*. Cham: Palgrave Macmillan.

Allemand, I., Brullebaut, B., Galia, F., & Zenou, E. (2017). Which board members when you innovate? Board selection as a strategic change for innovation. *Strategic Change*, 26(4): 311–322.

Anthony, S.D., Duncan, D.S., & Siren, P.M.A. (2014). Build an innovation engine in 90 days. *Harvard Business Review*, 92(12): 60–68.

Austin, R., & Devin, L. (2003). *Artful making: What managers need to know about how artists work*. Upper Saddle River, NJ: Financial Times Prentice Hall.

Bason, C. (2017) *Leading public design: Discovering human-centered governance*. Bristol & Chicago, IL: Policy Press.

Beauty at work. (n.d.). Retrieved from: www.beautyatwork.net – the website illustrates how beauty works and shapes the work that we do.

Beckman, S. (2020). To frame or reframe: Where might design thinking research go next? *California Management Review*, 62(2): 144–162.

Beckman, S., & Barry, M. (2007). Innovation as a learning process: Embedding design thinking. *California Management Review*, 50(1): 25–56.

Beckman, S., Gil, N., & Kutun, Ö. (2023). UK's embassy village: Collaborating across public, private, and nonprofit sectors to tackle rough sleeping. Berkeley Haas Case Series. Retrieved from: https://cases.haas.berkeley.edu/2023/07/embassyvillage/

Bell, E., Warren, S., & Schroeder, J.E. (Eds.) (2021). *The routledge companion to visual organization*. London & New York, NY: Routledge.

Berger, W. (2010). *CAD monkeys, dinosaur babies and T-shaped people: Inside the world of design thinking and how it can spark creativity and innovation.* London: Penguin Books.

Bloomberg. (2023, March 28). Idea generation – Nicole McLaughlin. Retrieved from www .bloomberg.com/news/videos/2023-03-28/idea-generation-nicole-mclaughlin

Bogers, M., Chesbrough, H., & Moedas, C. (2018). Open innovation: Research, practices, and policies. *California Management Review*, 60(2): 5–16.

Boyd, D., & Goldenberg, J. (2013). *Inside the box: A proven system of creativity for break-through results*. New York, NY: Simon & Schuster.

Brown, T. (2008). Design thinking: Thinking like a designer can transform the way you develop products, services, processes – and even strategy. *Harvard Business Review*, 86(6): 84–92.

Brown, T. (2009). *Change by design: How design thinking transforms organizations and inspires innovation.* New York, NY: HarperBusiness.

Brown, T., & Wyatt, J. (2009). Design thinking for social innovation. *Stanford Social Innovation Review*, 8(1): 31–35.

Buchanan, R., & Margolin, V. (1995). *Discovering design: Explorations in design studies.* Chicago, IL: University of Chicago Press.

Catmull, E., & Wallace, A. (2023). *Creativity, Inc.: Overcoming the unseen forces that stand in the way of true inspiration* (The Expanded Edition). New York, NY: Random House.

Chesbrough, H. (2020). *Open innovation results: Going beyond the hype and getting down to business*. Oxford: Oxford University Press.

Chesbrough, H. (2024). Open innovation: Accomplishments and prospects for the next 20 years. *California Management Review*, 67(1): 164–180.

Chiva, R., & Alegre, J. (2009). Investment in design and firm performance: The mediating role of design management. *Journal of Product Innovation Management*, 26(4): 424–440.

Chung, K.-w., Kim, Y.-J., & Bencuya, S. (2015). Hyundai motor company: Evolution of a design organization. *Design Management Review*, 26(3): 50–59. Published in a special issue on Organization Development and Design Management.

Cooper, R., Junginger, S. & Lockwood, T. (2009). Design thinking and design management: A research and practice perspective. *Design Management Review*, 20(2): 46–55.

DMI (n.d.). The value of design. *Design Management Institute*. Retrieved from: www.dmi .org/page/designvalue

Dodgson, M., & Gann, D.M. (2018). *The playful entrepreneur: How to adapt and thrive in uncertain times*. New Haven, CT: Yale University Press.

Dunne, D. (2018). *Design thinking at work: How innovative organizations are embracing design*. Toronto: Rotman-UTP Publishing.

Dunne, D., Eriksson, T., & Kietzmann, J. (2022). Can design thinking succeed in your organization? *MIT Sloan Management Review*, 64(1): 60–67.

Furr, N., & Dyer, J.H. (2014). Leading your team into the unknown: How great managers empower their organizations to innovate. *Harvard Business Review*, 92(12): 80–88.

Gardien, P., & Gilsing, F. (2020). Walking the walk: Putting design at the heart of business. *Design Management Review*, 31(1): 49–63.

Gemser, G., Calabretta, G., & Quint, E. (2023). Leadership to elevate design at scale: Balancing conflicting imperatives. *California Management Review*, 65(3): 48–72.

Govindarajan, V., & Trimble, C. *The other side of innovation: Solving the execution challenge*. Boston, MA: Harvard Business Review Press.

Guellerin, C. (2021). Design, ethics, and humanism. *Design Management Review*, 32(2): 44–49.

Hallonsten, O. (2023). *Empty innovation: Causes and consequences of society's obsession with entrepreneurship and growth*. Cham: Palgrave Macmillan.

Huang, Y., & Hands, D. (2022). *Design thinking for new business contexts: A critical analysis through theory and practice.* Cham: Palgrave Macmillan.

Ignatius, A. (2015). How Indra Nooyi turned design thinking into strategy. *Harvard Business Review*, 93(9): 80–85.

Iyengar, S (2023). *Think bigger: How to innovate*. New York, NY: Columbia Business School Publishing.

Johnson, S., Gatz, F., & Hicks, D. (1997). Expanding the content base of technology education: Technology transfer as a topic of study. *Journal of Technology Education*, 8(2): 35–49.

Kelley, D., & Kelley, T. (2013). *Creative confidence: Unleashing the creative potential within us all.* New Yrok, NY: Crown Business.

Kim, E., Beckman, S., & Agogino, A. (2018). Design roadmapping in an uncertain world: Implementing a customer-experience-focused strategy. *California Management Review*, 61(1): 43–70.

Kimbell, L. (2011). Rethinking design thinking: Part I. *Design and Culture*, 3(3): 285–306.

Kimbell, L. (2012). Rethinking design thinking: Part II. *Design and Culture*, 4(2): 129–148.

Knapp, J., Zeratsky, J., & Kowitz, B. (2016). *Sprint: How to solve big problems and test new ideas in just five days*. New York, NY: Simon & Schuster.

Kostyk, A., & Sheng, J. (2023). VR in customer-centered marketing: Purpose-driven design. *Business Horizons*, 66(2): 225–236.

Liedtka, J., Hold, K., & Eldridge, J. (2021). *Experiencing design: The innovator's journey*. New York: Columbia University Press.

Liedtka, J., Salzman, R., & Azer, D. (2017). Democratizing innovation in organizations: Teaching design thinking to non-designers. *Design Management Review*, 28(3): 49–55.

Liedtka, J., Salzman, R., & Azer, D. (2017). *Design thinking for the greater good: Innovation in the social sector*. New York, NY: Columbia Business School Publishing.

Lockwood, T. (Ed.) (2010). *Design thinking: Integrating innovation, customer experience, and brand value*. New York, NY: Allworth Press.

MacNeil, R.T. (2024). *Observing dark innovation: After neoliberal tools and techniques*. Bristol: Bristol University Press.

Magistretti, S., Dell'Era, C., Cautela, C., & Kotlar, J. (2023). Design thinking for organizational innovation at PepsiCo. *California Management Review*, 65(3): 5–26.

Martin, R. (2009). *The design of business: Why design thinking is the next competitive advantage*. Boston, MA: Harvard Business Review.

Martin, R. (2009). *Opposable mind: Winning through integrative thinking*. Boston, MA: Harvard Business Press.

Mau, B. (2020). *MC24: Bruce Mau's 24 principles for designing massive change in your life and work*. London & New York, NY: Phaidon Press.

Mintzberg, H. (2024). Four forms that fit most organizations. *California Management Review*, 66(2): 30–43.

Moldoveanu, M., & Martin, R. (2010). *Diaminds: Decoding the mental habits of successful thinkers*. Toronto: Rotman-UTP Publishing.

Munro-Smith, N. (2018). Making a difference with design thinking. *Design Management Review*, 29(1): 22–28.

Nagji, B., & Geoff, T. (2012). Managing your innovation portfolio. *Harvard Business Review*, 90(5): 66–74.

Nakata, C. (2020). Design thinking for innovation: Considering distinctions, fit, and use in firms. *Business Horizons*, 63(6): 763–772.

Ozkan, G. (2021). Design management as an effective user-centric management tool for organizations. *Design Management Review*, 32(3): 46–54.

Pink, D. (2006). *A whole new mind: Why right-brainers will rule the future*. New York, NY: Riverhead Books.

Porcini, M. (2013). A love letter. *Design Management Review*, 24(1): 58–64.

Porcini, M. (2023). *The human side of innovation: The power of people in love with people*. Oakland, CA: Berrett-Koehler Publishers.

Quint, E., Gemser, G., & Calabretta, G. (2022). *Design leadership ignited: Elevating design at scale*. Stanford, CA: Stanford University Press.

Recker, J., von Briel, F., Yoo, Y., Nagaraj, V., & McManus, M. (2023). Orchestrating human–machine designer ensembles during product innovation. *California Management Review*, 65(3): 27–47.

Riel, J., & Martin, R. (2017). *Creating great choices: A leader's guide to integrative thinking*. Boston, MA: Harvard Business Review Press.

Rossman, R.J., & Duerden, M.D. (2019). *Designing experiences*. New York, NY: Columbia Business School Publishing.

Schaefer, S. M., & Hallonsten, O. (2023). What's wrong with creativity? *Organization*, 31(5): 820–828.

Schweitzer, J., BenMahmoud-Jouini, S., & Fixson, S. (2023). *Transform with design: Creating new innovation capabilities with design thinking*. Toronto: Rotman-UTP Publishing.

Thomke, S., & Manzi, J. (2014). The discipline of business experimentation: Increase your chances of success with innovation test-drives. *Harvard Business Review*, 92(12): 70–79.

Thompson, L., & Schonthal, D. (2020). The social psychology of design thinking. *California Management Review*, 62(2): 84–99.

Tkaczyk, B. (2021). *Leading positive organizational change: Energize – redesign – gel*. London & New York, NY: Routledge.

Tkaczyk, B. (2022). Positive organization development: Design-inspired strategizing for co-creating positive organizational change. *Design Management Review*, 33(4): 12–17. Published in a special issue on Supports and Barriers to the Business of Design.

Tripp, C. (2013). Energizing innovation through design thinking. *Rotman Management Magazine*, 3: 71–75.

Trummer, J., & El Mahgiub, M. (2020). From creative outlet to perceived panacea: Can design deliver? *Design Management Review*, 31(1): 10–19.

Vojak, B.A., & Herbst, W.B. (2022). *No-excuses innovation: Strategies for small- and medium-sized mature enterprises*. Stanford, CA: Stanford University Press.

Yoo, Y., & Kim, K. (2015). How Samsung became a design powerhouse. *Harvard Business Review*, 93(9): 73–78.

Zhang, X., & Kim, T. (2022). Design-driven innovation with the JMGO brand. *Design Management Review*, 33(3): 44–50.

Zhang, X., & Kim, T. (2022). Radical innovation: Promoting sustainable dynamics for design business innovation. *Design Management Review*, 33(4): 23–32.

Module monitor and Consolidation III

Workshop III: Applications/review exercises

Self-check questions

You should now be able to answer Self-Check Questions 1–10

1 **True or false** Changing organizations is messy. The *failure* rate of *organizational change* programs is around 70% irrespective of whether they are driven by "mergers", "acquisitions", "downsizing", "de-layering", "IT", "total quality management", "business process re-engineering", or "culture change" initiatives.

2 **True or false** *Positive organization development* (OD), aiming at developing the organization's self-renewing capacity, refers to reforming and transitioning people, teams, and organizations to a desired future state.

3 True or false *Diagnostic OD* and *dialogic OD* are two sides of the same coin.

4 True or false Looking at organizational change from a human perspective, *energize, redesign,* and *gel* (ERG) – a positive, dialogic approach to methodologically shifting, transitioning, or transforming the what and/or how of an organization – helps mobilize the power of people to drive *strategic change.*

5 True or false *Design Thinking* is an innovation approach that revolves around the human experience, centering on understanding life, customer needs, rapidly prototyping solutions, and generating imaginative ideas. This methodology has the potential to revolutionize the development of products, services, processes, organizations, and organizational innovations.

6 True or false By employing Design Thinking, you *base your decisions* on the genuine needs and desires of customers, rather than relying solely on *historical data* or taking risky gambles driven by *instinct* rather than *evidence.*

7 True or false Design Thinking balances *desirability* ("what resonates with people and meets their needs effectively?"), *feasibility* ("what can be achieved from a technical standpoint within the reasonably foreseeable future?"), and *viability* ("what has the potential to be incorporated into a viable and sustainable business model?").

8 True or false Any tough innovation challenge can be tackled through *business design*: *empathy and deep human understanding* ("what's the opportunity?"), *concept visualization* ("what's the breakthrough idea?"), and *strategic business design* ("what's the strategy to deliver the vision?").

9 True or false Organizations have the opportunity and should actively leverage both internal and external sources of ideas and pathways to the market as they seek to propel their innovations forward. This describes *Open Innovation.*

10 True or false The ability to *simultaneously* hold two *opposing ideas* in your *mind,* and then reach a synthesis that contains elements of both but actually improves on each. This describes standard *analytical thinking.*

Individualized learning record

When you have finished Module III, try filling in this record of what you have learned.

1 If you manage across different countries, to what degree have you observed the need for different ways of engaging in organizational change/diverse approaches to organizational change in each country? Why is this the case?

What factors contribute to this necessity? Is leading organizational change positively valued highly all over the map? Are the "positive approach" and the values underpinning it relevant outside of the United States, where it was predominantly developed?

....

....

2   If major change had to be introduced in your enterprise, what do you believe would be the main barriers that would stand in its way, and how might positive/dialogic OD activity enable some of those barriers to be tackled? Does all change lead to learning?

....

....

3   "Design Thinking is Design as we've known it, in a new and much-expanded form". How far do you agree with this statement? Talk about similarities and differences between the two, if any.

....

....

4   Imagine 'n' Design Challenge 1: Imagine that you know someone who is a wheelchair user. One day, she confides in you that the three things she hates most about her wheelchair are: that "I can't go over curbs. I struggle to get up stairs. And when I am talking to someone, I am unable to look them in the eye". What would you do to improve her wheelchair?

....

....

5   Imagine 'n' Design Challenge 2: Imagine that your grandpa continues to use your grandma's prescription medications, and the other way around. They should carefully read the bottle labels, you advise. You hear them say that they can hardly even read the labels… How can you help them?

....

....

6   Imagine 'n' Design Challenge 3: Imagine that you'd like to get your teenage niece to quit smoking cold turkey. In reality, you'd like to convince a million more teens to give up smoking while you're at it. Now, simply telling them that "smoking kills" can actually make smoking seem more "cool" and more "rebellious". So, how can nonsmoking suddenly become trendy and rebellious?

....

....

7   Imagine 'n' Design Challenge 4: Imagine that you've always wished you could make a living doing something energizing and innovative. However, you ended up running a business that sells dog food. How can you elevate this into a higher calling?

    ....

    ....

8   Imagine 'n' Design Challenge 5: Imagine that you find yourself in a village where drinking water is in short supply. A short bike ride away is a lake, although the water is rather murky. Using nothing but your bike, how can you transport clean, usable water back to the village?

    ....

    ....

9   How can one use Design Thinking for social innovation and for the greater good? How can Design Thinking allow high-impact solutions to social problems to bubble up from below rather than being imposed from the top?

    ....

    ....

10 Discuss how an artist like Van Gogh, who struggled to make ends meet when he was alive, would feel about the cosmic sums his works command nowadays? Next, discuss whether the state should provide financial support for young designers. As an aside, do you think people should be "educated" to appreciate design a lot more?

    ....

    ....

Can-do checklist

Looking back, I have learned the following Key Terms:

Unit 5

- change (generative, organizational, positive, sustainable; aversion, confidence, drivers, failure, leadership, management, readiness)
- design thinking (collective)
- energize, redesign, and gel (ERG)

- learning (adaptive, continuous, culture, dialogic, emergent, generative, organizational, planned, vigilant)
- organization development (OD) (diagnostic, dialogic, generative, humanistic, positive, strategic)
- organizational energy (depleted, dysfunctional, negative, personal, positive, relational)
- organizational (un)learning vs. organizational forgetting
- organizational renewal (strategic)
- psychological safety (team)
- resistance to change (active, passive, constructive)
- response to change (affective, behavioral, cognitive, emotional, physical)
- super-flexibility (strategic)

Unit 6

- design (business/digital/service; human-/life-/user-centered; purpose-driven, responsible, strategic, sustainable)
- design discipline
- design ethnography
- design function
- design management
- design maturity
- design thinking (as mindset, as process)
- Innovation (empty, open, organic, radical, social)
- organization (designful, design-driven, design-led, design-minded)
- problem (ill-defined, well-defined, wicked)
- thinking (designerly, "inside the box", integrative, "outside the box", systems)

Module IV

Creating and managing WOW brands

Energizing your brand

7 WOW! It's cool!

Crafting a coolness strategy for your brand

"If no one hates it, no one really loves it" – Jessica Walsh

Sneak peek

Focus on: Key concepts and terms

Unit 7

- Brand: cool, graveyard, healthy, high-energy, iconic, luxury, niche cool, mass cool, *uncool*, with energy
- Brand associations
- Brand authenticity
- Brand awareness
- Brand coolness (strategy)
- Brand energy
- Brand equity
- Brand hate
- Brand health
- Brand heritage
- Brand image
- Brand loyalty
- Brand relevance
- Branded energizer
- Branding (strategic/strategy)
- Characteristics typical of cool brands: positively energizing, extraordinary/ useful, aesthetically appealing, high status, rebellious, original, authentic, subcultural, iconic, and popular

DOI: 10.4324/9781003508274-12

- Consumer behavior
- Economy: circular, sharing
- Energized differentiation
- Energizing the brand
- Fans and followers
- Founders
- Influences: behavioral, personal, psychological, social, cultural
- Intentions to buy/use
- Metaverse (immersive)
- Touchpoints: physical, virtual, social, digital, metaverse
- Users: exceptional/extraordinary (scientists, athletes, celebrities, explorers)
- Value package
- Word of mouth

Pause 'N' reflect: On the current issues and trends

Before you complete this unit, think about each of the following statements. Mark each statement:

V – if you *agree.*
X – if you *disagree.*
? – if you are *undecided.*

Your Take: Integrative Thinking	*Before doing Unit 7*	*After doing Unit 7*
1 Essentially, brands are logos, graphics, trademarks, or slogans.		
2 You can manage your brand by managing the touchpoints – any points of contact between you and your buyers.		
3 Successful branding leads to top-of-mind awareness, which is the degree to which a brand name favorably comes to mind when a consumer thinks about a specific product category.		
4 Additionally, strategic branding returns brand loyalty. When consumers demonstrate high brand loyalty, they regularly purchase products because they're satisfied with their performance.		

Your Take: Integrative Thinking	*Before doing Unit 7*	*After doing Unit 7*	
5 Apple users have high-quality emotional-social connections to the Apple community, and, consequently, to the company brand. In contrast, Samsung customers often choose Samsung not because they genuinely adore the brand but because they dislike Apple.			
6 Luxury firms can create and strategically manage authentic brands by tapping into connections (associations), conformity (iconicity), and consistency (constancy). To do so, enterprises need to harness their long-standing brand heritage, the enduring influence of their founders, and associations with exceptional users (for example, think: scientists, explorers, or passionate fans and followers).			
7 Yes, it's possible to craft a "coolness" strategy for your brand.			
8 Initially, brands become cool to a select group of informed insiders by being distinctive, authentic, rebellious, extraordinary, and visually attractive. Some of these "niche cool" brands eventually expand and gain a larger following, at which point they are referred to as "mass cool" and are seen as being significantly more well-known and iconic but less independent.			
9 Energizing a brand may be the most difficult task the majority of brands face. When you lose energy and the visibility that comes with it, you lose brand relevance and health. If amazing brands with energy are available, why consider one that is tired and has nothing fresh or exciting to offer?			
10 Brand coolness can transform product quality judgments into positive word of mouth and increased intentions to buy/ use the brand.			

After you have done the unit, repeat "Your Take". How has reading the unit clarified the ideas herein? How have your views, feelings and thoughts changed over time?

Lead-in

General discussion points

Individually or in buzz groups, think about:

1 What makes brands cool? What features and brand assets characterize cool brands?
2 Berkeley-Haas (US), Birkbeck Business School (UK), Imperial College Business School (UK), Stanford Graduate School of Business (US); Acqua di Parma, Amouage, Calvin Klein, Zara; Hyundai, Lexus, Mini, Tesla; Dunkin', McDonald's, Starbucks, Tim Hortons; Burberry, Ralph Lauren, Victoria's Secret, Under Armour – what emotions and feelings do you associate with each brand? What image is each brand trying to conjure up? What is the secret of the success of these brands? Select a few and outline a "customer profile" for a typical consumer of some of these brands.
3 How can a brand become cool, and stay cool? How can leaders create and sustain brand coolness in order to expand their customer base and boost sales?
4 In what ways are your attitudes toward brands different from those of your (grand)parents' generations? Give examples of how companies make their brands more attractive to your own generation's concerns, aspirations, goals, and lifestyle choices.
5 Why wasn't Google created by Microsoft, WhatsApp by AT&T or Netflix by Blockbuster?
6 Share your thoughts with your peers/team members. Discuss points of (dis)agreement.

Idea watch

Brands are not *just* product names, logos, graphics, or slogans. These are artifacts that can help with brand recognition, but a brand is much more than that. Brands are assets, with strategic value. Moreover, a brand can be thought of as a personality. Strong brand qualities help you differentiate yourself from the competition by clearly communicating what your enterprise stands for, making you instantly recognizable and memorable.

In fact, rather than thinking of Nike's brand as the swoosh or McDonald's brand as the golden arches, one thinks about brands as sets of associations that exist in consumers' heads. A brand does live in people's minds – it activates a mental frame in your brain which can be a mental image, a state, or a scenario. By way of illustration, a brand like Coca-Cola is more than simply this fizzy, caramel-colored drink that comes in a red can. For many, it's a set of actual memories. It represents closeness to your loved ones, friendship, and fun. So, it's more than an invitation to pause for refreshment when you say, "Let's have a Coke". It's really a kind way of expressing, "Hey, let's keep each other company for a bit". In addition, what impression do your consumers have of you? Friendly? Fun? What are your "touchpoints" with them? In this context, touchpoints is an employed method of communicating, or are occasions when a business or an organization is in physical, virtual, social or (immersive) digital contact with its customers, etc. or meets them.

At present, building a brand is simple. However, if you want to achieve brand leadership and want your brand to stand out from the crowd and the brand clutter, you must create a "*cool* brand".

Being cool has aided startup brands (such as Netflix) in "leapfrogging" established rivals (e.g., Blockbuster). Conversely, being *un*cool may damage even well-known brands (for example, Yahoo), consigning them to the case studies that serve as warnings.

Brand coolness is dynamic – periodically, brands move from *un*cool to "niche cool" to "mass cool" – and (on occasion) back to *un*cool. For this reason, companies need to manage these distinctions carefully.

It's possible to actually craft a "coolness" strategy for your brand based on the ten features that characterize cool brands, including being positively energizing and iconic.

Ultimately, brand coolness affects consumers' attitudes toward, satisfaction with, intentions to talk about, and readiness to buy/use the products associated with the brand.

Assumptions

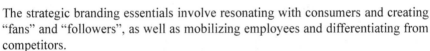

The strategic branding essentials involve resonating with consumers and creating "fans" and "followers", as well as mobilizing employees and differentiating from competitors.

To achieve this, brands need constant energizing and evangelizing. For instance, cool brands are found to share up to ten characteristics: among these, being energetic, authentic, and popular (see below in "Key elements").

On top of that, brand coolness can inform managerial decision-making. By systematically assessing and monitoring their brand's component-level coolness over time, across segments and against competitors (e.g., to what degree the individual components of brand coolness serve as strengths or weaknesses of the brand), companies can strategize how to boost their brand's coolness. This can be done, for example, by pre-testing and evaluating different marketing programs, by (re-)energizing and designing the brand, as well as by executing communication tactics designed for increasing or maintaining a brand's perceived coolness.

Key elements

Research by Richard Bagozzi and colleagues finds that consumers perceive cool brands to have the following WOW factors:

Positively energizing – Active, energetic, vigorous, and dynamic.
Extraordinary/useful – Awesome; high quality, and offering superior functional value.
Aesthetically appealing – Elegantly designed.

High status – Associated with high social class, luxury, and prestige.

Rebellious – Revolutionary, rule-breaking, disobedient.

Original – New, fresh; creative, imaginative; unusual, unconventional, unorthodox, groundbreaking, and pioneering.

Authentic – Genuine; behaving consistently and remaining true to its roots.

Subcultural – Associated with an autonomous group of people within a larger culture, often having beliefs or interests at variance with those of the mainstream.

Iconic – Widely recognized as cultural symbols and icons.

Popular – Very fashionable and liked by most people.

As David Aaker evangelizes, brands need to have life to stand out from the crowd. Brands with energy are:

Exciting – They give people a reason to talk about them (e.g., Tesla).

Engaging – They integrate into valued activities or lifestyles (e.g., Lego).

Innovative – They are continually at the forefront of innovation (e.g., 3M).

Purpose-driven – They are fueled by a higher purpose that inspires passion (e.g., Patagonia).

Brands with energy not only resist image decline but also maintain their ability to drive financial performance. For high-energy brands, boosts in energy and attitude correlate with increased stock returns. Thus, differentiation must be redefined as "energized differentiation", for, without energy, differentiation loses its impact. In the long run, energy taps the brand's future orientation.

 Thinking critically: Issues

Brand coolness is fluid – what is cool now may not be cool tomorrow. Case in point: prior to Facebook, MySpace dominated the social networking service landscape.

Moreover, coolness is a personal preference. Brands are only cool (or *un*cool) to the extent that customers think so. Take, for example, Apple and Samsung. Some see these as *really* cool brands, yet others view Apple and Samsung as *un*cool, owing to their perceptions of the brands as, say, less subcultural or less rebellious now.

Interestingly, although it seems that not *all* of the ten characteristics of cool brands are essential for every brand and every consumer segment, boosting any of these qualities can help make a brand look cooler. By way of illustration, Under Armour is increasingly viewed as cool and popular, especially with athletes, because its performance gear has extraordinary quality, signals positive energy and is aesthetically pleasing. Harley-Davidson is seen as iconic by a subculture of its "anti-social" bikers and it seems rebellious. Lexus, conversely, is cool because it has become a high-status symbol, as well as because of its extraordinary performance, design, and energy.

However, some qualities may even conflict with each other (e.g., "subcultural" with "popular"). Potentially, there might be a tension between "brand coolness" and, say, "brand hate", namely, "extreme negative affect" toward brands. Some studies classified "brand hate" emotions, indicating an illness in consumption cultures, in a "mild", "modest", and "severe" emotional format.

Also, of note is the fact that when a brand becomes super popular, it might actually lose its cool. Companies have to be careful to avoid over-exposure, which can damage the exclusive aspect of the brand image – especially in the case of luxury brands.

That said, unlike many other brands, luxury brands *can* enjoy surprisingly enduring success (think Louis Roederer's champagnes, including the legendary Cristal). Still, while remaining faithful to their history, they *must* innovate to remain relevant.

Energizing a brand, therefore, may be the most difficult tasks that the majority of companies face. The brand must generate and sustain enough energy to avoid fading into obscurity. Brands that are tired, personality-less, and not connected to innovation are fairly boring. As a result, when a brand lacks energy and visibility, it can become a "graveyard" brand – one that customers might have heard of, but one which is difficult to recall easily and cannot be considered straightaway.

In addition, nurturing strong "brand equity" is vital. Simply speaking, brand equity is the added value a brand name contributes to a product or service – this can be a tremendous source of leverage for launching new products (think: brand/line extensions), as well as a significant barrier to competitors. Yet, brand equities as measured by brand awareness, brand image and perceived quality may be declining sharply in time. A notable exception are those brands with energy, which can stay healthy while still driving financial returns.

At heart, strategic branding should be purpose-driven and so it should contribute to the greater good or to marketing pressing social issues – like advancing the *circular* or *sharing economy* or *consciously investing* in socially and environmentally friendly ways that are more cool for widespread adoption. Proactive digital reputation management will be vital, too.

Applications

Today's consumer views a product as a bundle of attributes, collectively known as the "value package". To understand consumer behavior, business leaders need to study major behavioral influences on consumer behavior, among others, psychological, personal, social, and cultural. If their brand does not score high enough for one or more of the elements of brand coolness, leaders may want to strategize and act – they must enhance the image of the brand with regard to the missing feature or qualities. Here are some possible strategies and tactics:

Positively energizing

There are two ways to energize the brand: energizing the business or creating a "branded energizer". By way of illustration, to energize the business, you can try innovating (this creates interest and visibility), involving customers (by asking your fans to upload and share their most fanatical videos and photos on social media when using your product), going retail (by opening a flagship store so as to offer story in a compelling and integrative way), holding publicity events (to generate a lot of buzz and energize conversation in the industry), and using promotions (to attract new customers). To create a "branded energizer" – a branded product, promotion, sponsorship, symbol, or program that, by association, significantly enhances and energizes a target brand – you can launch a branded sponsorship program, a social program, charitable global giving, or community and virtual volunteering.

Extraordinary/Useful

To build a sense of exceptional quality, instead of adopting incremental improvements, focus on creating high performance and breakthrough functional specifications that are leading-edge and game-changing – that which will deliver unrivaled positive customer experience or service.

Aesthetically appealing

Design products, processes and experiences that are appealing and beautiful.

High status

Glam up... by considering luxury positioning (e.g., luxury brands thrive on the perception that their products are not accessible to everyone, making ownership a status symbol), offering exclusive experiences (e.g., exclusive access to special events, limited-edition products, or VIP services), or using celebrity endorsements (symbolizing success).

Rebellious

Consider employing a spokesperson, for instance, who is renowned for questioning the status quo and for speaking his or her mind even when it challenges convention.

Original

Continuously introduce new methods, ideas or products, and try to stay one step ahead of the competition.

Authentic

A company's founder, heritage, and fans can be powerful tools in creating authentic brands, particularly legitimate luxury brands. So remind your passionate buyers, extraordinary users (e.g., scientists, athletes, celebrities, explorers), or your "fans" and "followers" (who actually use your products as social proof of your authenticity), of the history (e.g., long-standing tradition of quality craftsmanship, rooted in a specific time period and geography) and core values of your brand (such as excellence) and its founders (the lifetime passion and talent of the artisan or innovator who created it, whose name typically honors the brand, and whose physical and symbolic image is highly acclaimed).

Subcultural

Connect the brand to an admired subculture. Don't make it too niche, though. Make sure that it's genuine and that it doesn't diminish the brand's utility.

Iconic

Evangelize for your enterprise and what it has to offer. Use "strategic brand story-telling" that resonates with consumers (see below in Unit 8).

Popular

Make it very fashionable so that it's trending and loved by many.

Case alert! Case classic

Canada Goose

LOOK IT UP: Goldstein, G.A., & Carpenter, G.S. (2022). Legitimately luxurious: Creating authentic luxury brands. *Business Horizons*, 65(5): 631–642.

Your task: Based on the case of Canada Goose, an extreme weather outwear maker established in 1957, in Toronto, Canada, explain how an organization can draw on multiple sources of authenticity to successfully create a legitimate luxury brand. Make a list of the best strategies, tactics, and the key lessons learned. Are there any surprises? Can *your* enterprise enter the luxury market? Why (not)?

To record your critical insights, use the Case Analysis Record provided in Appendix 2. Report your research findings and good practices back to your peers/team members.

Greater good corner: Get ready to exercise your ethics

Take a stance: What would *you* do?

Dilemma and decision: It wows?

During a business trip to an economically developing country, you come across a very cool, authentic, original, and energizing product which you believe could be successfully marketed in your own country at a price that would be both attractive to the consumer and profitable for you. It wows! Yet, when you visit the plant which produces this product, you find that the working conditions of the workforce are substandard and the pay rates are low. The factory environment appears unsafe, and employees seem to be working long hours under difficult conditions.

Should you enter into a contract with them?

Time out: Journal entry

Thought Sparks: A few reflections, insightful ideas, actionable suggestions, strategic thinking, and key takeaways from this unit.

Learning never stops… So, pause for a few minutes and reflect in writing on your personal learning experience and beliefs. Through writing in your journal, you develop your awareness of your own beliefs and attitudes. Now, consolidate what you have learned in this unit.

1 How have your beliefs and ideas about creating and managing cool brands changed since you began the unit?

   ....

   ....

2 Thinking about the problems presented in the unit, write about whether you have found solutions to these problems.

   ....

   ....

3 How confident do you now feel about energizing your brand and engineering brand coolness?

....

....

4 What would you still like to have clarified? What remaining concerns do you have?

....

....

5 What more would you like to learn about the topic, now that you have completed this unit?

....

....

6 If you want, doodle/draw something about some high-energy brand *you're* crazy about. This can be as abstract as you wish.

....

....

Remember: It's particularly useful to re-visit journal entries several times and see how themes have recurred or your thoughts have changed over time. Now, repeat "Your Take".

Making connections: Related units and models

- U 1. **Behavioral economics and policy 101:** For humans (see pp. 9–26)
- U 3. **Strategic transformation:** Strategy choice-making (see pp. 61–81)
- U 4. **SOAR:** Possibility thinking in positive strategic dialog (see pp. 82–95)
- U 6. **Design-driven organization:** Human-centered design thinking and innovation execution (see pp. 122–139)
- U 8. **Once upon a time…** Strategic brand storytelling (see pp. 160–174)
- U 11. **So, you want to go global?** Becoming an instant international (see pp. 227–237)
- Add in more related models you may want to remember: _____.

Industry snapshot

www.canadagoose.com/ca/en/our-history.html

Deep dive: Main references and resources

Aaker, D. (2011). *Brand relevance: Making competitors irrelevant*. San Francisco, CA: Jossey-Bass.

Aaker, D. (2023). *The future of purpose-driven branding*. New York, NY: Morgan James Publishing.

Bagozzi, R.P., & Khoshnevis, M. (2022). How and when brand coolness transforms product quality judgments into positive word of mouth and intentions to buy/use. *Journal of Marketing Theory and Practice*, 31(4): 383–402.

Bendell, B.L., & Kristal, E.K. (2023). Five naming strategies to help tell your organization's story. *Business Horizons*, 66(3): 387–404.

Berry, L.L., & Seltman, K.D. (2007). Building a strong services brand: Lessons from Mayo Clinic. *Business Horizons*, 50(3): 199–209.

Bowers, A., & Reuber, R. (2018). Reputation management goes digital. *Rotman Management,* 4: 76–81.

Brown, V. (2021). Is coolness still cool? *Journal for Cultural Research*, 25(4): 429–445.

Bruun, A., Raptis, D., Kjeldskov, J., & Skov, M.B. (2016). Measuring the coolness of interactive products: The COOL questionnaire. *Behaviour & Information Technology*, 35(3): 233–249.

Bryson, D., Atwal, G., Hultén, P., & Heine, K. (2021). Antecedents of luxury brand hate: A quantitative study. *Strategic Change*, 30(1): 35–43.

Busche, L. (2024). *Brand psychology: The art and science of building strong brands*. London & New York, NY: Routledge.

Carpenter, G.S., & Barlier, X. (2021). Legendary luxury brands: Inventing the future by reaching to the past. *Academy of Marketing Science Review*, 11(3–4): 464–470.

Goldstein, G.A., & Carpenter, G.S. (2022). Legitimately luxurious: Creating authentic luxury brands. *Business Horizons*, 65(5): 631–642.

Grolleau, G., Evon, J., & Qian, Y. (2022). How fine wine producers can make the best of counterfeiting. *Strategic Change*, 31(5): 515–522.

Heine, K., & Atwal, G. (2022). Growing luxury brands through culture-driven innovation. *Strategic Change*, 31(5): 533–543.

Hsu, M. (2017). Neuromarketing: Inside the mind of the consumer. *California Management Review*, 59(4): 5–22.

Jiménez-Barreto, J., Correia Loureiro, S.M., Rubio, N., & Romero, J. (2022). Service brand coolness in the construction of brand loyalty: A self-presentation theory approach. *Journal of Retailing and Consumer Services*, 65: 102876.

Johnson, M., & Misiaszek, T. (2022). *Branding that means business*. London: The Economist.

Koskie, M.M., & Locander, W.B. (2023). Cool brands and hot attachments: Their effect on consumers' willingness to pay more. *European Journal of Marketing*, 57(4): 905–929.

Kucuk, S.U. (2021). Developing a theory of brand hate: Where are we now? *Strategic Change*, 30(1): 29–33.

Loureiro, S.M.C., Jiménez-Barreto, J., & Romero, J. (2020). Enhancing brand coolness through perceived luxury values: Insight from luxury fashion brands. *Journal of Retailing and Consumer Services*, 57: 102211.

Mizik, N., & Jacobson, R. (2008). The financial value impact of perceptual brand attributes. *Journal of Marketing Research*, 45(1): 15-32

Phau, I., Akintimehin, O.O., & Lee, S. (2022). Investigating consumers' brand desirability for upcycled luxury brands. *Strategic Change*, 31(5): 523–531.

Russell, C.A., Schau, H., & Bliese, P. (2019). Brand afterlife: Transference to alternate brands following corporate failure. *Journal of Business Research*, 97: 257–267.

Suzuki, S., & Kanno, S. (2022). The role of brand coolness in the masstige co-branding of luxury and mass brands. *Journal of Business Research*, 149: 240–249.

Taqi, M., Bagozzi, R. P., Tuğrul, T., & Yaprak, A. (2024). The phenomenon of brand hate: A systematic literature review. *Journal of Marketing Theory and Practice*, 1–28.

Thomas, S., & Kohli, C. (2009). A brand is forever! A framework for revitalizing declining and dead brands. *Business Horizons*, 52(4): 377-386.

Quartz, S., & Asp, A. (2015). *Cool: How the brain's hidden quest for cool drives our economy and shapes our world.* New York, NY: Farrar, Straus and Giroux.

Warren, C., Batra, R., Loureiro, S.M.C., & Bagozzi, R.P. (2019). Brand coolness. *Journal of Marketing*, 83(5): 36–56.

Whitler, K.A. (2021). *Positioning for advantage: Techniques and strategies to grow brand value.* New York, NY: Columbia Business School Publishing.

Yu, S., & Birss, D. (2018). *Iconic advantage: Don't chase the new, innovate the old.* New York, NY: Savio Republic.

8 Once upon a time... Strategic brand storytelling

"In the beginning was the Word" – John the Evangelist 1:1

Sneak peek

Focus on: Key concepts and terms

Unit 8

- Brand: community, differentiation, empathy, identity, leadership, position, promise, relevance, value
- Brand activism (strategy)
- Brand design (human-centered process)
- "Brand DNA" (personality, purpose, spirit, values, voice)
- "Brand evangelism"
- Brand storytelling (digital, strategic)
- Chief Evangelist Officer
- Communication (strategic)
- Customer/user journey
- Elements of a story (e.g., hero; goal; plot; setting; theme; the call to adventure; obstacle(s); crossing the threshold, tests, trials and tribulations; turning point; resolution)
- Hero-Goal-Obstacle dynamic
- H2H ("human-to-human")
- Media channels (e.g., social, digital, and traditional)
- Narrative (capital, process, thinking)
- Noise
- Points ("pain", high/"passion")
- Story (archetypes, elements, structure)

DOI: 10.4324/9781003508274-13

- Storytelling (digital, emotive, immersive, organizational, participatory, personalized, strategic)
- "Storytelling organization"
- Transmedia brand storytelling (strategy)
- Types of stories (heritage, contemporary, vision, and folklore)

Pause 'N' reflect: On the current issues and trends

Before you complete this unit, think about each of the following statements. Mark each statement:

V – if you *agree.*
X – if you *disagree.*
? – if you are *undecided.*

Your Take: Integrative Thinking	Before doing Unit 8	After doing Unit 8	
1 Every brand has a story to tell.			
2 Facts alone fall short. So, rather than making a sales pitch or overwhelming clients with information, use stories to move people and to foster an emotional–social connection.			
3 If truth be told, stories aren't the best strategic communication technique for distilling complex ideas to their core because they can be overly simplistic; for example, parable-style storytelling is often too basic.			
4 Organizational storytelling—with its narrative capital and process—can be a powerful and constructive tool in energizing brands, driving organizational change and consultation, increasing influence and support, creating strategic partnerships, building rapport, illustrating specific points to support larger goals, developing next-generation leaders, transferring knowledge, rightsizing, formulating short- and long-term strategies, communicating the vision for a strategic initiative, and managing crises.			

Your Take: Integrative Thinking	*Before doing Unit 8*	*After doing Unit 8*
5 Stories stick in people's memories for a very long time; as a result, all major organizations, religions, and philosophies employ stories and metaphors to impart their lessons.		
6 The three critical elements of brand stories are plot, character, and setting.		
7 Being visual is a powerful means of conveying a compelling brand narrative – a picture is worth a thousand words, and a video is more valuable than a million words.		
8 Transmedia provides an integrated storytelling experience that gradually draws you in as it unfolds over time. Transmedia storytelling strategically employs various media channels (e.g., social, digital, and traditional) to convey different elements of a brand's narrative. This approach allows brands to tell new kinds of stories in both a disciplined and innovative manner, creating a cohesive world that's presented synergistically and holistically.		
9 Customers can be an excellent source of stories. Plus, thanks to tech advances, brands can now engage customers in their narratives by allowing them to actively participate.		
10 Developing a successful brand design is more than just creating something that looks "cool". It's all about working out how to fire people's imaginations and enthusiasm while solving the problem they're confronted with.		

After you have done the unit, repeat "Your Take". How has reading the unit clarified the ideas herein? How have your views, feelings and thoughts changed over time?

Lead-in

General discussion points

Individually or in buzz groups, think about:

1 "Truth, naked and cold, had been turned away from every door in the village. Her nakedness frightened the people. When Parable found her, she was huddled in a corner, shivering and hungry. Taking pity on her, Parable gathered her up and took her home. There, she dressed Truth in story, warmed her and sent her out again. Clothed in story, Truth knocked again at the doors and was readily welcomed into the villagers' houses. They invited her to eat at their tables and warm herself by their fires" – *Jewish Teaching Story.* What does this Jewish teaching story mean to you? How true is this of modern storytelling in general?
2 How to tell a good story? What can a story do that facts can't?
3 Strong brands are built on a narrative. What goes into a great brand story?
4 What does your brand look, feel, and sound like? Can you tell *your* brand's story? Is your story easy to tell/pitch?
5 How, in today's hyper-connected world, can new digital tools and strategies help make your brand's story more positively energizing, relevant, and timely?

Share your thoughts with your peers/team members. Discuss points of (dis)agreement.

Idea watch

In this era of slide decks, posts and soundbites, emotive storytelling is our oldest and sometimes most *under*-appreciated form of strategic communication. Indeed, an emotionally gripping narrative is the most remembered and powerful means there is.

Given this, strategic storytelling is a disciplined, effective way of engaging with employees and clients and mobilizing them to drive business results. Therefore, to achieve brand leadership and to lead in a dynamic environment, business leaders and brand marketers should leverage the power of narrative thinking and media (esp. digital and social media) to tell epic brand stories.

Moreover, viable brand-building organizations are customer-obsessed organizations. In particular, conversations between brands and consumers are created when brands tell stories by effectively connecting their brand promise and purpose to customer "pain" and "passion" points.

In today's hyper-connected world, transmedia storytelling – a highly immersive, participatory and personalized digital storytelling approach that results in a coordinated story and entertainment experience that unfolds over multiple media channels (social, digital, and traditional) – should be integral to digital brand storytelling.

From a managerial or strategic branding perspective, this can be approached systematically. You can design a coherent and cohesive brand content campaign in three steps:

1 First, focus on crafting a credible and unique brand story, relevant for the target, as well as defining accurately the brand core purpose, personality, voice, spirit, and values ("brand DNA"),
2 Next, by coordinating content, format (visual and semantic design) and objectives across the distinct storytelling channels, formulate a strong and unified brand storytelling strategy, and…
3 Finally, communicate and implement your brand storytelling strategy framework in an integrative way – even if they present distinct but complementary objectives (for example, one version of its brand story shared through an app, a little different version on a podcast ad, and a third through social messaging), ultimately, the multiple channels should work in synergy by conveying the same storytelling throughout the entire "customer journey" (on- and off-line). After all, the user journey represents the real experience path of users as they interact with your product/service, which impacts the value of your brand.

 Assumptions

Brands needs energizing, as well as evangelizing.

To achieve this, living and leading brands are tapping into narrative thinking and strategic brand storytelling to cut through the competition and the "noise" (distractions in the brand communication environment that interfere with meaning transmission). By doing so, they create fervent brand communities and arm their followers with a rich vocabulary so they can communicate the brand to others.

For example, standout "storytelling organizations" – enterprises founded on storytelling such as Disney or Lego, are great at cultivating a storytelling culture throughout their organizations. Importantly, this culture extends across all domains and functions (storytelling is not just for marketing!). As a result, they have consistently told compelling stories – even if we don't purchase their stuff, we may be familiar with their brand stories and/or products.

One reason for this success is that the archetypes found in stories are timeless (see below in "Key elements"). Stories stick with us. They comfort us and connect us to new people. They wake up our imagination and cross cultural and linguistic boundaries.

Moreover, extraordinary brand marketers shine at strategic digital storytelling. They recognize that customer insights come first. In particular, they are adept at relating their brands to customer "high points" (positive experiences) and "pain points" (negative experiences). By following a structured narrative process and executing a transmedia storytelling strategy, they enhance brand resonance and loyalty.

Key elements

Stories are universal. Everybody tells them. In truth, from ancient mythology, classical literature to Hollywood blockbusters, practically every great story can be categorized into one of the seven archetypes. The archetypical stories are: "Overcoming the Monster", "Rags to Riches", "The Hero's Quest", "Voyage and Return", "Comedy", "Tragedy", and "Rebirth". Brands can also take up some archetype. By way of illustration, Nike's "Just do it" and the entire Nike story is about "defeating the monster that lives inside you", which is your limitations, apathy or inactivity. It's always important to know your genre. To help you master it, for example, study five good examples in your genre and three bad ones.

Aristotle, who lived more than 2,300 years ago, developed the classic "beginning-middle-end" story structure; it resembles how the human mind tends to arrange reality. Such a three-act structure is still widely used by, for example, Hollywood screenwriters today, namely, Act 1 (set-up: introducing characters, developing relationships, and establishing the hero's unfulfilled desire, which keeps the story moving); Act 2 (confrontation: encountering roadblocks that keep the main character from achieving their desire); Act 3 (resolution: the main character emerges transformed).

At bottom, a story is a hero's struggle against an obstacle to reach a goal (the "Hero-Goal-Obstacle" dynamic). Within the strong story structure, some other key elements of a story can be used:

Plot – Is the writer's choice of events and their design in time.

Setting – A story's setting is four-dimensional: Period (a story's place in time), Duration (a story's length through time), Location (a story's place in space), and Level of Conflict (the story's position on the hierarchy of human struggles).

Theme – Much deeper than a plot. It's a subject matter that is personal and that the creator and audience have an emotional connection to. A thematic area can be summed up in one or two words (e.g., family, finding hope). To craft a powerful theme, ask yourself: is it relevant, moral, debatable?

Hero – A hero is someone like us with a high stakes goal and/or high stakes need to change who drives the action forward through all obstacles to reach the goal. A hero is someone relatable (and/or likable yet flawed), whose struggle we can identify with (think, for example, quirks, nobility, personality, ambition, pain). They can be funny, charismatic, passionate, beautiful. The character, at the beginning, may have some kind of flaw or deficiency (e.g., knowledge, wisdom), they can be suffering (e.g., growing up with a narcissistic mother/tyrant father). They are driven and they won't quit. A hero is the one we root for. We love characters who learn and grow (e.g., growth in ability, strength, courage, nobility, some virtue). They're the heart of your story.

Goal – A goal is the organizing drive for the hero; it motivates the hero. Some categories of goals include love, prize, personal achievement, survival, rescue, escape, "beat the enemy", et cetera.

The call to adventure – Like an inciting incident, conventionally in the first act, it throws the protagonist's life out of balance, then (re-)energizes them to restore that balance.

Crossing the threshold, tests, trials and tribulations – The second act of a story begins when obstacles and challenges begat conflict, failure, and drama. This often leads the protagonist to experiment with changes. Specifically, an obstacle is something that challenges your hero externally as well as internally, to grow and change; it's the essence of dramatic storytelling. For instance, it may include: a human being vs. another human being, a human being vs. self, a human being vs. nature, a human being vs. society.

A turning point – The second act is brought to a close with this as a symbolic point of no return. The main character is now unable to see or act in the same way as previously.

A resolution – In the third act, the main character either triumphs spectacularly or fails tragically. Remember: know where you're headed. On that account, figure out your ending first.

🔊 Thinking critically: Issues

Everyone has a story to tell. Yet, having a message isn't enough. Customers only have so much spare time, focus, and interest. Besides, given the abundance of stories that are constantly bombarding us in today's hyper-connected society, it's very easy to become overwhelmed. In truth, very few brands genuinely succeed in breaking through the noise and competition. For this reason, you'll need to develop a narrative that overcomes our collective story weariness while coming up with effective methods to use it creatively and strategically.

The use of fanciful stories is not encouraged when the use of good storytelling is advocated. Something made up to make a terrible situation appear good is not what it's meant by when the term "story" is used. Instead, we're discussing stories that are so compelling and genuine that our fans' interests seem to be entwined with ours.

When it comes to managing the story process, strategic storytelling often begins at the top. Hence, it's no surprise that amazing brand-building enterprises tend to be led by visionary CEOs who could be called "Chief *Evangelist* Officers". They are like spokespeople for their brands and their future vision (e.g., Sir Richard Branson's Virgin Galactic's purpose is to democratize space, eventually making commercial space travel affordable and accessible to all). Importantly, in our social age, "brand evangelism" and the spreading of this good news is literally *everyone's* job (see below in "Applications").

On the subject of tech and telling your brand story, instead of first asking, "Should we use this or that platform?", start with: "What's the story we want to tell?" Afterward, puzzle out what platforms are best suited to engaging and communicating that story in the most effective manner.

At the same time, while customers look to brands to take a stand and contribute back to the community in trying times, enterprises face new and dynamic difficulties in an era marked by wars, political turmoil and a global pandemic. Brands that can't change to meet consumer expectations run the danger of damaging criticism on social media, declining sales, and boycotts. Recently, market-driven organizations have started to pursue a brand activism strategy through which they align themselves with a sociopolitical cause to boost their brand relevance and solidify their ties with customers. Having said that, this can be a risky strategy because by doing so, brands can generally alienate a significant part of their existing clientele.

It may sound possible to try and entirely reposition a brand, but this frequently ends in failure. So, perhaps, do not fundamentally change your brand narrative.

Ultimately, when crafting standout brand stories, stay human. Stop obsessing about what wows for B2B ("business-to-business") or even B2C ("business-to-consumer"). Remember that it's always about relational energy exchange and H2H ("human-to-human") connection; the focus of an H2H approach to brand storytelling being on the people without whom an enterprise would not be able to exist...

Applications

If you wish to develop your own human-centered brand design (see more in Unit 6 "Design-driven organization: Human-centered design thinking and innovation execution"):

First, think about your brand position – originate a strategy that provides brand purpose, identity, empathy, and energized differentiation.

Also, decide what associations – those that relate to your brand position – you want to evoke in people's minds. For example, take "cheap". Curiously, "cheap" can have positive *or* negative connotations. If your customers think *you are cozy, convenient* and *cheap*, it's a positive. If they say *you're cheap, dilapidated* and *faraway*, it's a negative.

Furthermore, "prototype" and "test". To develop a prototype design, think like designers – and think narratively. Build your solution (make something others can interact with) and test your design on customers (do they have the positive associations with your brand you wanted them to have?). Always implement some system(s) to track the results and evaluate progress, and, if needed, revise your storytelling strategy. Ultimately, reflect and log the key takeaways.

Practically, although content and style can vary greatly, as mapped by Kelly Smith and Michael Wintrob, brand and design strategists, stories typically adhere to four basic constructs: "heritage", "contemporary", "vision", and "folklore" – each creating genuine, long-lasting, ever-more-immersive experiences. Specifically:

Heritage stories explain the brand's origins and the reasons for its distinctive characteristics.

DO's

- Include origin story to breathe life into your brand.
- Spread it both internally and externally, allowing customers, stakeholders and employees to connect with the brand at creation.

Example:

Lots of people, including those who are *not* Dell users, can tell you that Dell's story began with a core purpose "that everybody should have easy access to the best technology anywhere in the world" and that Michael Dell started his business by putting together and selling upgrade kits for personal computers in his dorm room at the University of Texas. However, finding consumers who are familiar with the origins of Huawei may not be that easy.

Contemporary stories belong to or occur in the present and follow modern ideas or fashion in style or design.

DO's

- Make equity elements come to life.
- Communicate overall brand promise, as well as elements, method, business innovation, and technologies.

Example:

A good example of a company even more true to their shared mission is Starbucks, whose core purpose is "to inspire and nurture the human spirit – one person, one cup and one neighborhood at a time". Today, they find themselves in a position where, to reinvent themselves for the future, they must *modernize* and transform the Starbucks experience in their stores and recreate an environment that is relevant, welcoming and safe, and where they uplift one another with dignity, respect, and kindness. Executing their "Reinvention plan" includes delivering beverage innovation, expanding effortless digital convenience and digital tipping, introducing new apps, digital innovation through non-fungible tokens (NFTs), reinventing scheduling and decisioning tools, and developing personalized career paths for "partners" (employees).

Vision stories help imagine and "visit" an ideal future.

DO's

- Lead the now from a stretching view of the future.
- Create a meaningful, "positively deviant", as well as aspiring story of the future – rather than just another generic "me-too vision statement" that lacks distinctiveness.
- Energize stakeholders around your bold vision and engage a brand's most devoted fans and followers.
- Of note, try to show, rather than tell. Incidentally, if actions speak louder than words, could your vision story work with the sound turned off?
- Be flexible enough, revise it, and, as needed, accommodate changing circumstances (think: external impacts, core beliefs, trends).

Example:

Sir Richard Branson's Virgin Galactic, the world's first commercial spaceline, whose core purpose they're communicating is that they exist "to connect people across the globe to the love, wonder and awe created by space travel".

Folklore stories are stories of a community, created, driven, and *organically* spread by consumers (as "chief story crafters"), often via synergized opportunities for engagement (e.g., think: wiki practices and methods).

DO's

- Integration of organization and consumer via *co*-creation of social communities, values and attitudes (a brand community, made up of "brand loyalists", is a "space" for consumer integration).
- Include consumer perspectives throughout the brand story.
- Capitalize on folk stories, as well as popular beliefs, customs, and parodies.

Example:
IKEA, on its website, apart from sharing stories behind different products about where Ikea products are born (…in people's homes!) – told by the product designers, also celebrates inspiring stories by allowing a variety of real-life customers to share their own tales ("everyday rituals") – showing how they use Ikea products (e.g., press coffee, coffee spoon, coffee maker, mug) that improve their everyday lives (e.g., slow coffee ritual), often, without even mentioning the brand at all.

Remember: writing is re-writing. Thus, when you craft a story, always ask for honest feedback.

On top, as popularized by Guy Kawasaki, Apple's first Chief Evangelist Officer, adopt "brand evangelism" to share the good news and effectively promote brands, i.e., use strategic brand storytelling that genuinely resonates with consumers. It seems that customers who have a deeper social, spiritual, emotional connection with the brand ("brand empathy") deliver more value to the enterprise. So, evangelize for your enterprise and what it has to offer by means of:

schmoozing – for example, get out of your office, share your passions, follow up with people – and do favors,
public speaking – for instance, deliver quality content (omit the sales pitch!), customize the speech for your audience, focus on entertaining your listeners, tell stories, practice – and speak all the time,
social media – in particular, offer value when posting, be interesting, take chances, keep it brief, add drama, use hashtags – and keep on evangelizing.

Case alert! Case classic

Burberry

LOOK IT UP: Sull, D., Turconi, S., Zanjani, S. (2022). *Burberry's digital strategy (London Business School Case Collection)*. London: London Business School Publishing. Retrieved from: https://publishing.london.edu/cases/burberrys-digital-strategy/

Your task: Burberry, the original British luxury brand, debuted its first logo in 1900 and trademarked its iconic check pattern in 1920. For several decades, it was an established luxury brand for wealthy middle-class conservatives, and yet sales started to fall as the brand seemed to fall out of fashion. To reposition the Burberry brand in line with its luxury and exclusive heritage, perhaps, the brand's image may need renewing. How to achieve this?

Read the case "Burberry's digital strategy" and reflect on what Burberry, an iconic British luxury brand, needs to design to better narrate the essence of the "new" Burberry strategically, blending a contemporary vibe combined with classic British elitism? To what extent is the investment in digitizing the brand, harnessing technology, social media, and customer analytics paying off? Should Burberry continue to prioritize enhancing digital as a strategic capability, its social media presence, strategic brand storytelling, analytics, and e-commerce platforms?

Which moves are most likely to position the company for future profitable growth?

To record your critical insights, use the Case Analysis Record provided in Appendix 2. Report your research findings and good practices back to your peers/team.

Greater good corner: Get ready to exercise your ethics

Take a stance: What would *you* do?

Dilemma and decision: Cheap – For and against

You're a luxury sunglasses maker, having invested heavily in strategic branding and brand storytelling. Your brand represents not just high-quality craftsmanship, but also a commitment to sustainability, fair labor practices, and an ethical approach to luxury. Today, you're faced with the problem of cheap fakes of your most expensive models now flooding the market. These counterfeit products not only threaten your profits but also undermine the ethical principles your brand stands for, as they are often produced under questionable labor conditions with little regard for environmental impact.

Some believe that the way to handle it is to manufacture less expensive models (a) to develop the new customer base and (b) to beat counterfeit products. Develop arguments both *for* extension (e.g., people will only pay for fakes if no extension, new target audience, sales up...) and *against* the extension (e.g., to compete with fakes new marketing/pricing strategies needed, cheaper versions may actually validate fakes and erode the narrative of exclusivity and ethical luxury, emphasize quality, sales up only temporary, risk losing brand loyalists/brand image if...) What action(s) would you take?

Time out: Journal entry

Thought Sparks: A few reflections, insightful ideas, actionable suggestions, strategic thinking, and key takeaways from this unit.

Learning never stops... So, pause for a few minutes and reflect in writing on your personal learning experience and beliefs. Through writing in your journal, you develop your awareness of your own beliefs and attitudes. Now, consolidate what you have learned in this unit.

1 How have your beliefs and ideas about storytelling, narrative thinking and brand evangelism changed since you began the unit?

....
....

2 Reflecting on the problems presented in the unit, write about whether you have found solutions to these problems.

....
....

3 How confident do you now feel about strategic brand storytelling?

....
....

4 What would you still like to have clarified? What remaining concerns do you have?

....
....

5 What more would you like to learn about the topic, now that you have completed this unit?

....
....

6 If you want, doodle/draw something about strategic communication/brand storytelling. This can be as abstract as you wish.

....
....

Remember: It's particularly useful to re-visit journal entries several times and see how themes have recurred or your thoughts have changed over time. Now, repeat "Your Take".

Making connections: Related units and models

- U 2. **The kindness advantage**: Cultivating positively energizing leaders and followers (see pp. 27–53)
- U 4. **SOAR:** Possibility thinking in positive strategic dialog (see pp. 82–95)
- U 5. **Dialogic organization development (OD):** Leading positive organizational change (see pp. 103–121)
- U 6. **Design-driven organization:** Human-centered design thinking and innovation execution (see pp. 122–139)
- U 7. **WOW! It's cool!** Crafting a coolness strategy for your brand (see pp. 147–159)
- U 10. **Executive coaching:** Whoop it up! (see pp. 204–219)
- U 12. **Small world:** Are you a culturally intelligent organization? (see pp. 238–250)
- Add in more related models you may want to remember: _____.

Industry snapshot

https://uk.burberry.com/c/stories/

Deep dive: Main references and resources

Aaker, D. (2018). *Creating signature stories: Strategic messaging that energizes, persuades and inspires.* New York, NY: Morgan James Publishing.

Aaker, D., & Aaker, J.L. (2016). What are your signature stories? *California Management Review*, 58(3): 49-65.

Aimé, I. (2023). The dynamic construction of brand storytelling. *Journal of Strategic Marketing*, 31(7): 1243–1262.

Bardey, A.C., Turner, R., & Piccardi, P. (2022). Bargaining our emotions: Exploring the lived experience of purchasing luxury fashion counterfeit. *Strategic Change*, 31(5): 505–514.

Berthon, P.R., Lord Ferguson, S., Pitt, L.F., & Wang, E. (2023). The virtuous brand: The perils and promises of brand virtue signaling. *Business Horizons*, 66(1): 27–36.

Boyd, B. (2010). *On the origin of stories: Evolution, cognition, and fiction.* Cambridge, MA: Harvard University Press.

Cancellieri, G., Ferriani, S., & Cattani, G. (2023). Balancing valued tradition with innovation. *MIT Sloan Management Review*, 64(4): 3–5.

Carey, H., & Blume, M. (2023). Communicating visions for design: The STOVE framework. *Design Management Review*, 34(2): 30–37.

Cooper, H.B., Ewing, M.T., Campbell, C., & Treen, E. (2023). Hero brands, brand heroes: How R.M. Williams inspired a cult following and created a shared sense of meaning. *Business Horizons*, 66(3): 405–414.

Denning, S. (2011). *The leader's guide to storytelling: Mastering the art and discipline of business narrative.* San Francisco, CA: Jossey-Bass.

Egri, L. (2004). *The art of dramatic writing: Its basis in the creative interpretation of human motives.* New York, NY: Touchstone.

Feldman, J. (2006). *From molecule to metaphor: A neural theory of language.* Cambridge, MA: The MIT Press.

Green, M.C., & Brock, T.C. (2000). The role of transportation in the persuasiveness of public narratives. *Journal of Personality and Social Psychology, 79*(5): 701-721.

Heath, C. & Heath, D. (2008). *Made to stick: Why some ideas survive and others die.* New York, NY: Random House.

Joy, A., Zhu, Y., Peña, C., & Brouard, M. (2022). Digital future of luxury brands: Metaverse, digital fashion, and non-fungible tokens. *Strategic Change*, 31(3): 337–343.

Kawasaki, G. (2015). The art of evangelism. *Harvard Business Review*, 93(5): 108–111.

Keel, A.L., & Tran, A. (2023). Increasing small nonprofits' influence through strategic storytelling. *Business Horizons*, 66(3): 359–370.

Kemp, A., Gravois, R., Syrdal, H., & McDougal, E. (2023). Storytelling is not just for marketing: Cultivating a storytelling culture throughout the organization. *Business Horizons*, 66(3): 313–324.

Kerrison, M. (2022). *Immersive storytelling for real and imagined worlds: A writer's guide.* Studio City, CA: Michael Wiese Productions.

Landa, R., & Braun, G. (2024). *Shareworthy: Advertising that creates powerful connections through storytelling.* New York, NY: Columbia Business School Publishing.

Luffarelli, J., Mukesh, M., & Mahmood, A. (2019, September 12). A study of 597 logos shows which kind is most effective. *Harvard Business Review.* Retrieved from: https://hbr.org/2019/09/a-study-of-597-logos-shows-which-kind-is-most-effective

Mar, R.A., & Oatley, K. (2008). The function of fiction is the abstraction and simulation of social experience. *Perspectives on Psychological Science*, 3(3): 173-192

McKee, R. (1997). *Story: Style, structure, substance, and the principles of screenwriting.* New York, NY: HarperCollins.

McKee, R. (2003). Storytelling that moves people: A conversation with screenwriting coach Robert McKee. *Harvard Business Review*, 81(6): 51–55.

Merlo, O., Eisingerich, A.B., Gillingwater, R., & Cao, J.J. (2023). Exploring the changing role of brand archetypes in customer–brand relationships: Why try to be a hero when your brand can be more? *Business Horizons*, 66(5): 615–629.

Riley, C. (2021). *The Hollywood standard: The complete and authoritative guide to script format and style* (3rd edition). Studio City, CA: Michael Wiese Productions.

Rose, F. (2015, February 9). The power of immersive media. *Strategy+Business.* Retrieved from www.strategy-business.com/article/00308

Rose, F. (2024). *The sea we swim in: How stories work in a data-driven world.* New York, NY: W.W. Norton & Company.

Sawhney, M. (2019). Digital brand storytelling. In A.M., Tybout, & T. Calkins (Eds.), *Kellogg on branding in a hyper-connected world* (pp. 161–176). Hoboken, NJ: John Wiley & Sons, Inc.

Simmons, A. (2019). *The story factor: Inspiration, influence, and persuasion through the art of storytelling.* New York, NY: Basic Books.

Smith, K., & Wintrob, M. (2013). Brand storytelling: A framework for activation. *Design Management Review*, 24(1): 36–41.

Snyder, B. (2005). *Save the cat! The last book on screenwriting you'll ever need.* Studio City, CA: Michael Wiese Productions.

Speer, N.K., Reynolds, J.R., Swallow, K.M., & Zacks J.M. (2009). Reading stories activates neural representations of visual and motor experiences. *Psychological Science*, 20(8): 989-999.

Srivastava, S., Oberoi, S., & Gupta, V.K. (2023). The story and the storyteller: Strategic storytelling that gets human attention for entrepreneurs. *Business Horizons*, 66(3): 347–358.

Sull, D., Turconi, S., & Zanjani, S. (2022). Burberry's digital strategy (London Business School Case Collection). London: London Business School Publishing. Retrieved from: https://publishing.london.edu/cases/burberrys-digital-strategy/

Tkaczyk, B. (2017). Mind-based linguistics 101 for managers: How language really works. *European Financial Review*, 2: 24-29.
van Laer, T., de Ruyter, K., Visconti, L.M., & Wetzels, M. (2014). The extended transportation-imagery model: A meta-analysis of the antecedents and consequences of consumers' narrative transportation. *Journal of Consumer Research*, 40(5): 797–817.

Module monitor and Consolidation IV

Workshop IV: Applications/review exercises

Self-check questions

You should now be able to answer Self-Check Questions 1–10.

1 **True or false** *Branding* is a process of making use of symbols to strategically communicate the qualities of a product, created by a particular producer.

2 **True or false** To make sense of consumer behavior (various *behavioral facets* of the decision process by which customers come to purchase and consume products), companies need to research *psychological* (an individual's motivations, perceptions, ability to learn, and attitudes), *personal* (lifestyle, personality, and economic status), *social* (family, friends, opinion leaders, and coworkers), and *cultural* influences (culture, subculture, and social class).

3 **True or false** When looked upon as a *value package* for the buyer, a product is a bundle of value-adding attributes (such as prestige of ownership, and/or an ease of use) consisting of the right benefits, features, intangible rewards, and reasonable price.

4 **True or false** By being original, authentic, rebellious, exceptional, and aesthetically pleasing, brands first become *cool* to a limited subculture; these brands are referred to as *niche cool*.

5 **True or false** *Brand equity*, a formidable investment barrier to competitors, is the "surplus value" a brand name attaches and contributes to a product or service. It's vital to nurture strong brand equity because it can be a tremendous source of leverage for launching new products (think: brand/line extensions). Still, brand equities as measured by brand awareness, brand image, and perceived quality can be falling sharply sooner or later. A noteworthy exception are those positively energizing brands, which can continue to be healthy and retain their ability to drive good financial returns.

6 True or false Losing *energy* relevance is like losing brand health, which is also a threat to established brands. When a brand loses energy, it becomes worn, out-of-date, and rather uninteresting. It might still be a good offering and an adequate choice for your parents or grandparents but not up-to-date enough for you. It no longer fits. Furthermore, visibility goes down with energy. When considering a purchase, the brand is no longer among those that springs to mind. It is no longer relevant. However, in time, *brand energy* can have a positive and statistically significant direct effect on stock returns.

7 Multiple-choice The ways to effectively *evangelize* a brand and share the good news are (select one):

a   schmoozing
b   public speaking
c   social media
d   all of the above

8 True or false Your customers and your R&D employees cannot be very powerful *fountainheads for stories*.

9 True or false *Transmedia storytelling* allows a story to unfold across multiple media platforms.

10 True or false Red Bull's tag line, "Red Bull gives you wiiings", serves the *core purpose of the brand* well, meaning: "do extreme things".

Individualized learning record

When you have finished Module IV, try filling in this record of what you have learned.

1   What is a *brand* and how do brands acquire meaning?
    ....
    ....

2   How do *brands* influence *perceptions*, *preferences*, and *choices*?
    ....
    ....

3 Identify ten *components* that contribute to brands being seen as *cool*.

....

....

4 What can you do to *energize* and defend a *well-performing/premier* brand? What can you do to *revitalize* a *neglected* or *under-performing* brand?

....

....

5 *Evaluate* how customers perceive *your* brand – is it currently, for example, *niche cool*, *mass cool*, or *uncool*? Devise specific recommendations to strengthen your brand.

....

....

6 Search for *branding failure* on the Internet to find an example of a company that has experienced one. Take notes and then discuss with a partner.

....

....

7 What makes a *luxury* brand *authentic*? How can you manage authenticity over time? Can you think of innovations (e.g., cultural innovations) within the luxury sector?

....

....

8 The *story* connects, personalizes, and humanizes the *brand*, plus it helps build (global) *brand power*. Say why and how.

....

....

9 What steps can be taken to create a sustainable *brand story*?

....

....

10 How could you develop your own *personal brand*? How can you give your personal brand a *digital boost*? Now, craft your *personal brand statement*.

....

....

Can-do checklist

Looking back, I have learned the following Key Terms:

Unit 7

- brand: cool, graveyard, healthy, high-energy, iconic, luxury, niche cool, mass cool, *uncool*, with energy
- brand associations
- brand authenticity
- brand awareness
- brand coolness (strategy)
- brand energy
- brand equity
- brand hate
- brand heritage
- brand loyalty
- brand relevance
- branded energizer
- branding (strategic/strategy)
- characteristics typical of cool brands: energetic, extraordinary/useful, aesthetically appealing, high status, rebellious, original, authentic, subcultural, iconic, and popular
- consumer behavior
- energized differentiation
- energizing the brand
- fans and followers
- influences: behavioral, psychological, personal, social, cultural
- Intentions to buy/use
- touchpoints: physical, virtual, social, digital, metaverse (immersive)
- users: exceptional/extraordinary (scientists, athletes, celebrities, explorers)

Unit 8

- brand: community, differentiation, empathy, identity, leadership, position, promise
- brand activism (strategy)
- brand design (human-centered process)
- "brand DNA" (personality, purpose, spirit, values, voice)

- "brand evangelism"
- brand storytelling (digital, strategic)
- Chief Evangelist Officer
- communication (strategic)
- customer/user journey
- elements of a story (e.g., hero; goal; plot; setting; theme; the call to adventure; obstacle(s); crossing the threshold, tests, trials and tribulations; turning point; resolution)
- hero-goal-obstacle dynamic
- H2H ("human-to-human")
- narrative (capital, process, thinking)
- noise
- story (archetypes, elements, structure)
- storytelling (digital, emotive, immersive, organizational, participatory, personalized, strategic)
- "storytelling organization"
- transmedia brand storytelling (strategy)
- types of stories (heritage, contemporary, vision, and folklore)

Module V

Helping genuinely

Always aim higher

9 Professional management consulting for real people

The advice business demystified

"Start with character, intelligence, and industry" – Edwin G. Booz

Sneak peek

Focus on: Key concepts and terms

Unit 9

- Advice (business, expert, targeted, trusted)
- Boutique consulting firm
- Business process reengineering (BPR)
- Client (business, bill, centered, firm, win)
- Consultant (external/internal, independent, management, professional, role, strategy)
- Consulting (activity, assignment, cycle, design, engagement, firm, humble, industry, job, knowledge, management, methods, professional, project, proposal, rhetoric, robo, services, skills, strategy, work)
- Models (management, operational, strategic, tactical)
- Plan–do–study–act (PDSA) cycle
- Professional service firms (PSFs)
- Strategic dialogue
- Trust equation

DOI: 10.4324/9781003508274-15

Pause 'N' reflect: On the current issues and trends

Before you complete this unit, think about each of the following statements. Mark each statement:

V – if you *agree.*
X – if you *disagree.*
? – if you are *undecided.*

Your Take: Integrative Thinking	*Before doing Unit 9*	*After doing Unit 9*
1 When you are snowed under with urgent cases, dogged by pressing problems, or *too* involved with the issue, it's best to ask an outsider for advice, as they'll take an objective, fresh look at it.		
2 Consultants simply "play doctor" – they take the pulse of an enterprise, run a few tests, offer a smart diagnosis of the problem, and make detailed prescriptions for maintaining or improving its health.		
3 Consultancies win clients based on the assumption that there's a problem with the organization or that the organization needs a specialized service or task that they're unable to do "in-house". It's uncommon for consultants to decline a prospective contract, or they may identify a flaw in a company's operations even when there isn't one.		
4 "Implementation? I'm a consultant, and I don't know what to do! I'll produce a long report anyway" (management consultant)		
5 Big consulting companies can bill their clients up to $ 10 million each year for advice, regardless of whether it improves performance.		
6 "A consultant is someone who borrows your watch to tell you the time, and then keeps it" (client)		

Your Take: Integrative Thinking	Before doing Unit 9	After doing Unit 9
7 Using consultants may frequently go wrong due to insufficient clarity in briefing them and reluctance to collaborate directly with them on the project.		
8 "Why not outsource difficult decisions? This is gonna be politically *un*popular, so I'll bring in consultants; the blame will fall on them" (board member)		
9 ...and who audits the auditors?! There should be government inquiries running on audit firms. They need periodic evaluation to ensure the quality of their audits and to maintain confidence in that quality among program managers, legislators, and other audit groups.		
10 Any enterprise can set itself up as a consultant and solicit for work. The consulting industry is unregulated, and so inexperienced clients may end up paying "fat" fees for poor-quality services.		

After you have done the unit, repeat "Your Take". How has reading the unit clarified the ideas herein? How have your views, feelings and thoughts changed over time?

Lead-in

General discussion points

Individually or in buzz groups, consider the following discussion prompts:

1 Agree or disagree with this statement: "Sometimes it takes an expert to point out the obvious". What does it mean? Can you give examples of this phenomenon?
2 Why do you think organizations often outsource projects or tasks to external consultants? What do you think are some of the (dis)advantages of taking on external advisors? Have you had first-hand experience working alongside outside consultants?
3 How can an enterprise ensure that the right kind of management consultant or consultancy is recruited? What would be an appropriate sequence of steps when hiring an external consultant for any organization?

4 Have *you* ever worked as a consultant? What are some potential advantages and disadvantages of working as an external/internal consultant? Are the skills that internal and external consultants utilize similar? Discuss your experience.

5 *A management consultant is someone who...* Brainstorm a list of words to describe the attributes of a *professional* management consultant. Now, what about "an unprofessional professional" or "an advisor who can't be trusted"? Discuss the paradoxes. Are these apparent contradictions or real contradictions?

Share your thoughts with your peers/team members. Discuss points of agreement/disagreement.

 Idea watch

Management consulting is both an industry and a practice, making a substantial contribution to the world economy.

Despite its modern importance, this exciting yet misunderstood profession was still in its infancy when, in 1886, the Arthur D. Little consultancy firm was formed by a Massachusetts Institute of Technology (MIT) professor of the same name. In its original form, the company revolved around science, engineering, and innovation. In 1907, "other people's troubles are our business" became the Arthur D. Little slogan. Similarly, in Chicago, IL, in 1914, on the eve of World War I, a young college graduate in psychology named Edwin G. Booz went into business for himself. The company, originally under the name The Business Research Service, next became Booz Allen Hamilton, one of the earliest true management consultancies. Ed's first major client assignment was for the Illinois State Railroad, researching potential customer reaction to a rate increase. Ed frequently published articles about business practices and articulated the values of character and professionalism in his thought leadership. Principally, what differentiated those two consultancies from others at that time was their focus on people, rather than any particular theory, method, or tool.

Today, the advice business is booming worldwide. Professional service firms (PSFs), whether local or global, offer services, for a fee, to other organizations, in any sector locally, regionally, and globally, which often are unable to manage without expert, evidence-based, and trusted advice from (independent) consultants who objectively advise on strategy, executive human resource development (HRD), organization development (OD) and change, design, digital transformation, artificial intelligence (AI), tech and innovation management, risk, and policymaking (among other issues), and/or who help implement realistic, optimal and practical business solutions so as to create value for organizations collaboratively. Management consultants, often called "management analysts", apply knowledge techniques and assets, and research and recommend ways to improve an organization's efficiency and performance, and ensure positive change.

Besides, there are different ways consultants can work with organizations: in a (tech) expert role, a pair-of-hands role, a collaborative role, an orchestrator's role, an innovator's role, or in a facilitator's/teacher's role – in the service of producing human and organizational learning (and *un*learning). This will be conditional on management style, the nature of the assignment, and the personal choice of the consultant. At their core, best practice consultants develop the "human chemistry" needed for success.

On top of that, in particular, to create the most positive, human-to-human (H2H) client experience, and to continuously improve it, the role of *design* in consulting is growing significantly. Greater than the sum of its parts, intrinsically, a 21st-century consultancy is literally a "design consultancy" – a collective intelligence – made up of unique talent (people with diverse human capital and skill sets), context (designers, strategists and technologists synergizing their efforts in reinventing processes, models and the future of work) and a "hybrid" variety of experiences and industries (for example, a software company can become a transportation company; healthcare needs service design; management consulting needs data visualization, design research, ethnography, user experience (UX), experience strategy, and so on). That being the case, to maximize impact and capture greater value, the *corporate in*-sourcing trend is causing *design* consultancies to be quickly acquired. Even though all in-house teams are at risk of some of the same pushes that make running a design consultancy demanding, integrated teams can help achieve smoother program and project implementation. Besides, this suggests that, nowadays, design is regarded as a true strategic competency and a differentiator and that companies are interested in enhancing meaningful ROI that's *human*-centered, rather than just operationally "fixed".

Assumptions

As Peter Block, an OD consultant, enlightens us as to modern consulting, every time you offer advice to somebody who faces a choice, you are consulting.

Companies can be more successful if they can call on someone outside their own organizations for expert, targeted, evidence-based, and candid advice.

Consulting is a professional *helping* role. In this context, you as a consultant agree to only perform work that is necessary and something that you can do well – something that you're qualified to perform.

Furthermore, management consultancy is the *co*-creation of value for enterprises – with a creative human touch.

Professional consultants recognize that every client situation is truly unique – a blank canvas. While there are guiding principles that drive their actions (plus a comprehensive inventory of numerous theories, frameworks, tools and techniques to draw on), to achieve the best results – and results *that endure*, consultants keep on reinventing the process and renewing the connection. It can be said, therefore, that the process is both dialog- *and* diagnosis-driven.

Effective consultants act with integrity, and create and sustain a high-quality client-centered partnership – with the intent to empower them.

Notably, extremely good consultants happily (and openly) share know-how.

Building on this, great consultants know it starts with character – they see the quality of their character as a catalyst for transformation and continuing professional learning and development (L&D).

Brilliant consultants understand that the "magic" is not in the models, but rather in the "intangibles" – authenticity, the trust, the learning process, and the consultant's genuine relationship to the client.

Importantly, effective strategic decision-making only comes about through free and open choice. Successful execution requires internal commitment.

Ultimately, in consulting work, the assignment (typically performed as a project or executed as the ongoing support) is successful only if the client is better off after the engagement. This improvement/helping can take myriad forms. Among them are objective analysis, energizing the workplace and helping during a busy period (as consultants can temporarily absorb workloads from permanent employees), optimizing the workplace in support of the business goal, improving organizational efficiency, solving a difficult human or organizational performance problem, jump-starting a positive organizational change or delivering a learning program or an event, uncovering previously untapped sources of OD (as well as effectiveness and health), enhancing the knowledge base, raising the quality of management dialogue, producing a deliverable such as a report or a plan, making sure that strategic decisions and recommendations are driven by data and based on evidence, reinterpreting a complex issue so that it can be properly addressed, providing the language needed to facilitate organizational reform, transferring critical skills, tracking management trends, finding the sources of friction to the betterment of the entity, promoting and sharing next-practice thought leadership, controlling costs, carrying out the implementation work of a project or task by consultants themselves (*only if* previously formally agreed upon) without long-term commitments to the client company, crafting a winning HRD strategy, and so on.

 ## Key elements

Top qualities of a management consultant

To deliver on the promise (and never *over*-promise anything you know you can't deliver!) of providing high-quality, ethical, and expert advisory services, a consultant must hold or work on developing the following key qualities:

- *Consulting skills*: These include in-depth knowledge of value-adding performance consulting cycles and processes (from pre-entry, entry, and contracting, through analysis, design, development, delivery, program close and evaluation, and post-engagement learning). Moreover, they embody insight into research-backed practice and practice-informed research, consultancy and research techniques (quantitative and/or qualitative), scientific management methods and models (strategic, tactical, and operational), risk management, positive organizational change leadership, and evidence-based program and project management.
- *Technical* and *in-depth business expertise*: This encompasses not only insight into the client's specific business but also functional, industry expertise, and a global perspective.

- *Personal effectiveness*: The consultant should demonstrate a commitment to being helpful, collaborative, humble in inquiry, caring, emotionally resilient, and positive in manner and communication – expressing and receiving positive relational energy. Ideally, he or she should also have a winning mindset (but without arrogance), show genuine curiosity, paradoxical awareness, and the ability to super-flexibly navigate the Scylla and Charybdis of complexity and ambiguity; be accountable, authentic, analytical, entrepreneurial and resourceful; have good team and people skills and stakeholder focus, and be able to build and sustain client relationships and ultimately to elevate themselves to *trusted advisor* status; use design, whole systems and integrative thinking; be effective in negotiating genuinely, and managing difficult conversations and resistance; know-how to efficiently organize and prioritize tasks; be driven and able to travel frequently and adhere to extremely tight deadlines.
- *Learning agility*: This requires dedication to continued learning and to never-ending professional development, as well as to creating and leveraging new knowledge. Given the increasing professionalization of consulting, it's not surprising that you can now study Management Consultancy even at Masters level (Consider, for example, professional MSc "Human Resource Development and Consultancy" or MSc "Management Consultancy and Organizational Change" at the Birkbeck Business School, University of London).
- *Ethics*, *values*, and *behaviors*: The consultant's behavior should be guided by ethical decision-making, integrity, confidentiality, and adherence to a code of professional conduct (e.g., the IMC USA Code of Ethics). You as a professional management consultant will serve the interest of society and the consultancy profession, too.

The above-mentioned professional competencies may be viewed as "enabler tools" of a professional management consultant. Without them, the consultant will not be able to fully translate ideas into action. These days, an increase in the credibility of a consultant comes through rigorous consulting and ongoing demonstration of their practical contribution and long-term, high value to the business client and to organizational performance. Should these be met, the consultant will show true value and their professional practice will flourish.

The client: Who's the client?

The intricate consultant–client system can be made simpler by grouping the clients into three categories, as recommended by Peter Cockman, Bill Evans and Peter Reynolds, senior partners and management consultants:

- *Those who know*: They are aware of the problem(s) to be confronted.
- *Those who care*: They suffer from the problem(s) afflicting the enterprise.
- *Those who can*: They are the sponsors of the consulting assignment and have the power to green light the improvement project.

Each of these groups has an important role to play and a stake in the consulting collaboration. By way of illustration, the outcome will be rather poor if a consultant actively engages *those who know* and *those who care* only – without listening to *those who can*.

Trust

Equally important to the consultant-client relationship is the element of trust, which underpins successful collaboration. There are several facets to trust. For instance, I might believe your expertise and honesty ("credibility") but really dislike your selfish motives and that you're in it for the money only and that you don't genuinely care ("self-orientation"). I might trust your "reliability" (the repeated experience of links between promises and action; the repeated experience of expectations fulfilled), but greatly dislike your style of dealing with me, plus the fact that so many "difficult" subjects are barred from conversation ("intimacy"). To better understand the economics of connections, consider the following "trust equation" by Charles Green:

$$\text{Trustworthiness} = (\text{Credibility} + \text{Reliability} + \text{Intimacy})/\text{Self-orientation}$$

At heart, by assigning values to the four factors, the formula can be used to determine the amount of trust in a relationship, which can be especially helpful to you in comparing various relationships.

Trust is essential for fostering a productive consultant-client relationship, as it ensures that all parties are committed to the success of the project.

Management models: Strategic, tactical, and operational

To professionally help the client, a consultant's intervention needs to be realistic, disciplined, practical, creative, method-driven and evidence-informed. Nevertheless, the management consultant also needs to be vigilant in not allowing models to become overly mechanical or "robotic". That being said, for every new consulting project, consultants should approach the problem with a fresh, unbiased mindset that suits each client's unique situation.

Because it's not really possible to detail every management model used by consultants, let's only zero in on three example frameworks of strategic, tactical, and operational models.

Strategic models (*enterprise positioning/mobilizing*) can help frame the strategic position of an enterprise and give answers to strategic questions. For instance, to help formulate and progress strategy, consultants can use *strategic dialogue*, developed by Berenschot. This systematic methodology is composed of three phases (strategic questions) and seven steps. It's important to note that to go from strategy formulation to execution, various in-depth analyses need to be carried out for each step. Here's just an overview of this management model (representative analyses are simply put forward in brackets for consideration):

Phase 1: *What does your playing field look like?*

1 Strategic window and ambition (e.g., Greiner's growth model)

Phase 2: *Which game(s) do you want to play?*

2 Outside-in competitive analysis (e.g., Porter's five industry forces analysis)
3 Inside-out analysis (e.g., Porter's value chain analysis; the DuPont analysis)
4 Synthesis and strategic options (e.g., SWOT/SOAR analysis)
5 Appreciation and strategic choices (e.g., Scenario planning; risk/reward analysis)

Phase 3: *How do you play a winning game?*

6 Elaboration and planning (e.g., Strategic HRM model; Henderson and Venkatraman's strategic alignment model)
7 Execution and monitoring (e.g., The balanced scorecard)

Tactical models (*(re)design/enterprise*) are used to direct enterprise processes, resources, capabilities, and talent. They also address critical "how to" questions when researching and reengineering enterprises. By way of illustration, let's examine *business process reengineering (BPR)*. Specifically, having determined strategy, you may want to critically re-evaluate and radically redesign organizational processes. According to Michael Hammer and James Champy, consultants, BPR project can be led in four phases:

- **Phase 1**: *Define scope and establish goal(s)*
  Clear signals include hostility and redundant communication, e.g., too many meetings and emails.

- **Phase 2**: *Redesign process(es)*
  Priorities include efficiency measures, critical success metrics and output levels.

- **Phase 3**: *Determine management*
  Priorities include choosing management methods, determining reward systems, managing performance, continuing L&D.

- **Phase 4**: *Execute and consolidate*
  Priorities include leading a change initiative in a disciplined way, and consolidating gains by continuing to remove organizational processes and policies that inhibit change, and by establishing new, related programs.

Upon successful implementation of BPR, the enterprise may enjoy several tangible benefits like significant improvement in speed, quality and service; substantial reduction in costs and indirect labor; and marked increase in revenues.

Operational models (*execution*) are deployed to make the most effective use of the operational processes and actions, to help improve execution and transform organizations, and to implement next practices in enterprises. Case in point: *the plan–do–study–act (PDSA) cycle*. The PDSA cycle, advised by W. Edwards Deming, is composed of four stages: *plan*, *do*, *study*, and *act*. It's a simple and powerful methodology for developing, testing, and implementing changes to any process that will lead to continuous improvement and long-term organizational learning.

- **Plan**: Define the process, players, and expectations. Establish a challenging target for improvement and develop action plans to achieve the target. Consultants will need to analyze the current situation, describe process(es) and select the most promising solution(s).
- **Do**: Implement the plan on a trial basis by running disciplined experiments. By doing so, consultants will not use up all the resources, rather they will learn and see.
- **Study**: Check the results of the experiment. Did process performance improvement come? What else can be improved? Is further experimentation needed? In what shape and form?
- **Act**: Select the best change or solution. During this stage, the improvements are standardized, and the final plan is executed as a current best practice and communicated throughout the enterprise. What did you conclude from *this* cycle? Because PDSA means never being satisfied with the status quo, the whole cycle starts over again in an iterative process to identify other improvement opportunities or next practices.

The central proposition of PDSA is that improvement is the result of the application of knowledge – knowledge developed through a process of continued L&D.

🔊 Thinking critically: Issues

Love it or hate it, management consulting, remains an alluring yet misunderstood profession. While much is claimed of management consultancy by critics and celebrants alike, many still wonder exactly what management consultants *actually* do. The simple answer is that they uncover reliable intelligence and insights needed to drive smart decision-making. As organizations seek new ways to optimize the workforce, support business goals, increase revenues, maximize efficiency and control costs, demand for professional consulting services will only mushroom.

However, some have a love-hate relationship with consultants and are rather skeptical about the value of consultants' advice. This skepticism comes about because some consultants speak with a lot of clichés and buzzwords – and rebadge existing organizational practices (think: "agile", "lean", "scientific management", etc.), but may lack the specialized knowledge the business is seeking. Some critics say, consultants foment secrecy, or just snoop around to only produce a report that tells something that is already known. Unquestionably, "impression management" and introducing (or selling) management fashions and fads are core to some consultancies. Moreover, the consultant may simply be inexperienced in the industry/sector.

In terms of compensation, the typical billing and salary structure in consulting firms worldwide requires consultants to generate three times their salary in billings to clients. For instance, a consultant making $100,000 USD per year should generate annual fees of $300,000 USD. Typically, the first portion covers their salary, the second portion covers operational costs, and the final portion represents profits distributed among the partners. Despite being (astronomically) expensive, the consultant's fees are not typically based on the success of the project; there is very little to no assurance that the consultancy will be successful, depending on the signed contract and who is taking on the greater risk.

Beware of the idea that consultants will want to come do a preliminary research at your expense before they formulate their approach. Indeed, any consultancy would wish to work within the confines of their own know-how, as well as their own experience. You might not always want some tried-and-true method that has "worked miracles" for someone else, yet did so in contexts and conditions that are radically different from yours. Although successful prior experience is priceless, it may have relatively limited value if the organizational environment or the business scenario are significantly different.

Likewise, with so many consulting firms on the market and rising competition, it is often difficult to tell how they vary from one another or what a consultancy's unique selling points or "added value" could be. Even big and well-established consultancies can be ill-suited. Their wealth of experience across different industries and in multiple locations worldwide may eventually result in a popular "flagship" (cookie-cutter) product, which they may be hesitant to tweak, or even give up, whenever they come across anything new. In contrast, smaller, lesser-known but highly specialist consultancies (*boutique* consulting firms) may offer the same advice – or even more professional (and more personalized) services than more prestigious (and much more expensive!) consultancies.

Moreover, many today would criticize the term "professionalism" being applied to the professional services industry, especially management consulting. Interestingly, the word *profession* has its origins in Middle English (denoting the vow made on entering a religious order): via Old French from Latin *professio(n-)*, from *profiteri* "announce a belief" or "declare publicly", which derives from the notion of an occupation that one "professes" to be skilled in.

While professions like medicine or law can be held accountable for their actions (doctors or lawyers may not "profess" that they are high-quality "experts" without being held to standards of, say, "malpractice"), management consultancies somehow managed to "hack it" and avoid this by claiming that this is only "advice". Be that as it may, the situation gets more nuanced with the different types of consultancy activity, as Alexander Hehmeyer, a lawyer by profession, a former editor of the *California Law Review*, and Chairman of the Board, Advisor, and Chief Financial Officer (CFO) at Rootstock Software, a provider of cloud enterprise resource planning (ERP) manufacturing solutions, headquartered in San Ramon, California, elucidates:

> For example, in general or strategic consulting, there is no one "correct" strategy or course of action. So a general standard of care would apply to their work. Unless somehow there is gross negligence or deliberate sabotage or intent to harm or something like that, there would be no liability for advice that turns out to be wrong. Essentially, outcomes of strategic and general advice are inherently uncertain. However, management consulting for matters such as computer program implementation are different than strategic consulting, and should meet the same standards as doctors, lawyers and accountants. In actuality, they represent to clients that they are implementation experts. Therefore, they should be responsible for the outcome in most cases. Basically, if they fail to achieve an implementation and are proven incompetent or negligent – they can and should be liable. Of course, their engagement contract can try to exonerate them if they fail, but that only goes so far.

Ultimately, if the consultant's role is as impactful as many argue, we should be able to observe its merit in market values and economic reactions. Specifically, looking at how the stock market reacts to the public announcement of the hiring of management consultants and whether it differentially values clients on the basis of their financial profitability and the brand-name of the engaged consultant is an interesting thing to do. Evidently, most clients who publicize that they've hired management consultants do experience a rise in their market value. Research by Donald Bergh and Patrick Gibbons finds that the client firms that have the highest financial profitability show the biggest growth, by way of drawing from signaling theory. Be that as it may, their research suggests that stock market reactions to an organization's announcement that it has hired an external consultant do not seem to positively correlate with the consultancy's brand reputation. That is to say, clients hiring the most well-known global consultancies, such as Bain, Boston Consulting Group, Booz Allen Hamilton, McKinsey & Company, do not realize any different market response than those clients that engaged other advisory firms.

Looking to the future of the industry, it's recognized that by 2050 the advice business may differ from what it is now, possibly by increasing the use of AI-driven "robo-consulting", for example, in the domains of healthcare, law or finance.

 ## Applications

As it happens, the most productive engagements with an external consultant are carefully planned to balance sound research with creative application. To effectively execute consulting engagements, consultancy may have a "product" as well as a "process" orientation.

Methods used in consultancy

If they are to deliver reliable insights to their client, consultants must be familiar with different research techniques – both qualitative and quantitative. The following qualitative and quantitative techniques are commonly used in management consultancy:

Qualitative (phenomenological to cover a number of viewpoints). To gather necessary data, this approach uses:

- *ethnography* (participant observation),
- *interviews* (structured, semi-structured, and unstructured), and
- *ground work* (reviewing existing documentation, emails, reports, etc.).

Quantitative (empirical). To collect necessary data, this approach uses:

- *surveys* and *questionnaires,*
- *experiments* (for example, quasi-experimental design), and
- *business process modeling* and *simulations* (to model data, behaviors, enterprises, and their operations).

In practice, as more firms pay scrupulous attention to delivering concrete results through improved systems and processes, on consultancy projects, management analysts deploy both epistemological approaches through mixed research methods.

The consulting cycle

Managing co-active relationships with clients using the "consulting cycle" can come together as follows:

1 *Starting the client-centered intervention:* gaining entry
2 *Contracting* (both formal and psychological): clarifying expectations, negotiating each other's wants and offers, coping with mixed motivation – if any, surfacing client's concerns about exposure, loss of control, or just looking foolish
3 *Collecting and categorizing data,* and *feeding it back*
4 *Making sense* of organizational and human process data and *diagnosing the problem*: identifying scope and scale of the issues, plus using theories and models
5 *Generating options*: ask *what if? What would have to be true?*
6 *Execution*: facilitating and helping your client take action
7 *Extension, recycle* or *disengagement* (plus, knowledge transfer, retainer, and follow-up)
8 *Evaluating* the client-centric assignment, and *self-evaluating* (incl. project review and the lessons learned)

The client's perspective

Let's now zoom in on the client – here are some recommended steps and "best practice" in seeking real help from management consultants faster:

1 *Define the specific problem, project or specialist task(s).*
   What's the issue for which you're considering seeking outside help?
2 *Try working out how to solve the problem **without** turning to management consultants.*
   Management consultants can be high-priced and time-taking since they must thoroughly understand how your business operates, the organizational structure, the culture, the philosophy, practices and policies, the products, and a who's who of the key players in your organization. If you could only figure out an easier solution to tackle the issue, you might actually save both time and money. By way of illustration, conceivably, a senior executive who just left the company would come visit and spend a few days strolling around and mingling with people to help you see perhaps something new, to help you reframe or embrace the problem, or to prove that even if you haven't quite got the answer yet, you are on the right track. Alternatively, have one or two business school professors from a local business school over to lunch to discuss it, as long as you know and trust them. Go to the next step, if you're still sitting on the fence.
3 *Turn to professional management consultants.*
   Assuming you correctly worked out and got the issue, and given that you can explain it clearly to an "outsider", somebody who has never been inside your company, then, you may want to "brief" one or more management consultancies, and ask them to bid for the business and submit their written "proposals".
   Importantly, produce and present consultants with a clear and realistic brief, the foundation of your interactions with them, a framework from which they cannot deviate. The brief should include: a description of your enterprise, a description of the challenge, and of what you want to achieve really. As part of a preliminary screening process, the consultant's proposal should include: executive summary, their understanding of the problem, organization and the industry, any relevant evidence of expertise and experience of the consultancy in projects of this nature, a work-plan, timeline and quality control measures and success metrics, the team (incl. roles and experience), their approach, tools and models, the fees, the reports and any systems that will be delivered, and any input expected by you/the client company. (Note to client firm: *If you're not satisfied with any part of the consultancy proposal, don't hire them. Make certain that the "human chemistry" is right, too.*)
4 *Choose between alternatives.*
   Whether you continue with the advisors or execute your own rough-cut strategy is up to you to decide. Ask yourself: Can you afford it if the consultants are able to successfully deliver the intended outcome(s)? Do you have the

capabilities/management systems necessary to put your strategy into action? What's the timescale for this?

5 *Own the solution, if possible.*

Should you choose to continue working with the consultants, leading the ensuing step and continuously monitoring the execution should come high on your priority list. Moreover, if it can be done, make sure that local ownership of the solution is attained as soon as possible. Remember: the implementation will be smooth and more valuable only when the new arrangements are running well and possibly owned by your own enterprise.

Case alert! Case classic

Enron explained

LOOK IT UP: Seijts, G.H. (2016). Enron explained. *Ivey Business Journal*, March/April. Retrieved from https://iveybusinessjournal.com/enron-explained/

Your task: Read the *Ivey Business Journal* interview with Andrew "Andy" Fastow, former Enron CFO. Did anything surprise you?

Reflect upon the following:

"When we did these creative deals, they weren't hidden. We had parties to celebrate them. We got awards for them. Magazines wrote articles that extolled the virtues of them" – Andrew "Andy" Fastow, former CFO at Enron, an energy company employing 21,000 people and with revenues of $111 billion in 2000, named by *Fortune* magazine "America's Most Innovative Company" – for six consecutive years.

Is there sometimes only a very *fine line* between *creative* and *criminal*?

"Andy, *every single deal* you've done at Enron has been *approved*. Every deal is *technically* correct, and therefore by definition, whatever pops out the bottom is *not materially misleading*" – the head of Arthur Andersen's energy practice.

To gain a deeper understanding of the case, search online for Arthur Andersen, the accountants who audited Enron's accounts, to find out more about the advice they gave. Why was Arthur Andersen found guilty in the Enron case? To what extent did the Enron scandal cause the dissolution of Arthur Andersen, once one of the world's top five accounting firms?

"Businesses really do operate to a large degree in *grey* areas, so today's students will eventually be put in a position that pressures them to compromise principles. So they need to expect it and get ready for it because it's coming" – Andrew "Andy" Fastow, former Enron CFO.

Do you agree with this? Why or why not? Give your reasons.

Discuss your feeling about Andy Fastow. Can you understand his behavior and actions? Do you feel sympathetic toward him? Did his punishment fit the crime? What skills does he have that he could use to start a new career? If you were counseling Andy, what occupations would you recommend?

To record your critical insights, use the Case Analysis Record provided in Appendix 2.

Greater good corner: Get ready to exercise your ethics

Take a stance: What would *you* do?

Dilemma and decision: Consultant with a moral sense

StratCo (not its real name), a global strategy consultancy, is pleased with one of their key clients' performance, *GuardTech* (not its real name), a smart defense systems company. Since the consultants began advising GuardTech three years ago, the company has generated significant profits and a 15% growth rate. John Q. Public (not his real name), a senior strategy consultant at StratCo, was first made aware of a knotty problem when the GuardTech CFO requested him to lie to one of the company's partners about an investment. This served as the first red flag of governance risk. He said "No!" for moral reasons, ... and shortly after, his supervisor moved him to a different organization.

Not long ago, John discovered that GuardTech was committing sophisticated fraud and he suddenly finds himself in a moral bind: should he inform an independent financial regulator of what he knows? Both businesses are quite strong and even if he has evidence, his claims might not be believed and, if that is the case, he will never be able to land another consulting job...

Given John's moral dilemma, he faces two primary choices. What are the consequences of the two choices John Q. Public has?

If John chooses to report the fraud and notify a regulator, and they start an inquiry:

- He may be fired right away.
- He may be sued.

- He may be required to give a deposition in court against former coworkers and friends.
- Big fines may be imposed on executives of both companies and/or they could even end up in jail (monetary fines often don't work; a jail sentence *will* alarm executives).
- StratCo and GuardTech may collapse after the alleged massive fraud.

How might these consequences influence John's decision? What other potential consequences may follow from John's decision?

Alternatively, if John chooses to remain silent and to quit as a senior strategy consultant at StratCo…

- There's a chance the scam won't be brought to light – for a long time.
- He may certainly start working for another consultancy, but he'd have to lie about why he left StratCo. Yet, if the lie is exposed, he might be dismissed.
- He will feel guilty for failing to prevent this serious fraud.
- It's also likely that as time passes, things will grow much worse.

How might these consequences affect John's sense of responsibility and ethics? What other potential consequences may follow from John's decision? What other steps can John consider taking?

Now, what would *you* do? What do you recommend be done to resolve this issue?

Time out: Journal entry

Thought Sparks: A few reflections, insightful ideas, actionable suggestions, strategic thinking, and key takeaways from this unit.

Learning never stops… So, pause for a few minutes and reflect in writing on your personal learning experience and beliefs. Through writing in your journal, you develop your awareness of your own beliefs and attitudes. Now, consolidate what you have learned in this unit.

1 How have your beliefs and ideas about management consulting changed since you began the unit?

    ....
    ....
    ....

2 Thinking about the problems presented in the unit, write about whether you have found solutions to these problems.

....
....
....

3 How confident do you now feel about serving as a trusted management consultant?

....
....
....

4 What would you still like to have clarified? What remaining concerns do you have?

....
....
....

5 What more would you like to learn about the topic, now that you have completed this unit?

....
....
....

6 If you want, doodle/draw something you like about consulting. This can be as abstract as you wish.

....
....
....

Remember: It's particularly useful to re-visit journal entries several times and see how themes have recurred or your thoughts have changed over time. Now, repeat "Your Take".

Making connections: Related units and models

- U 1. **Behavioral economics and policy 101**: For humans (see pp. 9–26)
- U 3. **Strategic transformation:** Strategy choice-making (see pp. 61–81)
- U 4. **SOAR:** Possibility thinking in positive strategic dialog (see pp. 82–95)
- U 5. **Dialogic organization development (OD):** Leading positive organizational change (see pp. 103–121)

- U 6. **Design-driven organization:** Human-centered design thinking and innovation execution (see pp. 122–139)
- U 10. **Executive coaching:** Whoop it up! (see pp. 204–219)
- U 11. **So, you want to go global?** Becoming an instant international (see pp. 227–237)
- U 12. **Small world:** Are you a culturally intelligent organization? (see pp. 238–250)
- U 13. **Progress with purpose:** The "good" enterprise (see pp. 257–272)
- U 14. **Oops! I messed up.** Why good people do bad things every so often (see pp. 273–287)
- Add in more related models you may want to remember: _____.

Industry snapshot

Arthur Andersen. (n.d.). Retrieved from: https://en.wikipedia.org/wiki/Arthur_ Andersen

Enron. (2000). Retrieved from: https://web.archive.org/web/20000620173849/ http://www.enron.com/ at the Wayback Machine (archived June 20, 2000).

Deep dive: Main references and resources

Alvehus, J. (2021). *The logic of professionalism: Work and management in professional service organizations.* Bristol: Bristol University Press.
Anand, V., Glick, W.H., & Manz, C.C. (2002). Thriving on the knowledge of outsiders: Tapping organizational social capital. *Academy of Management Perspectives*, 16(1): 87–101.
Berenschot. (2002). *Het strategieboek I.* Amsterdam: Nieuwezijds. [*The strategy book I.*]
Berenschot. (2006). *Het strategieboek II: Nieuwe speelvelden.* The Hague: SDU. [*The strategy book II: New playing fields.*]
Bergh, D.D., & Gibbons, P. (2011). The stock market reaction to the hiring of management consultants: A signalling theory approach. *Journal of Management Studies*, 48(3): 544–567.
Berglund, J., & Werr, A. (2000). The invincible character of management consulting rhetoric: How one blends incommensurates while keeping them apart. *Organization*, 7(4): 633–655.
Bhatt, M., & Vakkayil, J. (2023). Belongingness on the go: Examining road warrior consultants' experiences of belongingness with their firms. *Canadian Journal of Administrative Sciences / Revue Canadienne des Sciences de l'Administration*, 40(4): 458–473.
Biggs, D. (2010). *Management consulting: A guide for students.* Hampshire: Cengage Learning.
Birkinshaw, J., & Lancefield, D. (2023, June 13). How professional services firms dodged disruption. *MIT Sloan Management Review.* Retrieved from: https://sloanreview.mit.edu/article/how-professional-services-firms-dodged-disruption/
Block, P. (2023). *Flawless consulting: A guide to getting your expertise used* (4th edition). Hoboken, NJ: Wiley.
BLS (Bureau of Labor Statistics). (2019). *Occupational outlook handbook: Management analysts.* Washington, DC: Bureau of Labor Statistics, U.S. Department of Labor. Retrieved from: www.bls.gov/ooh/business-and-financial/management-analysts.htm
Bourgoin, A., & Harvey, J.-F. (2018, July 27). How consultants project expertise and learn at the same time. *Harvard Business Review.* Retrieved from: https://hbr.org/2018/07/how-consultants-project-expertise-and-learn-at-the-same-time

Bourgoin, A., & Harvey, J.-F. (2018). Professional image under threat: Dealing with learning–credibility tension. *Human Relations*, 71(12): 1611–1639.

Boussebaa, M., Morgan, G., & Sturdy, A. (2012). Constructing global firms? National, transnational and neocolonial effects in international management consultancies. *Organization Studies*, 33(4): 465–486.

Bouwmeester, O., Versteeg, B., van Bommel, K., & Sturdy, A. (2022). Accentuating dirty work: Coping with psychological taint in elite management consulting. *German Journal of Human Resource Management*, 36(4): 411–439.

Buono, A.F. (2023). A humble giant: Reframing the management consulting challenge. *The Journal of Applied Behavioral Science*, 59(2): 197–201.

CIMC. (n.d.). Chartered Institute of Management Consultants. Retrieved from: www.cimcglobal.org

Clark, T., & Salaman, G. (1998). Creating the "right" impression: Towards a dramaturgy of management consultancy. *The Service Industries Journal*, 18(1): 18–38.

Clegg, S.R., Kornberger, M., & Rhodes, C. (2004). Noise, parasites and translation: Theory and practice in management consulting. *Management Learning*, 35(1): 31–44.

Cockman, P., Evans, B., & Reynolds, P. (1992). *Client-centred consulting: A practical guide for internal advisers and trainers*. London: McGraw-Hill.

Coghlan, D. (2024). *Edgar H. Schein: The Artistry of a reflexive organizational scholar-practitioner*. London & New York, NY: Routledge.

Collins, D. (2004). Who put the con in consultancy? Fads, recipes and "vodka margarine". *Human Relations*, 57(5): 553–572.

Craig, D. (2005). *Rip-off! The scandalous inside story of the management consulting money machine*. London: Original Book Co.

Crossan, M., Seijts, G., & Furlong, B. (2024). *The character compass: Transforming leadership for the 21st century*. London & New York, NY: Routledge.

David, R.J., Sine, W.D., & Haveman, H.A. (2013). Seizing opportunity in emerging fields: How institutional entrepreneurs legitimated the professional form of management consulting. *Organization Science*, 24(2): 356–377.

Evans, J., & Lindsay, W. (2020). *Managing for quality and performance excellence* (11th edition). Boston, MA: Cengage.

Evans, B., Reynolds, P., & Cockman, P. (1992). Consulting and the process of learning. *Journal of European Industrial Training*, 16(2): 7–11.

Fincham, R., Clark, T., Handley, K., & Sturdy, A. (2008). Configuring expert knowledge: The consultant as sector specialist. *Journal of Organizational Behavior*, 29(8): 1145–1160.

Fleming, P. (2023). "Never let a good crisis go to waste": How consulting firms are using COVID-19 as a pretext to transform universities and business school education. *Academy of Management Learning & Education*, 22(3): 425–438.

Furusten, S. (2009). Management consultants as improvising agents of stability. *Scandinavian Journal of Management*, 25(3): 264–274.

Gardner, H.K., Anand, N., & Morris, T. (2008). Chartering new territory: Diversification, legitimacy, and practice area creation in professional service firms. *Journal of Organizational Behavior*, 29(8): 1101–1121.

Glückler, J., & Armbrüster, T. (2003). Bridging uncertainty in management consulting: The mechanisms of trust and networked reputation. *Organization Studies*, 24(2): 269–297.

Groysberg, B., & Lee, L.-E. (2008). The effect of colleague quality on top performance: The case of security analysts. *Journal of Organizational Behavior*, 29(8): 1123–1144.

Haas, M.R. (2006). Acquiring and applying knowledge in transnational teams: The roles of cosmopolitans and locals. *Organization Science*, 17(3): 367–384.

Hammer, M., & Champy, J. (2006). *Reengineering the corporation: A manifesto for business revolution*. New York, NY: HarperCollins Publishers.

Harvey, W.S., Morris, T., & Müller Santos, M. (2017). Reputation and identity conflict in management consulting. *Human Relations*, 70(1): 92–118.

Heusinkveld, S., & Benders, J. (2005). Contested commodification: Consultancies and their struggle with new concept development. *Human Relations*, 58(3): 283–310.

Heusinkveld, S., & Visscher, K. (2012). Practice what you preach: How consultants frame management concepts as enacted practice. *Scandinavian Journal of Management*, 28(4): 285–297.

Hicks, J., Nair, P., & Wilderom, C.P.M. (2009). What if we shifted the basis of consulting from knowledge to knowing? *Management Learning*, 40(3): 289–310.

Höner, D., & Mohe, M. (2009). Client–consultant interaction: Capturing social practices of professional service production. *Scandinavian Journal of Management*, 25(3): 299–312.

IC. (n.d.). Institute of Consulting (Chartered Management Institute). Retrieved from: www.managers.org.uk/institute-of-consulting/

ICMCI (CMC-Global). (n.d.). International Council of Management Consulting Institutes. Retrieved from: www.cmc-global.org

IMC (IMC USA). (n.d.). Institute of Management Consultants USA. Retrieved from: https://imcusa.org

ISO. (n.d.). ISO 20700:2017 (Guidelines for management consultancy services). Retrieved from: www.iso.org/standard/63501.html

Jones, C., & Livne-Tarandach, R. (2008). Designing a frame: Rhetorical strategies of architects. *Journal of Organizational Behavior*, 29(8): 1075–1099.

Kantola, A., & Seeck, H. (2011). Dissemination of management into politics: Michael Porter and the political uses of management consulting. *Management Learning*, 42(1): 25–47.

Keidar, N. (2023). Cities and their gurus: The role of superstar consultants in post-political urban governance. *International Journal of Urban and Regional Research*, 47(2): 279–298.

Kipping, M., Bühlmann, F., & David, T. (2019). Professionalization through symbolic and social capital: Evidence from the careers of elite consultants. *Journal of Professions and Organization*, 6(3): 265–285.

Kipping, M., & Clark, T. (Eds). (2012). *The Oxford handbook of management consulting*. Oxford: Oxford University Press.

Kirkpatrick, I., Sturdy, A., Reguera-Alvarado, N., Blanco-Oliver, A., & Veronesi, G. (2019). The impact of management consultants on public service efficiency. *Policy & Politics*, 47(1): 77–95.

Kirkpatrick, I., Sturdy, A., Reguera-Alvarado, N., Blanco-Oliver, A., & Veronesi, G. (2022). The management consultancy effect: Demand inflation and its consequences in the sourcing of external knowledge. *Public Administration*, 100(3): 488–506.

Kirkpatrick, I., Sturdy, A., Reguera-Alvarado, N., & Veronesi, G. (2023). Beyond hollowing out: Public sector managers and the use of external management consultants. *Public Administration Review*, 83(3): 537–551.

Løwendahl, B.R., Revang, Ø., & Fosstenløkken, S.M. (2001). Knowledge and value creation in professional service firms: A framework for analysis. *Human Relations*, 54(7): 911–931.

Maister, D.H., Green, C.H., & Galford, R.M. (2021). *The trusted advisor* (20th anniversary edition). New York, NY: Free Press.

Mazzucato, M., & Collington. R. (2023). *The big con: How the consulting industry weakens our businesses, infantilizes our governments, and warps our economies*. London: Allen Lane.

MCA. (n.d.). Management Consultancies Association. Retrieved from: www.mca.org.uk

Mohe, M., & Seidl, D. (2011). Theorizing the client-consultant relationship from the perspective of social-systems theory. *Organization*, 18(1): 3–22.

Nanda, A., & Narayandas, D. (2020). What professional service firms must do to thrive. *Harvard Business Review*, 99(2): 98–107.

Nikolova, N., Reihlen, M., & Schlapfner, J.-F. (2009). Client–consultant interaction: Capturing social practices of professional service production. *Scandinavian Journal of Management*, 25(3): 289–298.

Noordegraaf, M. (2011). Risky business: How professionals and professional fields (must) deal with organizational issues. *Organization Studies*, 32(10): 1349–1371.

O'Mahoney, J. (2022). *Growth: Building a successful consultancy in the digital age*. London & New York, NY: Routledge.

O'Mahoney, J., Sturdy, A., & Galazka, A. (2021). Acquiring knowledge through management consultancy: A national culture perspective. *Journal of Management & Organization*, 1–20.

Pemer, F., Börjeson, L., & Werr, A. (2020). The role of chief executive tenure for public organizations' hiring of management consultants. *Governance*, 33(2): 269–285.

Phelan, K. (2013). *I'm sorry I broke your company: When management consultants are the problem, not the solution*. San Francisco, CA: Berrett-Koehler.

Ram, M. (2000). Hustling, hassling and making it happen: Researching consultants in a small firm context. *Organization*, 7(4): 657–677.

Richter, A., & Schröder, K. (2008). Determinants and performance effects of the allocation of ownership rights in consulting firms. *Journal of Organizational Behavior*, 29(8): 1049–1074.

Rousseau, J. (2015). The case for design consulting. *Design Management Review*, 26(3): 13–15.

Rummler, G.A., & Brache, A.P. (2012). *Improving performance: How to manage the white space on the organization chart*. San Francisco, CA: Jossey-Bass.

Sayyadi, M., Collina, L., & Provitera, M.J. (2023). The end of management consulting as we know it? *Management Consulting Journal*, 6(2): 7–10.

Schein, E. (2016). *Humble consulting: How to provide real help faster*. Oakland, CA: Berrett-Koehler Publishers.

Seijts, G.H. (2016). Enron explained. *Ivey Business Journal*, March/April. Retrieved from https://iveybusinessjournal.com/enron-explained/

Shaw, D. (2022a). *An ancient Greek philosophy of management consulting. Thinking differently about its assumptions, principles and practice*. Cham, Switzerland: Springer.

Shaw, D. (2022b). Would Plato have banned the management consultants? *Philosophy of Management*, 20(2): 101–111.

Söderlund, J. (2011). Pluralism in project management: Navigating the crossroads of specialization and fragmentation. *International Journal of Management Reviews*, 13(2): 153–176.

Strang, D., David, R.J., & Akhlaghpour, S. (2014). Coevolution in management fashion: An agent-based model of consultant-driven innovation. *American Journal of Sociology*, 120(1): 226–264.

Sturdy, A. (2011). Consultancy's consequences? A critical assessment of management consultancy's impact on management. *British Journal of Management*, 22(3): 517–530.

Sturdy, A., Clark, T., Fincham, R., & Handley, K. (2009). Between innovation and legitimation—Boundaries and knowledge flow in management consultancy. *Organization*, 16(5): 627–653.

Sturdy, A., & O'Mahoney, J. (2018). Explaining national variation in the use of management consulting knowledge: A framework. *Management Learning*, 49(5): 537–558.

Sturdy, A., Werr, A., & Buono, A.F. (2009). The client in management consultancy research: Mapping the territory. *Scandinavian Journal of Management*, 25(3): 247–252.

Sturdy, A., & Wright, C. (2008). A consulting diaspora? Enterprising selves as agents of enterprise. *Organization*, 15(3): 427–444.

Sturdy, A., & Wright, C. (2011). The active client: The boundary-spanning roles of internal consultants as gatekeepers, brokers and partners of their external counterparts. *Management Learning*, 42(5): 485–503.

Tkaczyk, B. (2018). Business leadership for the management consulting industry: A new model for the greater good. *Rutgers Business Review*, 3(1): 53–66.

Tkaczyk, B. (2018, October 3). Humanizing robo-consulting. *Association for Talent Development (Insights)*. Retrieved from: www.td.org/content/atd-blog/humanizing-robo-consulting

Tkaczyk, B. (2021). ERG strategizing: A professional approach to positive human resource and organization development consulting. In *Leading positive organizational change: Energize – redesign – gel* (pp. 47–74). London & New York, NY: Routledge.

Vogelpohl, A., Hurl, C., Howard, M., Marciano, R., Purandare, U., & Sturdy, A. (2022) Pandemic consulting. How private consultants leverage public crisis management, *Critical Policy Studies*, 16(3): 371–381.

Wallace, J.E., & Kay, F.M. (2008). The professionalism of practising law: A comparison across work contexts. *Journal of Organizational Behavior*, 29(8): 1021–1047.

Walton, M., & Deming, W.E. (1988). *The deming management method*. New York, NY: A Perigee Book.

Whittle, A. (2008). From flexibility to work–life balance: Exploring the changing discourses of management consultants. *Organization*, 15(4): 513–534.

Wright, C. (2009). Inside out? Organizational membership, ambiguity and the ambivalent identity of the internal consultant. *British Journal of Management*, 20(3): 309–322.

Wright, C., Sturdy, A., & Wylie, N. (2012). Management innovation through standardization: Consultants as standardizers of organizational practice. *Research Policy*, 41(3): 652–662.

Xie, W. (2023). Using Chinese wisdom to rekindle strategy consulting. *Management Consulting Journal*, 6(2): 16–20.

10 Executive coaching

Whoop it up!

"Everybody needs a coach" – Eric Schmidt

Sneak peek

Focus on: Key concepts and terms

Unit 10

- Championing
- Coach/coachee (link, relationship, partnering)
- Coaching (activity, behavioral, career, co-active, cohort, confidentiality, development plan, effective, elements, ethics, executive, executive leadership team (ELT), exercise, external, fad, formal, goal-focused, group, internal, mindset, life, one-on-one, organizational, peer, people-centered, positive leadership development, positive organizational change, positive psychology, presence, principles, professional, scenario, self-, services, session, skills, solution-focused, standards, strategy, supervision, team, tools, qualities, workplace)
- Coaching culture (benefits)
- Collage, coaching with
- Continuing professional development (CPD)
- Dialogic learning
- Feedback (constructive, honest)
- High performers
- Human resource development (HRD) (executive, strategic, strategy)
- Inquiry (humble, positive)
- Learning and development (L&D) (strategy)

DOI: 10.4324/9781003508274-16

- Listening (reflective, for possibility, supportive, with nuance and sensitivity)
- Mental contrasting with implementation intentions (MCII)
- Naming it
- Performance management process (PMP)
- Playback and check-in
- Positive psychology
- Questioning the status quo
- Sounding board (serve as a)
- Tracking
- Wish, happy outcome, obstacle, plan (WHOOP)

Pause 'N' reflect: On the current issues and trends

Before you complete this unit, think about each of the following statements. Mark each statement:

V – if you *agree.*
X – if you *disagree.*
? – if you are *undecided.*

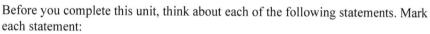

Your Take: Integrative Thinking	*Before doing Unit 10*	*After doing Unit 10*
1 We live in a culture of "telling". All (too!) often we *tell* others what we think they need to know or *should* do.		
2 Solution-focused coaching often differs from consulting.		
3 If I tell someone that I'm a coach, the instant question is: "In which sport?"		
4 Coaching is for failures!		
5 Coaching is a mark of my status – the company pays for my executive coach.		
6 Coaching is not just for problems...		
7 "Coaching is... not my job!" – Line Manager		
8 Executive coaching is a precision tool for optimizing the abilities of leaders.		

Your Take: Integrative Thinking   *Before doing Unit 10   After doing Unit 10*

9 "Executive coaching is a second career" – Soon-to-retire Executive		
10 People-centered coaching is a partnership that thrives on trust, confidence (without attitude), and forward progress.		

After you have done the unit, repeat "Your Take". How has reading the unit clarified the ideas herein? How have your views, feelings and thoughts changed over time?

Lead-in

General discussion points

Individually or in buzz groups, work on the following:

1 *Coaching is a talent development fad.* What do you think?
2 Have *you* ever experienced "executive coaching"? If yes, how did it go? Discuss your experience with a partner or your buzz group.
3 *Coaching is the creative art of facilitating the performance, learning and development (L&D) of another.* Does this description make sense? If so, explain why. What alternatives are there? Jot down your own definition of "coaching".
4 How to ensure high, ethical and consistent coaching standards – across the organization?
5 *The truly successful organization is a learning enterprise. Human resource development (HRD)/L&D has been charged to blueprint and lead the way to organization and individual renewal. In a nutshell, learning is the new form of labor.* Do you agree or disagree with this statement?

Idea watch

Executive coaching, one of the fastest-growing professions worldwide, grounded in dialogic organization development (OD) and the behavioral science of positive psychology, is co-active partnering between (internal or external) professional coaches and executive clients that helps executives to develop more rapidly toward a preferred future state, to set goals, take action, make better decisions, produce results, and to capitalize on their natural strengths and talents. Coaching energizes leaders to maximize their personal and professional potential. It's chiefly about (self-)awareness, discovery, and choice.

Beyond fostering appreciation, aha moments, and choice, coaching is goal-focused and increases performance. The goal-setting process, to ensure continuous L&D, has two parts: skill development and psychological development.

When designing the organizational L&D procedures for maximum performance delivery, the performance management process (PMP) should find an appropriate balance between centering on business targets and control, and achieving a motivating and developmental process for the individual(s) and teams. PMP, if professional, energizes, supports, recognizes and rewards organizational members in achieving their outstanding performance. Moreover, it enables the retention and development of accomplished and devoted individuals who will help the organization to attain both its short-term and longer-term goals. Coaching, a powerful dialogic learning process (it entails connecting with others in ways that lead to a developing awareness of the organizational culture and of how it normally attains its goals), can aid performance management immeasurably.

In line with the focus on performance management, high-performing enterprises have "coaching cultures". High performers are those organizations that perform as well as or better than their competitors in financial performance, employee engagement, customer/client satisfaction and growth potential for the upcoming five years – and, ideally, beyond. Those that strongly agree that their talent development functions enable them to attain their business goals are entities with coaching cultures. The most reported benefits of a coaching culture are: a boost in productivity and well-being, enhanced positive communication and meaning, raised employee engagement, improved collaboration and positive relationships and positive climate, heightened skills-to-performance transfer, demonstrated organizational commitment to strategic HRD, and greater change management success – if integrated with change management efforts.

Coaching, a powerful talent development method, is about inspiring people to do their best. Great coaches ask penetrating questions, listen actively, reflectively and attentively, and empathize. It doesn't mean having all the answers; it's about challenging coachees to come up with the answers on their own. Some popular areas of executive coaching expertise include:

- Behavioral coaching (incl. leader's behaviors, style, vision, practice, and executive presence)
- Career/life coaching (incl. coaching for "transition")
- Coaching for positive leadership development (incl. "leader as coach" program)
- Coaching for positive organizational change (incl. coaching for dialogic OD)
- Coaching for strategy (incl. strategizing to win)
- Executive leadership team (ELT) coaching (coaching ELTs to make sure that the team achieves its goals and intended outcomes)

Assumptions

You cannot force people to learn. The fundamental objective of organizational L&D/HRD is to drive collective progress by fostering collaborative, expert, and ethical stimulation and facilitation of learning and knowledge. This approach supports business goals and develops individual potential.

Coaching, an L&D/HRD method, is not just for problems.

The client is naturally creative, resourceful and whole.

The coach doesn't develop the client, but equips them to develop themselves. The coach is a catalyst, a key element in the process of accelerating lasting positive change.

The coach uses clear evidence-based methodology, but doesn't provide answers or advice. Rather than train, the coach energizes, asks, listens, and invites the client to figure out, ideate, choose, transform, and work out the solution themselves.

The client sets the agenda and takes effective action. The coach holds the client accountable for their actions and (baby) steps.

The coach/client link is a synergistic, professional, dynamic, individualized, trustful, respectful, and equal relationship – the coach and client are co-active collaborators.

In spite of the coach's close working relationship with the client, the coach is not a substitute colleague, fellow executive, business partner or best friend. A happy, healthy, and harmonious relationship is not built on being just "nice"; it's built on being real.

You don't need to work as a coach to deliver brilliant modern coaching. A leader-/manager-as-coach/team leader that uses and sees coaching as a skill-set, can be as successful in coaching as any certified coach.

Extremely good coaches take ownership of their learning and enhance their professional practice for they recognize that continuing professional development (CPD) is vital. For example, you can create your own coaching development plan and/or enroll for advanced training in coaching skills in business school. Given the increasing professionalization of coaching, it's not surprising that you can even study coaching psychology at Masters level (for example, MSc Career Coaching and Coaching Psychology at the Birkbeck Business School, University of London). As Marshall Goldsmith evangelizes, "to help others develop, start with yourself".

 ## Key elements

As shared by Mark Rittenberg, an executive coach and coach's coach, many leaders have mastered the critical analytical tools required for leadership, but far fewer excel in coaching others and unlocking their potential to achieve peak performance. For all that, leaders can learn to become super coaches for their people. Among others, the key coaching elements include:

Primary coaching skills

• Getting things ready – setting the ground rules; preparing the physical setting, also mentally continuing your preparations for the session, incl. self-management; recognizing the coachee's perspective; structuring (using, for example, the WHOOP model), and providing follow-up, to whatever degree necessary, to ensure sustainability.

- Championing – showing that you believe in the client and his/her abilities, and that everybody is capable of more so one should focus on potential rather than past performance (a person's past is no indication of his/her future).
- Questioning the status quo and naming it – delivering unwelcome news, managing conflict positively, and taking intelligent risks.
- Dialogic learning – having a growth mindset; leveraging the power of inquiry; having a heart-to-heart; facilitating successful people-centered interactions and handling issues humanistically; a transformation being more apt to be achieved through "generative conversations" and storytelling.
- Serving as a sounding board – being fully present, and providing an unconditional, non-judgmental, positive regard.
- Providing constructive feedback – offering continual help via reinforcing, refocusing and challenging.

Coaching tools

- Positive inquiry – asking curious open-ended questions: *Out of curiosity, what's on your mind?* (the "fire-up" question); *And what else?* (the "wonder" question); *I think I have a sense of the overall challenge/I think I understand some of what's going on with* [insert name of the person or the situation]. *What's the real challenge here for you?* (the "challenge" question); *What do you want?* (the "foundation" question); *Just so I know…How can I help?* (the "helping" question); *If you're saying Yes to this, what are you saying No to?* (the "action plan" question); and *What was most useful for you?* (the "reflection" question).
- Playback" and "check-in" as listening tools – play back, with empathy, what you've just heard (e.g., "let me make sure I heard you…"), and "check-in" to see if you heard it accurately.
- Tracking – by tracking the course of events or "blind spots" ("what/who has moved you?", "What have you learned?", "What are you feeling?", "What questions have come to the surface?"), it can become evident where the breakdown in a dialogue/partnership occurred.
- Picture collage as a creative coaching tool – an arts-based methodology that unlocks unconscious thinking, enabling profound psychological insight through a deeper and faster exploration of emotions and behaviors.
- Theatre-based techniques – warm-up activities, breathing and voice work, improvisational theatre activities, and personal value-forming stories.

Coaching qualities

- Human chemistry" (building and sustaining "high-quality connections" (HQCs))
- Humble inquiry (the gentle art of asking instead of telling)
- Listening with nuance and sensitivity – "reflective" listening ("What I hear you saying is…"); "supportive" listening ("I'm so sorry. This must be sooo frustrating"); "listening for possibility" ("So, what could you do now?")

- Positive energy and coaching presence – transferring physical, emotional, mental and spiritual energy
- Thinking on one's feet/having curiosity/paradoxical awareness
- Playfulness/humor/joy/fun as perspective
- Relaxation/breathing
- Eye contact
- Voice (*and* silence) – knowing how and when to use them
- Focusing
- Timing
- Intuition and awareness (incl. raising, self-, boundary awareness)
- Nonstop learning (incl. CPD)
- Confidentiality and ethics
- Appreciation and gratitude

Universal communication principles for human connection rooted in cultural anthropology

- Show up and choose to be fully present – energize and live in the moment.
- Pay attention to what has heart and meaning – empathize, and be full-, open-, strong-, clear-hearted.
- Tell the truth without blame or judgment – yes, be honest (but don't be brutal!).
- Be open to outcome, not attached to outcome – be super-flexible, and hold the dialogue open to creative problem-solving at all levels.

The WHOOP method elements

- **W**ish – A wish that is energizing, but possible to fulfill.
- **H**appy **O**utcome – The most desired outcome.
- **O**bstacle – Your major obstacle.
- **P**lan – A strategy for overcoming the obstacle.

 ## Thinking critically: Issues

Although coaching has recently seen explosive growth, it appears that evidence-based coaching is still the least understood L&D intervention. Tensions exist between the need to build a convincing business case for proposed L&D initiatives and the imperative to experiment to develop the new knowledge crucial for innovation and advancement.

Coaching is not just for problems. Effective modern coaching is not about fixing someone's problems, but it is about inspiring and tapping into their personal vision, capabilities, strengths, and talents.

The coach helps (extremely) good leaders further succeed. The coach addresses the client's *whole* life – both business *and* personal goals (clients are empowered to *choose!*) are integrated into the coaching to ensure balance, fulfillment, and life purpose are achieved.

In practice, coaching takes place either *pre-*, looking forward, energizing, and preparing somebody for the event they're about to handle (*What challenges do you expect?*, *How will you respond to this?*, *What could you do if...?*", or *post-*, looking back to reflectively and analytically embed lessons learned (*So, how did it go?*, *What happened that you never expected? What can you learn from that experience?*").

As for the logistics, formal coaching takes place at the client's site (board rooms), at the coach's office, or off-site (e.g., mountain retreats) – or, now, largely, in a virtual space, where coaches work with coachees through some video/call platform. Coaches may contract with clients for a fixed period of time, such as three/six/twelve/eighteen months.

On reflection, there are still marked variations in practice and in standards. Although leaders have a desire to be coached and the benefits of workplace coaching seem impressive for both employees and employers – as it enhances leadership and performance – not all organizations sponsor and manage formal coaching programs that are provided by internal/external professional coaches. Some of the reasons for not having a formal coaching program include:

- Lack of resources, such as time or money
- Lack of knowledge on how to administer the program
- Lack of leadership buy-in
- Organizational culture/size
- Lack of interest or availability from potential coaches/coachees
- Failure of a prior organizational coaching program
- A feeling that coaching isn't valued.

Other critical issues include, for example, whether it is enough to position coaching activities with line managers, viz., more often than not, to tack coaching on to an ever growing to-do list of line manager responsibilities' (*Can they coach their own staff, given the power relationship and the need for no bias in the coaching relationship?*), or, perhaps, to develop a clear, embedded, fully aligned strategy that deploys dedicated coaches to positively "infect" the entire organizational learning culture. The real world is hardly ever so clear-cut since managers have to mix coaching with direction anyway.

Investment in skilled *internal* coaching frequently results from a conviction that an internally run process is less expensive than *external* executive coaching. In this case, prudence is required. In fact, internal coaching can be more expensive in terms of training, of supervising the coaching process and of ensuring workloads are freed so that necessary time to coaching activity is dedicated.

Positive psychology coaching works. Of note, is the fact that optimism – positive expectations about the future based on past experiences – often differs from positive thinking that is based on little more than imagination or wishful dreaming. When it comes to attaining goals, positive thinking (or fantasizing) alone will *not* do the trick. Yes, dreaming about the future may relax you, measurably reducing systolic blood pressure, yet it can actually sap you of the energy you need to take action in pursuit of your goals. Specifically, positive thinking alone can deceive your mind into believing that you've already achieved your goal, decreasing your motivation to reach it. What works beautifully, though, is, what Gabriele Oettingen calls, "mental contrasting with implementation intentions" (MCII), a hybrid, balanced approach that mixes positive thinking *with* "realism". Paradoxically, the challenges we perceive to be the biggest roadblocks to realizing our goals can, in fact, serve to advance them. So, rather than merely dream, Gabriele encourages you to WHOOP – think of a **W**ish. After this, imagine the wish coming true for a little while (**H**appy **O**utcome), allowing your thoughts to roam and sway as they like. Change gears next. Now, picture the **O**bstacles that prevent you from achieving your dream for a few minutes. Lastly, come up with a **P**lan for overcoming those obstacles.

Organizationally speaking, coaching, as a social learning method, is only one way of achieving professional development. There are also other methods organizations can use for executive development that can help them prepare for the future of their careers. Some powerful talent development methods and customized series of development experiences include, for example, formal executive education (generic training rarely realizes strategic potential though, so go for targeted training); social learning (e.g., expert coaching, mentoring, and reverse-mentoring, team "pizza sessions"); on-the-job learning (for example, learning from project reviews); and assessment (collecting information and giving feedback to people about their behavior, communication, style, or skills). All should be part of HRD/L&D strategy.

Ethically speaking, you as a coach must respect and protect the confidentiality of your client's information – except as required by law. Besides, you as a coach must not participate in any sexual or romantic engagement with client(s), or sponsor(s) – the entity (including its representatives) buying and/or arranging or defining the coaching services to be delivered. Remember: in case of (potential) conflict of interest, you as a coach must resolve it by working through the issue with relevant parties, seeking professional assistance, suspending temporarily, or canceling the engagement so as to end the relationship.

 Applications

WHOOP is a science-backed mental strategy that people can adopt to express and fulfill their wishes, set preferences, and change their habits. The WHOOP technique can be used in *self*-coaching, *one-on-one* coaching, *peer* coaching, and *team* coaching.

I   First, name a **WISH** (big or small, long term, or short term) that is energizing, but possible to fulfill.

   Think about the next, say, 24 hours/4 weeks/12 weeks/6 months/12 months: *What is the one thing you would love to see come true?* Choose a wish that feels stretching to you but that you believe you can successfully implement within the specific timeframe.

   Record your wish in 3–6 words: _____

   _____.

II Next, determine the **happiest OUTCOME** and imagine this outcome.

Now, pause for a moment, close your eyes and imagine this most positive outcome. *What would be the nicest thing if your wish was realized? How will accomplishing your dream make you feel?* Visualize it as fully as you can.

Record your thoughts, and your outcome in 3–6 words: _____

_____.

III After that, zoom in on the major **OBSTACLE** that might get in your way – and examine it.

Now, take your time zeroing in on your chief obstacle. *What's holding you back, and what in you could be stopping you? A changing mood? A bad habit? Irrational thinking? Faulty logic? Feeling tired/stressed out? Are the constraints fixed, authentic, elastic, or illusionary?* Dig deeper – what is it really? Figure out your main (inner) obstacle.

Record your true (inner) obstacle in 3–6 words: _____

_____.

IV Lastly, make a **PLAN** of how to overcome the obstacle.

Finally, plan what you can do to surmount your obstacle. *What could you actually do to overcome/remove your obstacle?* Decide on one productive action you will take and/or one creative idea you can apply to overcome it.

Record your effective action/constructive idea in 3–6 words: _____

_____.

and craft your "if-then" plan: *If...* (the obstacle you named), *then I will...* (action or idea you named to overcome obstacle).

Take a break and re-imagine this "if-then" plan – then, just do it!

V **Dialogue building**: If you wish, write a short dialogue based on a typical challenge that you meet in your job. Personalize the dialogue as much as possible:

Coach:
Coachee:
Coach:
Coachee:
Coach:
Coachee:
Coach:
Coachee:
Coach:
Coachee:

When all is said and done, coaches can achieve enhanced effectiveness in instigating the desired positive transformation within organizations by acknowledging that the coaching journey should primarily revolve around the individual's personal vision of an ideal future. This approach is more fruitful than structuring the coaching process around merely addressing existing problems.

Case alert! Case classic

Caterpillar

LOOK IT UP: Anderson, M.C., Anderson, D.L., & Mayo, W.D. (2008). Team coaching helps a leadership team drive cultural change at Caterpillar. *Global Business and Organizational Excellence*, 27(4): 40–50.

Read this case study on how North American Commercial Division (NACD), the biggest of the four marketing divisions of Caterpillar, the world's largest manufacturer of construction equipment, used individual and team coaching to prepare their top leaders for a broad cultural initiative, helping them understand how to be more effective with each other, and then how to drive behavioral change across the business by embodying the principles of service.

Describe their "cultural journey". What kind of team coaching activities did they take part in? Was the "Leading with Insight" model effective? If you were to formally evaluate its application and impact, what would you say?

Reaction:

• Did people like it?

Learning:

• What did they learn?

Behavior:

• Did their behaviors change? Can they now apply the new learnings on-the-job?

Results:

• Was the business impact significant?
• What about the return on investment (ROI)?*
• What about the return on expectations (ROE)? What about other intangible benefits?

*By the way, is it justified to measure ROI on coaching, given the difficulties in quantifying coaching benefits? In this context, ROI measures the financial results of a learning program and is calculated as the net benefit (benefits minus costs) divided by the program costs, multiplied by 100 to convert it to a percent.

To record your critical insights, use the Case Analysis Record provided in Appendix 2.

Greater good corner: Get ready to exercise your ethics

Take a stance: What would *you* do?

Dilemma and Decision: "I'm surrounded by fools, idiots, and people less competent than me".

Here's a role play scenario for a "three-person coaching session".

You are coaching a senior level executive who is an ambitious, able overachiever. Just the same, he has an edge about people – he thinks everybody is incompetent and unprofessional. Basically, every time he builds a bridge, he tears it down. His dominance, narcissism, vanity, and arrogance in the office are damaging the organizational culture and making everybody obsessively anxious, insecure, stressed out, and mistrustful around him.

Would *you* coach this executive? Reflect on the ethical considerations of coaching a client whose actions could negatively impact others. How can you support the executive's development while also ensuring the well-being of his colleagues?

To practice coaching, role-play this scenario as a "coach" and a "coachee". The third person acts as an "observer and feedback-giver" – while observing the coaching session (if possible, record the live performance), evaluate the effectiveness of the session. To do so, go back to "Elements" above, and anatomize: the primary coaching skills, coaching tools, coaching qualities, universal principles, and, if used, the WHOOP technique elements. In the end, give honest feedback to the coach. Now, how did the coachee feel?

Time out: Journal entry

Thought Sparks: A few reflections, insightful ideas, actionable suggestions, strategic thinking, and key takeaways from this unit.

Learning never stops… So, pause for a few minutes and reflect in writing on your personal learning experience and beliefs. Through writing in your journal, you develop your awareness of your own beliefs and attitudes. Now, consolidate what you have learned in this unit.

1   How have your beliefs and ideas about executive coaching changed since you began the unit?

   ....
   ....

2   Thinking about the problems presented in the unit, write about whether you have found solutions to these problems.

   ....
   ....

3   How confident do you now feel about coaching executives and ELTs?

   ....
   ....

4   What would you still like to have clarified? What remaining concerns do you have?

   ....
   ....

5   What more would you like to learn about the topic, now that you have completed this unit?

   ....
   ....

6   If you want, doodle/draw something you like about professional coaching or helping. This can be as abstract as you wish.

   ....
   ....

Remember: It's particularly useful to re-visit journal entries several times and see how themes have recurred or your thoughts have changed over time. Now, repeat "Your Take".

Making connections: Related units and models

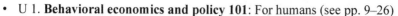

- U 1. **Behavioral economics and policy 101**: For humans (see pp. 9–26)
- U 2. **The kindness advantage**: Cultivating positively energizing leaders and followers (see pp. 27–53)
- U 3. **Strategic transformation:** Strategy choice-making (see pp. 61–81)
- U 4. **SOAR:** Possibility thinking in positive strategic dialog (see pp. 82–95)
- U 5. **Dialogic organization development (OD):** Leading positive organizational change (see pp. 103–121)
- U 6. **Design-driven organization:** Human-centered design thinking and innovation execution (see pp. 122–139)
- U 8. **Once upon a time...** Strategic brand storytelling (see pp. 160–174)
- U 9. **Professional management consulting for real people**: The advice business demystified (see pp. 181–203)
- U 12. **Small world:** Are you a culturally intelligent organization? (see pp. 238–250)
- U 14. **Oops! I messed up.** Why good people do bad things every so often (see pp. 273–287)
- Add in more related models you may want to remember: _____.

Industry snapshot

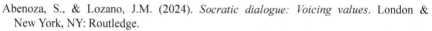

https://careers.caterpillar.com/en/life-caterpillar/life-at-caterpillar/

Deep dive: Main references and resources

Abenoza, S., & Lozano, J.M. (2024). *Socratic dialogue: Voicing values*. London & New York, NY: Routledge.

Anderson, M.C., Anderson, D.L., & Mayo, W.D. (2008). Team coaching helps a leadership team drive cultural change at Caterpillar. *Global Business and Organizational Excellence*, 27(4): 40–50.

Arrien, A. (1993). *The four-fold way: Walking the paths of the warrior, teacher, healer and visionary*. New York, NY: HarperCollins.

ATD. (2017). *Mentoring matters: Developing talent with formal mentoring programs*. Alexandria, VA: The Association for Talent Development.

ATD. (2020). *Managers as coaches: Boosting employee and organizational performance*. Alexandria, VA: The Association for Talent Development.

ATD. (2022). *Coaching: Enhancing leadership and performance*. Alexandria, VA: Association for Talent Development.

Bakhshandeh, B., & Rothwell, W.J. (Eds.). (2024). *Building an organizational coaching culture: Creating effective environments for growth and success in organizations*. London & New York, NY: Routledge.

Batista, E. (2015, February 18). How great coaches ask, listen, and empathize. *Harvard Business Review*. Retrieved from: https://hbr.org/2015/02/how-great-coaches-ask-listen-and-empathize

Berger, W. (2016). *A more beautiful question: The power of inquiry to spark breakthrough ideas*. New York, NY: Bloomsbury.

Boyatzis, R.E., & Jack, A.I. (2018). The neuroscience of coaching. *Consulting Psychology Journal: Practice and Research*, 70(1): 11–27.

Boyatzis, R.E., Smith, M.L., & van Oosten, E. (2019). *Helping people change: Coaching with compassion for lifelong learning and growth*. Boston, MA: Harvard Business Review Press.

Boyatzis, R.E., Hullinger, A., Ehasz, S.F., Harvey, J., Tassarotti, S., Gallotti, A., & Penafort, F. (2022). The grand challenge for research on the future of coaching. *The Journal of Applied Behavioral Science*, 58(2): 202–222.

Bungay Stanier, M. (2016). *The coaching habit: Say less, ask more & change the way you lead forever.* Toronto: Box of Crayons Press.

Clutterbuck, D., Whitaker, C., & Lucas, L. (2016). *Coaching supervision: A practical guide for supervisees*. London & New York, NY: Routledge.

Clutterbuck, D., Gannon, J., Hayes, S., Iordanou, I., Lowe, K., & MacKie, D. (Eds.). (2019). *The practitioner's handbook of team coaching*. London & New York, NY: Routledge.

Coutu, C., & Kauffman, C. (2009). What can coaches do for you? *Harvard Business Review Research Report*, 87(1): 91–97.

Downey, M. (2015). *Effective modern coaching: The principles and art of successful business coaching*. London: LID Publishing Ltd.

Doyle, N., & Mcdowall, A. (2023). *Neurodiversity coaching: A psychological approach to supporting neurodivergent talent and career potential.* London & New York, NY: Routledge.

Egan, T., & Hamlin, R.G. (2014). Coaching, HRD, and relational richness: Putting the pieces together. *Advances in Developing Human Resources*, 16(2): 242–257.

Fey, N., Nordbäck, E., Ehrnrooth, M., & Mikkonen, K. (2022). How peer coaching fosters employee proactivity and well-being within a self-managing Finnish digital engineering company. *Organizational Dynamics*, 51(3): 1–13.

Garvey, B. (2011). *A very short, fairly interesting and reasonably cheap book about coaching and mentoring*. London: Sage.

Goldsmith, M. (2003). Helping successful people get even better. *Business Strategy Review*, 14(1): 9–16.

Hackman, R. (2009). Why teams don't work: The HBR interview by Diane Coutu. *Harvard Business Review*, 87(5): 98–105.

Hackman, R., & Wageman, R. (2005). A theory of team coaching. *Academy of Management Review*, 30(2): 269–287.

Hall, J.A., Holmstrom, A.J., Pennington, N., Perrault, E.K., & Totzkay, D. (2023). Quality conversation can increase daily well-being. *Communication Research*, Online First: 1-25.

HBR. (2014). *HBR guide to coaching employees* (HBR Guide Series). Boston, MA: Harvard Business Review Press.

HCI/ICF. (2018). *Building a coaching culture for change management*. Cincinnati, OH: Human Capital Institute & Lexington, KY: International Coach Federation.

Hoffmann, B., Napiersky, U., & Senior, C. (2023). A sound case for listening. *Frontiers in Human Neuroscience*, 17: 1–3.

ICF. (n.d.). International Coach Federation. Retrieved from: www.coachingfederation.org

ICF. (2023). *The 2023 ICF global coaching study (GCS)*. Lexington, KY: International Coach Federation.

IOC. (n.d.). Institute of Coaching (IOC). McLean, Affiliate of Harvard Medical School. Retrieved from: www.instituteofcoaching.org

Jack, A.I., Passarelli, A.M., & Boyatzis, R.E. (2023). When fixing problems kills personal development: fMRI reveals conflict between real and ideal selves. *Frontiers in Human Neuroscience*, 17: 1–17.

Jacobs, R.L. (2003). *Structured on-the-job training: Unleashing employee expertise the workplace* (2nd edition). Oakland, CA: Berrett-Koehler Publishers.

Kimsey-House, K., Kimsey-House, H., Sandhal, P., & Whitworth, L. (2018). *Co-active coaching: The proven framework for transformative conversations at work and in life* (4th edition). Boston & London: Nicholas Brealey Publishing.

Knowles, S. (2021). *Positive psychology coaching*. Cham, Switzerland: Springer.

Knowles, S. (2022). *Coaching culture: Strategies for CEOs, organisational leaders, and HR professionals*. Cham, Switzerland: Springer.

Larcker, D., Miles, S., Tayan, B., & Gutman, M. (2013). *2013 executive coaching survey*. Stanford, CA: Miles Group & Stanford University.

Longenecker, C., & McCartney, M. (2020). The benefits of executive coaching: Voices from the C-suite. *Strategic HR Review*, 19(1): 22–27.

Lyons, P., & Bandura, R.P. (2021). Coaching to enhance learning and reinforce commitment. *International Journal of Evidence Based Coaching and Mentoring*, 19(2): 100–114.

Maltbia, T.E., Marsick, V.J., & Ghosh, R. (2014). Executive and organizational coaching: A review of insights drawn from literature to inform HRD practice. *Advances in Developing Human Resources*, 16(2): 161–183.

Oettingen, G. (2015). *Rethinking positive thinking: Inside the new science of motivation*. New York, NY: Current.

Passmore, J., Diller, S.J., Isaacson, S., & Brantl, M. (Eds.). (2024). *The digital and AI coaches' handbook: The complete guide to the use of online, AI and technology in coaching*. London & New York, NY: Routledge.

Passmore, J., Underhill, B., & Goldsmith, M. (Eds.). (2019). *Mastering executive coaching*. London & New York, NY: Routledge.

Rittenberg, M. (2012). *The leader as coach: Becoming an inspirational leader*. Berkeley, CA: Corporate Scenes.

Schein, E., & Schein, P.A. (2021). *Humble inquiry: The gentle art of asking instead of telling* (2nd edition). Oakland, CA: Berrett-Koehler Publishers.

Sevincer, A.T., Plakides, A. & Oettingen, G. (2023). Mental contrasting and energization transfer to low-expectancy tasks. *Motivation and Emotion*, 47: 85–99.

Swart, J., & Guirguis, C. (2023). *The coach's casebook: Skills, tools and techniques for effective coaching*. London: Kogan.

Tkaczyk, B. (2014). Daily check-ins stimulate self-improvement. *Talent Development*, 68(8): 72–73.

Tkaczyk, B. (2021). Team coaching for positive organizational change: Building and sustaining high-quality teams vie ERG. In *Leading positive organizational change: Energize – redesign – gel* (pp. 32–46). London & New York, NY: Routledge.

Watts, A. (2023). *Collage as a creative coaching tool: A comprehensive resource for coaches and psychologists*. London & New York, NY: Routledge.

Wheeler, S., & Leyman, T. (2023). *Playfulness in coaching: Exploring our untapped potential through playfulness, creativity and imagination*. London & New York, NY: Routledge.

Zander, R., & Zander, B. (2002). *The art of possibility: Transforming professional and personal life*. London: Penguin Books.

Module monitor and Consolidation V

Workshop V: Applications/review exercises

Self-check questions

You should now be able to answer Self-Check Questions 1–10

1 **True or false** There are different *helping* roles. Management *consultants* analyze; give recommendations and roadmaps; influence but have no direct power. *Managers* manage and have direct responsibility. *Mentors* can help with career development, advocacy, role modeling, personal and emotional guidance, strategies and systems advice, learning facilitation, and friendship. Forward-looking *coaches* develop and turn good and talented performers into excellent ones – they energize people to do their best and, by listening to them with great interest and asking them penetrating questions, challenge them to come up with answers on their own. *Therapists* go back, diagnose, and "fixes" dysfunctionality. Business *trainers* identify skills gaps and train employees. *Teachers* test, teach, test.

2 **True or false** *Management consultants* can bring chaos, noise, disorder in an organization.

3 **True or false** *Arthur D. Little* was created by Frederick W. Taylor.

4 **True or false** *Booz Allen Hamilton* was created by W. Edwards Deming.

5 **True or false** The consultant's *report* is the most *tangible deliverable*, and unless otherwise negotiated and included in the written *contract*, the *fee* may not cover *implementation*.

6 **True or false** *Self-coaching* and daily check-ins can stimulate self-improvement.

7 **True or false** *One-on-one* coaching is therapy.

8 **True or false** *Team* coaching is not a simple matter of coaching a collection of individuals, but a sophisticated process of coaching a system of interdependent individuals that must build synergistically to achieve a shared outcome.

9 **True or false** *Group* coaching can be a cost-saving option that too many enterprises fail to appreciate. So, to scale the benefits of coaching, create strategic "coaching cohorts" across levels, job functions, geographies, or business lines. When deployed professionally, group coaching can have

a high impact, maximize budget dollars, and energize employees (a much larger number of employees than one-on-one coaching) to develop both their positive leadership skills and high-quality connections (HQCs).

10 True or false *WHOOP* stands for **w**onder, **h**igh **o**ptimism, **o**utcome, and **p**erformance.

Individualized learning record

When you have finished Module V, try filling in this record of what you have learned.

1   Edgar Schein evangelized that if we are truly committed to being helpful, it's critical to have an honest curiosity about the client's (or colleague's or subordinate's) issue and a genuinely caring attitude. Do you agree? Explain why.

....

....

2   The management consultancy industry is vibrant but not easy to quantify. W. Edwards Deming used to say: "In God we trust. All others bring data". Now, do you believe consultants can be objective when evaluating the strategies they have helped to execute/have executed?

....

....

3   Is it common practice to use consultancy firms in your country? Which business sectors spend most/least money on consultants (agriculture, arts and entertainment, banking and financial services, communications services, construction, educational services, energy, healthcare, manufacturing, public administration, retail industry, utilities, ...)? If you were the Managing Director, would you take the consultant's advice? Why (not)?

....

....

4   Brainstorm words and phrases to describe coaching. Besides, brainstorm arguments for and against coaching. By the way, does your organization have a formal coaching program? If so, give details.

Look at the following "collocations" that commonly go together (collocation is the way words combine with other words to form strong and frequent "word partnerships"):

behavioral coaching, career coaching, coaching culture, coaching cohort, coaching development plan, coaching elements, coaching ethics, executive coaching, external/internal coaching, coaching fad, goal-focused coaching, group coaching, coaching mindset, life coaching, one-on-one coaching, peer coaching, positive leadership development coaching, positive organizational change coaching, positive psychology coaching, coaching presence, coaching principles, coaching scenario, self-coaching, coaching services, coaching session, coaching skills, solution-focused coaching, coaching standards, strategy coaching, coaching supervision, team coaching, coaching tools, coaching qualities.

Pick five collocations that are relevant to you, and write notes about your own learning experience. Next, give a mini-presentation to your team/group on an experience you had/you'd like to have of excellent coaching/on an experience you had of very bad coaching.

5   How would you rank (from 1 to 3) the relative importance of the coach being (a) expert in the coachee's job, (b) older than the coachee, and (c) the direct line manager.

6   Coaching scenario: Your coaching client is a female consultant who tells you, "No matter how many great ideas I contribute, my voice is just not heard. They don't take me seriously, and they discount my opinions". Start coaching her. Work with your colleague and role-play this coaching scenario as a Coach and Coachee.

7   Coaching exercise: "Soul portrait". Ask your coachee the following client profile questions:

1   What do you want me to know about you?
2   What are the values that get you up every morning?
3   What's the deepest dream for yourself?
4   What's holding you back?
5   What do you want to be remembered for?
6   How can I be your hero coach today?

8   Coaching exercise: "Saying Yes – Saying No"

By saying YES to:	I'm saying NO to:
1	....
2	....
3	....

By saying NO to: I'm saying YES to:

1 ....
2 ....
3 ....

9 How beneficial might coaching as a "helping" process for performance management be – or is it – in your enterprise, and what reliable evidence is there to support your assessment here?

10 The International Coaching Federation (ICF) revised the expression of its organizational core values as to what it means to represent the highest standards of professional coaching. The new ICF values include:

- Professionalism – We commit to a coaching mindset and professional quality that encompasses responsibility, respect, integrity, competence, and excellence.
- Collaboration – We commit to develop social connection and community building.
- Humanity – We commit to being humane, kind, compassionate, and respectful toward others.
- Equity – We commit to use a coaching mindset to explore and understand the needs of others so we can practice equitable processes at all times that create equality for all.

At heart, the core values should be more than just words on paper. They should empower and energize coaches and leaders as coaches to – always – work professionally and ethically. Do you live those universal values daily? If so, how?

Can-do checklist

Looking back, I have learned the following Key Terms:

Unit 9

- advice (business, expert, targeted, trusted)
- boutique consulting firm
- business process reengineering (BPR)
- client (business, bill, centered, firm, win),
- consultant (external/internal, independent, management, professional, role, strategy)

- consulting (activity, assignment, cycle, design, engagement, firm, humble, industry, job, knowledge, management, methods, professional, project, proposal, rhetoric, robo, services, skills, strategy, work)
- models (management, operational, strategic, tactical)
- plan–do–study–act (PDSA) cycle
- professional service firms (PSFs)
- strategic dialogue
- trust equation

Unit 10

- championing
- coach/coachee (link, relationship, partnering)
- coaching (activity, behavioral, career, co-active, cohort, confidentiality, development plan, effective, elements, ethics, executive, executive leadership team (ELT), exercise, external, fad, formal, goal-focused, group, internal, mindset, life, one-on-one, organizational, peer, people-centered, positive leadership development, positive organizational change, positive psychology, presence, principles, professional, scenario, self-, services, session, skills, solution-focused, standards, strategy, supervision, team, tools, qualities, workplace)
- coaching culture (benefits)
- collage, coaching with
- continuing professional development (CPD)
- dialogic learning
- feedback (constructive, honest)
- high performers
- human resource development (HRD) (executive, strategic, strategy)
- inquiry (humble, positive)
- learning and development (L&D) (strategy)
- listening (reflective, for possibility, supportive, with nuance and sensitivity)
- mental contrasting with implementation intentions (MCII)
- naming it
- performance management process (PMP)
- playback and check-in
- positive psychology
- questioning the status quo
- sounding board (serve as a)
- tracking
- wish, happy outcome, obstacle, plan (WHOOP)

Module VI

Global management strategies

Going places

11 So, you want to go global?

Becoming an instant international

"Own shares either in good ships, or in none at all. Make your ship attractive, then good people will join it and it will be well manned. Make your ship ready to sail at the beginning of summer and travel during the best part of the year, and always have reliable equipment on board. And never stay out on the high sea in autumn, if it is within your powers. Take good care of all these things – then there is hope that all will turn out well, with God's mercy" – From The Vikings' Guide to Good Business: On How to Do Business Overseas and Succeed (translated from the original 13th-century text by Bernard Scudder).

Sneak peek

Focus on: Key concepts and terms

Unit 11

- Born globals (BGs)
- Developing/developed economies
- Enablers of (early and rapid) internationalization
- Global mindset
- Global startups
- High-tech companies
- Industrial clusters
- Instant internationals
- International new ventures (INVs)
- Knowledge intensity
- "Leapfrog" technologies/leapfrogging
- Mergers and acquisitions (M&A) strategies
- Research and development (R&D): in-house (domestic) vs. external (abroad)
- Scaling (blitz, efficient, fast)

DOI: 10.4324/9781003508274-18

> • Speed
> • "Stage" model of internationalization
> • "Trickle-up" innovation (reverse innovation) strategy
> • Volatility, uncertainty, complexity/chaos, and ambiguity (VUCA)

Pause 'N' reflect: On the current issues and trends

Before you complete this unit, think about each of the following statements. Mark each statement:

V – if you *agree.*
X – if you *disagree.*
? – if you are *undecided.*

Your Take: Integrative Thinking	*Before doing Unit 11*	*After doing Unit 11*
1 Launching international business (usually selling products abroad) soon after their inception is not a brilliant strategy for young, entrepreneurial startups. As a startup, before internationalizing through export, you should always prioritize home markets before anything else.		
2 Domestic operations record has become seen as steadily less and less relevant for successful new international entrepreneurship.		
3 Gradual internationalization is just dead, period.		
4 If you're a high-tech "born global" (BG), an international new tech venture or a global tech startup, it's customary to seek international operations from or near your formation.		
5 International entrepreneurship implies creating competitive advantage by leveraging multiplex international resource configurations.		

Your Take: Integrative Thinking	*Before doing Unit 11*	*After doing Unit 11*
6 International entrepreneurs need to foster human capital in each country where they operate.		
7 It seems that maturing, tech-based, BG companies may survive through mergers and acquisitions (M&A).		
8 Frontier markets are irrelevant – innovations in economically poor countries cannot transform global markets.		
9 Innovation and learning move from economically rich countries to economically poor countries.		
10 Innovation knows no geographic boundaries. Established companies can master "trickle-up" (reverse) innovation strategizing, too. This involves creating products in Brazil, China, or India and then adapting them for developed economies, and/ or distributing them globally, in order to capitalize on opportunities in emerging markets and to create value segments in wealthier countries.		

After you have done the unit, repeat "Your Take". How has reading the unit clarified the ideas herein? How have your views, feelings and thoughts changed over time?

Lead-in

General discussion points

Individually or in buzz groups, consider what it takes to create a successful international new venture (INV). Think particularly about:

1 The advantages/disadvantages of early and rapid internationalization.
2 How to design a business model that facilitates extremely rapid development, navigates critical strategic moves at each level of scale, and deals with the management issues that come as your firm expands?
3 The entrepreneurial capabilities and "knowledge-creative" assets and resources for necessary INV success (e.g., people, technology, brand's energized

differentiation, partnerships, collective design thinking, strategic organizational learning).
4   What key strategic management systems and processes must be in place (consider, for example, research and development (R&D), manufacturing, strategic talent management and HRD, marketing, IT, emergency/crisis communication and the incident management system, open innovation).
5   The role of networked service ecosystems, industrial clusters, and "knowledge towns" (research universities and colleges well-placed to inform business) as talent magnets in launching and growing "born-global" (BG) firms.

Share your thoughts with your peers/team members. Discuss points of agreement/disagreement.

 Idea watch

Some small or medium-sized companies manage to play to win on the global stage very early on, frequently far sooner than their more powerful rivals.

Not long ago, quite a few newly established firms (mostly small to medium-sized enterprises) went international within a few years of formation, even while still being quite minor at home. These so-called BGs can swiftly hit very high percentages of international revenues – indeed, sometimes 100% of their total sales.

As noted by Alina Kudina, George Yip and Harry Barkema, BGs, also known as INVs or "*instant* internationals", are typically regarded as enterprises that, from inception, endeavor to gain major competitive advantages from the use of assets and the sale of outputs in multiple locations worldwide (e.g., Airbnb, Inc., East India Company, Energizers, LLC, Logitech, Ormat Technologies, Zara).

Quantitatively speaking, BGs are specifically business entities that, within two to three years of their founding, have attained a share of overseas sales of at least 25%.

One of the secrets to starting and growing massively valuable businesses is "scaling", not just *efficient* scaling (where efficiency only is put first) or *fast* scaling (where speed alone is prioritized), but, what Reid Hoffman and Chris Yeh call, "blitzscaling" in particular. "Blitzscaling", an aggressive growth strategy, is a specific set of practices for energizing and managing hyper-growth; an accelerated path to the stage in a startup's life-cycle where the most value is created. New business ventures that have learned how to blitzscale prioritize speed and market dominance over efficiency in the face of uncertainty. This enables a firm to innovate and to rapidly progress from "startup" to "scaleup" at a furious pace that captures market opportunities.

 Assumptions

The dominant logic holds that, before expanding abroad, most multinational companies experience rapid domestic market growth.

The conventional strategy for internationalization has been referred to as a "stage" model, in which a business first establishes a firm foothold in its home market before looking into opportunities for expansion into neighboring countries in the region. The company then goes on to expand internationally as its knowledge and experience with foreign markets increase (think: BP, Microsoft or Santander).

Interestingly, the lack of a robust home market often forces some (high-tech) enterprises to go global right away, making them *instant internationals*. In reality, if they don't go overseas, they may not be able to actually survive, and they might just fail.

Key elements

Market conditions – New ventures sometimes get "pushed" to go global because their home market for their products or services is small or non-existent. Early and rapid internationalization is frequently one of their means of survival.

Global winning aspiration – A fearless mindset, exhibiting a determination and willingness to take bold action and achieve spectacular results – globally. Think about what is an easy/hard-fought win for you – and – against whom?

Prior international experience of the founders – The founders are experienced in international business. They can dynamically "sense, seize, and reconfigure" international business opportunities.

Knowledge intensity – The majority of R&D can be done in-house – domestically, but some businesses undertake a sizable portion of their R&D externally – abroad. If you decide on developing products domestically, you should always strive to stay alert to the latest market developments by strategically learning (and *un*learning) from foreign markets as well.

The degree of technology acquisition from overseas – Performance and technology acquisition are correlated, i.e., businesses that acquire some technology from foreign operations perform better than those that depend on domestic in-house R&D only.

Hard-to-copy-and-substitute ("leapfrog") technology – Another crucial enabler is that these enterprises' leading-edge new technologies are frequently exceedingly challenging to copy and substitute. As a result, BGs are often able to "leapfrog" established firms – that is to say, to significantly improve their position by moving quickly past or over the rest of the market.

Why choose you over the competition? – What is your customer value proposition? How is your competitive advantage linked to your "where-to-play" choices? Perhaps, rather than competing on the basis of having lower costs than the other players in your industry, you should try winning on the basis of brand differentiation.

Develop super-flexible workforce – Increasingly, leaders get thrown into a VUCA mess – characterized by volatility, uncertainty, complexity/chaos, and ambiguity. Therefore, it is now essential for people to become super-flexible – to simultaneously be able to *positively* embrace novelty, non-linearity and paradox, as well as *strategically* mitigate risk and turbulence, navigate the chaos, boost strategic resilience, renew their business – and create winning change.

Tapping into social capital, trust-based networks, and "knowledge-creative" (service) ecosystems – Your global operations will be more successful if you have a professional network of people you can rely on. Plus, knowing well and trusting the people who run your international offices is critical for keeping a competitive edge in the market later on. It turns out that trust acts as a kind of "glue" when doing business abroad. On top of that, think about knowledge-creative (service) ecosystems as talent magnets – that is to say, people, culture, and place (e.g., Silicon Valley in the San Francisco Bay Area, Greater Cambridge Area Cluster, or Dubai Internet City).

Thinking critically: Issues

In general, doing business abroad is significantly harder than doing business at home. So, why not stay at home as much as possible?

The reasons for the emergence of INVs may differ for businesses from big markets (such as the US), medium-sized markets (such as the UK), and small markets – often poor in natural resources, but very rich in human capital (such as Israel). Indeed, expanding quickly overseas may be a smart winning strategy for a firm operating in a field with very little domestic market potential (or if it is considering starting a business in a market where there is minimal home demand).

Industry-wise, high-tech firms are especially prone to the BG effect and conducive to early and rapid internationalization. Yet, in an increasingly globalized business environment, high-tech BG companies also have lessons to teach other companies across industries.

"Blitzscaling" is not a one-size-fits-all strategy. It poses risks and problems linked to, for example, cash burn, maintaining quality, complying with regulations, and sustaining corporate culture amid hyper-growth. In today's turbulent "bear market", new hyper-growth initiatives should know how critical it is to keep these risks in mind and tweak their scaling strategy as needed.

Furthermore, consider what happens to BG firms when they grow up. It may be that maturing, tech-based, BG enterprises will need to adopt a much more aggressive M&A strategy than they already apply in order to continue being successful.

Ultimately, established corporations can embrace "trickle-up" (reverse) innovation, too. Although the dominant logic maintains that innovation comes from the US, travels to Europe and Japan, and then gravitates to economically poor countries, today, as C.K. Prahalad evangelizes, we're starting to see a reversal of that flow. To be specific, innovation can now be seen or used first in developing nations, before spreading to the industrialized, developed ones – as practiced, for example, by GE Healthcare, Nestlé, PepsiCo, and Procter & Gamble.

Applications

The market

The market in your home country is too small to support the scale at which you need to operate.

Customers

The majority of your potential clients are international, multinational, and global corporations.

Sector

You operate in a knowledge-intensive, knowledge-creative, and, preferably, high-tech sector.

Tech advances

Having the most technically advanced offering in the world is critical to maintaining your competitive edge.

Products and services

Your product or service benefits significantly from network effects or first-mover advantages.

Key managers

You have critical executives with worldwide business expertise.

Key capabilities

You know your key capabilities, and you recognize the strengths and weaknesses within your teams. You can identify future capability requirements and determine which skills to develop in-house, outsource, acquire – or automate.

Case alert! Case classic

Logitech

LOOK IT UP: Oviatt, B.M., & McDougall, P.P. (1995). Global start-ups: Entrepreneurs on a worldwide stage. *Academy of Management Perspectives*, 9(2): 30–43.

Your task: Search for the *Logitech* case to learn more about this. Make a list of the best strategies and the key lessons learned from Logitech, a global leader in designing products and experiences that connect people to the digital world around them. Are there any surprises? If yes, explain why. Report your research findings, insights, and good practices back to your peers/team members.

To record your critical insights, use the Case Analysis Record provided in Appendix 2.

Greater good corner: Get ready to exercise your ethics

Take a stance: What would *you* do?

Dilemma and decision: Corporate espionage

Your foreign competitor, in the booming space sector, has made a significant global tech advancement that will raise the caliber of their product, lower the cost of their production, and render *your* product *un*competitive. Someone comes up to you at a trade fair and offers to sell you the specifics of the research that your rival conducted and that contributed to the breakthrough.

What would *you* do?

Time out: Journal entry

Thought Sparks: A few reflections, insightful ideas, actionable suggestions, strategic thinking, and key takeaways from this unit.

Learning never stops… So, pause for a few minutes and reflect in writing on your personal learning experience and beliefs. Through writing in your journal, you develop your awareness of your own beliefs and attitudes. Now, consolidate what you have learned in this unit.

1   How have your beliefs and ideas about BGs, scaling and internationalization changed since you began the unit?

....

....

2   Thinking about the problems presented in the unit, write about whether you have found solutions to these problems.

....

....

3   How confident do you now feel about launching an INV?

....

....

4 What would you still like to have clarified? What remaining concerns do you have?

....

....

5 What more would you like to learn about the topic, now that you have completed this unit?

....

....

6 If you want, doodle/draw something you like about going global or blitzscaling. This can be as abstract as you wish.

....

....

Remember: It's particularly useful to re-visit journal entries several times and see how themes have recurred or your thoughts have changed over time. Now, repeat "Your Take".

Making connections: Related units and models

- U 3. **Strategic transformation**: Strategy choice-making (see pp. 61–81)
- U 4. **SOAR**: Possibility thinking in positive strategic dialog (see pp. 82–95)
- U 5. **Dialogic organization development (OD)**: Leading positive organizational change (see pp. 103–121)
- U 6. **Design-driven organization:** Human-centered design thinking and innovation execution (see pp. 122–139)
- U 7. **WOW! It's cool!** Crafting a coolness strategy for your brand (see pp. 147–159)
- U 9. **Professional management consulting for real people:** The advice business demystified (see pp. 181–203)
- U 12. **Small world:** Are you a culturally intelligent organization? (see pp. 238–250)
- U 13. **Progress with purpose:** The "good" enterprise (see pp. 257–272)
- Add in more related models you may want to remember: _____ .

Industry snapshot

www.logitech.com/en-us/about.html

Deep dive: Main references and resources

Agarwal, N., & Kwan, P. (2018). Pricing mergers with differential synergies. *Strategic Change*, 27(1): 3–7.

Agarwal, N., Kwan, P., & Paul, D. (2018). Behavioral merger and acquisition pricing: Application to Verizon mergers with AOL and Yahoo. *Strategic Change*, 27(1): 9–21.

Almor, T. (2011). Dancing as fast as they can: Israeli high-tech firms and the great recession of 2008. *Thunderbird International Business Review*, 53(2): 195–208.

Almor, T., Tarba, S.Y., & Margalit, A. (2014). Maturing, technology-based, born-global companies: Surviving through mergers and acquisitions. *Management International Review*, 54(4): 421–444.

Bartlow, A.C., & Harris, T.B. (2021). *Scaling for success: People priorities for high-growth organizations*. New York, NY: Columbia Business School Publishing.

Burnell, D., Neubert, E., & Fisher, G. (2023). Venture tales: Practical storytelling strategies underpinning entrepreneurial narratives. *Business Horizons*, 66(3): 325–346.

Cavusgil, S., & Knight, G. (2015). The born global firm: An entrepreneurial and capabilities perspective on early and rapid internationalization. *Journal of International Business Studies*, 46(1): 3–16.

Galpin, T. (2020). *Winning at the acquisition game: Tools, templates, and best practices across the M&A process*. Oxford: Oxford University Press.

Gomes, E. (2020). Mergers, acquisitions, and strategic alliances as collaborative methods of strategic development and change. *Strategic Change*, 29(2): 145–148.

Gomes, E., Alam, S., Tarba, S.Y., & Vendrell-Herrero, F. (2020). A 27-year review of mergers and acquisitions research in 27 leading management journals. *Strategic Change*, 29(2): 179–193.

Govindarajan, V., & Trimble, C. (2012). *Reverse innovation: Create far from home, win everywhere*. Boston, MA: Harvard Business Review Press.

Hoffman, R., & Yeh, C. (2018). *Blitzscaling: The lightning-fast path to building massively valuable companies*. New York, NY: Currency.

Jennings, J., & Haughton, L. (2002). *It's not the big that eat the small…It's the fast that eat the slow: How to use speed as a competitive tool in business*. New York, NY: HarperCollins Publishers.

Knight, G., Koed Madsen, T., & Servais, P. (2004). An inquiry into born-global firms in Europe and the USA. *International Marketing Review*, 21(6): 645–665.

Kudina, A., Barkema, H., & Yip, G. (2008). Born global. *Business Strategy Review*, 19(4): 38–44.

Kumar, N. (2009). How emerging giants are rewriting the rules of M&A. *Harvard Business Review*, 87(5): 115–121.

Kuratko, D.F., Holt, H.L., & Neubert, E. (2020). Blitzscaling: The good, the bad, and the ugly. *Business Horizons*, 63(1): 109–119.

Nambisan, S., & Luo, Y. (2022). *The digital multinational: Navigating the new normal in global business*. Cambridge, MA: The MIT Press.

Oviatt, B.M., & McDougall, P.P. (1994). Toward a theory of international new ventures. *Journal of International Business Studies*, 25(1): 45–64.

Oviatt, B.M., & McDougall, P.P. (1995). Global start-ups: Entrepreneurs on a worldwide stage. *Academy of Management Perspectives*, 9(2): 30–43.

Prahalad, C.K. (2009, April 6). 5 tips for trickle-up innovation from C.K. Prahalad. *Bloomberg*. Retrieved from: www.bloomberg.com/news/articles/2009-04-06/5-tips-for-trickle-up-innovation-from-c-dot-k-dot-prahalad

Scudder, B. (1997). *The vikings' guide to good business: On how to do business overseas and succeed* (Translated from the original 13th-century text). London: Gudrun.

Senor, D., & Singer, S. (2009). *Start-up nation: The story of Israel's economic miracle*. New York, NY & Boston, MA: Twelve.

Staley, D.J., & Endicott, D.D.J. (2023). *Knowledge towns: Colleges and universities as talent magnets*. Baltimore, MD: Johns Hopkins University Press.

Tallman, S., & Koza, M.P. (2024). *Global strategy in our age of chaos: How will the multinational firm survive?* Cambridge: Cambridge University Press.

Weber, Y., Tarba, S.Y. & Öberg, C. (2014). *A comprehensive guide to mergers & acquisitions: Managing the critical success factors across every stage of the M&A process*. Upper Saddle River, NJ: FT Press.

Yates, L.K. (2022). *The unicorn within: How companies can create game-changing ventures at startup speed*. Boston, MA: Harvard Business Review Press.

Zámborský, P., Yan, Z.J., Michailova, S., & Zhuang, V. (2023). Chinese multinationals' internationalization strategies: New realities, new pathways. *California Management Review*, 66(1): 96–123.

12 Small world

Are you a culturally intelligent organization?

"Love your neighbor as yourself" – Romans 13:9

Sneak peek

Focus on: Key concepts and terms

Unit 12

- Cultural, administrative, geographic, economic (environmental, risk) distance framework (CAGE(er))
- Cultural characteristics/dimensions: power distance, uncertainty avoidance, individualism/collectivism, masculinity/femininity, time orientation, and indulgence/restraint
- Cultural intelligence (CQ)
- Cultural shock
- Cultural variations
- Cultural-awareness training course
- Culture (national, organizational)
- Emotional stages associated with an overseas assignment: honeymoon-culture shock/crisis-recovery-adjustment
- Evangelization (universal)
- Implicit forms of organizations: a pyramid of people, a well-oiled machine, a village market, and the family
- Internationalization
- Globalization
- People management and development practices
- Regionalization
- Stereotyping

DOI: 10.4324/9781003508274-19

Pause 'N' reflect: On the current issues and trends

Before you complete this unit, think about each of the following statements. Mark each statement:

V – if you *agree.*
X – if you *disagree.*
? – if you are *undecided.*

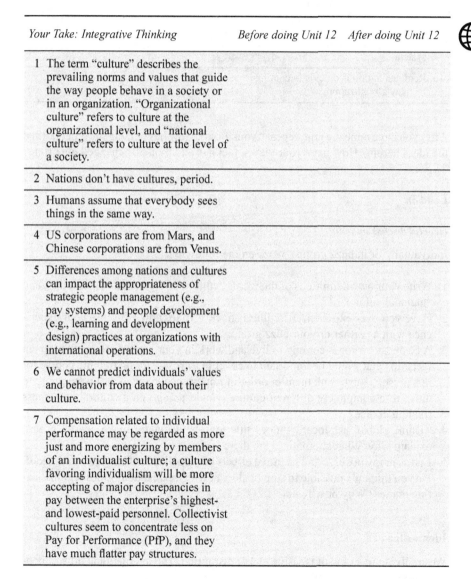

Your Take: Integrative Thinking	*Before doing Unit 12*	*After doing Unit 12*
1 The term "culture" describes the prevailing norms and values that guide the way people behave in a society or in an organization. "Organizational culture" refers to culture at the organizational level, and "national culture" refers to culture at the level of a society.		
2 Nations don't have cultures, period.		
3 Humans assume that everybody sees things in the same way.		
4 US corporations are from Mars, and Chinese corporations are from Venus.		
5 Differences among nations and cultures can impact the appropriateness of strategic people management (e.g., pay systems) and people development (e.g., learning and development design) practices at organizations with international operations.		
6 We cannot predict individuals' values and behavior from data about their culture.		
7 Compensation related to individual performance may be regarded as more just and more energizing by members of an individualist culture; a culture favoring individualism will be more accepting of major discrepancies in pay between the enterprise's highest- and lowest-paid personnel. Collectivist cultures seem to concentrate less on Pay for Performance (PfP), and they have much flatter pay structures.		

Your Take: Integrative Thinking	*Before doing Unit 12*	*After doing Unit 12*
8 Self-actualization tends to be more of a motivator in highly individualist societies than in those where "keeping face" within group relationships is a primary social expectation.		
9 When formulating and executing international strategies, always take account of distance. Distance can derail the process – this is primarily due to geography and different legal systems.		
10 Regionalization is quickly becoming the new globalization.		

After you have done the unit, repeat "Your Take". How has reading the unit clarified the ideas herein? How have your views, feelings and thoughts changed over time?

Lead-in

General discussion points

Individually or in buzz groups, work on the following:

1 Write your own definitions of the words "culture", "organizational culture", and "national culture".
2 Have you ever experienced "culture shock"? If so, how? Discuss your experience with a partner or your buzz group.
3 A business visitor is coming to live and work in your country. Share the top ten facts/tips that would be important to cover in a cross-cultural training course for this person. Next, rank them in order of importance. Now, if you were going to move to a completely different culture, would *you* go on a cultural-awareness training course?
4 "Think global, act local" – does this long-held mantra make sense? If yes, explain why. What alternatives are there?
5 List as many positive and negative effects of globalization that you can think of. Do you think it's possible to stop or slow down globalization? Does regionalization matter? Why or why not?

Idea watch

We are living in a time of massive global disruption. The international flow of people, information, funds, and goods and services for commercial purposes continues to grow. Internationalization leads to more international customers, suppliers and partners. The process of worldwide economic integration in international markets is known as "globalization". The rise and proliferation of multinational corporations are both a result and cause of globalization. Of note, global markets are also consolidating into regional hubs ("regionalization"). Therefore, market leaders need to act on this too – or they may get left behind.

Organizations that operate in more than one country, regardless of their level of global participation, must acknowledge that countries are not identical – they differ in terms of many cultural characteristics. Culture is usually referred to as shared attitudes, beliefs and assumptions about how the world works and what values are worthwhile pursuing. According to Geert Hofstede, a national culture, aka "collective mental programming" of the people in an environment, distinguishes one nation from another and has the following dimensions: high or low power distance, high or low uncertainty avoidance, individualism/collectivism, masculinity/femininity (motivation toward achievement and success), long-term or short-term orientation, and indulgence versus restraint.

These cultural elements may be used to create a successful approach for interacting and cooperating with people from various nations. National culture differences can be crucial, and failing to recognize them can lead to business failure and career repercussions for individual leaders.

Over and above that, cultures can affect the appropriateness of strategic people management and people development practices. For instance, HR practices that work in the US may fail or backfire in another country with different shared values and assumptions. Therefore, organizations must train leaders to recognize and manage cultural differences.

Assumptions

People from other cultures may behave and respond in quite different ways than you are accustomed to.

Cultural variations and the major dimensions of cultural difference between workplaces based in different countries become apparent when a company starts to operate internationally.

Key elements

Power distance – This refers to the extent to which people in a particular culture acknowledge and expect that power in institutions and organizations is (and should be) distributed unequally. In countries with large power distances, including Malaysia and the Philippines, the culture defines it as normal to maintain great disparities in power. In countries with small power distances, such as Austria and Canada, people work to remove inequalities. Differences in power distance can be observed, for example, in the way individuals converse with one another. Mexico and Syria are high-power-distance nations where formal titles are used to address one another (*Señor* Martinez for *Mr.* Martinez; *Aanisa* Hoda for *Miss* Hoda).

On the other end of the spectrum, in the UK and the US, most of the time, people address one another a lot more informally – by their first names – which might be considered situationally inappropriate in other countries.

Uncertainty avoidance – This reflects the degree to which people in a culture feel nervous or threatened by uncertain and ambiguous circumstances, and thus create institutions and norms to strive to avoid them. In countries with high uncertainty avoidance such as Greece and Poland, people seem to prefer structured situations and clear instructions. In countries with low uncertainty avoidance such as Denmark or Ireland, people are a lot more comfortable with uncertainty and ambiguity and therefore much more willing and ready to take risks.

Individualism (and *collectivism*, on the other side of the continuum) – Individualist cultures (for example, Australia) tend to prioritize personal interests and those of their immediate family, but collectivist cultures (for example, South Korea) have a tighter social structure in which each person is loyal to and respects the wider group to which they belong.

Masculinity (and *femininity*, on the other end of the spectrum) – In a masculine culture (think: Hungary), the dominant values are said to be ambition, assertiveness, competition, performance, and the acquisition of money and wealth, while in a so-called feminine culture (think: Norway), values such as the quality of life, maintaining personal relationships, and caring for the weak and the environment are cherished.

Time orientation (originally termed "Confucian dynamism") – Cultures with a long-term orientation (the focus of cultural values is on the future), like China, value perseverance and saving because they know that these characteristics will pay off in the long run. Cultures with a short-term orientation (those who emphasize the past and the present) encourage reverence for previous traditions, as well as fulfilling societal obligations in the present, as in Nigeria.

Indulgence (*versus* restraint) – An indulgent society (for example, Sweden) values the satisfaction of human needs and desires with regard to living life and having fun. Such societies have a positive attitude and tend toward optimism. Furthermore, they place a greater value on leisure time, well-being, and the freedom to act and spend money as they like. A restrained society (for example, Russia) sees the value in curbing one's desires and withholding pleasures to align more with rigid social norms. Positive emotions are less openly expressed, and happiness, freedom and leisure are not as valued (for the majority).

Ultimately, countries, based on some comparatively clear cultural differences, can be clustered and categorized into four implicit forms of organizations:

- **A pyramid of people** (countries with large power distances and high uncertainty avoidance, including Guatemala, Russia, and Serbia, relying strongly on hierarchy and clear instructions from superiors),
- **A well-oiled machine** (countries with small power distances and high uncertainty avoidance, including Austria, Finland, and Germany, depending on rules, procedures, and clear structures),

- **A village market** (countries with small power distances and low uncertainty avoidance, including Denmark, Ireland, and the UK, meeting the demands well as they arise), and
- **The family** (countries with large power distances and low uncertainty avoidance, including China, Indonesia, and the Philippines, where issues are continually settled by "going to the boss", who is like a father to an extended family, resulting in a concentration of authority without structuring of activities).

Thinking critically: Issues

Culture is communication. While American formalization, Japanese centralization, and European socialization each have distinct approaches, a universally effective method—whether in Denver, Kyoto or Amsterdam—is the use of storytelling, parables, legends, and "evangelization". As advocated by Edgar Schein, these techniques are instrumental in winning hearts and minds, fostering widespread acceptance of a unified mission and shared purpose within an organization. Evangelization relies on the power of shared beliefs and the deployment of ambassadors, often referred to as corporate apostles, who are tasked with spreading these ideas and ensuring their adoption across the business.

However, it's critical to avoid exaggerating the significance of cultural differences or stereotyping. Oftentimes, a widely held and fixed image or idea of a particular type of person or culture is oversimplified.

In addition to Geert Hofstede's model, there are various other frameworks available that assist in understanding cultural differences and navigating cross-cultural management, such as those developed by Edward T. Hall, Erin Meyer, Harry C. Triandis, and Fons Trompenaars. For all that, getting the possible cultural variations and differences right is no guarantee for building and sustaining high-quality connections, as no two individuals are alike.

As Sverre Lysgaard reports, based on interviews with 200 Norwegian Fulbright grantees to the US, at the individual level, the emotions that come with an international assignment tend to progress in phases such as:

- **"Honeymoon"** (the euphoria of the new culture),
- **Culture shock/Crisis** (feelings of disorientation when you experience a new culture),
- **Recovery** (when you recover from culture shock),
- **Adjustment** (you accept and enjoy – or at worst, "endure" – the host country's culture).

At the organizational level, organizations with high levels of what Soon Ang and colleagues call "cultural intelligence" (CQ) – the capability to understand, relate and function successfully in complex, culturally diverse situations – are much better equipped to navigate the complexity of today's multicultural world more effectively.

Even though cultivating multinational flexibility in employees is a must-have for any multinational company that plans on entering another culture, misunderstandings can *still* happen.

Besides, nations consist of clusters of "sub-cultures". So it's important to stress variability *within* nations in the expectations of employees.

On top of that, distance can be created by more than just culture. On that account, when crafting your international strategy, the CAGE framework developed by Pankaj Ghemawat can assist you in navigating potential pitfalls. Accordingly, apart from:

- **C**ultural differences – ethnicities, values, norms, trust, social responsibility, also think,
- **A**dministrative differences – the political environment, the legal system, currency, corruption, business dispute resolution,
- **G**eographic differences – the physical distance between countries, time zones, climates, access to nearby markets,
- **E**conomic differences – the infrastructure (including the availability and quality of real estate, telecom and IT, transportation network, power supply), corporate taxes, natural/financial resources, income inequality, human capital, skill pool, labor costs and current average wages for managers and skilled workers, vendor landscape, and innovation.

When doing your CAGE analysis, don't forget to also consider environment and risk profile, so that it's CAGEer:

- **E**nvironment – business environment (e.g., compatibility with prevailing business culture and ethics), government support (policy on foreign investment, bureaucratic and regulatory burden), living environment (overall life quality, prevalence of HIV infection, and serious crimes per capita), accessibility (flight frequency).
- **R**isk profile – disruptive events (political unrest, risk of labor uprising, and natural disasters), security (armed confrontation, terrorism, risks to personal security and property from fraud, or government arresting its political opponents), intellectual property (IP) theft (strength of data and IP protection regime), regulatory (the rule of law vs. the rule of power, government attacks on media freedom, stability, fairness, and efficiency of legal framework), macroeconomic risk (cost inflation, currency fluctuation, and capital freedom).

Applications

Cultures can have a significant impact on organizations and the appropriateness of strategic people management and development approaches. Specifically, cultural characteristics can affect the success of a learning and development (L&D) program and its design. For example:

Power distance

High-power-distance countries want trainers to be "gurus" who transfer expert wisdom. L&D professionals are required to be authoritative and take the initiative in the room.

Uncertainty avoidance

Cultures high in uncertainty avoidance want formal, structured educational contexts. There is less tolerance for spontaneous behavior and a facilitative style.

Individualism

Individualism-driven cultures expect engagement in exercises and questioning to be decided by status in the organization or culture.

Masculinity

Female trainers tend to face less resistance in low-masculinity countries. In addition, feminine cultures value high-quality connections with other trainees.

Time orientation

Long-term oriented cultures will have learners who are likely to accept development plans and projects.

Indulgence

Learners based in an indulgent society will appreciate experiential (e.g., outdoor learning) or social learning methods (e.g., technical team "pizza sessions", reverse-mentoring, "virtual coffees" or team-centered coaching), whereas trainees based in a restrained society will see more value in formal education (e.g., traditional classroom teaching).

Case alert! Case classic

Skyworks Solutions (US) and ZTE (China)

LOOK IT UP: Young, M.N., Bruton, G.D., Peng, M.W., & Yu, X. (2022). U.S. corporations are from Mars, Chinese corporations are from Venus. *Business Horizons*, 65(4): 505–517.

Your task: Relations between US and Chinese corporations are becoming more tense.

By examining the relations between Skyworks Solutions (US), an innovator of high-performance analog semiconductors with an ambitious vision of connecting everyone and everything, all the time, and ZTE (China), a leader in telecommunications and information technology, you will discover how differences in the key domains of corporate governance, underlying corporate philosophy, innovation, and commercial dispute resolution contribute to this strained relationship.

Further, make notes on some of the broad strategies available to (US) managers for engaging with Chinese corporations. Discuss the pros and cons of each of the approaches.

What other strategies and tactics can you come up with? Report back.

To record your critical insights, use the Case Analysis Record provided in Appendix 2.

Greater good corner: Get ready to exercise your ethics

Take a stance: What would *you* do?

Dilemma and decision: Just "normal" business?

You're a British oil and gas major seeking new oil reserves and want to gain access to the Russian market but is unable to do so without a Russian partner. Your Russian partner seeks tech and management know-how for their Russian upstream business. Therefore, you form a joint venture JV with the Russians. However, you are now engaged in a business dispute with the Russian shareholders of your (JV), a group led by Russian billionaires and oligarchs. This environment is extremely volatile, uncertain, chaotic, complex, and ambiguous (VUCA).

The Russian shareholders want the JV's CEO to be fired, a British executive whom you appointed. The Russian shareholders claim that you are not appropriately managing costs, and are obstructing efforts to expand the JV outside of Russia because that would compete with your own activities. They further allege that you are hiring too many high-earning expats in Russia. Ultimately, they want to reduce capital investment spending, but pay dividends instead. Additionally, the JV is having issues with the Russian government and top officials over employee visas and exploration licenses.

From your point of view, the JV is a significant part of your global oil and gas business, representing almost one-quarter of your oil output. The resolution of disputes between the partners and with the government will have long-term consequences for you and your operations in Russia. This will also impact Russia's public reputation for attracting foreign investment. You begin to think: Is this just "normal business in Russia"? Who wants you out? Is it, for example, the Russian government or the oligarchs? What could you do? For instance:

- Sue your Russian partner for breaching the shareholder agreement?
- Take the dispute to the highest levels in the Russian government?
- Ask the British government for assistance?
- Accept a Russian CEO?
- Recognize it wasn't smart to even think you could operate legitimately in Russia, cut your losses and leave?

Discuss and decide on a potential course of action. What are the problems associated with agreeing to each of these options above?

Time out: Journal entry

Thought Sparks: A few reflections, insightful ideas, actionable suggestions, strategic thinking, and key takeaways from this unit.

Learning never stops... So, pause for a few minutes and reflect in writing on your personal learning experience and beliefs. Through writing in your journal, you develop your awareness of your own beliefs and attitudes. Now, consolidate what you have learned in this unit.

1 How have your beliefs and ideas about national cultures changed since you began the unit?

....

....

2   Thinking about the problems presented in the unit, write about whether you have found solutions to these problems.

....

....

3   How confident do you now feel about interacting with and building and sustaining high-quality connections (HQCs) with people from different countries?

....

....

4   What would you still like to have clarified? What remaining concerns do you have?

....

....

5   What more would you like to learn about the topic, now that you have completed this unit?

....

....

6   If you want, doodle/draw something you like about cultural variations or your own national culture. This can be as abstract as you wish.

....

....

Remember: It's particularly useful to re-visit journal entries several times and see how themes have recurred or your thoughts have changed over time. Now, repeat "Your Take".

Making connections: Related units and models

- U 2. **The kindness advantage:** Cultivating positively energizing leaders and followers (see pp. 27–53)
- U 3. **Strategic transformation**: Strategy choice-making (see pp. 61–81)
- U 5. **Dialogic organization development (OD):** Leading positive organizational change (see pp. 103–121)
- U 8. **Once upon a time…** Strategic brand storytelling (see pp. 160–174)
- U 9. **Professional management consulting for real people:** The advice business demystified (see pp. 181–203)
- U 10. **Executive coaching:** Whoop it up! (see pp. 204–219)

- U 11. **So, you want to go global?** Becoming an instant international (see pp. 227–237)
- U 14. **Oops! I messed up.** Why good people do bad things every so often (see pp. 273–287)
- Add in more related models you may want to remember: _____.

Industry snapshot

www.skyworksinc.com/About/
www.zte.com.cn/global/about/corporate_information.html

Deep dive: Main references and resources

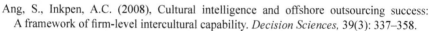

Ang, S., Inkpen, A.C. (2008), Cultural intelligence and offshore outsourcing success: A framework of firm-level intercultural capability. *Decision Sciences,* 39(3): 337–358.

Anglès, V. (2019). Doing business in China: Challenges and opportunities. Global Business and Organizational Excellence, 38(2): 54–63.

Bartlett, C.A., Ghoshal, S. (2002). *Managing across borders: The transnational solution.* Cambridge, MA: Harvard Business School Press.

Brett, J.M., & Mitchell, T.D. (2022). *Searching for trust in the global economy.* Toronto: University of Toronto Press.

Frynas, J. G., Mol, M. J., & Mellahi, K. (2018). Management Innovation made in China: Haier's Rendanheyi. *California Management Review*, 61(1): 71–93.

Garavan, T., McCarthy, A., & Morley, M. (2016). *Global human resource development: Regional and country perspectives.* London & New York, NY: Routledge.

Ghemawat, P. (ed.) (2007). Differences across countries: The CAGE distance framework. In *Redefining global strategy: Crossing borders in a world where differences still matter* (pp. 33–64). Boston, MA: Harvard Business School Press.

Greeven, M.J., Xin, K.R., & Yip, G.S. (2023). How Chinese companies are reinventing management. *Harvard Business Review*, 101(3–4): 104–112.

Hall, E.T. (1959). *The silent language.* Garden City, NY: Double Day & Company, Inc.

Hall, E.T. (1983). *The dance of life: The other dimension of time.* New York, NY: Anchor Books.

Hofstede, G., Hofstede, G.J., & Minkov, M. (2010). *Cultures and organizations: Software of the mind* (3rd ed.). New York, NY: McGraw Hill.

Hofstede Insights. (n.d.). Retrieved from: www.hofstede-insights.com/country-comparison/ – the website explains how different countries "score" on different cultural dimensions.

Livermore, D., Van Dyne, L., & Ang, S. (2022). Organizational CQ: Cultural intelligence for 21st-century organizations. *Business Horizons*, 65(5): 671–680.

Lysgaard, S. (1955). Adjustment in a foreign society: Norwegian Fulbright grantees visiting the United States. *International Social Science Bulletin,* 7(1):45–51.

Mahadevan, J. (2017). *A very short, fairly interesting and reasonably cheap book about cross-cultural management.* London: Sage.

Meyer, E. (2014). *The culture map: Breaking through the invisible boundaries of global business.* New York, NY: PublicAffairs.

Minkov, M., & Kaasa, A. (2022). Do dimensions of culture exist objectively? A validation of the revised Minkov-Hofstede model of culture with World Values Survey items and scores for 102 countries. *Journal of International Management*, 28(4): 100971.

O'Neil, S.K. (2022). *Globalization myth: Why regions matter.* New Haven, CT: Yale University Press.

Schein, E. (2004). *Organizational culture and leadership.* San Francisco, CA: Jossey-Bass.

Steiber, A., Corvello, V., & Ghosh, S. (2023). International acquisition processes: A cultural analysis of GE Appliances' business transformation. *Business Horizons,* 66(2): 171–180.

Tolbert, A.S., McLean, G.N., & Myers, R.C. (2002): Creating the global learning organization (GLO). *International Journal of Intercultural Relations.* 26(4): 463–472.

Triandis, H.C. (1995). *Individualism and collectivism.* London & New York, NY: Routledge.

Trompenaars, F., & Hampden-Turner, C. (2021). *Riding the waves of culture: Understanding diversity in global business* (4th edition). Hew York, NY: McGraw-Hill.

Trompenaars, F., & Wooliams, P. (2010). Tango to intercultural integration: Reconciling cultural differences in mergers, acquisitions, and strategic partnerships. *Intercultural Management Quarterly,* 11(2): 3–7.

Williamson, P.J., Guo, B., & Yin, E. (2021). When can Chinese competitors catch up? Market and capability ladders and their implications for multinationals. *Business Horizons,* 64(2): 223–237.

Wong, P., & Neck, P. (2015). When east meets west: A harmonised model for performance and institutional alignment to manage knowledge practitioners, their productivity in a knowledge-based economy. *International Journal of Contemporary Management,* 14(1): 7–26.

Xu, D., Zhou, K.Z., & Chen, S., (2023). The impact of communist ideology on the patenting activity of Chinese firms. *Academy of Management Journal,* 66(1): 102–132.

Young, M.N., Bruton, G.D., Peng, M.W., & Yu, X. (2022). U.S. corporations are from Mars, Chinese corporations are from Venus. *Business Horizons,* 65(4): 505–517.

Zhang, L. (2023). *Understanding Chinese corporate governance: Practical guidance for working with Chinese partners.* London & New York, NY: Routledge.

Module monitor and Consolidation VI

Workshop VI: Applications/review exercises

Self-check questions

You should now be able to answer Self-Check Questions 1–10

1 **True or false** *Born globals* are firms less than 20 years old that internationalized on average within three years of founding and generate at least 25% of total sales from abroad.

2 **True or false** The four *VUCA* characteristics are: volatility, uncertainty, chaos, and anxiety.

3 **True or false** "*Innovations* no longer merely spread from wealthy to less-developed economies in a single direction. They can also flow in *reverse*". This refers to the practice of *trickle-up innovation*.

4 **Multiple-choice** *Logitech* was founded in 1981 in (select one):

  a *Taiwan*, and quickly expanded to *Silicon Valley*, USA

  b *Hong Kong*, and quickly expanded to the *UK*

c *Lausanne, Switzerland*, and quickly expanded to the *Silicon Valley*, USA

d *Silicon Valley*, USA, and quickly expanded to the *Middle East*

e *Gdansk, Poland*, and quickly expanded to *Ireland*, the *UK, Canada*, and the *USA*

5 **True or false** *Leapfrogging* happens when a country skips over traditional stages of development in favor of either jumping directly to the newest technologies right away (stage-skipping) or pursuing an alternative course of technological advancement that involves developing emerging technologies that offer novel advantages and opportunities (path-creating).

6 **Multiple-choice** *CQ* means (select one):

a cultural information system

b cultural variation

c cultural intelligence

d culture shock

e stereotyping

7 **True or false** The six *cultural dimensions* developed by Geert Hofstede that allow different national characteristics to be classified or mapped are: society (individualism vs. communitarianism), achievement orientation (achievement/egalitarian/what people do vs. ascription/hierarchical/who people are), time orientation (monochronic/sequential vs. polychronic/synchronic), rules (universalism/following rules vs. particularism/"it depends"), emotions/disagreeing (affective/confrontational vs. neutral/avoiding confrontation), and human desires/having fun (indulgence vs. restraint).

8 **True or false** If there is low-*power distance*, schemes for employee participation are more likely to flourish.

9 **True or false** Leadership in a *collectivist* society will tend toward the group rather than the *individual*.

10 **True or false** *CAGE* stands for cultural, aspirational, geographic, and ethical differences between countries that organizations should address when crafting international strategies.

Individualized learning record

When you have finished Module VI, try filling in this record of what you have learned.

1 A born-global firm – is it a myth, magic, or reality? What are some of the enablers of internationalization? What drives companies to venture

overseas early on? Should every startup go global? What will a typical global startup look like in 5, 10, or 15 years?

....

....

2   For many, "Silicon Valley" and "startup" are synonymous. In fact, a dispro-portionate number of business ventures that have grown from garage start-ups into global giants are headquartered in Silicon Valley. What is the secret to these startups' remarkable success? Can this be replicated in any region?

....

....

3   If you're not a born global, but an established market leader, to what extent do you still keep emerging giants on your radar screen? How much time, energy, and attention do you invest in monitoring the moves of small but rapidly growing and super-innovative rivals from developing countries?

....

....

4   Edgar Schein defines organizational culture as: "A distinctive aspect of the way that an organization functions, which shapes its overall performance as well as the feelings which individuals have about it, is its culture. This is the pattern of basic assumptions developed by an organization as it learns to cope with problems of external adaptation and internal integration. These assumptions are taught to new members as the correct way to perceive, think, and feel in order to be successful. They cover a wide range of issues: how to dress, how much to argue, how far to defer to the boss's authority, what to reward and what to punish, are some of them". Now, what are the differences between "organizational culture" (Cf. E. Schein) and "national culture" (G. Hofstede)?

....

....

5   Analyze national culture and, for example, consumer purchasing patterns. Evidence suggests that, for instance, in a country that scores high on mas-culinity, more "status" products such as high-priced watches and jewelry are sold. Yet, in a high uncertainty avoidance culture, which values purity and basic products, there will be more sales of mineral water, fresh fruit,

and pure sugar. Individualist cultures spend less on food, while collectivist cultures spend more on food – food plays a key social function in the latter. Now, consider the products purchased in your household over the last month – is your purchasing pattern in harmony with your national culture?

....

....

6 Can enterprises truly be culturally intelligent? If so, explain how. How to develop organizational CQ?

....

....

7 Design and implement an L&D program for a global workforce (think: language, culture, delivery method, learning styles, gap assessment, time zones, costs, tools, connectivity, technology, evaluation). How to create the global learning organization?

....

....

8 Multinational corporations are often targeted by social activists, who organize protests against their seeming avarice and the detrimental impact they have on some of the cultures in which they operate. What are the arguments for and against this point of view?

....

....

9 Tesla seeks to further explore going into Europe and has narrowed down the countries to the Czech Republic, Germany or Poland. Use the CAGE(er) framework to choose which would be a better strategic possibility. Explain your reasons.

....

....

10 Chinese companies are reinventing management. What can Western companies learn from innovative Chinese companies when doing business with the new China?

....

....

Can-do checklist

Looking back, I have learned the following Key Terms:

Unit 11

- born global (BG)/international new ventures (INVs)/instant internationals
- enablers of early and rapid internalization
- "leapfrogging"
- scaling (blitz, efficient, fast)
- speed
- stage model of internationalization
- trickle-up innovation (reverse innovation) strategy
- volatility, uncertainty, complexity/chaos, and ambiguity (VUCA)

Unit 12

- cultural, administrative, geographic, economic (environmental, risk) distance framework (CAGE(er))
- cultural characteristics/dimensions: power distance, uncertainty avoidance, individualism/collectivism, masculinity/femininity, time orientation, and indulgence/restraint
- cultural intelligence (CQ)
- cultural shock
- cultural-awareness training course
- culture (national, organizational)
- emotional stages associated with an overseas assignment: honeymoon-culture shock/crisis-recovery-adjustment
- evangelization (universal)
- forms of organizations (implicit): a pyramid of people, a well-oiled machine, a village market, and the family
- globalization
- regionalization
- stereotyping

Module VII

Behavioral ethics

Achieving ethical practice for the greater good

13 Progress with purpose

The "good" enterprise

"If humanity today succeeds in combining the new scientific capacities with a strong ethical dimension, it will certainly be able to promote the environment as a home and a resource for all..." – Pope John Paul II

Sneak peek

Focus on: Key concepts and terms

Unit 13

- Capitalism (compassionate, conscience, conscious)
- Chief sustainability officer (CSO)
- Code of ethics
- Common good
- Corporate social responsibility (CSR; strategic)
- Economy (circular, "good", humane, "of Communion", solidarity-based, sharing)
- Environmental, social, corporate governance (and technology) (ESG(T))
- Fragility, conflict, and violence (FCV)
- "Good" enterprise
- People, planet, prosperity, peace, and partnership (PPPPP)
- Progress with purpose
- Regenerative business model
- Sustainability (forces driving; human, talent, environmental, governance, financial)

DOI: 10.4324/9781003508274-21

Pause 'N' reflect: On the current issues and trends

Before you complete this unit, think about each of the following statements. Mark each statement:

V – if you *agree.*
X – if you *disagree.*
? – if you are *undecided.*

Your Take: Integrative Thinking	Before doing Unit 13	After doing Unit 13
1 Humans should be at the very center of the economy.		
2 Although it might appear to be a modern trend, businesses have actually been engaging in "compassionate capitalism" for almost a thousand years. Historically, prosperous entrepreneurs frequently used their accumulated wealth to support their communities.		
3 ESG stands for economy, standardization, and globalization.		
4 There is an emerging consensus that enterprises should prioritize long-term sustainability over short-term profit.		
5 Sustainability is about the company's regenerative business model, namely, how its products and services strategically support sustainable development.		
6 All market participants (SMEs, large, "public interest" organizations) should be obligated to disclose non-financial as well as diversity information (aligned with and benchmarked against the sustainability objectives such as environmental, social, and governance goals).		

Your Take: Integrative Thinking   Before doing Unit 13   After doing Unit 13

7	Established multinationals have no problem delivering superior financial returns while serving the interests of all stakeholders.		
8	The Progress with Purpose approach equalizes financial goals with environmental goals, as well as the health, happiness, well-being, and welfare of the workforce and consumer. It radiates positive influence through its high-quality connections (HQCs) with various stakeholders.		
9	Individuals and enterprises should shift society toward becoming *more sustainable* rather than *less unsustainable*. If human beings can learn to work with natural systems rather than exploit them, both humans and nature will flourish.		
10	Enterprises can advance human, organizational, and stakeholders' flourishing through the inherent dignity found in work.		

After you have done the unit, repeat "Your Take". How has reading the unit clarified the ideas herein? How have your views, feelings and thoughts changed over time?

Lead-in

General discussion points

Individually or in buzz groups, think about:

1 *The "good" enterprise should establish an organizational culture based on...* (e.g., trust, giving, sharing, the inherent dignity found in work, care, integrity, good conduct, social values, mutual respect, shared responsibility, openness, regeneration, justice, transparency, etc.). What other qualities could you suggest? Can you think of any "good" enterprises?
2 In contrast to Henry Ford, Milton Friedman advanced the doctrine as a theory of business ethics (the Friedman Doctrine, *aka* the Shareholder Theory) that states that "an entity's greatest responsibility lies in the satisfaction of the shareholders", meaning that the enterprise should continually strive to maximize

its revenues to boost shareholder returns, and that the one and only social responsibility of business is to make profits. What is *your* take?

3 In what ways, if any, do you believe that an organization is responsible to the following groups: shareholders, employees, suppliers, customers, and the general public? Can you think of any other stakeholders?

4 Socially responsible investors ("impact investors") are people who are concerned with where their money is going. Like everybody else, they aspire to a secure financial future – but not at the price of their ethical, purpose-driven or social values. They're environmentally altruistic rather than economically opportunistic – they want the enterprises in which they invest to share a common value system, to be socially, morally, and environmentally responsible and to think of the long-term effects of their business transactions. Are you a socially responsible investor?

5 Could, for example, banks reassess their lending/advisory/investment policies concerning sustainability-sensitive projects? Specifically, should they have companies that manufacture tobacco, biological, chemical or nuclear weapons, gambling companies, mining companies, and/or fossil fuel companies in their fund portfolios or invest in morally questionable national economies?

Share your thoughts with your peers/team members. Discuss points of (dis) agreement.

Idea watch

The "good" enterprise – becoming a force for the "Common Good".

"No job is more vital to our society than that of the manager", as Henry Mintzberg put into words. This view is also echoed by John Paul II who emphasized that "the degree of well-being that society enjoys today would be impossible without the dynamic figure of the entrepreneur". The world of business needs to be transformed into a positive force for the Common Good – that is to say, the sum total of social conditions which allow people, either as groups or individuals, to reach their fulfillment more fully and more easily. In this context, the conventional belief is that the well-being of the community is inseparable from the moral, social, and spiritual aspects of an individual's life. In fact, the common good impacts on the life of all. It requires good judgment from each individual, with an even greater responsibility placed on those in positions of authority.

In today's knowledge-creative economy, enterprises of all sizes, in all industries, are under growing pressure to uphold social and ethical standards from the public, investors, and the government. While organizations bang the drum of ethical policies, mere policies are no longer enough.

The "good" enterprise, an entity viewed as a community and defined by personal connections, as part of a humane economy – the "good" economy (the "Economy of Communion") that nurtures the creation of *shared* value for a flourishing society, lives and breathes ethical behavior – the behavior that always seeks to make sure that its effects have the greatest positive impact (looking ahead beyond the managed destruction or regeneration of the natural world) and the least negative impact on the most people possible in society (both inside and outside the enterprise) and the planet Earth (recognizing and valuing Nature's bias toward plentifulness and waste-free living). It also cultivates a culture of joy, kindness, helping, giving, sharing, caring, compassion, forgiveness, sacrifice, and gratitude.

Of note is the fact that "flourishing" involves employee thriving (think: positive energy, vitality, and learning), happiness (think: high spirts and positive emotions), engagement (think: work satisfaction and self-motivation), and stakeholders' flourishing (think: the best possible experience and functioning of every specific stakeholder).

Consequently, a sustainable business should become "values-driven" *as well as* finance-driven". Thus, the "good" enterprise has the potential to thrive both commercially *and* ethically. To achieve this balance between short-term profitability and long-term sustainability (serving diverse stakeholder interests to shape an enterprise's sustainably financial and creative future), consider incorporating the following five sustainability building blocks:

- **Human** sustainability (think: human well-being) – recognizing that the human person is at the center of the economy; investing in the well-being of everyone you connect with and championing a happiness, human-centered and ethics-based product/service portfolio;
- **Talent** sustainability (think: talent retention) – putting people first by empowering socially diverse people to personally and professionally flourish, to pursue their aspirations and to achieve their full potential;
- **Environmental** sustainability (think: environmental preservation) – caring for and being resource and "planet positive", committed to giving back more to the planet than you take, and working hard toward a better future;
- **Governance** for sustainability (think: effective governance) – sustaining professional governance;
- **Financial** sustainability (think: financial stability) – delivering spectacular financial returns.

This will help guarantee *progress, sustainable performance with purpose*, which, in turn, will help regenerate and renew your business and boost your bottom line – serving people, planet, prosperity, peace, and partnership (PPPPP) in equal measure.

Assumptions

Business is a noble vocation, and "conscience capitalism" cares about the conditions that foster dignity and flourishing at the human, organizational, societal, and natural environmental levels. It holistically and systematically appreciates the interconnectedness between people, enterprises, and society – "conscious capitalist" enterprises simultaneously mix together real-time profitability, solidarity, sustainability reporting and long-term positive impact.

Interestingly, Adam Smith, the universally acknowledged founding father of modern economics, advocated for self-interest not because he thought humans were fundamentally self-seeking ("Homo *economicus*"); on the contrary, he recognized the need of everyone of us making "rational efforts to further our material well-being". He argued that "Benevolence" cannot exist without "prudence" – without first raising capital, the benevolent have nothing to distribute ("Homo *moralis*"). Following this logic, businesses exist to create wealth – whether by their goods or services – that helps the "good" (solidarity-based, sharing) economy (the "Economy of Communion") thrive, which is necessary for the stability, sustainability, happiness, prosperity, and advancement of humanity.

In this context, the Economy of Communion (EOC) is a positive force for the world. It transforms work environments and brings about social change through everyday, human-centered decision-making, and action. For these enterprises (regarded as "communities"), leading *positive* sustainable change means "humanizing" the economy by consistently privileging the creation and sustenance of high-quality connections (HQCs) over profit-maximizing, and by putting profits in common and leveraging them to address "wicked" social problems. Furthermore, it means "humanizing" enterprises through business practices, policies, and philosophies that respect the inherent dignity of every human being, and that are intended to remove barriers between business partners.

On that account, groundbreaking "good" enterprises embrace social missions like nonprofits, yet generate revenue streams to pursue their missions like for-profit entities. To succeed both commercially *and* ethically, they're "values-driven" *as well as* finance-driven"; in other words, they can *sustainably* balance the short and long terms.

Ultimately, the goal of sustainability is to (re-)energize and sustain a human-friendly ecosystem on the planet. Currently, sustainability seems to be making a shift from addressing "deficits gaps" (living and organizing *less unsustainably*) to instead addressing "abundance gaps" (becoming *more sustainable*).

The dynamic forces that powerfully impact organizations' sustainability and business ethics agenda include: an explosion of sustainable innovation and entrepreneurship, social/humanitarian movements, globalization of businesses, the media, gradual evolution of more ambitious policy-making on sustainability, environmental concerns, the talent war to attract and retain an environmentally aware workforce, stakeholder power, socially responsible investing legislation, sustainability-related reporting, codes, and benchmarking – alternatives to the mainstream stock market benchmarks. For example, consider, the Dow Jones Sustainability World Index (DJSI World), which represents the top 10% of the biggest 2,500 companies in the S&P Global Broad Market Index based on long-term environmental, social, and governance (ESG) criteria. Today, it can be said that many investors seek out socially conscious investments, making the DJSI World a popular benchmark for private wealth managers. Another such index is the FTSE4Good Index Series. This index is a collection of ESG stock indexes created and maintained by the Financial Times Stock Exchange-Russell Group (FTSE). The purpose of such indexes is to highlight enterprises that score highly in measures of strategic corporate social responsibility (CSR) or citizenship.

Key elements

Our world is fast changing, prompting enterprises all over the world to reconsider what it means to be winning, where people, the environment and money all play a role. The organization of the future that is daring enough to transform its business model and become regenerative will prosper. This entails an enterprise operating in a way that constantly re-energizes and renews itself, leverages its values, and positively impacts on PPPPP.

ESG(T) represents environmental, social, governance (and technology). This is often regarded as a measure of sustainability. ESG(T) is at the core of numerous organizations' business models – it's about how their products and services strategically support sustainable growth – progress with purpose. What's more, it's about enterprise risk management (ERM) – that is to say, how it carries out its own operations to keep negative impacts to a minimum. Ultimately, ESG(T) may be critical for business decision-making.

Environmental – Our environment is significantly impacted by global production and consumption. Manufacturing anything on a large scale might potentially lead to climate change, resource depletion, waste, pollution, deforestation, and biodiversity loss.

Social – Companies have a responsibility for their employees, as well as their impact on the societies in which they operate – for instance, in terms of helping, giving, sharing, caring, human dignity, workplace conditions, justice, employee voice and rights, and diversity.

Governance – Governance can act as a check on bribery and fraud, modern slavery, massive executive compensation, tax evasion, and internal control. Corporate governance is critical to the growth of businesses and offers long-term advantages to employees, shareholders, and society. One method of doing this is paying attention to boosting accountability and openness in communications between the enterprise and its shareholders on topics such as board structure and shareholder voting rights.

Plus,

Technology – The ESG agenda, according to some, has to be expanded to properly take into account technology challenges as well. Therefore, the extended framework can be abbreviated as ESGT, with T standing for technology. For example, think: massive tech shifts, artificial intelligence (AI), cybersecurity, cybercrime, robotic processing, fake news, dark web, data miming, bioengineering, surveillance, digital power concentration or regional digital inequality.

Naturally, you can make regeneration and renewal core to your business and try to embed ESG(T) into your everyday operations.

Thinking critically: Issues

Some will claim that given the power and assets that many enterprises (particularly those who are global players) and their shareholders have accumulated through their operations in free-market economies, their owners have a moral responsibility to use at least some of those resources to help out the less fortunate in society. On the other hand, others believe that "the business of business is business" and, therefore, any enterprise exists in order to succeed as a business.

Certainly, capitalism is under siege from all sides… As a result, we can no longer solely pursue consumption-driven economic growth. To reimagine the capitalist system, CEOs need to rethink, reinvent and reposition their enterprises and pledge to focus on all stakeholders and the planet, and not just profit. Admittedly, *becoming* a better corporate citizen isn't simple (think: fragility, conflict, and violence (FCV), market failure, structural unemployment, extreme poverty, the erosion of trust, corruption, social risk in supply chains, as well as anti-sustainability rhetoric); however, it's doable.

Besides, there will *always* be critics of your executing sustainability philosophies, policies, and practices – both inside *and* outside your enterprise. If your *inside* critics, especially at the top of your organization, don't want to adopt the idea of the "good" enterprise ever, then perhaps they shouldn't stay on the executive leadership team (ELT) much longer. In order to implement the purpose-driven strategy, CEOs must create support networks and learn how to address attacks from *outside* pressure groups, too. By way of illustration, if some skeptical non-governmental organizations (NGOs) doubt and claim that your sustainability effort amounts to little more than window dressing, and if that's the case indeed!, be honest and make clear that you are implementing something new and be upfront about your tardiness. Moreover, to champion the "good enterprise", as part of the "good" economy, you may join forces with other organizations – even competitors – in your sector. Primarily, go for local, connected solutions. Think: partnerships.

Importantly, being "good" doesn't mean just funding charitable programs to make yourself feel and/or look "good". Likewise, nowadays, more and more enterprises are increasingly drawing up codes of ethics to guide behavior – at all levels. Surely, codes, professional standards and qualifications can help define and achieve ethical practice – but they won't guarantee it. Although most organizations declare they have ethical policies, having impressive-sounding mission statements, policy statements, and beautifully crafted codes of ethics isn't enough. Remember: ethical codes are *only* legitimate *if* they're appreciated and freely practiced by the vast majority of people. Therefore, enterprises need to cultivate ethical company culture – it's essential for ethics to permeate both the organizational culture and the hearts and minds of its employees.

On balance, although ESG-aligned investing ("impact investing") seems promising, we shouldn't have *un*realistic expectations. Using threats of divestment to transform corporate behavior or corporate citizenship may prove rather unsuccessful, and enterprises that are demonstrably "good" do not consistently deliver high returns. Most significantly, societal ills cannot be cured by business and finance alone; business, the state, and civil society all need to serve distinct, complementary responsibilities to design the sustainable future we want – and to build a flourishing society.

What's more, business schools and executive education need to get a lot more serious about sustainability and ethics too. For example, as many organizations are not living up to their own "green" rhetoric, enterprises and executives alike seek a greater focus on teaching responsible business and ethics. Consequently, more programs such as an MBA in *Sustainability* Leadership/ or an MBA in *Purpose* Economy should be launched – with modules including, but not limited to: The "Good"/*Humane* Economy, "the Economy of *Communion*", "the *Common Good*", *Behavioral* Economics, *Regenerative* Business, *Humanizing* the Enterprise, *Heart-based* Leadership, *Dialogic* Organization Development, Leading *Positive* Organizational Change, Organizational *Energy*, Business as a *Calling*, *Principled* Entrepreneurship, *Social Innovation* Startups, *Talent* Development, Leading with *Integrity*, *Positive* Followership, *Virtuousness* in Organizations, The *Conflict-Positive* Enterprise, Organizational *Recovery* and *Healing*, *Flourishing*, *Spirituality* at Work, *Behavioral* Ethics, *Ethical* Management Consulting, *Cultural* Intelligence, *Productivity* through *Strengths*, Creating *Sustainable* Value, The Science of *Happiness*, *Beauty* at Work, and Imagining *Hope*, etc.

Finally, when businesses fully integrate ESG frameworks into their company strategy and operations, a stand-alone Chief Sustainability Officer (CSO) job would be redundant. Nonetheless, until that day comes, it is critical to adapt and evolve the CSO role.

On top of that, ESG is being given bad press too, and some say that with good reason, for the absence of common definitions, especially for the S. Therefore, while the acronym ESG may, at some point, perhaps vanish, the question of how to balance profits *and* virtues will – and *should* – stay with us forever.

Applications

Examples of *good* enterprise practices in positive strategic transformation may include the following (for more information and details, see the PepsiCo case on which this part is based on: Nooyi, I., & Govindarajan, V. (2020). Becoming a better corporate citizen: How PepsiCo moved toward a healthier future. *Harvard Business Review*, 98(2): 94–103):

Be careful what words you choose to communicate your sustainability program

Communicate your purpose-driven initiative in a way that is clear to everybody. Be careful with the language in your sustainability reports and disclosures, as these are often full of warm, fuzzy generalizations. It has to sound real *and* sincere and actually *be* so. Hence, in order to demonstrate your genuine dedication to guaranteeing human, talent, environmental and governance sustainability in addition to superior financial performance, do not play down the message with mere three-letter acronyms (TLAs) such as CSR, ESG or DEI (diversity, equity, and inclusion)… Instead, genuinely communicate an *understandable* (and *true!*) message. As an aside, have you read your company's CSR report lately? If yes, what do you think of it? Does it use *passion, commitment, engagement, trust, equity, governance, credibility*, etc? Have some of these words become CSR "buzzwords"? Is it just full of waffle?

Make sure the board is on your side

Although they will hold you accountable for delivering on your purpose-led strategy, ensure that your board of directors is behind you all the way.

Think gigatrends and behave from the "outside-in"

Start by designing your strategy from the outside-in. Analyze mega-trends (think: geopolitics, financial inclusion, the talent war, hyper-connected workplace, AI, robots and automation, clean tech arms race between nations, the rise of activism, human migration – and social unrest, well-being, environment and climate fluctuations, urban development, social risk in supply chains, distribution of food, scarcity of natural resources) and future-proof your company by developing "future back" strategies.

With early actions, positively model the required new attitudes

For the company to see that the purpose-driven approach is more than simply a passing fad, make a strong move early on. For instance, institute a "chairperson award" to publicly and empathically recognize and honor staff who sincerely practice the enterprise's aspirational ethical standards. Additionally, call off a new product launch or investment into a new territory, regardless of the internal pushes or expenses incurred, if the product or action is not in harmony with organizational ethics. Further, designate your new strategy ambassadors. Contrary to popular belief, you do not need to create or appoint a CSO. If you hire one, the new strategy may fall more on that person's shoulders than on anybody else's, and you want everybody to "own" it.

Build new capabilities to nurture the purpose-driven aspiration

To execute your novel purpose-driven program, build fresh capabilities – bring in people from across sectors, cultures, experiences, demographics, generations, intelligences, insights, relationships, and backgrounds. For instance, create prominent leadership roles and hire outsiders (e.g., chief design officer, chief scientific officer). This will send a strong message to your organization (*and* your industry) that you are serious about developing the radically divergent individual and organizational talent capabilities (e.g., being human-centered, ethics-led, sustainability-focused, research-based, practice-informed, etc.).

Localize your strategic transformation implementation

Even though a purpose-driven approach must be consistent across all of your business operations geographies, make your program "local" in character.

Implant the greater good within your organization's DNA so it becomes an essential characteristic of who you are

While leading positive sustainable change may be kicked off by the CEO, it won't endure if it's not ingrained in your organizational DNA. To heighten employees' awareness of and to mobilize their support for your sustainable performance with a purpose agenda, the best strategy is to:

1 Start at the top: Organizational ethics and sustainability concern leadership, thus workshops for ELTs are a good place to start, ideally employing a dilemma-based learning and development (L&D) approach. Use: executive coaching, role play, problem-solving, simulations, case studies, and interactive videos.
2 Cascade the training throughout the enterprise: Next, co-ordinate training for all other staff. Designate a champion for each key business unit. Herein, especially make use of competent line managers who are best positioned to be familiar with the challenges their front-line personnel need to respond to every day. Mix dilemma-based e-learning with face-to-face methods.
3 Deploy specialist learning and development interventions as appropriate: Provide high-risk functions such as emergency operation center, public information office, procurement, health and safety with specialized L&D opportunities. Follow it with an e-learning exercise to test understanding and application of learning so as to enable L&D staff and senior management to evaluate the results of the targeted learning.

Case alert! Case classic

PepsiCo

LOOK IT UP: Nooyi, I., & Govindarajan, V. (2020). Becoming a better corporate citizen: How PepsiCo moved toward a healthier future. *Harvard Business Review,* 98(2): 94–103.

    Your task: Read the *PepsiCo* case over again to now dig deeper and uncover facts which can be substantiated.

    Make a list of all the challenges that PepsiCo needed to respond to when executing a program called Performance with Purpose (PwP).

    Next, consider PepsiCo's performance (e.g., financial performance, female leadership, healthfulness of its offerings, investments in R&D, environmental performance).

Are there any surprises? If yes, explain why. Report your research findings, insights, and good practices back to your peers/team members.

To record your critical insights, use the Case Analysis Record provided in Appendix 2.

Greater good corner: Get ready to exercise your ethics

Take a stance: What would *you* do?

Dilemma and decision: Planet positive vs profit negative

You're a local manufacturer, and your R&D department informs you that it is feasible to re-engineer your production process to eliminate environmental harm. However, this change would significantly increase your product costs, making your offerings much more expensive than those of your rivals.

What would you do? Consider the pros, cons, and consequences of your decision.

Thought questions:

How would your decision affect your responsibility toward the environment, your employees, and the community? Would prioritizing profit over environmental sustainability compromise your ethical standards? Conversely, could the increased costs and potential loss of market share lead to downsizing or other negative impacts on your workforce? How do you balance your duty to shareholders with your ethical obligations to society and the planet?

Time out: Journal entry

Thought Sparks: A few reflections, insightful ideas, actionable suggestions, strategic thinking, and key takeaways from this unit.

Learning never stops... So, pause for a few minutes and reflect in writing on your personal learning experience and beliefs. Through writing in your journal, you develop your awareness of your own beliefs and attitudes. Now, consolidate what you have learned in this unit.

1 How have your beliefs and ideas about the "good" enterprise/Common good/sustainability changed since you began the unit?

....

....

2 Thinking about the problems presented in the unit, write about whether you have found solutions to these problems.

....

....

3 How confident do you now feel about championing progress with purpose?

....

....

4 What would you still like to have clarified? What remaining concerns do you have?

....

....

5 What more would you like to learn about the topic, now that you have completed this unit?

....

....

6 Visit https://thecompanycube.org and and engage with the "company cube". Roll the cube, read the prompts, and reflect on how they align with your work and values. Live out the principles you discover, share your insights with your peers, and immerse yourself in the experience. Enjoy the process and have fun!

....

....

Remember: It's particularly useful to re-visit journal entries several times and see how themes have recurred or your thoughts have changed over time. Now, repeat "Your Take".

Making connections: Related units and models

- U 1. **Behavioral economics and policy 101**: For humans (see pp. 9–26)
- U 2. **The kindness advantage:** Cultivating positively energizing leaders and followers (see pp. 27–53)
- U 3. **Strategic transformation:** Strategy choice-making (see pp. 61–81)

- U 4. **SOAR:** Possibility thinking in positive strategic dialog (see pp. 82–95)
- U 5. **Dialogic organization development (OD)**: Leading positive organizational change (see pp. 103–121)
- U 6. **Design-driven organization**: Human-centered design thinking and innovation execution (see pp. 122–139)
- U 9. **Professional management consulting for real people**: The advice business demystified (see pp. 181–203)
- U 11. **So, you want to go global?** Becoming an instant international (see pp. 227–237)
- U 14. **Oops! I messed up.** Why good people do bad things every so often (see pp. 273–287)
- Add in more related models you may want to remember: _____.

Industry snapshot

www.pepsico.com/who-we-are/our-commitments/pepsico-positive

Deep dive: Main references and resources

Akgiray, V. (2019). *Good finance: Why we need a new concept of finance*. Bristol: Bristol University Press.

Casson, C., Casson, M., Lee, J., & Phillips, K. (2020). *Compassionate capitalism: Business and community in medieval England*. Bristol: Bristol University Press.

Chen, C. (2022). *Work pray code: When work becomes religion in Silicon Valley*. Princeton, NJ: Princeton University Press.

The Company Cube (n.d.). Retrieved from: https://thecompanycube.org – it's is a new cooperative strategy for business success. Its objective is to transform work environments and bring about positive social change through daily, decision-making and action.

Davies, R. (2023). *What is philanthropy for?* Bristol: Bristol University Press.

Dessart, L., & Standaert, W. (2023). Strategic storytelling in the age of sustainability. *Business Horizons*, 66(3): 371–385.

Dyllick, T., & Muff, K. (2016). Clarifying the meaning of sustainable business: Introducing a typology from business-as-usual to true business sustainability. *Organization & Environment*, 29(2): 156–174.

Eccles, R.G., & Taylor, A. (2023). The evolving role of chief sustainability officers. *Harvard Business Review*, 101(4): 76–85.

Economy of Communion (EOC). Economia di Comunione (EdC). Rome: Movimento dei Focolari. (n.d.). Retrieved from: www.edc-online.org/en/ – the EOC project, a worldwide humanitarian initiative, irrespective of religious allegiance, is a concrete effort to address urgent social problems by establishing and nurturing enterprises that are integral parts of their communities, unlike the consumerist economy. The project asks member firms to commit, after an appropriate investment in the sustainability of the business, a part of their profits to direct aid for those in need and another part toward cultivating a culture of kindness, helping, giving, profit sharing, caring, serving and gratitude.

Edwards, M.G., Lindberg, A., Larsson, M., & Angel, J. (2024). *Regenerative business voices: Values-based entrepreneurship for sustainable enterprises*. London & New York, NY: Routledge.

Fiaschi, D., Giuliani, E., Nieri, F., & Salvati, N. (2020). How bad is your company? Measuring corporate wrongdoing beyond the magic of ESG metrics. *Business Horizons*, 63(3): 287–299.

Ford (2013, September 5). Ford's legacy of sustainability. Retrieved from: https://media. ford.com/content/fordmedia/fna/us/en/features/ford-s-legacy-of-sustainability.html

Fu, R., Tang, Y., & Chen, G. (2020). Chief sustainability officers and corporate social (ir) responsibility. *Strategic Management Journal*, 41(4): 656–680.

Gallagher, J., & Buckeye, J. (2014). *Structures of grace: The business practices of the economy of communion*. Hyde Park, NY: New City Press.

Gulati, R. (2022). *Deep purpose: The heart and soul of high-performance companies.* New York, NY: Harper Business.

Harrison, N.E., & Mikler, J. (2022). *Capitalism for all.* Albany, NY: SUNY Press.

Hasan, R., & Yu, Z. (2020). Capitalism leading to unhealthy food consumption. *Strategic Change*, 29(6): 633–643.

Hiller, A., & Goworek, H. (2023). *Ethical consumption: A research overview.* London & New York: Routledge.

Hoffman, A.J. (2022). *Management as a calling: Leading business, serving society.* Stanford, CA: Stanford Business Books.

IJMR. (2023). Grand societal challenges: The contributions of business, management and organisation studies. *International Journal of Management Reviews*, 25(2): 231–409.

John Paul II. (1991). *Centesimus annus.* Rome. Retrieved from: www.vatican.va/content/ john-paul-ii/en/encyclicals/documents/hf_jp-ii_enc_01051991_centesimus-annus.html

Keeley, T. (2022). *Sustainable: Moving beyond ESG to impact investing.* New York, NY: Columbia University Press.

Klein, P.G., Holmes Jr. R.M., Foss, N., Terjesen, S., & Pepe, J. (2022): Capitalism, cronyism, and management scholarship: A call for clarity. *Academy of Management Perspectives*, 36(1): 6–29.

Lavie, D. (2023). *The cooperative economy: A solution to societal grand challenges.* London & New York, NY: Routledge.

Lynch, M. (2021, February 1). Seven forces driving a sustainable business revolution. Retrieved from: www.ivey.uwo.ca/sustainability/news/2021/01/seven-forces-driving-a-sustainable-business-revolution/

Malnight, T.W., & Buche, I. (2023, October 27). How your company's social purpose can also drive profit. *Harvard Business Review*. Retrieved from: https://hbr.org/2023/10/ how-your-companys-social-purpose-can-also-drive-profit

Mazzucato, M. (2023). Governing the economics of the common good: From correcting market failures to shaping collective goals. UCL Institute for Innovation and Public Purpose, Working Paper Series (IIPP WP 2023–08). Forthcoming in *Journal of Economic Policy Reform*. Retrieved from: https://www.ucl.ac.uk/bartlett/public-purpose/ wp2023-08

Mazzucato, M. (2024). Governing the economics of the common good: from correcting market failures to shaping collective goals. *Journal of Economic Policy Reform*, 27(1): 1–24.

Nooyi, I., & Govindarajan, V. (2020). Becoming a better corporate citizen: How PepsiCo moved toward a healthier future. *Harvard Business Review*, 98(2): 94–103.

Pearson, G. (2020). *Remaking the real economy: Escaping destruction by organised money.* Bristol: Policy Press.

Porter, M., Serafeim, G., & Kramer, M. (2019, October 16). Where ESG fails. *Institutional Investor.* Retrieved from https://www.institutionalinvestor.com/article/b1hm5ghqtxj9s7/ Where-ESG-Fails

Posner, M. (2023, January 31). How to make ESG investing real and meaningful. Retrieved from: www.ethicalsystems.org/how-to-make-esg-investing-real-and-meaningful/

Prahalad, C.K. (2010). *The fortune at the bottom of the pyramid: Eradicating poverty through profits* (Fifth edition). Upper Saddle River, NJ: Wharton School Publishing.

Quinn, R.E., & Thakor, A. (2019). *The economics of higher purpose: Eight counterintuitive steps for creating a purpose-driven organization.* San Francisco, CA: Berrett-Koehler Publishers.

Rasche, A., Morsing, M., Moon, J., & Kourula, A. (Eds.). (2023). *Corporate sustainability: Managing responsible business in a globalised world.* (2nd ed.). Cambridge: Cambridge University Press.

Rodin, J., & Madsbjerg, S. (2021). *Making money moral: How a new wave of visionaries is linking purpose and profit.* Philadelphia, PA: Wharton School Press.

Sachs, J. (2015). *The age of sustainable development.* New York, NY: Columbia University Press.

Sheehan, N.T., Vaidyanathan, G., Fox, K.A., & Klassen, M. (2023). Making the invisible, visible: Overcoming barriers to ESG performance with an ESG mindset. *Business Horizons*, 66(2): 265–276.

Smith, A. (1759). *The theory of moral sentiments.* London: Pantianos Classics.

Sustainable development: Sustainable development goals (SDGs). (n.d.). New York, NY: The United Nations. Retrieved from: https://sdgs.un.org/goals

Tirole, J. (2017). *Economics for the common good.* Princeton, NJ: Princeton University Press.

Wilson, S, & McCalman, J. (2017). Re-imagining ethical leadership as leadership for the greater good. *European Management Journal*, 35(2): 151–154.

14 Oops! I messed up

Why good people do bad things
every so often

"Integrity is doing the right thing, even when no one is looking" – C.S. Lewis

Sneak peek

Focus on: Key concepts and terms

Unit 14

- Bias (confirmation, conformity, overconfidence, self-serving)
- CEOs/executives (Machiavellian, narcissistic, overconfident, psychopathic)
- Dissonance (cognitive/moral)
- Ethics (behavioral, business, neuro, organizational)
- Ethical decision-making process (six steps)
- Examen (daily)
- Executive derailment
- External pressures (social, organizational)
- Framing (emotional)
- Happiness gap
- Incrementalism
- Internal psychological biases and mental shortcuts
- Moral imagination
- Multiple minds
- Neuroethics
- Noise
- Self (best, could-, ideal, moral, should-, want-)
- Situational factors (general, temporal)
- Summum Bonum ("the supreme good")
- System 1 thinking: (almost) automatic, emotional, and intuitive

DOI: 10.4324/9781003508274-22

- System 2 thinking: more rational and conscious
- Test ("big brother", "breaking news", front-page, generalizability, "mirror")

Pause 'N' reflect: On the current issues and trends

Before you complete this unit, think about each of the following statements. Mark each statement:

V – if you *agree*.
X – if you *disagree*.
? – if you are *undecided*.

Your Take: Integrative Thinking	*Before doing Unit 14*	*After doing Unit 14*
1 *Organizational* ethics helps define what an enterprise is and what it stands for. *Behavioral* ethics, the science of moral decision-making, looks into why and how people make the choices that they do.		
2 We often think that when the time comes, we will act more ethically than we really do.		
3 The incentives for innovative entrepreneurs, when it comes to praising the qualities of their inventions, are enormous. Therefore, since they cannot avoid it, sometimes, they will overpromise (or *slightly* misrepresent) their products.		
4 Overconfidence can actually derail. For example, Enron was frequently hailed as "the most innovative" US firm. Its personnel were known as "the smartest guys in the room". They put in a great deal of effort to formulate its RICE (**R**espect, **I**ntegrity, **C**ommunication, **E**xcellence) code of ethics. When indications of the enterprise's financial misdeeds – and its near failure – started to come to light, at first, Enron staff was surprised and quite scandalized that anybody could doubt the ethics and lawfulness of the organization's operations.		

Your Take: Integrative Thinking	*Before doing Unit 14*	*After doing Unit 14*
5 Executives who are narcissists, Machiavellians or psychopaths are dysfunctional and pathologically destructive. A narcissistic, tyrannical, malignant, and "productive" "leader" is the main threat to the successful productivity, teamwork, innovation, optimization, and harmony of the enterprise.		
6 CEO pay is out of line – executives of large corporations take significant pay raises at a time when their companies are showing no signs of a return to profitability. Growing inequality is just unjust and unethical.		
7 Some spend more time at work than at home; office romance has challenged sexual norms at work. Yet, you can't legislate love – you don't want to develop "romance policies" at work.		
8 Moral values are the final line of defense against fraud and misconduct when market competition produces negative pressures and rules and when regulations fail.		
9 Very few multinational enterprises have unethical practices.		
10 Ethical norms across different national cultures vary, making international standards difficult to implement.		

After you have done the unit, repeat "Your Take". How has reading the unit clarified the ideas herein? How have your views, feelings and thoughts changed over time?

Lead-in

General discussion points

Individually or in buzz groups, think about:

1 Are you more ethical than your competitors, co-workers, and peers?
2 *An ethical business leader should be...* (good, fair, responsible, truthful, reliable, trustworthy, just, open-minded, transparent, etc.). Why is it hard to be the kind of person your dog thinks you are? Why do good people sometimes mess up?

3   Part of the high failure rate of innovative startups may be the result of problems with the entrepreneurs themselves, their "overconfidence" in particular. Has "overconfidence" ever gotten *you* into a troubling situation?

4   Express your opinion on the following: Individuals who are morally corrupt struggle to form lasting friendships due to the unhealthy relation with themselves and others. If you *can* avoid it, don't hire narcissists, Machiavellians or psychopaths. If you have them, never promote them.

5   A business person, found guilty of cheating his customers, was ordered by a judge in California to take a business ethics course as part of his sentence. This novel and unorthodox approach of justice delivery has significant consequences for organizational or business ethics. Will taking a business ethics course as a form of punishment, equivalent to prison, increase the likelihood of future moral (or at the minimum legal) behavior? Should all leaders take courses in professional ethics?

Share your thoughts with your peers/team members. Discuss points of (dis)agreement.

 Idea watch

Ethics goes beyond just preventing you from being put behind bars. *Behavioral ethics*, an emerging field, as explained by leading business ethicists Max Bazerman and Ann Tenbrunsel when studying "blind spots", seeks to understand *how* individuals truly behave when confronted with ethical dilemmas and *why* we often act in ways that contradict our intended ethical standards.

The very word *ethics* is derived from the Greek word *ethos*, which refers to a person's fundamental orientation toward life. Originally, *ethos* meant "a dwelling place". For Aristotle (384–322 BC), a student of Plato (429–347 BC), one of the first philosophers to shape the ethics of Western civilization from a *secular* orientation, who held the view that humans are, by nature, rational beings, and who maintained that the good person is the one who lives most rationally and whose moral judgments and social conduct are the result of reflection and reason, and not of instincts, *ethos* evolved to convey "an inner dwelling place", or what is today termed "inner character". The Latin translation of *ethos* is "mos, moris", from which comes the word *moral* in English. During Roman times, the focus changed from internal character to overt behavior – acts, routines, and practices.

Apart from the secular tradition, ethics has also *religious* roots. For example, St. Augustine (354–430), who synthesized the philosophy of Plato with Christianity (Plato was a disciple of Socrates (469–399 BC) and the teacher of Aristotle), held the view that we may transcend our underlying immoral nature and we shall eventually be reconciled in God's City in Paradise, if we allow ourselves to be led to God via faith. Through divine grace, the humanity's wicked inclinations could be overcome. He viewed ethics as an enquiry into the *Summum Bonum*: "the supreme good", which brings about the happiness all humans seek. In this regard, his moral thought is more in line with the "eudaimonistic" virtue ethics of the classical Western tradition (*eudaemonism* being a system of ethics that bases moral value on the likelihood that good actions will produce happiness). For St. Augustine, happiness consists in the enjoyment of God, a reward granted in the hereafter for virtue in this life; virtue itself is a gift from God, and is founded on love, rather than on the wisdom cherished by philosophers.

Another leading Christian philosopher, Thomas Aquinas (1224–1274), integrated Aristotelian philosophy with Christian theology. According to Aquinas, all humans are gifted with a natural desire to be good. He taught that this inclination could be latent in a person and could even be corrupted. However, he believed it was in everybody and that it could not be destroyed. Aquinas said that it goes against human nature to resist God's pull, and that we shall fulfill our nature and be absolutely good if we allow ourselves to follow God. Moreover, by practicing this goodness in our everyday lives, we shall be moral and shall experience the most profound meaning of which we are capable.

Whether based on secular thought or religious belief, ethical concerns seem relevant in all aspects of life – personal *and* professional. In truth, living ethically results in living a more meaningful personal and professional life – the "good" legacy you want to be remembered for.

In many respects, your "moral self" is the core of who you are. Indeed, morality is the primary criterion used when people judge their closest peers – moral character has greater clout than expertise, extroversion or social confidence.

The most recent advancements, for example, in neurorobotics, artificial intelligence (AI), metaverse, space exploration, autonomous transportation, gene-editing, cloning and the like; a dysfunctional side of executive leadership (overconfidence, narcissism, Machiavellianism, tyranny or psychopathy); as well as unethical behavior of some at Arthur Andersen, Enron, FTX, Theranos, Wirecard AG… make the need for ethics all the more clear and urgent.

As it happens, business education is fragmented and deficient in "day-to-day" ethics – although researchers have long studied the various complex ways that people form judgments and business ethics courses *are* offered (which, like philosophy or theology, they often seek to instruct individuals on how to think about several moral problems) – these often ignore research- and evidence-based *behavioral* ethics that looks into why and how humans make the (un)ethical choices that they do – every day.

Behavioral ethics insights, based on research findings from fields such as behavioral psychology, cognitive science, and biology – and more recently, from *neuro*science (note: *neuro*ethics, a relatively new approach, uses the tools of neuroscience to examine how we make ethical choices; it is also the investigation of the ethics of neuroscience), can help understand the primary reasons why good people sometimes choose to do bad things – for instance, *how come a good kid from a good home, who graduates from a sought-after business program from an elite business school, ultimately participates willingly in some massive business scam?*

Assumptions

Our moral assessments are not always right.

As much as we may want to think we act rationally – and with integrity, ha!, according to behavioral ethics research (*behavioral* ethics differs from traditional philosophy – rather than concentrating on how individuals *should* behave, behavioral ethics looks into *why* humans behave the way they do), humans are often, say, "predictably *ir*rational". This means that many decisions are taken without much conscious thought – based on emotions (intuitive/automatic "System 1", as called by Daniel Kahneman) – rather than after thoroughly examining a circumstance (logical "System 2" thinking, as described by Daniel Kahneman).

There are several reasons why those who make unethical choices are instinctively affected by the following three types of forces:

- First, by **internal psychological biases and mental shortcuts** that often blind us to our moral character failings (e.g., "overconfidence bias" – our tendency to *over*estimate and to be more confident in our own abilities and in our capacity to act ethically than is *objectively* reasonable; "confirmation bias" – our inclination to look for or read into data that confirms our own views, pre-existing beliefs, hypotheses or expectations; "self-serving bias" – the tendency humans have to interpret information in ways that serve their own *self*-interest or reinforce their *pre*-existing beliefs; "incrementalism" – the *slippery slope* down which people's activities go from minor technical breaches, *cutting corners* – to bigger, more serious wrongs; or "framing" – the frame of reference through which we approach ethical problems influences how we respond to them),
- Second, by **external social and organizational pressures** (e.g., "conformity bias" – instead of using your own independent ethical judgment, you tend to *follow the herd*, i.e., behave as people around you do; or practice "obedience to authority" – trying to blindly please those in charge – even if getting on with their *wish list* goes against your own moral code), and
- Third, by **general situational, as well as temporal situational factors** that commonly go unnoticed (for example, *prosocial* behavior is more likely to occur when you're feeling *really good*. If you're *time-pressured*, you're more likely to engage in more unethical behavior. When you're *being watched*, you're more likely to behave more nicely. If you're being *fatigued*, you're more likely to cheat. If you're reminded of *money* ("money priming"), you adopt a mindset of professionalism, business, and productivity, and you're less likely to be caring or warm). This means that shaping conditions is as critical as forming moral character.

Unfortunately, sad to say, we are *morally fallible*, but we fail *even* more when the pressures and factors create room for failure – these three types of forces can cause a disconnect between your "ideal self" (or "best self") and your *actual* behavior.

All in all, generally, white-collar fraudsters don't end up in jail because they erroneously believed it was all right to engage in money laundering or tax evasion. They get often jailed because they made poor ethical choices – they *chose* wrongly.

Key elements

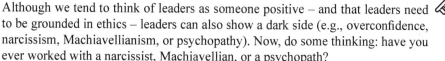

Although we tend to think of leaders as someone positive – and that leaders need to be grounded in ethics – leaders can also show a dark side (e.g., overconfidence, narcissism, Machiavellianism, or psychopathy). Now, do some thinking: have you ever worked with a narcissist, Machiavellian, or a psychopath?

Overconfidence (our inclination to overestimate our ethical competence and moral character, displaying greater confidence than what can be substantiated by objective evaluation) can lead us to act too hastily and without proper "System 2" thinking – this is when we are most inclined to engage in unethical behavior.

By way of illustration, **narcissists** need admiration. They tend to be entitled and arrogant. They believe they are better than other people. The need for praise and domination pushes narcissistic CEOs to predictable – and derailing – behaviors that can negatively affect organizations' bottom lines (e.g., awarding extravagant rewards and awards, protecting loyal management team members who flatter CEOs and defending them despite disappointing enterprise performance). They also erode collaboration and prevent teams from succeeding.

Machiavellians are deceptive, distrusting, and manipulative.

Psychopaths enjoy hurting and bullying people to distract attention from their own selfish activities.

Organizations can guard against dysfunctional CEOs by, for example:

- seeking 360-degree feedback about the CEO;
- preventing the CEO from also serving as board chair;
- having a talented (and ethical) chief operating officer (COO);
- having a strong committee, independent of the CEO, that selects board members; and
- making sure that board members have additional organizational information sources other than the CEO.

These "Dark Triad" personalities (narcissists, Machiavellians, and psychopaths) and the leadership dysfunctions presented in this unit by no means represent the whole spectrum of the dark side of leadership. Taken together, such patterns of behavior are textbook examples of "executive derailment" – what happens when leaders allow their natural negative impulses to go unchecked.

Thinking critically: Issues

Traditional ethics education addresses itself solely to themes that Aristotle, Plato, Socrates, and many others grappled with over 2,000 years ago. However, there hasn't been much development, at least in certain areas. For instance, because of the "overconfidence" bias, some leaders will frequently dismiss ethical issues – some may just believe that, having taken a standard ethics course, they have well-formed character and so they *will* do the right thing when faced with ethical dilemmas. In reality, standard ethics education can have a detrimental effect on some leaders – they may become overconfident in their capacity to behave morally as a result of it – even more so in comparison to others. Therefore, what needs to be nurtured in *behavioral* ethics education is moral humility, *not* moral confidence.

Typically, wherever there is judgment, there may be "noise" – variability in judgments that should be identical – surely a flaw in human judgment. To illustrate this, consider two judges in the same courthouse imposing radically different punishments on persons who have committed the same crime. Imagine for a moment that the same judge renders various rulings based on whether it's Monday, Friday, morning, or afternoon, for example.

Importantly, there is a difference between "moral judgments" (re the moral decisions and challenges of others) and "moral action decisions" (the decisions *you* take about how to behave when you are caught in a moral dilemma). When *you* take a moral action decision, it is expected that you *will* think on it much more, in particular, you will try to *imagine* and "picture" several consequences that might arise from the different moral options you're contemplating.

Now and then, we have a tendency to be of "multiple minds". In one sense, we aspire to live moral lives and do the right thing (the *should* self). At the same time, we also seek things like fun or power (the *want* self). For example, we invest in gym memberships – a lot, yet we grossly *over*estimate how frequently we'll *really* work out. Furthermore, to find creative solutions that keep their integrity intact, when contemplating moral dilemmas, instead of asking "What *should* I do?", prompting people to consider "What *could* I do?" (i.e., the "could" self) can help them generate moral insight, as well as boost "moral imagination" – that is, *creatively* imagining the full range of options while coming to moral decisions.

Moreover, emotions *are* a significant factor in making moral judgements – nonetheless, not all "negative" emotions (e.g., disgust) are bad *or* immoral. As it happens, some negative emotions such as "guilt" or "shame" can be quite "healthy" – and they can actually reduce unethical behavior. "Regret" can be the pathway to our best life – by understanding what people *regret* the most, one can understand what they perhaps *value* the most. Indeed, looking backward moves us forward.

Regarding values, especially "sacred values" are commonly acknowledged to be a vehicle for ethical decision-making. For that reason, they will almost never be compromised since they are seen as obligations as opposed to variables to be considered while arriving at decisions. In truth, ethical issues often start with and/ or come down to sacred values clashes.

However, it's quite easy to criticize glaring offenders like the "charismatic" Elizabeth Holmes of Theranos. What we often overlook, though, is the numerous individuals who enabled and backed their unethical or criminal behavior. Whether we acknowledge it or not, in almost every instance of this nature, there existed a network of complicitors, including business partners, staff, financiers, media outlets, and more. Remember, elements of emotional-like empathy are talents, rather than values. Demonstrating sensitivity to others' feelings does not necessarily indicate genuine concern for them. For instance, an individual might employ empathy as a tool for charming and seducing, while others may use it to effectively manage a group of individuals with strong egos.

On top, tackling corruption cannot rely exclusively on adequate institutional structures. Anti-corruption reforms alone are not enough – especially in nations undergoing institutional and economic transitions and transformations (e.g., countries of the former Soviet Bloc suffering from the "happiness gap" – citizens being less satisfied with their life than their Western neighbors). It also requires public participation and social support. Research finds that improved living conditions foster higher civic engagement, make people better citizens and more conformed to institutional regulations. As expected, happier citizens, with better access to socio-economic resources, tend to be more obedient to their public authority and more compliant with rules put in place to govern that society.

Applications

Modern cultures don't celebrate moral leaders. Yet, consistent evidence suggests that authentic, servant, and moral leaders typically outshine leaders who are amoral or immoral. Likewise, organizational ethics pays – an investment in ethics translates to the bottom line, productivity, and reputation.

Having said that, everyone's "ethical warning lights" can sometimes go off, so even good people with the best intentions can make poor ethical choices. Impulsive, short-term thinking is often caused by emotions. As emotions run high when ethics are at issue, you can apply this straightforward decision process to help guide you in making ethical judgments and think long term. The six-step ethical decision-making process includes:

Step 1. Pause 'n' think: Don't react. First, just pause for a moment and reflect.

Step 2. Collect necessary facts: You can now gather all the data and factual information. Is the decision you're making critical? Who's involved? Should it wait? Could it wait? What's at risk?

Step 3. Brainstorm possible solutions: Your decision is only as good as your best alternative. Use "moral imagination". Spend some time coming up with as many solutions as you can.

Step 4. Judge: This is the moment to consider your decision in light of ethics. To ensure that your judgment is *un*clouded, seek an ethics mentor – it is helpful to run things past others (building a "behavioral risk team" may be a great idea too).

Step 5. To avoid self-deceptive rationalization, try using the following ultimate tests:

a The generalizability test: How would you feel about everybody acting in this way?

b The "big brother" test: If you had known you were being filmed/watched, would you have done the same thing?

c   The front-page story/social media test: Picture the front page of the most popular newspaper or social media with your planned action… If it was *un*ethical, would you choose to do so?

d   The "breaking news" test: When in doubt, consider this: "Would I be A-OK if this decision made it to the 12 p.m. breaking news?" Avoid doing it if not!

e   The "mirror" test: If you look in the mirror after making the decision, would you be perfectly happy with yourself?

Step 6. Continuously review, reflect, and learn from moral challenges:

At the end of the day, do an "examen" exercise. Review the day in a posture of gratitude. This involves contemplation and moral evaluation of one's thoughts and conduct, typically performed on a daily basis. It's a short reflection back over the day, recalling events and taking note of your feelings and emotions. Recognize energizers/de-energizers from the day. Look with hope for a new tomorrow. The chief purpose is to become more aware of the ways you act and to live a more positive, ethical, and meaningful life.

Case alert! Case classic

Theranos Inc.

LOOK IT UP: Bó, E.D., & Xu, G. (2021). Theranos: How did a $9 billion health tech startup end up DOA? UC Berkeley Haas Case Series. Retrieved from: https://cases.haas.berkeley.edu/2021/02/theranos/

Your task: Read the Theranos case and think about the repercussions of the uncontrolled pursuit of entrepreneurial success in highly innovative fields, and the role of moral values as a defense against corporate fraud.

Write a *Causes and Effects* essay – composed of four parts/paragraphs. In Para 1: introduce the topic. In Para 2: describe problem and its causes with examples/explanations. In Para 3: describe effects with examples/explanations. In Para 4: summarize and give your opinion.

To record your critical insights, use the Case Analysis Record provided in Appendix 2. Report your research findings and good practices back to your peers/team members.

Greater good corner: Get ready to exercise your ethics

Take a stance: What would *you* do?

Dilemma and decision: The story of Adam and Eve

Eve was Adam's manager (she had just hired him), working at a consultancy. Both of them were single and interested in each other. She was smart and confident, and he was "Prince Charming". After a training program, they went out to a local bar one night. Afterward, she invited him to her place, and they grew closer that evening. The following day, the two drove to work together. Eve was worried that word of the romance might get out; but Adam boasted that they had slept together... Eve was embarrassed...

Adam and Eve continued working on a "special" consultancy job. This meant, throughout the workday, they spent an awful lot of time together. They would go eat lunch together, hold meetings (often behind closed doors), and work nearly entirely together.

Coworkers got irritated of Adam's excessive attention. Plus, they felt abandoned by Eve, their manager.

The special project led up to a presentation to the firm's partners. Adam delivered the presentation, with Eve coaching him effectively "behind the scenes". The partners were WOWed and so Adam was given the green light to implement his proposal. Rumors began to circulate that Adam was up for a promotion – "sleeping his way to the top". All kinds of slanderous rumors began, and team morale hit rock bottom...

Later, Eve broke up with Adam, and he began seeing an MBA intern... Still and all, Eve's professionalism was questioned. All of the rumors had reached the founder, and he lost trust in Eve, and so she eventually left the firm. Adam stayed with the firm and got promoted though...

Thought questions:

- What could Adam and Eve have done differently to handle this situation ethically and more professionally?
- What distinguishes hierarchical romances from workplace peer romances? Is dating a junior/senior ever OK? Why (not)?
- Should Adam have also received a penalty?
- Do you believe Adam's success at work is a direct outcome of his relationship with Eve? If so, does Adam still merits that job?

- Where's the line between workplace romance and hostile work environment/ sexual harassment?
- When should HR step in?

Task:

Now, your task is to craft an "intra-office dating" policy. List the dos and don'ts of love in the office. Consider, for example: public displays of affection (PDA); "dress for success"; peer-dating; romances with higher-ups/subordinates; unwanted sexual advances (via technology); sexual harassment being the result of an office relationship break-up, et cetera.

Time out: Journal entry

Thought Sparks: A few reflections, insightful ideas, actionable suggestions, strategic thinking, and key takeaways from this unit.

Learning never stops... So, pause for a few minutes and reflect in writing on your personal learning experience and beliefs. Through writing in your journal, you develop your awareness of your own beliefs and attitudes. Now, consolidate what you have learned in this unit.

1   How have your beliefs and ideas about ethics changed since you began the unit?
....
....

2   Reflecting on the problems presented in the unit, write about whether you have found solutions to these problems.
....
....

3   How confident do you now feel about applying behavioral ethics and the simple (yet powerful) six-step process to help guide you in reaching ethical decisions?
....
....

4 What about behavioral ethics would you still like to have clarified? What remaining concerns do you have?

....

....

5 What more would you like to learn about the topic, now that you have completed this unit?

....

....

6 If you want, doodle/draw something about behavioral ethics. This can be as abstract as you wish.

....

....

Remember: It's particularly useful to re-visit journal entries several times and see how themes have recurred or your thoughts have changed over time. Now, repeat "Your Take".

Making connections: Related units and models

- U 1. **Behavioral economics and policy 101**: For humans (see pp. 9–26)
- U 2. **The kindness advantage**: Cultivating positively energizing leaders and followers (see pp. 27–53)
- U 9. **Professional management consulting for real people**: The advice business demystified (see pp. 181–203)
- U 10. **Executive coaching**: Whoop it up! (see pp. 204–219)
- U 12. **Small world**: Are you a culturally intelligent organization? (see pp. 238–250)
- U 13. **Progress with purpose**: The "good" enterprise (see pp. 257–272)
- Add in more related models you may want to remember: _____.

Industry snapshot

Theranos.(2018).Retrievedfrom:https://web.archive.org/web/20180828113917if_/ https://theranos.com/ at the Wayback Machine (archived August 28, 2018)

Deep dive: Main references and resources

Andriani, L., & Ashyrov, G. (2022). Corruption and life satisfaction: Evidence from a transition survey. *Kyklos: International Review for Social Science*, 75(4): 511–535.

Babiak, P., & Hare, R.D. (2006). *Snakes in suits: When psychopaths go to work.* New York, NY: HarperCollins.

Bagozzi, R.P., & Verbeke, W.J.M. (2012). Exploring the minds of managers: Insights from three neuroscience studies. In K.S. Cameron, & G.M. Spreitzer (Eds.), *Oxford handbook of positive organizational scholarship* (pp. 138–151). New York, NY: Oxford University Press.

Bazerman, M.H. (2023). *Complicit: How we enable the unethical and how to stop.* Princeton, NJ: Princeton University Press.

Bazerman, M.H., & Tenbrunsel, A.E. (2012). *Blind spots: Why we fail to do what's right and what to do about it.* Princeton, NJ: Princeton University Press.

Biasucci, C., & Prentice, R. (2021). *Behavioral ethics in practice: Why we sometimes make the wrong decisions.* London & New York, NY: Routledge.

Bó, E.D., & Xu, G. (2021). Theranos: How did a $9 billion health tech startup end up DOA? University of California Berkeley Haas Case Series. Retrieved from: https://cases.haas.berkeley.edu/2021/02/theranos/

Boddy, C.R. (2024). Insights into the Bernie Madoff financial market scandal which identify new opportunities for business market researchers. *International Journal of Market Research*, 66(1): 149–167.

Brown, G., & Peterson, R. (2022). *Disaster in the boardroom: Six dysfunctions everyone should understand.* Cham: Palgrave MacMillan.

Chatterjee, A., & Pollock, T.G. (2017). Master of puppets: How narcissistic CEOs construct their professional worlds. *Academy of Management Review*, 42(4): 703–725.

Choi, Y., Ming, W., & Phan, J. (2022). Narcissistic leaders: The good, the bad, and recommendations. *Organizational Dynamics*, 51(3): 1–12.

Christie, R., & Geis, F.L. (1970). *Studies in Machiavellianism.* New York, NY: Academic Press.

Clark, C. (2021). *Giving voice to values in the boardroom.* London & New York, NY: Routledge.

Cragun, O.R., Olsen, K.J., & Wright, P.M. (2020). Making CEO narcissism research great: A review and meta-analysis of CEO narcissism. *Journal of Management*, 46(6): 908–936.

Ethical Systems (n.d.). *Ethics pays.* NYU Stern School of Business. New York, NY. Retrieved from: www.ethicalsystems.org/ethics-pays – the website makes academic research accessible to businesspeople.

Fausti, S. (2015). *Occasione o tentazione?* Milan: Ancora.

Gentile, M.C. (2010). *Giving voice to values: How to speak your mind when you know what's right.* New Haven, CT: Yale University Press.

Gilmour, N., & Hicks, T. (2023). *The war on dirty money.* Bristol: Policy Press.

Kahneman, D. (2011). *Thinking, fast and slow.* New York, NY: Farrar, Straus and Giroux.

Kahneman, D., Sibony, O., & Sunstein, C. R. (2021). *Noise: A flaw in human judgment.* New York, NY: Little, Brown Spark.

Kilduff, G.J., Galinsky, A.D., Gallo, E., & Reade, J.J. (2016). Whatever it takes to win: Rivalry increases unethical behavior. *Academy of Management Journal*, 59(5): 1508–1534.

Kiser, S.B., Coley, T., Ford, M., & Moore, E. (2006). Coffee, tea, or me? Romance and sexual harassment in the workplace. *Southern Business Review*, 31(2): 35–49.

Maccoby, M. (2000). Narcissistic leaders: The incredible pros, the inevitable cons. *Harvard Business Review*, 78(1): 68–77.

Maccoby, M. (2007). *Narcissistic leaders: Who succeeds and who fails.* Boston, MA: Harvard Business Review Press.

Markowitz, D.M., Kouchaki, M., Hancock, J.T., & Gino, F. (2021). The deception spiral: Corporate obfuscation leads to perceptions of immorality and cheating behavior. *Journal of Language and Social Psychology*, 40(2): 277–296.

McLean, B., & Elkind, P. (2013). *The smartest guys in the room: The amazing rise and scandalous fall of Enron* (10th anniversary edition). New York, NY: Portfolio/Penguin.

Nakamura, Y.T., Hinshaw, J., & Yu, D. (2024). The role of empathy in developing ethical leadership: Neurobiology and video-based approaches. In D.F. Russ-Eft, A. Alizadeh (Eds.), *Ethics and human resource development* (pp. 449–468). Cham: Palgrave Macmillan.

Navis, C., & Ozbek, O.V. (2016). The right people in the wrong places: The paradox of entrepreneurial entry and successful opportunity realization. *Academy of Management Review*, 41(1): 109–129.

Ong, M., Lee Cunningham, J., & Parmar, B.L. (2024). Lay beliefs about homo economicus: How and why does economics education make us see honesty as effortful? *Academy of Management Learning & Education*, 23(1): 41–60.

O'Reilly, C., Cao, X., & Sull, D. (2023). CEO personality: The cornerstone of organizational culture? *Group & Organization Management*, 0(0).

O'Reilly, C., Chatman, J.A., & Doerr, B. (2021). When "me" trumps "we": Narcissistic leaders and the cultures they create. *Academy of Management Discoveries*, 7(3): 419–450.

Pearce, J. A., II. (2010). What execs don't get about office romance. *MIT Sloan Management Review*, 51(2): 37–44.

Sguera, F., Bagozzi, R.P., Huy, Q.N., Boss, R.W., & Boss, D.S. (2018). The more you care, the worthier I feel, the better I behave: How and when supervisor support influences (un) ethical employee behavior. *Journal of Business Ethics*, 153: 615–628.

Straker, K., Sean, P., Erez, N., & Cara, W. (2021). Designing a dangerous unicorn: Lessons from the Theranos case. *Business Horizons*, 64(4): 525–536.

Taub, J. (2021). *Big dirty money: Making white collar criminals pay*. New York, NY: Penguin.

Vaidyanathan, B. (2019). *Mercenaries and missionaries*. Ithaca, NY: Cornell University Press.

Wood, M.S., Scheaf, D.J., & Dwyer, S.M. (2022). Fake it 'til you make it: Hazards of a cultural norm in entrepreneurship. *Business Horizons*, 65(5): 681–696.

Zhang, T., Gino, F., & Margolis, J.D. (2018). Does "could" lead to good? On the road to moral insight. *Academy of Management Journal*, 61(3): 857–895.

Module monitor and Consolidation VII

Workshop VII: Applications/review exercises

Self-check questions

You should now be able to answer Self-Check Questions 1–10.

1 **True or false** Leaders should help to shift *sustainability* from a focus on people and organizations being *more sustainable* to becoming *less unsustainable*.

2 **True or false** Achieving sustainability requires a fundamental change from the traditional *take–make–waste* (TMW) economy to a more ethical

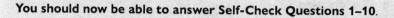

"*circular* economy" (CE). CE principles (such as sharing, reducing, reusing, recycling, repairing, redesigning, or repurposing existing materials and products as long as possible) can drive *sustainable growth*.

3 **True or false** It's still possible to follow rules and commit fraud.

4 **Multiple-choice** Our tendency to be more optimistic about our capacity to act ethically than our moral character objectively justifies. This illustrates (select one):

a confirmation bias
b conformity bias
c overconfidence bias
d self-serving bias

5 **Multiple-choice** Over-claiming, or falsely taking credit for, contributions to the enterprise is a typical red-flag behavior of (select one):

a a narcissist
b Machiavellian
c psychopath
d all of the above

6 **Multiple-choice** They are content to play the role of "puppeteer", quietly pulling the strings, and they don't necessarily need to be the center of attention. This usually describes (select one):

a narcissists
b Machiavellians
c psychopaths
d all of the above

7 **Multiple-choice** Not only do they take pleasure in hurting people, but they also purposefully utilize humiliation and bullying to shift other people's attention away from their hidden selfish behaviors. It's a prototypical behavior pattern of (select one):

a narcissists
b Machiavellians
c psychopaths
d all of the above

8 **Multiple-choice** The ability to, at the same time, be morally good and thriving by envisioning the full range of possibilities in a specific circumstance for the purpose of resolving an ethical dilemma relates to (select one):

a moral imagination
b moral muteness

c   moral philosophy

d   moral relativism

9 Multiple-choice Distinctive ways of describing the same information usually activate different emotions. The sentence that "the odds of survival three months after the neurosurgery are 90%" is more comforting than the equivalent statement that "mortality within three months of neurosurgery is 10%", which is the classic example of (select one):

a   emotional framing

b   groupthink

c   growth mindset

d   neuroethics

10 Multiple-choice A *code of ethics* is a great way to remind personnel and others of an organization's core beliefs and values. According to behavioral research, implementing an honor code can improve an organization's ethical behavior; "best practices" for a code of ethics include (select one):

a   simplicity is preferable to complexity

b   rather than depending on "experts", try engaging employees in the formulation and revision of the code

c   to resolve ethical issues, managers, and employees should actually use the code

d   the code ought to be persistently strengthened and consistently communicated organizationally wide – and, if needed, periodically, revised

e   all of the above

Individualized learning record

When you have finished Module VII, try filling in this record of what you have learned.

1 Consider any organization that is regarded as a "good corporate citizen". What forces, in your opinion, led the company's owners or corporate management to pursue this status, and how long do you believe it will likely last, given, for example, the current economic climate's challenges?

....

....

2   Governments throughout the world are proposing legislation to stop food corporations from marketing junk food to kids. How far should the food industry be held responsible for people's *health* problems? What can such companies actually do to move toward a healthier future? If you were the CEO of one of the food corporations, what would you see as the risks ahead of your business, and what would be its social responsibility? Now, instead of banning fast food altogether, what can be done to encourage customers to switch to healthier food options?

....
....

3   Many agree that differences in rates of pay according to value or effort are reasonable, although certain pay discrepancies are utterly "obscene". What criteria would you recommend for establishing pay differentials within a company that are viewed as both just *and* effective in being able to recruit, select, and retain talented candidates from the labor market?

....
....

4   Humans should not be exploring space. The massive *investments* in *space exploration* aren't justified in view of the human *misery* on Earth. Write a *For and Against* essay.

....
....

5   An investment in *ethics* translates to *profit, productivity,* and *prestige.* Taking into account varied arguments, explain how, and produce the business case.

....
....

6   "Thou shalt not steal" (Exodus 20:15) is one of the *Ten Commandments.* What about a sick mother stealing to feed a starving child – can she be excused? What about a boy stealing medicine for his sick and poor mother – can he be excused?

....
....

7   Socrates challenged the Greek way of life by provoking many into thinking about: *"The unexamined life is not worth living".* Do *you* (dis)agree with Socrates?

....
....

8 Plato held a virtue-based eudemonistic view of ethics, like most other ancient philosophers. That is to say, happiness or well-being (*eudaimonia*) is the highest aim of moral thought and conduct, and the virtues (*aretê*: "excellence") are the dispositions/skills needed to attain it. Do *you* (dis) agree with Plato?

....
....

9 Peter Drucker recommended that after a company has 1,000 people, work rules should be established to optimize efficiency and act as a guide for employee behavior. Now, you've been hired by a new globally expanding enterprise. Your CEO has requested that you to concisely comment on the usefulness of a *Code of Conduct* for all the personnel in the future. Write a report (500 words) in which you:

- give an explanation of the desirability/necessity of such a future Code of Conduct,
- make clear how it would benefit both the enterprise and its employees, and
- outline possible areas of content.

....
....

10 Moral development. How do you *develop character*?

- Who in your life has positively influenced your character development? (Family, friends, role models, etc.)

....
....

- What books, movies, and other media have helped you become a *better* person? (The Bible, *Don Quixote*, The Book of Mormon, *The Little Prince*, The Quran, The Torah…?)

....
....

- The "mirror test": What kind of person do you see when you look into the mirror every morning? What image of yourself has shaped your values and guided your life? (Note: *When our thoughts/values and actions are inconsistent, we experience (cognitive/moral) dissonance, which causes mental stress and discomfort. People will ideally resolve the issue by ceasing their unethical behavior and living according to their own ("good") self-image. However, many often overcome the dissonance by finding strategies to continue doing bad things while still believing that they are good people*).

Can-do checklist

Looking back, I have learned the following Key Terms:

Unit 13

- capitalism (compassionate, conscience, conscious)
- chief sustainability officer (CSO)
- code of ethics
- common good
- corporate social responsibility (CSR; strategic)
- economy (circular, "good", "of Communion", solidarity-based, sharing)
- enterprise risk management (ERM)
- environmental, social, corporate governance (and technology) (ESG(T))
- fragility, conflict, and violence (FCV)
- "good" enterprise
- people, planet, prosperity, peace, and partnership (PPPPP)
- progress with purpose
- regenerative business model
- sustainability (forces driving; human, talent, environmental, governance, financial)

Unit 14

- bias (confirmation, conformity, overconfidence, self-serving)
- CEOs/executives (Machiavellian, narcissistic, overconfident, psychopathic)
- dissonance (cognitive/moral)
- ethics (behavioral, business, neuro, organizational)
- ethical decision-making process (six steps)
- examen (daily)
- executive derailment
- external pressures (social, organizational)
- framing (emotional)
- happiness gap
- incrementalism
- internal psychological biases and mental shortcuts
- moral imagination
- multiple minds
- neuroethics

- noise
- self (best, could-, ideal, moral, should-, want-)
- situational factors (general, temporal)
- Summum Bonum ("the supreme good")
- system 1 thinking: (almost) automatic, emotional, and intuitive
- system 2 thinking: more rational and conscious
- test ("big brother", "breaking news", front-page, generalizability, "mirror")

Appendix 1

Case study grid

Unit	Case Organization	Focus/Mgmt Model/ Creative Strategy	Sector/Industry	Setting
1	The Royal Borough of Greenwich	Behavioral insights; a behavioral/nudge strategy; nudging-style policy; reducing anti-social behavior	Local government, public sector	UK
2	Starbucks	Kindness advantage; investing in humanity; heart-based leadership; building and sustaining high-quality connections (HQC); gratitude; compassion; well-being	Retail trade, food services	USA
3	Tennis Canada	Strategizing to win; strategic transformation; strategy choice-making	National governing body of tennis within Canada	Canada
4	John Deere	SOARing for sustainability	Agriculture, construction, forestry, turf care equipment, services	USA
5	General Motors (GM)	Dialogic OD; leading positive organizational change; negotiating change; reframing resistance to change; cognitive linguistics	Automotive	Poland

(*Continued*)

Unit	Case Organization	Focus/Mgmt Model/ Creative Strategy	Sector/Industry	Setting
6	Hyundai Motor Company	Design organization; design thinking; developing design capabilities; innovation execution	Automotive	South Korea
7	Canada Goose	Creating a legitimate luxury brand; sources of luxury brand authenticity	Performance luxury apparel	Canada
8	Burberry	Strategic brand storytelling; digital strategy and transformation; growth strategy	Fashion, luxury	UK
9	Enron	Consulting; behavioral ethics; dark side of leadership; overconfidence	Energy, commodities, services	USA
10	Caterpillar	Leadership team coaching for cultural change; leading with insight	Engineering, manufacturing, construction, mining, energy, marine and rail	USA
11	Logitech	Global management; global startups; entrepreneurship; rapid internationalization; born global (BG)	Electronics, tech, software	Switzerland/ USA
12	Skyworks Solutions & ZTE	Global management; national cultures; corporate governance, philosophy, innovation, business dispute resolution	Tech, semiconductors, telecom, mobile communications	USA/China
13	PepsiCo	Sustainability; performance/winning with purpose; the "good" enterprise; corporate citizenship	Food, snack, and beverage	USA
14	Theranos	Behavioral ethics in practice; dark side of leadership; narcissism; overconfidence; entrepreneurship; fraud	Healthcare services, health tech, personalized medicine, medical diagnostics	USA

Appendix 2

Case analysis record

Enhance and structure your approach to case study analysis, note-taking, planning and strategizing, using the Case Analysis Record (CAR) sheet. When studying a case, complete the CAR sheet by identifying the key points you may want to record and their sequence. Photocopy multiple CAR sheets so you have them readily available for any case study you come across – keep these sheets in a dedicated folder or binder for easy access. The completed CAR sheets will serve as a valuable resource when reviewing past cases or preparing for similar future cases.

Case:			**Date:**	
Who:	**Where:**	**Why:**	**Importance:**	**H M L**
What:	**When:**	**How:**	**Urgency:**	**H M L**
Define strategic problem:				
Assumptions:				
Case data analysis:	Industry (segments/ structure)	Customer value (channels/end customers)	Costs/capabilities	Competitors
Frame strategic choice:	Criterion 1 ____%	Criterion 2 ____%	Criterion 3 ____%	Criterion 4 ____%
Ch 1				
Ch 2				
Ch 3				

(Continued)

Generate possibilities:	Purpose	"Playing field"	Competitive advantage	Capabilities/ mgmt systems
P 1				
P 2				
P 3				
Specify conditions:				
Identify barriers:				
Test barriers:				
Your decision:				

Action plan:	Activity	Start date	Time to complete	Resources

Missing info/ reflection:				

Appendix 3

Summary propositions

Module I: Breathing humanity and new life into organizations – humanizing the enterprise

Unit 1. Behavioral economics and policy 101: For humans

1.1   This unit deals with behavioral science, behavioral economics, behavioral insights, as well as policy – and advances the A.S.S.E.T. framework (*A*ttract attention, *S*treamline, *S*ocialize, *E*nergize, *T*iming counts).

1.2   It's based on the recognition that real people ("humans") diverge from the idealized models found in traditional economics textbooks ("econs"). Instead, we often demonstrate inherent irrationality, relying on various cognitive shortcuts to navigate our daily lives.

1.3   Our decisions are often influenced by unconscious cognitive biases and processes (for example, "anchoring", "loss aversion" or "social proof"), which are systematic errors in thinking that affect our decision-making across various situations.

1.4   The unit highlights the concept of "nudging". A "nudge" refers to any aspect of the choice architecture that alters people's behavior in a predictable manner without restricting choices or significantly changing their economic consequences.

1.5   For a nudge to be considered beneficial, the intervention should be simple and cost-effective. It's crucial to understand that nudges do not impose mandates.

1.6   Nudging can help address and overcome "last-mile" challenges, which occur when consumers are making actual decisions.

1.7   The unit also looks at "libertarian paternalism", "defaults", "incentives", "friction costs", and "over-choice", among others.

Unit 2. The kindness advantage: Cultivating positively energizing leaders and followers

2.1   This unit explores the strategies and dynamics of positively energizing leadership and followership, plus the kindness advantage (kindness can be a "small act", an "event", or an "intervention").

2.2 Historically, academic attention in organizational studies and management research has heavily favored the analysis of leaders. Many presume that the success or failure of organizations depends solely on effective leadership.

2.3 Nevertheless, leadership represents just one component. Positive followers also hold significant importance – effective leadership cannot exist without co-active followership.

2.4 In practice, the effectiveness of true leaders hinges on kindness and their skill in engaging, building and sustaining high-quality connections (HQCs) with others and their followers.

2.5 Positive leadership, characterized by compassionate, empathetic, kind-hearted, and heart-based approaches, is a central component of Positive Organizational Behavior (POB). POB focuses on exploring and leveraging the positive aspects of human resource strengths, talents, and psychological capacities.

2.6 Primarily, positive leadership involves the process of energizing others to collaborate harmoniously to achieve significant objectives and to lead people and organizations toward a brighter future.

2.7 Notably, the aspiration to make a positive impact on others for the benefit of the organization also serves as a crucial indicator of "executive potential".

2.8 Interestingly, children do recognize that extremely good leaders are *good* people above all else. Surprisingly, studies indicate that even infants as young as 21 months old can discern between two distinct forms of social power: that of "leaders" based on *respect* and that of "bullies" based on *fear*. Moreover, at just 17 months old, infants expect leaders to address within-group misbehavior and to confront wrongdoers so as to rectify the situation, while they do not hold the same expectation for non-leaders. Additionally, five-year-old children perceive leaders as more responsible, rather than entitled, in comparison to non-leaders, demonstrating an early understanding of power dynamics and social structures. Children also deem "leaders" who take more than they give and contribute less toward shared objectives as unacceptable. The heart of the matter is: even very young infants prefer those who behave prosocially (a *helping* scenario) versus antisocially (a *hindering* scenario).

2.9 The unit also encompasses topics such as "gratitude", "generosity spectrum" ("givers", "matchers", "takers"), "psychological capital" (PsyCap), "spiritual capital", "the heliotropic effect", "flow", "personal energy", "relational energy", "positive organizational energy", and "toxic" and "tyrannical leadership".

2.10 Furthermore, the unit provides practical resources like motivating daily "check-ins" (daily reflections), practicing "loving-kindness meditation", and creating a "map of positive relationship networks".

2.11 Ultimately, both positive leadership and positive energy are crucial for producing positive performance in organizations and the workforce.

Module II: Strategizing for the future – setting, communicating, and executing a positive strategy

Unit 3. Strategic transformation: Strategy choice-making

3.1 This unit examines how strategy, decision-making, and strategy choice-making *really* work.

3.2 There exists a myriad of approaches to crafting strategy, each reflecting the individual perspectives of strategists.

3.3 Crucially, the success of a firm's winning strategy is influenced by both *external* factors (such as industry structure, profitability, and market dynamics – as the economic structure of an industry is *not* an accident) and *internal* factors (including valuable resources, dynamic capabilities, and management systems). Consequently, in an environment characterized by rapid change, devising and implementing successful strategies requires a more holistic, integrative perspective.

3.4 Importantly, a plan or planning is not a strategy. Strategy requires hard choices – it's a pattern in a stream of decisions.

3.5 Ultimately, each organization and Chief Strategy Officer (CSO) must address fundamental questions, among others: What is our winning aspiration?, Where to focus efforts and where to play?, How to win (do we compete on low cost or differentiation?), What capabilities are necessary?, and What management systems, structures, and measures are essential?

3.6 The unit also identifies essential strategy principles and concepts such as operational effectiveness, strategic execution, strategic transformation, value proposition, competitive edge, Michael Porter's five forces framework, the resource-based view (RBV) of the firm, dynamic capabilities, strategy as design, open strategy, emergent strategies, scenario planning, and strategy as practice (S-A-P).

Unit 4. SOAR: Fueling possibility thinking in positive strategic dialog

4.1 This unit investigates the process of setting, communicating, and executing a positive strategy through the SOAR framework (*S*trengths, *O*pportunities, *A*spirations, *R*esults).

4.2 SOAR represents a dynamic, innovative, strengths-centered, and solution-focused framework that adopts a participatory, whole system (stakeholder), co-creative approach to framing strategic thinking.

4.3 SOAR emphasizes the formulation and implementation of a positive strategy by identifying strengths, fostering creativity and innovation to capitalize on opportunities, energizing individuals and teams to articulate winning aspirations, and delivering positively deviant performance that is performance far above the norm – and spectacular results.

4.4 Backed by Positive Organizational Scholarship (POS), a sub-discipline within Management and Organizational Studies focused on the science and practice of that which is positive, flourishing and life-giving in organizations, the SOAR framework offers a flexible approach to positive dialogic organization development (OD) and learning. It serves as a platform for constructive, generative dialog, visioning, facilitating strategic assessment and the generation of innovative action strategies and thriving.

4.5 This unit provides a compilation of powerful SOAR questions and inquiries that organizations and strategists can use when strategizing for the future and strategizing to win positively.

4.6 This unit also looks at SWOT analysis (*S*trengths, *W*eaknesses, *O*pportunities, *T*hreats), balanced scorecard, future perfect strategy, blue ocean and red ocean strategy.

Module III: Organization development and design innovation – tools for dramatic change

Unit 5. Dialogic organization development (OD): Leading positive organizational change

5.1 This unit addresses dialogic organization development (OD), and leading positive organizational change by means of the *e*nergize, *r*edesign, and *g*el (ERG) framework.

5.2 Some common drivers of transformation encompass factors such as emerging competition, organizational restructuring, technological change, mergers and acquisitions (M&A), expansion, and downsizing.

5.3 OD is a process of planned and emerging interventions applying principles from behavioral and organizational sciences to change a system and improve its effectiveness, carried out in alignment with humanistic values, participation, choice, and development – so that the organization and its employees learn and develop.

5.4 While many change initiatives are traditionally designed and implemented from the top-down perspective (diagnostic OD), there are also purpose-driven change endeavors that emerge from "below" and gradually spread upward (dialogic OD).

5.5 Dialogic OD is considered a human-centered reaction to the *de*humanizing consequences of scientific management methodologies.

5.6 Positive OD diverges from the inclination to simply "fix" organizational and individual shortcomings.

5.7 Ultimately, in leading positive organizational transformations, positive OD necessitates a transition toward positive organizational energy (*energize*), collective design thinking (*redesign*), and strategic super-flexibility (*gel*).

5.8 The unit also discusses topics such as change readiness, strategic organizational renewal, strategic organizational learning and unlearning, and reactions – including both response and resistance to change.

Unit 6. Design-driven organization: Human-centered design thinking and innovation execution

6.1   This unit includes topics such as strategic business design, design ethnography, design management, design innovation, and adopting a design thinking approach.

6.2   Specifically, it explores design-driven organization, human-centered design thinking, and innovation execution strategies, in particular.

6.3   Design thinking (DT) represents a powerful repeatable creative problem-solving method comprising essential steps (*empathize, define, ideate, prototype, test*) and nuances crucial for those aiming to effectively generate value through innovation.

6.4   Design thinking serves as both a mindset and a process for discovering deep user insight and exploring opportunities through rapid prototyping and experimentation.

6.5   The focus is on big ideas and growth achieved via organic radical innovation.

6.6   Integrating the principles of strategic design thinking can enhance your organization's existing innovation, design maturity, and business development processes.

6.7   This process, in addition, has the potential to harness and boost the creative capabilities of all staff members.

6.8   This unit also covers *integrative* thinking, thinking *inside* and *outside* the box, *systems* thinking, "wicked" problems, *open* innovation, and *empty* innovation.

**Module IV: Creating and managing
WOW brands – energizing your brand**

Unit 7. WOW! It's cool! Crafting a coolness strategy for your brand

7.1   This unit teaches how to craft a coolness strategy for your brand – and how to manage "wow" brands.

7.2   It explores aspects such as brand authenticity and brand heritage, brand energy, brand health and brand relevance, and methods for energizing the brand such as energizing the business and/or creating a "branded energizer" – a branded product that by association significantly boosts the reputation and visibility of a target brand.

7.3   In contemporary times, building a brand may seem straightforward. Nonetheless, to attain brand leadership and differentiate your brand amidst the multitude and saturation of brands, it is imperative to cultivate a "cool brand".

7.4   It's feasible to develop a "coolness strategy" for your brand, drawing from ten distinctive attributes that define cool brands. These encompass being: *positively energizing, iconic, extraordinary/useful, aesthetically pleasing, of high status, rebellious, original, authentic, subcultural,* and *popular.*

7.5   Brand coolness is fluid, with brands transitioning from being "uncool", to achieving "niche cool" or "mass cool" status, and sometimes reverting to being *un*cool again. Consequently, companies must navigate these shifts attentively.

7.6   In the end, brand coolness influences consumers' perceptions, contentment with, willingness to discuss – and inclination to purchase or use the products linked to that brand.

7.7   The unit also touches upon strategic branding, the process of establishing authentic luxury brands, in particular.

Unit 8. Once upon a time… Strategic brand storytelling

8.1   This unit considers the "storytelling organization" (think, for example, Disney or LEGO). It covers strategic brand storytelling, strategic narrative development, and organizational storytelling.

8.2   Strategic storytelling entails a structured approach to and disciplined strategy for connecting with both employees and clients, energizing them to contribute toward achieving business objectives.

8.3   As such, in order to attain brand leadership and excel in a constantly evolving landscape, business leaders and Chief Evangelist Officers (CEOs) should harness the potential of narrative thinking, transmedia brand storytelling, and various media platforms, particularly digital and social media, to narrate compelling and epic brand stories.

8.4   Narratives hold a universal appeal, with most exceptional stories fitting into one of seven archetypes. These archetypical stories include "Overcoming the Monster", "Rags to Riches", "The Hero's Quest", "Voyage and Return", "Comedy", "Tragedy", and "Rebirth".

8.5   While the specifics of content and presentation may differ significantly, stories generally adhere to four fundamental constructs: "heritage stories", "contemporary stories", "vision stories", and "folklore stories".

8.6   This unit also identifies the concept of "brand evangelism". Specifically, the ways to effectively evangelize a brand are: schmoozing, public speaking, and social media.

8.7   It also touches upon brand activism as a strategy.

Module V: Helping genuinely – always aim higher

Unit 9. Professional management consulting for real people: The advice business demystified

9.1   This unit addresses management consulting and professional service firms (PSFs).

9.2   Management consulting encompasses both an industry and a practice. It involves co-creating value for businesses, making a substantial contribution to the global economy.

9.3 Management consultants, frequently referred to as management analysts or trusted advisors, utilize various knowledge, techniques and resources to research and recommend methods for improving an organization's effectiveness and performance – facilitating positive transformations.

9.4 Consulting is a professional helping role – consultants commit to executing only essential tasks within their expertise. Consultants may assume various roles, such as an expert, a collaborator or a facilitator/educator.

9.5 The consulting assignment (often conducted as a project or executed as ongoing support) is deemed successful solely if the client is better off after the engagement. This enhancement can manifest in various ways, including objective analysis, aiding during peak periods (where consultants can alleviate temporary workloads of permanent staff), streamlining the workplace to align with business objectives, delivering a learning program, resolving challenging human or organizational performance issues, producing deliverables like reports, or formulating winning strategies.

9.6 Advisory firms employ various management frameworks, comprising strategic models (like Strategic Dialogue), tactical models (such as Business Process Reengineering (BPR)), and operational models (e.g., the Plan–Do–Study–Act (PDSA) cycle). Consultancy methods encompass both qualitative and quantitative approaches.

9.7 Top qualities of a management consultant include adept consulting skills, specialized and profound business knowledge, personal effectiveness, positive relational energy, learning agility, and adherence to ethical standards (including ethical decision-making, integrity, confidentiality, and observance of a professional code of conduct).

9.8 This unit also discusses the client's perspective, the trust equation, the consulting cycle, plus the role of design in consulting and advice business.

Unit 10. Executive coaching: Whoop it up!

10.1 This unit deals with executive coaching. Recognized as a powerful talent development strategy and one of the fastest-growing global professions, it is based on dialogic organization development (OD) principles and positive psychology behavioral science.

10.2 Executive coaching involves collaborative engagement between professional coaches (either internal or external) and executive clients – so as to facilitate their rapid progression toward desired goals.

10.3 Executive coaching, a robust executive human resource development (HRD) method, extends beyond problem-solving.

10.4 This process aids leaders in goal setting, decision-making, and leveraging their natural strengths to achieve desired outcomes.

10.5 It serves as an effective tool in executive learning and development (L&D), energizing executives to maximize their personal and professional potential.

10.6 Excellent coaches are *not* robotic – they ask penetrating questions, engage in active, reflective, and attentive listening, and demonstrate empathy. They do not necessarily provide all the answers, but, rather, encourage coachees to discover solutions independently through challenging them.

10.7 Several common forms of coaching include one-on-one coaching, behavioral coaching, career coaching, executive leadership team coaching, coaching for strategy, group coaching, and life coaching.

10.8 Key coaching skills involve, for example, acting as a sounding board and offering constructive feedback.

10.9 Various coaching tools encompass positive and appreciative inquiry, tracking, utilizing "playback" and "check-in", and employing collage as a creative coaching tool.

10.10 Qualities of effective coaching comprise applying humble inquiry, maintaining a positive energy and strong coaching presence, thinking on one's feet, incorporating playfulness to offer alternative perspectives – and listening with sensitivity and nuance.

10.11 Some fundamental principles of communication include, for instance, focusing on what holds significance and emotional resonance, and conveying honesty without assigning blame or judgment.

10.12 This unit also illustrates a useful coaching technique known as the WHOOP method (*W*ish, *H*appy *O*utcome, *O*bstacle, *P*lan), rooted in *m*ental *c*ontrasting with *i*mplementation *i*ntentions (MCII).

10.13 Ultimately, high-performing enterprises have "coaching cultures".

10.14 The advantages of instilling a coaching culture are plentiful. These include increased productivity and well-being, improved positive communication and sense of purpose, heightened employee engagement, enhanced collaboration and positive relationships within the workplace, improved transfer of skills to performance, evident organizational dedication to strategic HRD, and heightened success in change management initiatives when aligned with such efforts.

Module VI: Global management strategies – going places

Unit 11. So, you want to go global? Becoming an instant international

11.1 This unit covers global management strategies, with a specific focus on initiating an international new venture (INV) during periods characterized by volatility, uncertainty, complexity, and ambiguity (VUCA).

11.2 Born Globals (BGs), aka "instant internationals", are typically companies that, from the outset, aim to achieve significant competitive benefits by utilizing resources and selling products or services in various locations around the globe.

11.3 Industry-wise, high-tech companies are particularly susceptible to the born-global effect and are favorable for early and swift international expansion. They frequently have the ability to surpass established firms rapidly, effectively "leapfrogging" ahead in the market.

11.4 One of the key factors in initiating and expanding highly valuable businesses lies in the concept of "scaling", which goes beyond mere *efficient* scaling or just *fast* scaling.

11.5 Instead, it emphasizes "blitzscaling", an aggressive growth strategy that entails specific practices for stimulating and handling hyper-growth. Blitzscaling offers an accelerated route to the phase in a startup's development where the most significant value is generated.

11.6 Businesses that have mastered blitzscaling, prioritize speed and market dominance over efficiency, particularly when faced with uncertainty.

11.7 This approach allows companies to innovate and swiftly transition from the "startup" phase, to the "scaleup" phase – seizing market opportunities at a rapid pace.

11.8 Yet, "blitzscaling" is not universally applicable as a strategy. It presents risks associated with factors such as cash burn, maintaining quality, adherence to regulations, and preserving corporate culture amidst hyper-growth.

11.9 The unit also brings up global innovation. Innovation is no longer limited to spreading from affluent to less-developed economies in a unidirectional manner. It can also flow in the opposite direction, a phenomenon known as "trickle-up innovation" or "reverse innovation".

Unit 12. Small world: Are you a culturally intelligent organization?

12.1 This unit delves into the topics of going global, culture, organizational culture and national culture, and the culturally intelligent organization.

12.2 The global movement of individuals, data, capital and commodities for commercial purposes is steadily expanding.

12.3 "Internationalization" results in an increase in international clientele, collaborators, and suppliers.

12.4 The phenomenon of worldwide economic integration in global markets is referred to as "globalization". The emergence and expansion of multinational corporations are both consequences *and* catalysts of globalization.

12.5 It's noteworthy that global markets are also consolidating into regional centers, a process known as "regionalization".

12.6 Businesses operating in multiple countries, irrespective of their extent of global involvement, need to recognize that countries vary significantly in terms of their cultural attributes. Consequently, individuals from different cultures may exhibit behaviors and reactions that diverge from what they are accustomed to.

12.7 National culture, aka the "collective mental programming" of people within a particular environment, sets one nation apart from another and encompasses various dimensions. These dimensions include levels of power distance, uncertainty avoidance, individualism versus collectivism, masculinity versus femininity (motivation toward achievement and success), long-term versus short-term orientation, and indulgence versus restraint.

12.8 Moreover, countries can be grouped into four implicit forms of organizations based on distinct cultural differences: a "pyramid of people" (e.g., Serbia), a "well-oiled machine" (e.g., Switzerland), a "village market" (e.g., Ireland), and the "family" (e.g., Hong Kong).

12.9 Emotions associated with an abroad assignment tend to progress in the following phases: honeymoon-culture shock/crisis-recovery-adjustment.

12.10 Of note, organizations with high level of "cultural intelligence" (CQ), which denotes the ability to comprehend, connect and operate successfully in culturally diverse environments, are considerably more adept at navigating the intricacies of today's multicultural global landscape.

12.11 It's worth mentioning that when developing your international strategy, the CAGE framework can aid in avoiding potential issues. CAGE stands for *c*ultural differences, *a*dministrative differences, *g*eographic differences, and *e*conomic differences.

Module VII: Behavioral ethics – achieving ethical practice for the greater good

Unit 13. Progress with purpose: The "good" enterprise

13.1 This unit advocates achieving ethical practice – for the greater good.

13.2 It highlights *progress with purpose* and the "good" enterprise – becoming a positive force for the "Common" good – a notion representing the entirety of societal circumstances enabling individuals or groups to more fully and effortlessly achieve their potential.

13.3 Traditional thought holds that the well-being of the community is intertwined with the moral, social, and spiritual dimensions of an individual's existence.

13.4 Indeed, the common good significantly influences everyone's life. It necessitates sound decision-making by each person, with businesses bearing an even greater responsibility for corporate social responsibility (CSR) to enhance their role as good corporate citizens.

13.5 Engaging in business is a noble calling, and "conscience capitalism" prioritizes creating conditions conducive to dignity and prosperity across human, organizational, societal, and environmental realms. Enterprises practicing conscious capitalism blend immediate profitability with considerations of solidarity, sustainability and long-term beneficial effects – thereby contributing positively to people, the planet, prosperity, peace, and partnership (PPPPP).

13.6 Today, "impact investors" are individuals genuinely interested in the destinations of their investments.

13.7 A sustainable business ought to prioritize values alongside financial considerations. Therefore, the concept of a "good" enterprise, seen as a community and characterized by interpersonal relationships, within a humane economy – the "good" economy (the "Economy of Communion") – holds promise for flourishing both commercially *and* ethically.

13.8 The fundamental components of sustainability encompass human sustainability (think: human well-being), talent sustainability (think: talent retention), environmental sustainability (think: environmental preservation), governance sustainability (think: effective governance), and financial sustainability (think: financial stability).

13.9 ESG(T) stands for *E*nvironmental, *S*ocial, *G*overnance (and *T*echnology), commonly associated with sustainability. ESG(T) lies at the heart of many organizations' business models, focusing on how their offerings strategically promote sustainable development – progress with a clear purpose.

13.10 Ultimately, integrating ESG(T) into daily operations allows for the establishment of a regenerative business model at the core of the enterprise.

Unit 14. Oops! I messed up. Why good people do bad things every so often

14.1 This unit explores ethics, behavioral ethics, neuroethics, and the process of ethical decision-making, addressing itself specifically to why good people do bad things every so often.

14.2 Our moral judgments are occasionally flawed. Individuals who make unethical decisions are often influenced by three types of forces: internal psychological biases and mental shortcuts (such as "confirmation bias", "self-serving bias", "incrementalism", or "framing"); external social and organizational pressures (like "conformity bias" or "obedience to authority"); and general situational or temporal factors (such as being tired or watched, money priming or time pressure).

14.3 The unit also emphasizes the distinction between "system 1 thinking" – characterized by automatic, emotional and intuitive responses and "system 2 thinking" – which is more deliberate, rational, and conscious.

14.4 Some leaders exhibit negative traits such as narcissism, Machiavellianism or psychopathy – derailing others. Additionally, the "overconfidence bias" refers to our inclination to have greater confidence in our ethical capabilities than is objectively warranted by our skills and moral integrity.

14.5 Among other issues, the unit also examines notions like "moral imagination" – which involves creatively envisioning various options during moral decision-making, "cognitive dissonance" – which refers to the mental discomfort and stress individuals experience when holding contradictory ideas simultaneously, and the "happiness gap" – representing the disparity or difference between people's perceived levels of happiness and their actual satisfaction with life.

Appendix 4

Answers to self-check questions

Self-check assessment exercises will help you review your understanding of the core concepts and frameworks presented before moving on to further materials. Reflecting on and comprehending the answers to these questions will contribute to ensuring complete mastery of the concepts and frameworks.

To maximize your learning and engagement, complete other assignments in the Playbook as well. These will add value by stimulating the development of your research-based skills. They have been designed to facilitate the transfer of theory to practice.

Module Monitor I (Units 1–2): Self-check questions

1 True, **2** True, **3** True, **4** True, **5** True, **6** True, **7** True, **8** False, **9** False, **10** False

Module Monitor II (Units 3–4): Self-check questions

1 False, **2** False, **3** True, **4** True, **5** True, **6** True, **7** False, **8** False, **9** False, **10** True

Module Monitor III (Units 5–6): Self-check questions

1 True, **2** True, **3** False, **4** True, **5** True, **6** True, **7** True, **8** True, **9** True, **10** False

Module Monitor IV (Units 7–8): Self-check questions

1 True, **2** True, **3** True, **4** True, **5** True, **6** True, **7** (d), **8** False, **9** True, **10** True

Module Monitor V (Units 9–10): Self-check questions

1 True, **2** True, **3** False, **4** False, **5** True, **6** True, **7** False, **8** True, **9** True, **10** False

Module Monitor VI (Units 11–12): Self-check questions

1 True, **2** False, **3** True, **4** (c), **5** True, **6** (c), **7** False, **8** True, **9** True, **10** False

Module Monitor VII (Units 13–14): Self-check questions

1 False, **2** True, **3** True, **4** (c), **5** (a), **6** (b), **7** (c), **8** (a), **9** (a), **10** (e)

An open invitation

Let's engage

Way to go! You now have a really good understanding of key models, tools, concepts, and creative strategies being taught in world's leading MBA programs from the University of Berkeley-Haas School of Business, the Carlson School of Management-the University of Minnesota, Gies College of Business-the University of Illinois Urbana-Champaign, the Central Saint Martins-Birkbeck Business School, Graduate School of Management-Kyoto University, to the Ivey Business School at Western University and the University of Toronto's Rotman School of Management.

If you like your new guide to getting ahead, why not spread the word to the world? For example:

- You can post something on your favorite social media platforms – LinkedIn, X (formerly Twitter), Instagram, or Facebook, for instance.
- You can tell your friends, colleagues, teachers, fellow students, and even your CEO at work.
- You can write a review on Amazon.

Thank you kindly for helping me help more leaders to put the greatest ideas taught in the best business schools into action.

If you'd like more personalized help, let's engage. There are different ways that I engage with individuals, organizations, and business schools – worldwide: as an executive coach, a trusted strategy, organization development, executive leadership and strategic human resource development consultant, a keynote speaker, and an executive education/(executive) MBA teacher-scholar.

I am also very happy to take (video) calls and emails from media on areas related to my research and am aware of the needs to respond to interested journalists in a timely manner. These should be directed to me: **email**: bart_tkaczyk@berkeley.edu or **follow** on X (formerly Twitter): @DrBTkaczykMBA

I look forward to hearing your experiences and perspectives as you apply these cutting-edge management frameworks and MBA concepts and to continuing our energizing executive learning and professional development conversation.

Gratefully,
Bart Tkaczyk

About the author

Bart Tkaczyk, a Fulbright Scholar at the University of California at Berkeley (the No. 1 public university in the world), is a Managing Member with Energizers, LLC, which consults to CEOs and senior executives of major corporations on the design and leadership of strategic transformation. Dr. Tkaczyk is an Executive Member of the Academy of Management, an award-winning human resource development consultant (trained at Birkbeck, University of London in the UK), a strategist (trained at the Rotman School of Management, University of Toronto in Canada), a design thinker and business innovator (trained at the University of Minnesota's Carlson School of Management in the USA), a professional executive coach (trained at the Berkeley-Haas School of Business in the USA), and a certified case method instructor and case writer (trained at the Ivey Business School-Western University in Canada), among others.

Working across industries worldwide, Dr. Tkaczyk's strategy consulting, executive education and coaching, leadership, human resource and organization development, and public speaking engagements have included projects with AstraZeneca, Bahrain Society for Training & Development, Byblos Bank Group, Central Bank of Oman, Chipita S.A., Cisco Systems, Dubai Police, the Estée Lauder Companies, Fluor, HP, International Federation of Training and Development Organisations, Johnson & Johnson, Lotos, Majarra, Minth, Moody's Analytics, Oracle, Orange, Qatar National Bank, Saudi Aramco, Takeda Pharmaceutical Company, UNESCO, the United Nations (HQ), and more.

Dr. Tkaczyk has published in leading outlets in Canada, the UAE, the UK, and the USA, including *Arab Investor, California Management Review (Insights), Design Management Review, Development and Learning in Organizations,* **Emerald**, *European Business Review, European Financial Review, Global Business and Organizational Excellence, Harvard Business Review (Arabic), Ivey Business Journal, Leadership Excellence, Routledge, Rutgers Business Review, Strategic Change, Strategic HR Review, Talent Development,* **Wiley**, and *The World Financial Review*, among others.

Dr. Tkaczyk's professional associations and service, on both sides of the Atlantic, include: the Academy of Management (AOM) in the USA; the Association for Talent Development (ATD) in the USA; the British Academy of Management (BAM); and the Chartered Institute of Personnel and Development (CIPD) in the UK.

Bart is happily married to the very wonderful Oleńka and is a very involved dad to little Zosia. He enjoys hiking, imaginative contemplation exercises, creative writing, learning Arabic, and developing his martial art skills (Kali) in his spare time and having Sunday afternoon tea with his family and friends. Moreover, he is passionate about effective methodologies in executive education, teaching MBA students, behavioral economics and insights, organizational psychology, positive organizational scholarship, strategizing, humanistic management, talent development, managerial cognition, applied imagination and collage as a creative learning technique, human happiness, cognitive science and linguistics, artificial intelligence, good parenting, and good work – for the common good.

Visit drtkaczyk.com
Follow @DrBTkaczykMBA
Email bart_tkaczyk@berkeley.edu

Also by Bart Tkaczyk
Leading Positive Organizational Change:
Energize – Redesign – Gel (Routledge, 2021)

Index

Printed in the United States
by Baker & Taylor Publisher Services